The Videomaker Guide to Digital Video and DVD Production
Second Edition

The Videomaker Guide to Digital Video and DVD Production
Second Edition

From the Editors of
Computer Videomaker Magazine

Introduction by Matt York, Publisher/Editor

Preface by Stephen Muratore, Editor in Chief

ELSEVIER

AMSTERDAM • BOSTON • HEIDELBERG • LONDON • NEW YORK • OXFORD
PARIS • SAN DIEGO • SAN FRANCISCO • SINGAPORE • SYDNEY • TOKYO
Focal Press is an imprint of Elsevier

Focal
Press

Focal Press is an imprint of Elsevier
200 Wheeler Road, Burlington, MA 01803, USA
Linacre House, Jordan Hill, Oxford OX2 8DP, UK

 Recognizing the importance of preserving what has been written, Elsevier prints
its books on acid-free paper whenever possible.

Library of Congress Cataloging-in-Publication Data

The Videomaker Guide to Digital Video and DVD Production / from the editors of Computer
    videomaker magazine; introduction by Matt York, publisher/editor; preface by
    Stephen Muratore, editor-in-chief.—2nd ed.
        p. cm.
    Includes index.
    ISBN 0–240–80566–6 (pbk.: alk. paper)
    1. Digital cinematography – 2. Digital video – Handbooks, manuals, erc.
    3. DVDs – Handbooks, manuals, etc. I. Computer videomaker
    TR860.V53 2004
    778.59 – dc22   2004002003
British Library Cataloguing-in-Publication Data
A catalogue record for this book is available from the British Library.

ISBN: 0-240-80566-6

For information on all Focal Press publications
visit our website at www.focalpress.com

04 05 06 07 08 09 10 9 8 7 6 5 4 3 2 1

Printed in the United States of America

This book is dedicated to Thomas Jefferson for his commitment to pluralism, diversity and community. He would be happy to see readers of this book exercising freedom of the electronic press.

Civil liberty functions today in a changing technological context. For five hundred years a struggle was fought, and in a few countries won, for the right of people to speak and print freely, unlicensed, uncensored and uncontrolled. But new technologies of electronic communication may now relegate old and freed media such as pamphlets, platforms and periodicals to a corner of the public forum. Electronic modes of communication that enjoy lesser rights are moving to center stage.

Ithiel de Sola Pool
Technologies of Freedom
(Harvard University Press, 1983)

Contents

Preface

Eight years since the publication of the first edition, the editors of *Computer Video-maker Magazine* are proud to present the third edition of *The Computer Videomaker Handbook*. Like the first two editions, this edition of the *Handbook* takes you from the planning of videos all the way through the final phases of their production. However, this edition was assembled from materials written more recently for *Videomaker Magazine*. Most of the contents of this book did not appear in the previous editions: this really is a new book. Also, we couldn't send it to press without adding a section on a very popular new development: DVD and CD authoring. Following the speedy acceptance of DVD players in homes everywhere, videographers have developed a zeal for delivering their videos to family, friends and clients on DVD, videoCD and CD-ROM. The last section of this edition will fuel that zeal with the information necessary for getting started.

As we did with the previous edition, we have supplemented this book with a companion Web page all its own. The Web page contains links to streaming video clips that illustrate various techniques discussed in the *Handbook*. If the site holds a streaming video relevant to a given chapter, you will find this icon

near the title on the first page of that chapter. To access the page of clips, go to http://www.videomaker.com/handbook. When asked for a password, type "effects" without quotation marks.

The *Handbook* can be read cover to cover as a comprehensive course on the art and science of videography. It can be used also as a handy field reference: the simple organization and index should make it easy for you to find answers to your questions, and the glossary will define the arcane terms of the art.

Affordable digital tools have made it easier than ever before to create high-quality video messages and deliver them to ready audiences. Let this book be your aid whenever you use these tools. Whether you are a weekend hobbyist or a practicing professional, the *Videomaker Handbook* will help you use your talent and your equipment to their fullest.

—*sm*

Introduction:
If you are new to making video: Welcome!

Matt York
Publisher of Computer Videomaker Magazine

The craft of making video is an enjoyable one. Whether video production is for you a pastime, a part-time moneymaker or a full-time occupation, I am certain that you will enjoy the experience of creating video. There are many facets to video production. Each brings its own pleasures and frustrations, and each will stretch your abilities, both technical and artistic.

Video is a wonderful communication medium that enables us to express ourselves in ways unlike other media. Television is pervasive in our society today. The chance to utilize the same medium that the great TV and film producers have used to reach the masses is an incredible privilege. Video is powerful. Video is the closest thing to being there. For conveying information, there is no medium that compares with video. It overwhelms the senses by delivering rich moving images and high-fidelity sound. Having grown up with TV, many of us lack the appreciation for its power. Compared with radio or print, television profoundly enhances the message being conveyed. For example, reading about a battlefield in war can be less powerful than hearing a live radio report from a journalist with sounds of gunfire, tanks, rockets, incoming artillery fire and the emotions from an anguished reporter's voice. Neither compares with video shot on a battlefield.

It is amazing that you can walk into a retail store, make a few purchases in a few minutes and walk out with all of the essential tools for producing video. For less than $2,000, you can buy a DV camcorder and a personal computer and suddenly, you have the capacity to create video that rivals a television station. The image and sound quality of a DV camcorder is better than broadcast television as viewed on an average TV. The transitions and special effects, available with any low-cost video editing software package, exceed the extravagance of those used on the nightly news.

There was a time when any message conveyed on a TV screen was perceived as far more credible than if it were conveyed by other media (i.e. print or audio cassette). While that may no longer be as true, video messages are still more convincing to many people.

Once a highly complex pursuit, video editing is now just another software application on a personal computer. We all realize that simply using video editing software doesn't make someone a good TV producer any more than using Microsoft Word makes one a good writer. However, the ability to edit video in your own home or office is so convenient that it enables more people to spend more time developing their skills.

One of the most rewarding experiences in video production is getting an audience to understand your vision. The time between the initial manifestation of your vision and the first screening of the video may be just a few days or several years, but there is no more satisfying (or nerve-wracking) feeling than witnessing an audience's first reaction to your work.

PART I

Video Gear

A guide to essential equipment: what to buy, how it works.

1
Camera Buttons and Controls

Dr. Robert G. Nulph

It's easy for first-time camcorder owners to be intimidated by all of the buttons and controls that seem to sprout from every recess and surface of a new camcorder. Believe me, if you don't know how to focus, adjust your iris or when to select a different shutter speed you are not alone. In this column, we will give all you beginners an overview of the various buttons, controls, dials and knobs common to camcorders.

Power, Eject & Record Buttons

Somewhere on the camcorder, there is a power switch. This switch often includes a save, standby or neutral position so that the camera goes into a power save mode when not recording, to preserve battery life. If your camcorder goes into the standby or save mode, simply push the standby button to power it back up. Power switches sometimes have a "lock" feature that prevents you from turning the camera on accidentally. To disengage this lock, press in the power switch to move it. The power

switch might also be part of the switch that changes the mode of the camcorder from camera to playback VCR.

The eject button is also a standard feature on all camcorders. This button, often colored blue, can be found most anywhere on the camcorder. Usually they are located on the side, top or bottom of the camcorder near the tape door. By pressing this button, you can eject your tape or open the tape door so that you can insert your tape into the tape carriage. On many camcorders, the door opens and the tape carriage then pops or slides out. If this is the case with your camcorder, when loading the tape into the camcorder, slide your tape into the carriage, then let the camcorder pull the tape inside before closing the outside door. This allows you to make sure that the camcorder firmly seats the tape into its internal mechanism.

All camcorders have a record button, of course. This button is usually red and is located where your thumb sits when holding the camcorder in your right hand. Some camcorders also have a record button on top or in the front for easier access when using the camera with a tripod. The record button starts and stops recording while in camera mode. On some cameras, the record button also acts as a record/pause button when your camcorder is in the VCR mode.

Focus

The buttons, knobs or dials that control the lens and the picture are perhaps the most important controls on the camera. As a beginner, you may tend to let the camera do the work in Auto mode. However, as you get used to your camcorder and do more shooting, you may want to switch it to manual so that you can take greater control of your focus.

The focus button or dial is usually located on or near the lens but, on some camcorders, it is on the side of the casing. By setting the camera for automatic focus, you let your camera do the focusing, sending out an infrared beam, computing the distance and setting the lens. This sounds great, but in practice, there are many problems with it. Anything that moves across the lens will cause it to change focus and, even though your subject may not change position, the camera is constantly checking the focus and changing it. This constant check and rechecking of the focus, causes your picture to drift in and out of focus and is a major drain on your battery.

If you are not comfortable focusing manually, let the camera focus automatically, then switch to manual. This effectively locks the focus until you change it again. Some camcorders allow you to hold the manual focus button down so that the camera focuses using its auto function. Then, when you release the button the camera enters the manual focus again so that it won't auto-fluctuate (see Figure 1.1).

Zoom

The zoom control is usually a couple of buttons, a slider or a rocker switch on top

Figure 1.1 *One good way to use the focus controls (if you aren't confident doing it yourself) is to let the camera automatically focus and then switch the focus to manual (i.e. lock the focus).*

of the camera. These buttons have the letters W for Wide (zoom out) and T for Tight (zoom in). You can also think of these as aWay and Towards. These buttons change the focal length of the optical system, which control how close or far away your subject looks. The zoom can be a very helpful feature, but be careful not to overuse it. Its primary use should be in setting the image size before you begin recording; try not to zoom during recording. Recorded zooms often don't look very good unless your camcorder has a variable speed zoom and you practice a lot using it.

Iris (Aperture)

Some camcorders have an iris or aperture control dial (see Figure 1.2). The iris controls the amount of light that enters the camera. By turning the dial, you can make the image brighter or darker. Aperture is measured in f-stops (e.g. f/1.8–f/16), with larger numbers indicating smaller openings. Some camcorders do not have

Figure 1.2 *The iris controls the amount of light that enters the camera. By turning the dial, you can make the image brighter or darker.*

Figure 1.3 *Stop Motion— Fundamentally, shutter speed controls the amount of light that is coming into the camera.*

explicit iris controls and instead adjust the overall exposure through some combination of iris and electronic amplification (gain).

Manual aperture control can be handy when your subject is standing against a bright background. The camera automatically reads the scene as being bright, so it closes the iris, making your subject very dark. By turning the iris control dial, you can make your subject brighter (with the background likely becoming overexposed). Many cameras have an explicit backlight button that may help you do this semi-automatically. You can avoid using the backlight button if you watch your backgrounds and change your shooting location. Always try to place your subject so that the background is a little darker than the subject. You can usually make your subject brighter by turning him so he almost faces the sun. You can also reduce the brightness of the background by zooming in on your subject.

Shutter Speed

Fundamentally, shutter speed controls the amount of light coming into the camera, with faster shutter speeds letting in less light (see Figure 1.3). Faster speeds also decrease the amount of blur for fast moving subjects. This comes in very handy when you slow the video down in your editor.

Without the shutter speed control, the slowed-down video would show blurred motion. By increasing the shutter speed, the motion will be crystal clear, even if the image is paused.

The one problem with higher shutter speeds is that it decreases the amount of light that enters the lens. If shooting outdoors at midday, this is not much of a problem, as the sun provides a lot of light. Indoors, however, you will have to add light if you want to use the high-speed shutter function.

White Balance

The white balance button is a necessary feature on a camcorder. This button sets the electronics of the camera so that they see colors accurately (see Figure 1.4). Surprisingly perhaps, different kinds of light sources (fluorescent, the sun, incandescent bulbs) produce slightly different colors of light. To use the white balance button, point your camera at a white piece of paper or cloth after you set up your shot. Press the white balance button and you'll see an icon in the viewfinder blink off and on. When the camera is white balanced, it will stop blinking. Make sure you white balance every time you change position or light sources. Watch out for a subtle, periodic cycling of automatic white balance under fluorescent

Figure 1.4 *The white balance button is a necessary feature on a camcorder. This button sets the electronics of the camera so that they see colors accurately.*

Figure 1.5 *Record Review—You might also find a record review button that you can press to check what you just recorded. When you press this button, the camcorder rewinds the tape and plays back your last few seconds of footage.*

lights, especially when using slower shutter speeds.

VCR Controls

Most camcorders have basic VCR controls built into them. These controls include Rewind, Fast forward, Play, Pause and Stop. You might also find a record review button that you can press to check what you just recorded (see Figure 1.5). When you press this button, the camcorder rewinds the tape and plays back your last few seconds of footage. The camera does

not have to be in the VCR setting to do this, making it a very handy function.

Clicking Off

We've cover the most common camcorder buttons, but your camcorder may have a few more buttons. Read over your manual and experiment using the different settings. If you've had your camcorder for a while, but have only shot in auto mode, it may be time to take more control of your camcorder. Have fun and enjoy making springtime videos.

Sidebar 1

Direct Focus

On still cameras, the focus ring is often mechanical, and a turn actuates a direct change in the position of the optics. On almost all camcorders, the focus ring is not mechanical. Instead, the movement of the focus ring by your hand translates into an electronic signal that then translates into the movement of the lens. This makes the focus ring seem mushy and unresponsive to changes.

Sidebar 2

Menus

Camera designers are faced with a dilemma: too many buttons can be baffling, yet too few restrict a videographer's freedom. Design engineers have attempted to solve this issue by putting the most commonly used controls on the body of the camera and placing seldom-used items in electronic menus. More advanced cameras tend to have more buttons, while simpler point-and-shoot models tend to have more menus. If your camera doesn't have a button that is listed in this article, check the on-screen menu.

2
A Quick Guide to Video Formats

Larry Lemm

There are lots of video formats in use today. They come in a myriad confusing names that all sound alike. If you've ever wanted to find out the differences between VHS, S-VHS, VHS-C and S-VHS-C keep reading. If you're curious about the distinctions between 8mm, Hi8, Digital8 and DV then this guide to the video formats will be very helpful.

For each type of videotape, there are some important features to examine. First, there's the picture quality of the format, which is expressed in lines of resolution. The more lines of resolution you have, the better your picture will look. Next is audio dub. Audio dub is the ability to record audio over existing video without erasing the video portion. Next is the format's ability to resist generation loss, or the video noise that occurs when you copy a tape. Combine these features with factors like tape length and size of the tape (and camcorder) and you have a pretty good idea of the features that differentiate the formats. Let's take a closer look at them format by format.

The VHS Family

The VHS family is very popular. JVC introduced it, and JVC still holds allegiance to the format. A good indication of this is that JVC is the only company that still makes an S-VHS-C camcorder.

VHS and VHS-C play in home VCRs, and S-VHS offers good audio and picture quality. The recording methods of all VHS formats is very similar. There are separate control, audio and video tracks on the tape. Embedded into the video track are separate stereo hi-fi audio tracks (see Figure 2.1). These hi-fi tracks record superior audio as compared to the linear audio track, but since it is embedded in the video track it cannot be audio dubbed. Let's take a look at each of these VHS formats.

VHS

This is one format that practically everyone knows and uses to some extent. VHS is the big ole videotape that your home

7

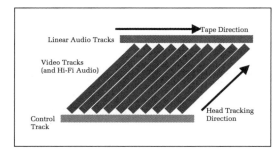

Figure 2.1 *The VHS format family have Hi-Fi stereo audio embedded in the video signal but a monaural linear audio track is available for audio dub while keeping video intact.*

VCR uses, and for some technologically-inhibited individuals, this is enough of a reason to use a camcorder that records in VHS. The simple ability to shoot a tape and stick that tape right into their VCR is the most important feature in these peoples' minds.

Almost every videographer will end up using VHS for distribution copies, but besides that last step in the video production cycle, professionals will avoid VHS like the plague. You'd think that it might be because of VHS's large overall size, but it's really because VHS has a low overall picture quality, maxing out at about 250 lines of resolution. VHS also has horrible generation loss, making the editing of VHS tapes a tricky endeavor for linear editors.

VHS-C

Once, one of the main complaints against full-sized VHS was the size of the tape, and the corresponding large size of the VHS camcorder. So JVC introduced a reduced-sized VHS and called it VHS-C (or compact VHS). On the plus side, it could play in a regular VCR with an adapter. By reducing the size of the cassette, they also reduced the length of time it could play. Size and length are the most significant differences between VHS and VHS-C.

S-VHS

S-VHS or Super VHS is an improved version of standard VHS. It looks similar (with the only visible difference being an extra slot in the tape case to verify that it is a high-band tape), but it offers superior video quality, and more editing flexibility.

S-VHS offers almost twice the video resolution of VHS. It'll give you up to 400 lines of resolution. Most S-VHS equipment also supports S-video connections. S-video connectors keep the video signal separated into grayscale (luminance) components denoted as (Y) and color (chrominance) components denoted as (C). This Y/C, or S-video, signal has less generation loss when making copies so it holds up better in the editing process than standard VHS. Finally, S-VHS supports LTC and VITC timecode which is essential in linear editing and very handy for computer editing if your system has machine control features. Unfortunately, you will find these timecode features only on professional models.

S-VHS-C

This format is dwindling. JVC is only company that currently makes S-VHS-C camcorders. The format has the same pros of S-VHS: better resolution, S-video connections and timecode, and the overall size reduction of VHS-C. However, it has a shorter maximum length of tape.

The 8mm Family

Just as VHS is JVC's baby, 8mm is Sony's. 8mm offers the reduced tape(and camcorder) size that VHS-C enjoys, but without the short recording length that haunts VHS-C. Many consumers complain that, with this format, you have to be technologically minded enough to connect your camcorder to your TV set to watch home videos, or get an 8mm VCR specifically for the purpose.

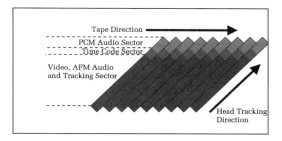

Figure 2.2 8mm formats embed audio into the video signal only which makes it impossible to make an audio dub without disrupting the video.

Hi8 and 8mm tapes use AFM audio which is embedded in the video signal in a fashion that is similar to the hi-fi audio track in VHS. In addition, Hi8 tape has a PCM audio sector and a time code sector (see Figure 2.2).

8mm

In many ways, 8mm is great for videographers that just want to shoot some video of the family around the house and not edit. It is small, so the camcorder won't break your back lugging it around. The video quality of 8mm is about the same 250 lines of resolution that VHS offers. It has roughly the same recording time. The AFM audio on 8mm is mono, but it sounds good to the ear. All in all, as long as you don't want to edit, 8mm is great.

If you do edit though, especially if you do linear editing, 8mm shows its weaknesses. First, 8mm suffers from generation loss when making copies the same as VHS. Next, 8mm doesn't offer timecode. Worst of all, 8mm cannot do audio dubs.

Hi8

Just as S-VHS is an improved version of VHS, Hi8 is an improved version of 8mm. It offers 400 lines of video resolution, like S-VHS. Hi8 camcorders generally use Y/C

connections also like S-VHS, so the format suffers less generation loss than standard 8mm. The format also supports timecode (though not many models have this feature), which is essential for accurate linear editing or nonlinear tape logging. The Hi8 format, as with 8mm, embeds the audio into the video so audio dub is not possible without disrupting the video. Bottom line: if you want an inexpensive, good looking analog picture, Hi8 does a good job with a small camcorder.

Digital8

Sony introduced Digital8 a couple of years ago. This format falls in the 8mm family, but also in the digital crew that we'll get to below. It's here because it uses Hi8 tape, but we'll give it the full treatment below.

The Digital Crew

The biggest shift in video over the last five years has been the digital migration. With the plummeting cost of high-quality nonlinear editing gear, digital video is the future. Right now, the two major players on the digital front are the firmly established Mini DV and the somewhat established Digital8. And the experimental new video formats of MiniDisc and DVD-RAM are finding their way into camcorders.

All digital camcorders convert the image into a series of ones and zeros instead of a complex analog signal. There are no significant differences in the tape used between analog and digital formats, which is more than underscored by the fact that Digital8 uses Hi8 tape (see Figure 2.3).

Mini DV

Mini DV is a solid video format. It offers extremely high quality video and audio and has virtually no generation loss. In addition, the tape is so small that Mini DV camcorders can be extraordinarily small

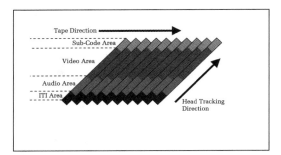

Figure 2.3 *Time code, date and time, reside in the Sub-code Area. The Insert Track Information (ITI) area is used for insert edits.*

and portable, yet still offer long recording times.

Mini DV delivers up to 525 lines of video resolution. On the downside, you'll occasionally experience artifacts with the way Mini DV compresses video. It is especially noticeable in patterns, but also shows up in some high action shots. The untrained eye may not catch these blocky, "pixilated" artifacts as they flash through the picture quickly, but after you start to look for them, they may become noticeable.

There are four parts to a Mini DV track: video, audio, subcode and ITI (Insert and Tracking Information). The video and audio are self-explanatory. The subcode holds timecode, date and time and track numbers. The ITI holds information for doing video insert edits.

For audio, Mini DV offers two modes: a 16-bit stereo pair, or two 12-bit stereo pairs (four 12-bit tracks total). The 16-bit option offers better quality (on a par with CD), while the 12-bit option lets you do audio dubs later to the additional tracks.

Perhaps the most-important feature of Mini DV is that it can use FireWire to transfer the digital bit stream directly to another tape, or to a hard-drive for editing. Because you are just transferring the ones and zeros that make up the serial stream, you lose no audio or video quality when you do it. That means no generation loss. Any way you slice it, Mini DV is top-notch for consumer video.

Digital8

The consumer-friendly Digital8 uses many of the same principals as Mini DV, but writes that information onto more-common Hi8 tapes instead of the specialized Mini DV tapes. It also offers an easy upgrade path for owners of current 8mm and Hi8 camcorders who want to be able to edit current stock of video on a computer. Digital8 uses a Hi8 tape, but records information in a manner almost identical with that of Mini DV. It also includes the FireWire port that makes Digital8 NLE-friendly.

The video quality of Digital8 comes in at the same 525 lines of resolution that Mini DV has to offer. The biggest difference is that Digital8 doesn't offer the 12-bit audio mode that supports audio dub (which is found on the Mini DV). This isn't very important if you plan on using a computer-based editor with your Digital8 because most NLE systems have multiple tracks for audio.

A big plus for the format is that you can play Hi8 and 8mm analog tapes on a Digital8 camcorder and by running it through the FireWire port convert it to digital. This won't change the original quality of the video signal, but it will allow you to bring your old analog footage into a computer editor with a FireWire port.

Mini Disc and Beyond

The future offers even more options for digital video. Sony has a camcorder that uses its Mini Disc as a storage medium, and soon Hitachi will introduce a DVD-RAM camcorder.

The Mini Disc camcorder stores video in MPEG-2 video and offers four 12-bit audio tracks. Perhaps the most striking feature of the only Mini Disc camcorder is that it has built-in editing. This could be an ideal format for the Web videographer.

Hitachi will soon introduce a DVD-RAM camcorder. This uses a removable DVD disc that stores ultra-high quality MPEG-2 video. Expect long recording times, high video quality and Dolby Digital 16bit audio.

So Many Standards

A healthy and competitive technological market is to blame for the diversity of video formats we have today. As camcorders get smaller and cheaper and have better video quality, we still hold on to the older, larger formats because they too have their own advantages. Before shopping, take stock of your needs. Whether you need an inexpensive cam to help you start shooting or a feature-rich one that supports editing well, you will find there is a camcorder for you.

Sidebar 1

DV vs D8

Face it. If you want to edit your video after you shoot it, then you need to take a hard look at a digital camcorder. Let's take a head-to-head comparison between Mini DV and Digital8.

- *Picture quality*. Mini DV and Digital8 have nearly identical picture quality when used in camcorders with similar optics and CCDs. However, there are no 3-CCD Digital8 camcorders. 3-CCD camcorders split the video signal up into its component Red, Green, Blue (RGB) parts giving superior color separation which means more when it comes to picture quality than lines of resolution do.
  Advantage: Mini DV (When used in 3-CCD camcorder)

- *Audio quality*. Mini DV supports either two 16-bit or four 12-bit audio tracks, while Digital8 only has the two 16-bit. However, both formats have excellent sound.
  Advantage: Tie

- *Video flexibility*. Both formats allow for cloning (making an exact digital copy), via FireWire to transfer video information. Digital8 can also play analog Hi8 tapes (and encode them through the FireWire port).
  Advantage: Digital8

- *Audio flexibility*. When using the four 12-bit audio tracks, Mini DV supports audio dub, while Digital8 does not.
  Advantage: Mini DV

- *Cost of operation*. Mini DV tapes are generally a bit more expensive than Hi8 tapes, but can record a few more minutes of video.
  Advantage: Digital8 by a little

- *Camera cost*. Digital8 cameras have a much lower price than Mini DV on the intro level, so it's less cost prohibitive to get into Digital8 video.
  Advantage: Digital8

Sidebar 2

Format Categories

Another Way to Sort Out the Format Differences
Consumer camcorders can be classified into three categories that don't necessarily coincide with their format. They are:

1. Standard grade analog including VHS, VHS-C and 8mm.

2. High grade analog including S-VHS, S-VHS-C and Hi8.

3. Digital including MiniDV and Digital8.

In general, the main differences between standard and high grades of analog camcorders are image and audio quality. High grade formats noticeably increase image resolution and audio fidelity over standard grade.

The digital formats record a digital signal that significantly increases resolution over high grade analog. Overall, increased image quality, combined with a greater diversity of features, will generate higher price tags among the different format categories.

3
How DV Works:
Technical Feature

Bill Fisher

Ladies and gentlemen, step right up! Inside this tent you'll have a remarkable opportunity to get closer than ever before to digital video, otherwise known as DV. I'll give each of you an unusual close-up look at the mechanics of DV, at the various DV formats on the market and at the reasons DV can do so much, so well. So follow me into the tent of wonders!

Look—the journey is already beginning. We're now shrinking, small enough to penetrate the inner workings of a DV camcorder. Let's enter through the lens housing and start exploring.

Light, Sound and Current

As we move through the zoom lens, note that at this point, digital video is a lot like analog video. Light and sound enter the camera through a lens and microphone and then a computer transforms the real world into electronic signals.

Digital and analog part ways fairly soon, however. The tiny silicon charge-coupled device (CCD) at the end of the lens barrel uses hundreds of thousands of pixels to make DV look incredibly sharp and clean, with around 500 lines of potential resolution (or more, in three-chip pro cameras).

From Analog to Digital

Next we come to the circuit boards, which do an enormous amount of the work of making your DV footage look and sound fantastic. The software coding and computer components contained in the boards produce a digital replica of each moment of video and audio in the analog-to-digital conversion process. There is also circuitry that works in reverse, for playback on your television. It's the "digital" part of DV that puts this technology head and shoulders above consumer analog video formats. Digital video is pure data, not analog signals, allowing pristine and endlessly repeatable transmission of high-resolution data through an all-digital pathway.

Doing the Math

All consumer digital video formats (Mini DV, Digital8, DVCAM and DVCPro) utilize the same basic data format and data rate (25 Mbps) to encode and decode 30 fps NTSC video data.

• *Sampling.* DV encoding hardware samples each frame of video for luminance (brightness) and chrominance (color) information. It uses 4:1:1 (Y:U:V or YUV) sampling for this operation (see Figure 3.1). The hardware scans each line of every 720×480 video frame, taking four pixel samples of luma information (Y) for every one pixel sample it takes of chroma information (U and V). That cuts down on extra data and also provides the right mix of luma and chroma detail to satisfy our eyes, which are more sensitive to brightness (luma) than color (chroma).

• *Compression.* The DV brain then mathematically compresses each resampled frame of video to speed throughput and save storage space on tapes and hard drives. This is accomplished with a 5:1 DCT (discrete cosine transform) mathematical algorithm that discards as much unnecessary image information as possible while retaining much of the quality of the original image.

• *Audio.* A separate sampling process takes the audio signal (after pre-amplification) and turns it into data as well. An audio sample rate of 48 kHz (with a 16-bit depth per sample) produces a single track of high-fidelity digital stereo audio (2 channels). Alternately, a 32 kHz sample rate with a 12-bit depth yields two stereo tracks (4 channels total), one of which can be used for voiceover narration.

• *Vital data.* All of this pristine but compressed digital information is bundled with additional vital pieces of generated data. This information includes time code, time/date information and digital pilot tone signals to replace the conventional control track of analog video, which the DV format lacks.

• *Error correction.* Also added to the data mix are error correction bits. Digital video data travels in tiny packets and the DV hardware adds unique codes that verify and correct corrupted data bits.

Express Delivery

The whole package is finally bundled in data packets compliant with the DV standard. Every one of these packets—each the size of a single DV track—contains four independent regions: a subcode sector for time code and other data, a video sector, an audio sector and a sector for insert editing and track data (see Figure 3.2). These packets move at a rate of 25 Mbps (megabits per second), which translates to roughly 3.5 MB of disk storage space per second of DV video.

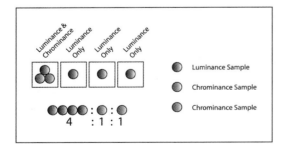

Figure 3.1 4:1:1 Sampling—DV Encoding hardware samples each frame of video for luminance (brightness) and chrominance (color) information taking four pixel samples of luma information (Y) for every one pixel sample it takes of chroma information (U and V).

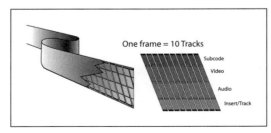

Figure 3.2 10 Tracks, 1 Frame—Each frame of DV video is made up of 10 tracks, each of which is divided into four subsections.

Where the Action is

We've seen the brains, but now we've come to the brawn—the spinning drums that record data onto the tape and read it off. The drum that houses the heads is a polished metal cylinder that's angled in the cassette compartment and rotates at a very high rate. Rollers hold the tape against the drum's grooved surface, where a number of electromagnetic heads make slanted swipes across the surface of the tape, recording tracks of data that correspond exactly to the DV packets described above.

Everything about this system is microscopic and is measurements are in microns, or thousandths of a millimeter. In fact, the record heads are so small, the tracks are so narrow and the data they contain is so densely packed, that a minute of digital video—about 200 MB of information— occupies less than two meters of tape. Put another way, a DV cassette can hold about 13 GB of digital information.

The Skinny on Digital Formats

Everything up to this point is common to the 25 Mbps Mini DV (DV25), Digital8, DVCAM and DVCPro formats. When it comes to recording to tape, however, manufacturers have developed several different ways to store the data (see Figure 3.3).

Mini DV tape comes in a 55 mm wide plastic cassette to fit consumer camcorders. The tape itself is 6.35 mm wide and is coated with metal that was deposited using an evaporated processing technique (ME) (see Figure 3.3). It moves at a rate of about 19 mm per second, with a track width of 10 microns. The typical 60-minute Mini DV cassette is about 70 m long and stores around 13 GB of data. The closely-related standard DV tape (designed for use in VTRs) is the same tape format, but comes in a cassette that's twice as big and holds as much as 180 minutes of tape.

DVCAM (Sony) and DVCPro (Panasonic) formats are modified DV25

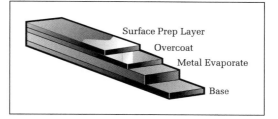

Figure 3.3 *Physical Format—Metal Evaporated (ME) Mini DV tapes have a number of physical layers protecting the important data layer.*

for the professional market. They use a wider track pitch for greater reliability and move the tape past the heads much faster. Both formats offer as much as three hours of running time on a single cassette.

The DVCPro format has several other pro-level features. DVCPro tapes use a metal particulate (MP) process instead of ME. Unlike Mini DV and DVCAM, DVCPro can use optional linear tracks at the top and bottom edges of the DV tape to record analog time code and audio information.

The Digital8 format also has idiosyncrasies. Larger than Mini DV tape, Digital8 records onto 8 mm and Hi8 tape. The key difference is that in a Digital8 camcorder, the tape moves twice as fast as in its analog relatives, and the signal is digital. The Digital8 format is backward-compatible with the analog 8 mm format. That's a big plus if you have a closetful of legacy 8 mm gear and tapes (see Figure 3.4).

Decks

Most of what you've seen here applies to digital VTRs as well. Decks use the same processing system as camcorders to understand analog and digital signals. Where decks differ from, and usually outshine, camcorders is their mechanical robustness and their multiple digital and analog input/output capabilities. These units also offer format cross-compatibility: many DV, DVCAM and DVCPro decks can play back all of the different tape formats.

25Mbps DV Tape Formats			
Tape	Pitch (microns)	Tape speed (in mm/sec)	Cassette dimensions (mm)
MiniDV	10	18	66×48×12
DVCam	15	28	66×48×12
Digital8	16	29	95×63×15
DVCPRO	18	34	98×65×15

Figure 3.4 *All consumer digital video formats utilize the same basic data format and data rate (25 Mbs) to encode and decode 30 fps NTSC video data.*

Output and Beyond

We conclude our tour at the camcorder's FireWire connection. And that's appropriate, because FireWire is a big part of DV's success. FireWire is a data transfer protocol like USB or Ethernet. FireWire moves dense packets of data at extremely high rates, and that makes it perfect for moving DV data between camcorder and computer. The DV/FireWire one-two punch has created a real revolution in consumer video, enabling all-digital desktop video production.

Parting Advice

As you leave this tent of wonders, make sure to remember that all DV equipment, from the most economical camcorder to the most elaborate high-end VTR, makes use of basically the same computational brain. And as for the many differences, don't worry about the underlying technology. Whether your DV comes in the form of a pro camera with a giant lens, a portable deck with an LCD screen or a palm-size camcorder for travel, there's a digital heart in all of these devices.

Sidebar 1

Standards

FireWire, like DV, is an international standard (IEEE-1394) that technology manufacturers have agreed to abide by in the interest of compatibility. But that doesn't mean that everyone agrees on what to call the standard. Apple Computer, which played a large role in developing the technology, named it FireWire and Sony dubbed their version i.LINK.

Sidebar 2

Longevity

Anyone who's used analog formats has seen dropouts and other signs of signal loss resulting from faults on the magnetic tape or from recording problems. When it comes to longevity, expect analog tapes to last at best 15 years before they start to degrade. Error correction built into DV eliminates many dropouts, but what about longevity? Since DV tapes use magnetic material to record data, you'll see gradual deterioration of these signals, too, though error correction can make up for some loss. Fortunately, it's easy to make perfect backup clones of DV tapes via FireWire.

4
Dissecting a Digital Camcorder

Scott Anderson

Dooley may be a little crusty, but he's the kind of guy you can trust with your camcorder. So when mine broke, he was the man to fix it. This was the perfect chance to learn the inside story about this amazing piece of technology, from the moment that the light hits the lens to the final TV output (see Figure 4.1).

"There's a lot of technology crammed into this little thing," said Dooley, who actually seemed to glow when he talked tech. "It has lenses, motors, gyros, microphones, a clock, a tape deck, a computer and a TV. Not to mention a dozen input and output jacks. It's a robot-operated entertainment center in the palm of your hand. So, how did you break it?" he asked.

"I didn't break it; it just stopped working," I said, somewhat defensively.

"Well, let's crack 'er open," Dooley replied. "And don't worry, I won't hurt your baby. Now hand me that tool kit."

I passed him a large kit containing everything from a basic screwdriver to a space-age remote control. In a few seconds he had the back off the camcorder and was pulling its guts out.

"Here's where it all starts," he said, holding up my precious zoom lens. "The lens is one of the most important, and expensive, parts of the camcorder. No amount of electronic wizardry can make up for a crummy lens."

He pointed at two small gray cylinders alongside the lenses. "See these? These are little motors to control the autofocus and the zoom," he said. "Essentially, this is a sophisticated robot eye that responds to what the camcorder brain tells it to do (see Figure 4.2). Yours has an optical stabilizer built into the lens; a squishy prism that uses a tiny gyroscope to keep the image steady."

"What's that?" I asked, pointing to a chip the size of a postage stamp on a tiny circuit board.

Shaking Hands with My CCD

"That's the CCD," he said, "a chip that converts light to electricity. These things

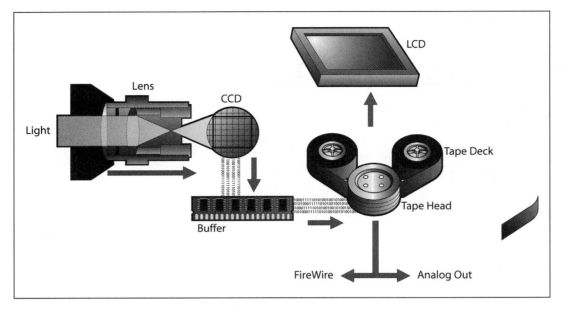

Figure 4.1 *Video out—this greatly simplified diagram may give you some idea of the complexity of getting a picture from the world at large to a place where we can see and edit it.*

Figure 4.2 *The lens—more than just glass for concentrating light, modern camcorder lenses have complex servos and gears for zooming and focusing.*

have been around for almost 25 years, but they keep getting better. It's a grid of tiny light sensors that engineers call photo-sites and computer-folks call pixels. The new ones are more sensitive for low-light situations and have more pixels for higher resolution. The more light that hits a photo-site, the greater the voltage output."

"But won't that just give you black and white? How do they see in color?" I asked.

"Well, there are basically two ways, but they both work by splitting the light into red, green and blue," Dooley said. "One technique uses prisms to split up the light and send it to three different CCDs. That's hot stuff, but expensive and bulky. Your camcorder just has one CCD, and it puts different-colored filters over the pixels," he said, handing me a diagram of a colored grid (see Figure 4.3).

"But this thing is mostly green," I replied. "Won't everyone come out looking seasick?"

"Actually, the eye sees better in the green part of the spectrum, so that grid works great. But if you think about it, this technique cuts into your resolution. You need to combine three mono-colored pixels to get one colored pixel. Software helps to smooth things out, but the more pixels you can get in your CCD, the better your final resolution. Typically, a camcorder has 300,000 to 500,000 pixels, but some new ones have a megapixel (1 million pixels). You could shoot HDTV with that kind of resolution."

"I want one!"

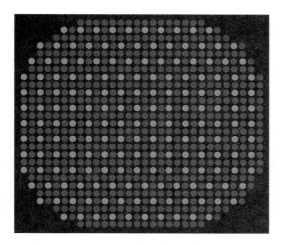

Figure 4.3 *The retina—the CCD records the light that is focused by the lens in discrete pixels.*

"Save your money, bud," Dooley growled. "Most megapixel CCDs are just for still images and HD cams ain't cheap. Now pay attention. These CCDs are scanned just like a TV, pixel by pixel, row after row. The output creates a varying voltage that travels through an analog-to-digital converter. Can you guess what that does?"

"Converts analog to digital?" I asked with a smirk.

"You're smarter than you look, pal. That digital signal gets stored in what they call a memory buffer, which is really just like computer RAM," Dooley said. "Once you have it in the buffer, you can use all kinds of software tricks on it. Some camcorders even throw in digital special effects, but I see yours doesn't."

"Naw, I like to do my effects on the computer," I said.

"Your camcorder uses optical stabilization, but some camcorders also use this buffer to stabilize the image," he said. "The software finds a feature and tries to keep it nailed down. If the camera shakes, the software electronically moves the image in the opposite direction to cancel the motion. That uses up some pixels around the border though, which dings your resolution a bit. The image is also used to determine exposure. There are at least two ways to do that. One electronically changes the amount of time that the CCD is allowed to gather light. The other way is to control a physical iris with another tiny motor.

"Your camcorder also uses this digital image to focus," he continued. "It has software that checks on the contrast of the image and controls the focusing motors. As long as the contrast increases, it will keep shifting the focus. But as soon as the contrast starts to go down, it knows it just passed the sweet spot, and it backs up a notch for perfect focus. There are other focusing methods; the most common uses an infrared beam. It just measures how long it takes light to bounce off your subject and then calculates the distance from that. It works just fine, but other infrared sources can fool it, like candles or fires.

"Finally," he went on to say, "another software program compresses the image by a factor of five before it gets saved to tape."

The Tape Deck

Dooley reached into the camcorder and pulled out the tape deck. I fervently hoped he knew how to put that thing back.

"That brings us to the tape deck part of the camcorder," he said. "Here, tiny write heads spinning at high speed lay down the digitized image track, along with the captured audio. The heads are little electromagnets, and as the pixels are read out of the buffer, the signal magnetizes the tape (see Figure 4.4).

Figure 4.4 *The head—the play/record head spins at a high rate of speed and is divided into a number of horizontal tracks.*

Figure 4.5 *In and out—the interface between the analog world and the camcorder is most often bi-directional on many modern DV camcorders.*

"That's really the end of the camcorder story," Dooley said, "except for how you get the video out again. For that, you need to read the tape back. This is just like the write process in reverse. The tape goes by the read head and every little magnetic spot on the tape converts back into bits of data. This is digital data, which is very robust stuff. Since a bit of data is binary— on or off—it's difficult to swamp it with noise. Even if noise does manage to destroy a bit, there are extra bits reserved for error-correction, which means that you can count on a reliable, 100-percent perfect recording and playback. It is this fact that makes digital so remarkable. No matter how many times you copy it, there is no generation loss like there is with analog video.

"On the way out, the video image is again stored in the buffer. Now, you can run it into a computer with a FireWire connection and edit it if you want. But if you just want to display it on a TV, you need to convert the digital image back to analog, the only thing a typical TV can handle (see Figure 4.5). What do you suppose they use for that, my friend?"

"A digital to analog converter?" I proposed.

"Right again, genius. That same circuit can also send a signal to the LCD viewfinder on your camcorder. It's interesting that although both CCDs and LCDs come from the computer world, they are both usually wired for analog inputs and outputs. So, your digital camcorder is really a hybrid, with a lot of conversion going on between the analog and digital worlds."

"Pretty soon, you can expect a fully digital signal path, which will give even better results. In the end, you'll still need to convert to analog for standard viewing, but soon, even the TVs will be digital."

Dooley surveyed the entrails of my camcorder strewn across the table. "Well, that about sums it up," he said. "Except for one thing. Your camcorder has something you don't see very often."

Dooley held up the tape unit. "This thing seems to have a toaster in it. Or at least someone must have thought so. Otherwise, why would there be a piece of bread in the cassette holder?"

"What?" I yelped. "No way, unless the twins got into it ..."

"You should keep your kids away from this thing, Anderson. Hand me the tweezers."

Dooley fiddled around a bit and then triumphantly plucked out a hardened chunk of bread squished into the shape of a DV tape. "It should work a whole lot better now," he said.

Sidebar 1

Quality Issues

The Lens

Lens quality. This is the most important part of your camcorder and usually the most expensive. It doesn't matter how many lines of resolution you have if the image is out of focus. Premium optical coatings do a better job of preventing color fringing and reflections.

Zoom. An important aspect of a lens is its zoom capacity. Modern optics are computer-designed and incredibly complex. Keep in mind that big zoom ranges may sacrifice optical quality and speed, and long zoom settings will require a tripod or an image stabilizer.

Stabilizer. Optical stabilizers let you use those zoom settings to the max, and they don't sacrifice CCD resolution the way electronic stabilizers might.

Speed. Faster lenses capture more light, so you can take shorter exposures. This is especially important for shooting sports events and low-light situations.

The Microphone

We tend to concentrate on the video parts of a camcorder, but the audio is just as important. Fortunately, audio is much easier and cheaper to deal with. Audio data is just a fraction of the size of the video data.

It's difficult to put a high-quality microphone on such a small object. Nevertheless, camcorder makers have done a decent job within a tight budget and even tighter spaces. If you're looking for better quality, look for an input jack for an external microphone. Then you can hook up whatever you want, including remote mikes.

The CCD

There are two things to look for in a CCD: the resolution and the sensitivity. The resolution depends mostly on how many pixels the CCD has, but is reduced somewhat if electronic image stabilizing is used. The more CCD chips you have, the better. For sensitivity, choose a low-lux CCD that can see well even in low light conditions.

Sidebar 2

WARNING! Don't Try this at Home!

The Editors of *Videomaker* do not recommend opening your camcorder's case under any circumstances. Doing so will certainly void your warrantee, and may cause permanent damage to the camera or personal harm to you. We recommend that you always (and only) have your video camera repaired by a trained professional.

5
All About Lenses

Jim Stinson

Without passing through a lens, the light falling on your camcorder's CCD would be as empty of information as a flashlight beam. The camcorder's lens converts incoming light from a gaggle of unreadable rays to an ordered arrangement of visual information—that is, a picture. It's the lens, then, that makes video imaging possible. Without it, your camcorder would record an image of blank white light.

All videos are successions of individual images, each made by forcing light to form a recognizable picture on a flat surface. You can do it with just a tiny hole in the wall of a darkened room, but it's easier to use a lens.

A lens does far more than just render light into coherent images; it also determines the visual characteristics of those images. For this reason, every serious videographer should know how lenses work and how to use them to best advantage.

A Little Background

As long ago as ancient Greece, people noticed that when they put a straight pole into clear water, the part of the pole below the water line seemed to bend. The mathematician Euclid described this effect in 300 BC. But it wasn't until 1621 that the scientist Willebrord Snell developed the mathematics of diffraction. Diffraction is the principle stating the following: when light passes from one medium to another—say from water to air or air to glass—it changes speed. And when light hits a junction between two media at an angle, the change in speed causes a change in direction.

Lenses, which refract light in an orderly way, were perhaps unintended side effects of glass blowing: if you drop a globule of molten glass onto a smooth, plane surface it will naturally cool into a circle that's flat on the bottom and slightly convex on top—an accidental lens. Look through this piece of junk glass and behold: things appear larger.

Now, hold the glass between the sun and a piece of paper and you can set the sheet on fire—but only if the glass-to-paper distance is such that all the sun's rays come together at a single point on the paper.

At some unknown moment somebody thought, "*Hmmn*, if it works with the sun, maybe it'll work with other light sources, too." In a darkened room, this someone held the glass between a piece of paper and an open window. Sure enough, at a certain lens-to-paper distance, a pinpoint of light appeared.

But then a bizarre thing happened. When the experimenter slowly increased the glass-to-paper distance, an actual picture of the window appeared, small, to be sure and upside down, but so detailed that they could see that tree outside, framed in the opening. (You can try this yourself with a magnifying glass.)

Back to the Present

If you've ever seen a cutaway diagram of a modern zoom lens, you have a grasp on how far we've come from that first accidentally dropped blob of glass.

The camcorder zoom may contain a dozen pieces of glass or more. Some of these permit the lens to zoom, some make the lens more compact by "folding" the light rays inside it, and some correct inescapable imperfections called lens aberrations.

But since you didn't sign up for an advanced physics seminar here, we'll pretend that the camcorder zoom is a simple, one-element lens. We can do this because the basic idea is exactly the same: when a convex lens refracts light, the light's rays converge at a certain distance behind the lens, forming a coherent image on a plane still farther back.

The plane on which the focused image appears is the *focal plane*; the place where the light rays converge is the *focal point*, and the distance from the focal point to the axis of the lens is the *focal length. Note*: contrary to common belief, the focal length is *not* the distance from the lens to the focal plane.

Your camcorder's image-sensing chip sits at the focal plane of the system, behind the actual lens.

Notice also that Figure 5.1 shows an additional measurement: *maximum aperture*, or, in plain language, the lens' ability to collect light. Get comfortable with lens *aperture, focus* and *focal length*, and you've got everything you need to know about camcorder lenses. So let's run through'em.

Open Wide

The *aperture* of a camera controls how much light enters the lens. In one way, a lens is just like a window: the bigger it is, the more light it admits. But a lens isn't quite as simple as a window, because the amount of light that gets in is also governed by its focal length (the distance from the lens to the focal point).

For this reason, you can easily determine maximum aperture—the ability of a lens to collect light. Use this a simple formula: *aperture = focal length divided by lens diameter*.

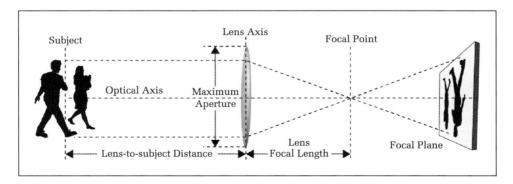

Figure 5.1 *The geometry of a simple lens.*

For example: if a 100 mm lens has a diameter of 50 mm, then 100 divided by 50 is 2. The lens' maximum aperture is 2, expressed as "f/2." Lens apertures are "f stops."

Since the amount of shooting light varies from dimly lit rooms to bright sunshine, all lenses have mechanical *iris diaphragms* that progressively reduce the aperture in brighter light. Your camcorder's auto exposure system works by using this diaphragm to change the lens' working aperture. In other words, the iris is changing the effective diameter of the lens.

These changes occur in regular increments called "stops," as noted. Each one-stop reduction in aperture size cuts the light intake in half. Most consumer camcorders fail to indicate these f stops. But some units—as well as most familiar single-lens reflex film cameras—indicate f stops by a string of cryptic digits: 1.4, 2, 2.8, 4, 5.6, 8, 11, 16, 22.

Why use these peculiar numbers to label f stops? Simple: long ago, lenses with maximum apertures of f/2 were very common, so f/2 became the starting point. F/1.4 is the square root of f/2; and if you look at the other f stop numbers you'll see that each is a multiple and/or root of another. (Some figures are rounded off: f/11 is not precisely a multiple of f/5.6.)

Just as confusing, these strange numbers appear to work backward. As the f stop number gets bigger, the aperture gets *smaller*. F/22 is the smallest common aperture and f/1.4 (or even 1.2) is the largest.

Why should you care how big the hole is in your camcorder lens? Because the working aperture has important effects on image quality and depth of focus. For critical applications, lenses create better images in the middle of their range of apertures. But for videographers, the crucial concern is the effect of aperture on focus.

Lookin' Sharp!

Before we can explain how aperture affects focus, we need to see what focus is and how the lens does it.

To start with, remember that the focal plane is the *one and only* plane on which the light rays create a sharp (focused) image. If you look at Figure 5.1 again, you'll see that the subject, the lens axis, the focal point and the focal plane are all in a fixed geometrical relationship. That is, you can't change one without affecting the others. You can't move the lens closer to the subject without changing the path of the light rays. And if you do that, you change the position of the focal plane.

In Figure 5.2a, the subject is a long distance from the lens, and its image appears sharply on the focal plane. Since the camcorder's CCD is on that plane, the recorded image is in focus.

Figure 5.2b shows what happens when you move closer to the subject. The geometry of the light rays moves the focal plane forward *away from the CCD*. The result? When the rays do hit the CCD they no longer form a sharp image. You're out of focus.

The solution: change the position of the lens to compensate for the shift in subject distance. As you can see from Figure 5.2c, doing this returns the focal plane to the CCD's position and the image is back in focus again.

This is exactly what happens in your camcorder lens. Lens elements move forward and backward to focus the incoming light on the CCD. Most camcorder zoom lenses feature *internal* focusing: the lenses move inside a fixed-length lens barrel. Most still cameras use *external* focusing: you can actually see the lens grow longer as its front element moves forward for closer focusing.

What's In Focus?

If you adjust the lens to focus on a subject near the camera, then the distant background will often go soft. That's because every lens at every aperture and focusing distance has what's called a certain *depth of field*. Here's how it works. Strictly speaking, the lens focuses perfectly only

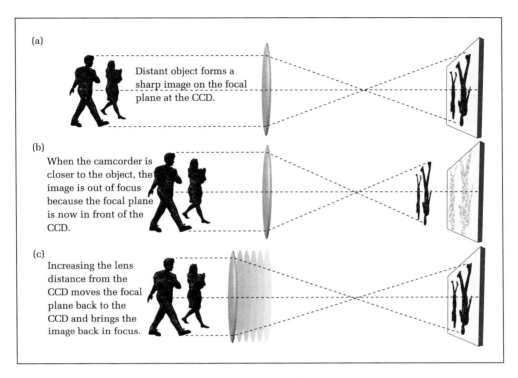

(a)

Distant object forms a sharp image on the focal plane at the CCD.

(b)

When the camcorder is closer to the object, the image is out of focus because the focal plane is now in front of the CCD.

(c)

Increasing the lens distance from the CCD moves the focal plane back to the CCD and brings the image back in focus.

Figure 5.2 *How (and why) a lens' focus is changed.*

on one plane at a certain distance from it. Objects receding from that plane—or advancing from it toward the lens—are all technically out of focus.

But in reality, objects up to a certain distance behind or in front of this imaginary plane still appear sharp to the human eye. This sharp territory from in front of the focal distance to behind it is depth of field.

Two factors govern the extent of the depth of field: 1) the focal length of the lens and 2) the working aperture. Since we've already covered aperture, let's see how it affects depth of field.

Each drawing of Figure 5.3 represents a picture made with the same lens, at the same distance from the subjects, and focused on the same person, the woman. The only variable is the aperture. As you can see, the higher the f stop, the greater the depth of field.

In Figure 5.3a, the stop is very high (f/22) and all three subjects are sharp. In

Figure 5.3b, the aperture widens to the middle of its range (f/5.6). Now the depth of field is more shallow and the man and the tree are at its front and back boundaries. They're starting to lose sharpness.

Open the aperture all the way to f/1.4 (Figure 5.3c) and the depth of field is quite narrow. Though the woman remains sharp, the man and the tree are just blurs. Once again, the higher (smaller) the f stop, the greater the depth of field, and vice versa.

As noted above, depth of field is also governed by the focal length of the lens. But first, we need to see what that geometrical abstraction *focal length* really means to practical videographers.

The Long and Short of It

The focal length of a lens affects three important aspects of the image: *angle of view, depth of field* and *perspective*.

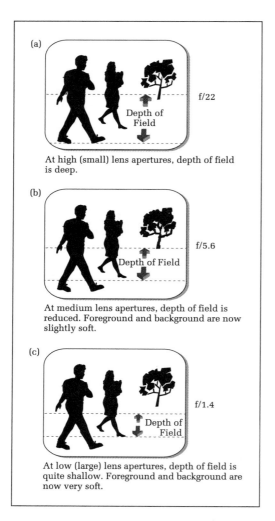

(a) At high (small) lens apertures, depth of field is deep.

f/22

Depth of Field

(b) At medium lens apertures, depth of field is reduced. Foreground and background are now slightly soft.

f/5.6

Depth of Field

(c) At low (large) lens apertures, depth of field is quite shallow. Foreground and background are now very soft.

f/1.4

Depth of Field

Figure 5.3 *Lens aperture affects the depth of field (all shots made at the same focal length and focused on the woman).*

The angle of view gives the lens its name.

In Figure 5.4, a wide-angle lens (here an angle of 85 degrees) includes a great deal of territory. A normal lens (here 55 degrees) is less inclusive; and a telephoto lens has a very narrow angle of view indeed (here 12 degrees). So, at any distance from the subject matter, the wider the lens angle, the wider the field of view.

Incidentally, the angles selected for Figure 5.4 are only typical examples. Each category—wide, normal and narrow (telephoto)—includes a range of angles.

So while 12 degrees is a narrow angle, 9 degrees is also a narrow angle, though slightly more extreme.

As a videographer, you exploit the differences in lens angle of view all the time. For example: shooting a birthday party you may zoom out to your widest angle, to include more of the scene when the small room won't let you move the camcorder farther back from the action.

Going Soft

Earlier, we noted that lens aperture affects depth of field. Now let's see how lens *focal length* also affects depth of field.

As you can see in Figure 5.5, the wider the angle, the greater the depth of field.

In bright sunshine, a wide-angle lens will hold focus from a couple of feet to the horizon. At the other extreme, in dim light a telephoto lens may render sharp subjects through only a few inches of depth. Notice that we include the light conditions because aperture and focal length working together always govern depth of field. But the rule is, at *any* aperture, the wider the lens angle, the greater the depth of field, at any distance from the subject.

Take special note of that last phrase, *at any distance from the subject.* When some photographers can't get enough depth of field they think, "Hey, no problem: I'll increase my depth of field by going wide-angle."

Wrong! If you widen the angle you *will* increase depth of field, but you also reduce the size of the subject in the frame. To return it to its former size in the wide-angle view, you must move the camera closer. What's wrong with that? There's one last rule of focus we haven't mentioned yet: at *any* focal length (and any aperture too), the closer the lens is to the subject, the less depth of field in the image.

See the problem? Moving closer to compensate for the smaller image effectively wipes out the depth gained from going wide-angle. It's a wash.

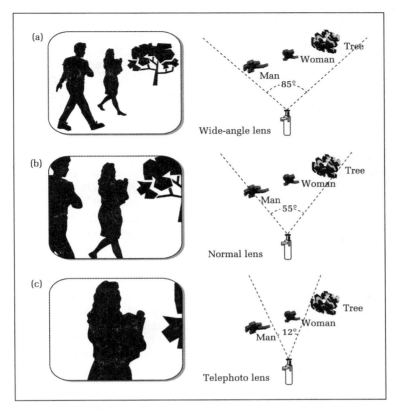

Figure 5.4 *Lens focal length affects angle view (camera is the same distance from subjects in all shots).*

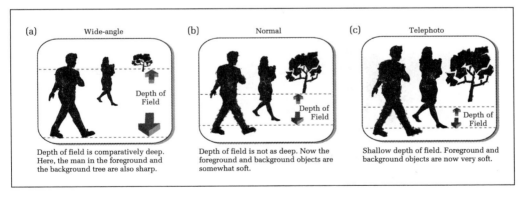

Figure 5.5 *Lens focal length affects the depth of field (all shots made at the same aperture and focused on the woman).*

We said that widening the angle decreases the subject size, and that leads us to the most dramatic effect that focal length has on the image: *perspective*.

Perspective and Focal Length

Perspective is the depiction of apparent depth—a phantom third dimension in a two-dimensional image.

In the real world, even people with only one functional eye can gauge distance, because the farther away objects are, the smaller they appear. Moreover, they diminish in size at a certain rate because of the geometry of the human optical system.

But other optical systems, such as camcorder lenses, may have very different geometries, and objects may shrink much faster or slower than they do in human vision. The perspectives of different lenses depend entirely on their focal lengths.

As you can see, wide-angle lenses exaggerate apparent depth.

Objects shrink quickly as they recede. Normal focal lengths imitate the moderate perspective of human vision (which, of course, is why we call them "normal"). Telephoto lenses reduce apparent depth. Background objects look much bigger and the space between them and the foreground appears compressed.

As the ground plans beside the drawings in Figure 5.6 show, you have to move the camera in order to achieve these different effects. As you change from wide-angle to telephoto, you must pull back so that the reference figure in the foreground (the man) remains the same size and in the same position in the frame. If you simply zoomed in from the first camera position, you would instead get the effect shown in Figure 5.4.

Wide-angle lenses can deliver very dramatic results. People and vehicles moving toward or away from the camera appear to

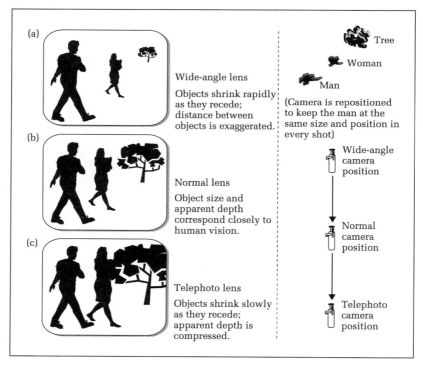

Figure 5.6 *Lens focal length affects relative object size and apparent depth (man, woman and tree are all the same height).*

hurtle past. A roundhouse punch swoops toward the lens like an incoming meteor.

But since they exaggerate depth, wide-angle lenses have drawbacks as well. Get too close to people's faces in wide angle and their noses will grow to elephant size.

On the opposite side, telephoto lenses can make great compositions on the screen by stacking up pictorial elements. For instance, if you want to dramatize congestion and pollution, get an extreme telephoto shot of a freeway at rush hour, viewed head-on. Because you're squeezing a mile's worth of cars into 100 yards of apparent depth, you make a bad problem look ten times worse.

Telephoto shots are great for suspense. Near the climax of Ferris Buehler's Day Off our hero must make it home through neighborhood backyards before his parents arrive. In one suspenseful telephoto shot, Ferris runs straight toward the camera—and runs, and runs, and runs—without seeming to make any progress. It's the telephoto focal length lens, of course, that compresses the distance he's actually covering.

What's What Here?

So far we've talked about wide-angle, normal and telephoto focal lengths without actually naming any. So what's a wide-angle lens, anyway: 8 mm, 28 mm, 90 mm, 200 mm? The answer: *all of the above*. For a full-size VHS camcorder, wide angle is 8 mm; for a 35 mm still camera it's 28 mm; for a 4×5 studio view camera it's 90 mm; and for an 8×10 behemoth it's 200 mm. In other words, the perspective delivered by a certain focal length lens depends on the size of the image it creates.

If you draw a picture of it, it looks like another dose of geometry; don't worry, it's really just common sense. The image created by a lens has to fill the camera's frame, right? But the frame is rectangular and the lens is round. That means that the lens diameter must slightly exceed the diagonal of the frame.

Conveniently, lens designers discovered long ago that for any size format, "normal" perspective is produced by a lens focal length slightly greater than the frame diagonal. That's why a 15 mm lens is normal on a camcorder with a half-inch chip, but a 35 mm still camera takes a 50 mm lens instead. (On the larger camera a 15 mm lens would be an ultra-wide.)

What does this mean to you and how do you interpret the lens markings on your camcorder? To understand the answer, you need to know what your camcorder lens is and how it works.

Zoom!

Unless you're using an older style, C-mount lens camera, or a surveillance camera discarded from a convenience store, your camcorder comes with a zoom lens. A zoom lens allows you to shift between focal lengths without changing lenses. In addition, it possesses two critical characteristics:

You can set the zoom lens at any and every focal length between its extremes. That means, if your camcorder lens ranges from 8 to 80 mm, you could, theoretically, set it at a focal length of 43.033 or 78.25 mm.

The zoom lens remains at the same focus throughout its zoom range. Focus on your subject at any focal length and the subject will stay in focus if you zoom in or out. *Note*: some inner focus lenses do not have this capability.

Okay, so your zoom lens is marked, say, 8–80 mm. What does that mean? What's wide-angle, normal and telephoto in that range?

8 mm would be wide-angle, about 15 mm would be normal and 80 mm would be telephoto. But regardless of what's normal for a given lens, the smaller the number (8 mm in this case), the wider the angle. The larger the number (here 80 mm), the tighter the angle.

Today many compact cameras use 1/3-inch CCDs, so their zoom lenses feature shorter focal ranges. In this format, a normal focal length is around 10 mm, a wide-angle setting would be 5 mm, and a strong tele-photo would be 50 mm.

For example: the Canon XL1 Mini DV camcorder has a 16 : 1 zoom that ranges from 5.5–88 mm. By contrast, the Fujix H128SW Hi8 camcorder's 12 : 1 lens ranges from 4.5–54 mm. Both have 1/3-inch CCDs.

As you can see, knowing what focal lengths mean can affect your choice of camcorder. The Canon offers you a longer telephoto; the Fujix a wider wide-angle. But to interpret the numbers, you have to start with the size of the CCD. 10 mm is a "normal" focal length for a 1/3-inch CCD, while 15 mm is considered normal for a 1/2-inch CCD. Once you figure out your normal focal length, you can roughly calculate wide-angle and telephoto lengths as percentages of normal:

- 35 percent of normal: extreme wide-angle.

- 50 percent of normal: wide-angle.

- 70 percent of normal: mild wide-angle.

- 200 percent of normal: mild telephoto.

- 400 percent of normal: telephoto.

- 500 percent of normal: long telephoto.

As you can see, even the simplest lens on the simplest camcorder is a miracle of mod-ern optical technology. A long, long way from that accidental glop of molten glass.

6
Image Stabilizers: The Technology that Steadies Your Shots

Robert J. Kerr

If you want steady pictures, use a heavy camera. Unfortunately, today's VHS-C and 8 mm camcorders fly in the face of this general rule of thumb; they're so light, the slightest external vibration can affect the quality of their images.

Enter the image stabilizer. Developed specifically to address this problem, these nifty gadgets now grace many small, light-weight camcorders. In this chapter, we'll examine the types of image stabilization systems and how they work.

A Short Stability History

I suppose that even the cave artists back at the dawn of pre-history had trouble freezing images of fast-moving antelope in their minds before they attempted to draw the beasts accurately on their cave walls. Portrait painters, too, have dealt with the problem of fidgety subjects; perhaps even famed Civil War photographer Matthew Brady cursed the artillery shells shooting past him during his long exposures.

Getting a steady image has been a problem for artists, photographers, cinematographers and videographers for as long as these arts have been practiced.

In the earliest days of photography, the size and weight of the camera and the long exposure time made the tripod *de rigeur*; it was the only way to achieve steady images. As film speed increased, so did portability; cameras such as the hand-held Kodak Brownie brought portable photography to every family. The relatively wide-angle lens further reduced the sensitivity to small camera movements. Still, the motion to depress the shutter trip lever required a steady hand for a steady picture.

That was then, this is now. Today's very fast film and electronic flash make steady still photographs the rule.

On to the silver screen. The first cinematographers also used heavy cameras mounted on tripods. Later, the shoulder supported 16 mm cameras also proved heavy enough to provide steady images— if the cinematographer stood still.

Filmmakers got around this limitation by mounting cameras on automobiles and airplanes to capture moving shots. They laid down dolly track, much like train rails, to allow smooth camera movement in action scenes. In the 1970s, Garret Brown invented the Steadicam™, a stabilization device cinematographers on the move used to keep shots steady via an elaborate counter balance. Again, the success of the Steadicam™ depended on its significant mass.

The story was much the same for early television cameras, whose weight and size also required tripod mounting. Resourceful engineers developed massive camera mounts that panned and tilted effortlessly and glided smoothly across studio floors.

With the late 1970s came the introduction of lightweight battery operated videotape recorders. Getting steady video pictures with these early models—shoulder-mounted or hand-held—was a problem. A problem aggravated by addition of the zoom lens with its telephoto capability some time later. Various "body brace" mounts appeared on the market for those who wanted to improve the steadiness of their videos, but the light weight of the cameras made them very sensitive to body or other external motion.

The next major coup: the appearance of the solid state electronics color camera for broadcast news gathering. This 25-pound shoulder-mounted camera could be held reasonably steady at moderate focal lengths of the zoom, but required great stamina on the part of the cameraperson. Not to mention that long focal length shots were a real problem.

The Steadicam™ mount developed for the movies could be used for video cameras, but television applications proved infrequent. Advances in solid state electronics made studio cameras smaller and lighter; the addition of housings and heavy zoom lenses kept them heavy enough to provide smooth operation. Enter the 1980s and the rapid growth of the portable color camera/recorder and camcorder industries. Light weight was a priority; the introduction of the CCD camera chip made VHS-C and 8 mm video cameras smaller than ever. The palmcorder overtook the steadier, larger shoulder-mounted models; its small size—coupled with a zoom lens—made steady pictures a problem. Fortunately, the same technology also supplied the microcircuit advances needed to provide the solution.

About this time, Garret Brown invented a smaller, lighter version of his Steadicam™ stabilization device. The ever-popular Steadicam JR™ helps to stabilize the images of camcorders weighing less than 5 pounds. It completely isolates the camera from rotational body movements, thanks to a delicate balancing system featuring a low-friction gimbal between the camera and the support handle.

This device, although useful, is not one you'd carry with you on vacation. It will fold to a shoulder mount configuration, but is best applied to specific shooting problems you can plan in advance. When properly deployed, the Steadicam JR™ can yield steady video pictures.

Not too long ago, numerous manufacturers including Panasonic, JVC, Hitachi, Sony and Canon introduced different systems that reduce image jitter problems. Unlike the Steadicam JR™, these systems are integrated into the camcorder itself and do not employ any external hardware.

There are two main image stabilization systems: optical stabilization and electronic stabilization.

The All Electronic System

The electronic system operates by first reducing the area of the CCD chip from which the video image is read (See Figure 6.1). This smaller image then increases in size to fill the whole screen. The exact area scanned then shifts electronically to compensate for unwanted external movement of the camera. Since this system does not actually sense the movement of

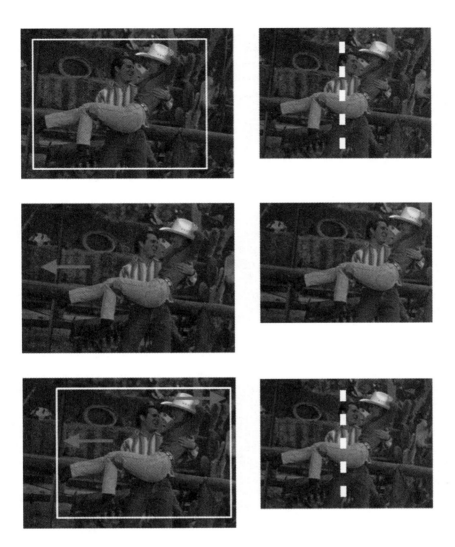

Figure 6.1 *Electronic image stabilization.*

the camera it must sense camera shake from the image only. The trick is to tell camera movement from movement of the subject.

Some manufacturers use a motion detection method based on fuzzy logic. How much to compensate for movement is a decision based on comparing the two images. An image freezes in computer memory and divides into numerous quadrants. A processor compares the differences between the individual quadrants of the frozen image and the current image. If all quadrants change in the same direction, the processor deduces that camera

movement caused the differences between the current and stored images. The area of the CCD being scanned then shifts in the opposite direction to cancel the movement.

Changes in fewer than all quadrants indicate subject rather than camera movement and no compensating action occurs. If quadrant analysis indicates that both the subject and the camera moved, fuzzy logic calculates the image shift needed just to compensate for the camera movement.

One criticism of this system: the loss in image quality brought about by reducing the number of pixels used to create the picture. This loss is noticeable to varying degrees on most camcorders, virtually invisible on others. By the time the video signal goes to the tape and back, especially on standard 8 mm and VHS models, image loss is negligible. Most videographers will find the added stability to be worth the tradeoff.

Optical Image Stabilization

Optical stabilization operates very differently from the electronic system. Instead of sliding an undersized image around the CCD camera chip, the optical system corrects for camera movement before the image reaches the chip. This way, the full resolution of the CCD occurs at all times. The result: no image degradation.

The key optical component is a variable bend prism. As light passes through a prism, it bends in the direction of travel. The amount of bending—known as *refraction*—is a function of the angle at which the light strikes the "in" side of the prism, the relative angle of the "exit" side and the refractive properties of the prism material.

Refraction is what you see when you look at an object at the bottom of a pool or

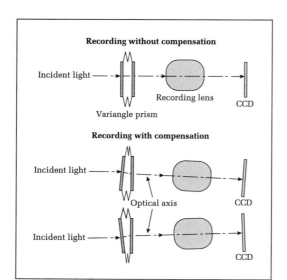

Figure 6.2 *Optical stabilization system.*

stream. If you look straight down on the object, the light reflected from it passes straight through the surface of the water. No bending or refraction occurs, and you see the object in its actual position. If you view the object in the pool or creek from an angle, thanks to refraction you'll think the object is considerably higher than it really is. If you've ever been spear fishing you'll know what I mean. Try to spear fish from above the water, and you'll have to aim the spear below the spot where you "see" the fish.

Back to the prism. When you think prism, you probably think about how it breaks up light into the color spectrum. Like how raindrops make a rainbow. You see the rainbow because different colors of light bend by differing amounts as they pass through the prism.

Rainbows may be pretty, but they're not so desirable in image stabilization systems; to eliminate any potential rainbow problems manufacturers choose prism materials carefully and restrict the angle of refraction to no more than 1.5 degrees.

The prism used in the optical stabilization system is a unique variable angle design consisting of two glass plates joined at the circumference by a flexible bellows. A silicone fluid with controlled refractive properties fills the space between the lenses (see Figure 6.2).

When the two plates are parallel, light passes through undisturbed. If, however, the plates contract at any point on the perimeter, the light path bends away from the compressed area. Thus the system can actually *steer* the optical image by manipulating the prism.

The next step: how the system can tell when to perform such steering.

The optical system requires two motion sensors, one for pitch (tilting up and down) and the other for yaw (panning side to side). The sensors amplify and process the motion signals to determine where and how to move the image. The results convert to electric current applied to two drive actuators, one for pitch and one for yaw. These actuators adjust one of the glass plates in the prism relative to the other, directing the image back to its proper position on the CCD sensor.

Field Testing the Two Systems

The easiest way to show how effective these two image stabilization systems are is to test them under adverse conditions. In this case, the test consisted of video recorded on a road of moderate roughness by one camera equipped with electronic image stabilization and then by a second, fitted with optical stabilization.

I did the videotaping from the passenger side of a car, while my business partner drove. We completed one complete trip over the test course for each camcorder. We used a medium telephoto zoom setting to exaggerate the effects of camera motion. Then we brought the tapes back to the studio and compared results.

Both systems provided extraordinary improvement in the stability of the image. With either type of camera, shots of the cars ahead of us stayed steady in the picture—even as the dashboard of the test vehicle shifted up and down at the lower part of the picture. Certainly video from moving vehicles proves much more usable when you engage the image stabilizers.

The optical system makes no use of video information, so it cannot wrongly interpret moving objects as camcorder motion. The same is not true, of course for the digital system. The question was, how well would its fuzzy logic compensate for an actual moving subject combined with camera pitch and yaw? The answer: fuzzy logic did an excellent job; road images remained steady—even when the car dashboard bounced up and down in the lower part of the picture.

Being almost completely mechanical, the optical system experiences some inevitable delay as its components move and adjust. This makes it somewhat slower to respond to quick jolts, but this does not adversely affect normal operation. A happy by-product of the mechanical system: its remarkable smoothness.

The electronic system is very fast, and tried to compensate for even the most instantaneous bumps in the road. Some image jump occurred, as though the electronics eventually gave up on fixing the jump and instead started fresh with a new image.

An interesting test result with both systems pan or tilt actions, with the stabilizers engaged, the movement of the image in the viewfinder lagged behind the camera movement, or "floated." The effect is only noticeable when moving the camera while looking in the viewfinder; I didn't notice it when viewing the recorded videotape. This simply tends to demonstrate that two dramatically different approaches provided almost exactly the same satisfactory result.

Cynic that I am, I tend to view a lot of "features" on the higher priced camcorders simply as opportunities for the video department salespersons to move customers to higher priced models.

Not so, however, for the two image stabilizers described here. They work, and prove very useful in many situations, particularly hand-held "shots of opportunity."

And So

Image stabilization is a feature well worth having, particularly on today's small, lightweight camcorders. Use it, and your images will be easier to watch; shoot handheld telephoto shots without it, and—well, just try it. You'll see what we mean.

7

Solar Panel Imaging: Secrets of the CCD

Loren Alldrin

Buried deep within your camcorder lies a fabulous image sensor that sets it apart from most other image-capturing devices. This image sensor is called a charge-coupled device—that's CCD to you and me.

If you're like most videographers, you probably don't know much about this hidden treasure. And that's a shame. Knowing the hows and whys of CCDs can help make your videography more effective. It can help you differentiate one model from another and decide which camcorder to buy. Moreover, CCD sensors benefit from some of the fastest-advancing technology in camcorders; know the future of sensors and you can peek into the very future of camcorders.

The Short Explanation

Defining the CCD is, uh, simple: a CCD, or interline transfer charge-coupled device, is a tightly-packed array of tiny photo-diodes consisting of silicon oxide and alternating P and photosensitive N semiconductor

regions on an N-type substrate. Every 1/60th of a second, a transfer pulse triggers a vertical transfer CCD lying between pixel rows to sweep accumulated charges out to the horizontal transfer register (H-CCD) and output amplifier. Newer designs employ an additional P+ embedded photodiode to improve signal-to-noise ratio by controlling irregular dark currents (see Figure 7.1).

Don't worry—that definition went over my head, too. Try this: imagine a huge grid made up of rows of solar panels. Each square-foot panel sits atop a small battery. Only a few inches separate each panel from those to its north and south. About a foot of space lies between one column of panels and the next; within that space you'll find a small pathway running next to each column, as well as along the bottom of the grid. The grid encompasses hundreds of panels in each direction, stretching for about 1/4 of a mile on a side.

When light strikes the panels, they charge their individual batteries. Panels exposed to more light charge faster, while

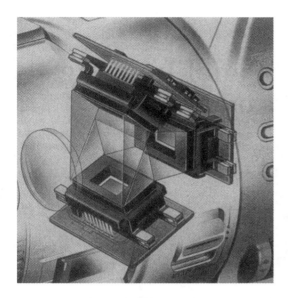

Figure 7.1 *Three-chip designs from Sony and Panasonic use three CCD sensors arrayed around a light-splitting prism.*

cleanliness required for making sensors is truly superhuman; most CCDs come from completely automated factories where humans play minor supporting roles. A tiny speck of dust, harmless enough to us, can actually shut down the CCD manufacturing process.

The batteries represent the buildup of charges in the pixel. Since CCD pixels are photosensitive, they create a charge in proportion to the light striking them. Lots of light makes for a greater charge, while darkness leaves them with little more than the small random charges we call noise. Smaller pixels gather less light and generate weaker charges; a principle manufacturers must address to produce smaller chips and pixels. More on that later.

The trucks mimic the action of the vertical transfer registers, electronic roadways that carry charges out of the active sensing area of the CCD. These registers are necessary because the record electronics do not read charges directly from individual pixels. Instead, charges move en masse down the vertical transfer registers until they reach the edge of the chip.

The conveyor belt is like the horizontal transfer register, which unloads the charges from its vertical counterpart. The horizontal transfer register carries charges off the CCD along the edge of the sensor. Their destination: the amplifiers and specialized circuits that process the signal before recording (see Figure 7.2).

The high-paid managers represent the camcorder's record electronics, processing and modifying signals for recording on magnetic tape. Specialized chips combine color and brightness information into one signal, boost its level and then send it on to the record heads.

Generating a final report on the status of the solar grid could take hours—depending on the speed of the trucks and whether or not those high-paid managers get stuck in an important meeting. In a camcorder, however, videotape records a "final report" from the CCD sensor sixty times per second. If only our government worked that fast.

those in the dark build up little or no charge. After a given period of time, tiny trucks drive down between the vertical rows of panels to measure each battery's charge. The trucks then quickly discharge the battery they're measuring and move on to the next panel. When the trucks reach the end of the row, they dump their information onto a conveyor belt. This belt carries the data from the panels back to a central station. It's here that high-paid managers combine the individual measurements, evaluating the electrical output of the grid. Their final report looks a whole lot like a video image.

To relate this rather loose analogy to an actual CCD, first we need to reduce the size of the solar grid by a factor of about 75,000. Most of today's CCDs measure a mere 1/3-inch from corner to corner, and even smaller 1/4-inch designs are on the horizon.

In our little analogy, solar panels serve as the individual pixels. Today's sensors actually boast hundreds of thousands of these pixels, etched onto the top of a silicon wafer by chemical and photographic processes. The machine tolerances and

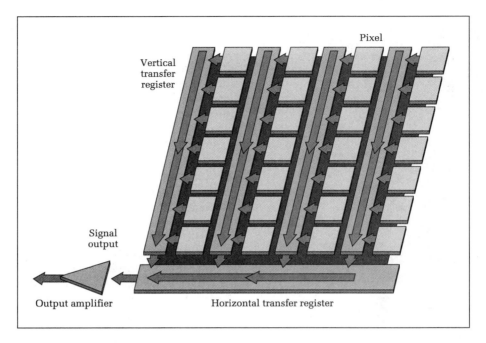

Figure 7.2 *In a standard CCD sensor, pixels feed charges to vertical transfer registers. These in turn feed the horizontal transfer register. From there, signals move through an amplifier to the record electronics.*

Sensor Overload

When a solar panel receives too much light, it overcharges its battery. The truck tries to read this abnormally high value, only to cook its tiny charge meter in the process. When the truck gets to the bottom of the row, it picks up a new charge meter, but until then severe damage can occur. All the readings it currently holds, as well as all subsequent measurements, are wrong. They all read maximum on the charge meter.

Something similar occurs when a given area of a CCD receives too much light. The vertical transfer register overloads, muddling all the charges for that row. This creates a bright, vertical smear in the image, extending out above and below the offending spot. You've probably seen this before, especially when shooting a bright spot of light against a dark background.

This type of image smear is unique to CCD sensors. Metal oxide semiconductor (MOS) sensors read each pixel directly, doing away with the need for vertical

transfer registers and their associated image smearing. Regardless, MOS sensors have fallen out of favor with manufacturers, probably due to higher manufacturing costs. New CCD designs address the bleed problem, resulting in chips less prone to streaking.

Shutter Shenanigans

Though you've heard the term high-speed shutter tossed about; there's actually no such component in the lens/sensor assembly. This term comes from the sensor's ability to mimic the effects of a film camera's fast shutter speed. In a film camera, opening the shutter's blades for a very short period of time exposes the film to a brief snippet of light. Thus a film camera can freeze even the fastest motion.

To understand how this works in a video camera, let's go back to the solar panel scenario. In just minutes, it will be time to measure the grid. But instead of letting the panels finish gathering a complete charge, the trucks sweep through the grid to discharge all the batteries. When the trucks return to collect measurements, the panels have been charging for just a few minutes. Output is lower, but management can still get a picture of the grid's status.

This is what happens with a camcorder's high-speed shutter. No mechanical blade assembly snaps open and shut; instead, the camcorder gives the pixels less time to charge before whisking their signals off to the recorder. If you select an extremely fast shutter speed, say 1/10,000th of a second, the pixels charge up as usual during the first 99 percent of the record cycle. Then, just 1/10,000 of a second before recording, the sensor discharges the pixels. What's recorded on tape is a brief slice of time, representing only the last tiny bit of the record cycle. Since most subjects don't move very far in 1/10,000th of a second, a high-speed shutter freezes the action. Whereas a single frame of an airplane propeller made at 1/60th of a second might show a blur, a single frame of the propeller made at 1/10,000th could show it standing still, each blade distinct.

Two matters to keep in mind when shooting with a high-speed shutter:

1. *Lighting.* Since pixels have so little time to charge, the intensity of the light must be greater to produce a usable image. The higher the shutter speed, the brighter the light required. Shooting at 1/10,000th of a second requires strong daylight. A more conservative setting of 1/2,000th of a second still requires sunlight or strong indoor lighting.

2. *Depth of field.* Because it needs more light, high-speed shutter forces the camcorder's iris to open up. This in turn reduces depth of field, a boon to creative videographers whose camcorders lack manual iris control.

If you want to soften the background behind your subject, reduce your depth of field by increasing shutter speed.

Some camcorders offer a slow-speed shutter, which has the exact opposite properties of high-speed. Slow-speed shutter delivers an image in less light, though much more image smear results. If you're shooting a stationary subject in extremely low light, slow-speed shutter may deliver an improved image. At the very least, you can use it as a unique special effect.

Here's how it works: The trucks servicing our solar array still sweep through the panels to gather readings; they simply don't discharge the batteries completely before reading the charge. This allows the panels to build up a greater charge, boosting the resulting values. Since the batteries retain some residual charge, each reading includes some values from the previous cycles. In the same way, a camcorder in low-speed shutter mode allows the pixels' charge to build up for longer than just one record cycle. It effectively "averages" the light, making fast-moving subjects smear and bleed.

Shrinking CCD Panels

Let's say that the owner of the field that contains the solar array wishes to sell off some of his land, leaving the panels with about 40 percent less area. We can't reduce the number of panels, so there's only one solution—make them smaller. To pack the same number of panels on our now-shrunken plot of land, we must cut them down to just over 7 inches per side. We buy new, smaller trucks and a shorter conveyor belt and fire up the new array. The managers are not happy.

Seems the scaled-down array now puts out about 40 percent less energy. These are lean times, and a cut in output simply won't do. The high-paid managers hire a few high-paid engineering consultants to increase the panels' sensitivity.

There you have it: the plight of the shrinking CCD. Like a tiny solar panel, a pixel's output is a function of its surface area. Shrink the pixel, and its sensitivity suffers. When sensitivity falls, so does the camcorder's low-light performance and resistance to video noise. But manufacturers can't ignore the benefits of smaller sensors—they achieve the same depth of field with smaller lenses. Smaller lenses in turn make for smaller camcorders, and smaller camcorders seem to sell better.

The solution: the microlens. Basically a tiny, translucent bubble formed over each pixel, the microlens gathers incident light that would have otherwise missed the pixel's active sensing area. CCD makers form microlenses into the CCD itself, increasing the effective area of the pixel without actually making it any larger. Thanks to the microlens, 1/3-inch CCDs are now a reality. This microlens technology is so effective, in fact, that a 1/3-inch sensor with microlenses may outperform the larger 1/2-inch designs—like realizing even more output from our solar array after placing a glass canopy over each panel.

Another way to offset the effect of smaller pixels is through better amplification. Noise is an enemy to any kind of electrical signal, and smaller signals are the most prone to it. Amplifying a signal just as it leaves the pixel reduces noise and strengthens output. At the time of this writing, manufacturers are experimenting with a new type of CMOS (complementary metal oxide semiconductor) sensor invented by NASA/JPL called the APS CMOS (Active Pixel Sensor) that places an amplifier at each photosite.

These technologies have led to sensors a scant 1/4-inch across—a big step toward the next generation of ultra-compact camcorders.

Smaller or Better

The same technology that allows sensors to shrink allows advances in the other direction as well. If pixels offer improved sensitivity at a smaller size, then CCD makers can pack more pixels on the same size chip. Once manufacturers increase the pixel count of a given sensor, they face a tough decision. They can use the additional pixels for a higher resolution video image, or they can employ them for special image effects at the standard resolution.

Electronic Image Stabilization (EIS) is a good example of such an effect. An increase in pixel count from 410,000 to 470,000 allows the camcorder to use just the central 90 percent of the chip for imaging without resolution loss. Move this region in opposition to the camcorder's movement, and you reduce shake on handheld shots. Whereas previous EIS schemes resulted in an inevitable loss of resolution, this system shows no noticeable softness of the image.

Color Blind

Some of you may remember from your high school science class that solar panels respond only to the amount of light striking them, not the color of the light. In the same way, CCD pixels are colorblind. So how does a camcorder record a color image?

Camcorders with a single CCD sensor use a mosaic color filter placed over the pixels. Imagine a huge stained-glass window lying over our solar panel array. This window alternates panes of color—either red, green and blue or their complements, yellow, magenta and cyan. Each solar panel sits directly under a colored pane, and responds only to that color of light. When the managers tally up the charges, they make note of each panel's color.

By tracking which pixels see which color, a camcorder extracts both a luminance (brightness and detail) and chrominance (color) signal from a monochrome sensor. Color filters are relatively easy to add to a CCD, though they compromise both color and brightness portions of the video signal. Because there are a limited number of pixels responding to a given color, chrominance has only about one quarter the resolution of the luminance signal. Placing a colored filter over the pixels also reduces their sensitivity and low-light performance.

There are better, albeit more expensive, ways to coax color information out of monochrome sensors. The best system is the one professional cameras have used for years—three sensors, or chips, with one sensor devoted to each of the three primary colors. Just behind the lens, a precision-made prism splits the incoming light into its red, green and blue components. Some manufacturers use an array of dichroic mirrors to sift the light; these coated mirrors reflect only a certain color, letting the rest pass.

Because there's no color filter clouding the sensors in three-chip designs, resolution does not drop. With a chip "specializing" in each primary color, hues are very accurate and natural. The result: a better picture than a single CCD can deliver.

Future CCDs

The trend toward smaller CCDs will most likely die with current 1/4-inch designs. Sensors of this size will work with incredibly small lenses, making the transport and tape medium itself the biggest obstacles to further camcorder downsizing.

Manufacturers will undoubtedly continue in the other direction, toward larger sensors with increased resolution. Chips with pixel counts approaching one million allow for special effects and electronic stabilization without resolution loss. The advent of HDTV and the growing popularity of today's 16:9 formats will drive the market toward ultra-high resolution sensors. HDTV cameras already have 2/3-inch sensors with over two million pixels.

Advances in sensors drive other areas of the video market as well. Camera resolutions are already much greater than those of camcorder transports. As sensors evolve far beyond the recording ability of camcorders, consumers will push for new video signal formats. Sensor evolution shows no sign of slowing. As long as there's a sun in the sky sending light to CCD pixels and solar panels alike, better sensors will be here to capture it. The future of sensors is bright indeed.

8

Filter Features: Camcorder Filters and How to Use Them

Michael Rabiger

Although widely available, filters aren't used much on camcorders—probably because they are not fully appreciated. Consider this: what other camcorder accessory helps you to soften picture contrast, reduce depth of field, change color intensity, shoot day-for-night, cut through haze, create star or flare effects, control reflections from glass or water, darken the sky, compose vignettes—even create fog where none exists?

Filters allow you to do all of this—and at very little expense.

Filter Principles

Filters for videography operate on two different principles. One type uses subtraction, permitting some colors of light to pass through while absorbing others.

To determine what color a filter passes, hold it up to white light: its color is the color of light it conducts. What isn't conducted is absorbed, along with a certain amount of heat traveling with the light.

The second type of filter uses the principle of diffusion, allowing all light to pass but intentionally modifying how it emerges. The low contrast filter, for example, takes bright illumination from image highlights, dispersing it into shadow areas without significantly changing image resolution.

Colored filters were in use even before color film. In black-and-white photography a red or orange filter blocking blue light darkens a blue sky, rendering a cloud formation into a dramatic white sculpture against an inky heaven. On sunny days, when indirect or "fill" light contains blue sky light, an orange or yellow filter can darken shadow areas by discriminating against their blue content.

If you are shooting video for eventual black-and-white, or taping a nightmarish color sequence, consider color filtering. You can use a color monitor to test your ideas before you shoot.

Kelvin Conversion

Most color film emulsions render colors accurately under one of two main sources of light. One emulsion balances to daylight, assumed to be 5,400 degrees on the Kelvin scale; the second balances for studio lights at 3,200 degrees Kelvin.

Daylight color temperature fluctuates depending on the time of day and location on the globe. It rises to 10,000 degrees Kelvin on a mountaintop, and plummets to a ruddy 1,800 at sunrise or sunset. You can check source-light color temperature with a color temperature meter.

The Kelvin Scale involves the concept of heating a black object. As its temperature rises it emits the progression of colors—red, orange, yellow, green, blue, indigo, and violet—that emerge from a prism used to split white light into its component colors. You can memorize the "roygbiv" sequence by remembering that colorful character Roy G. Biv.

Light also exists above and below the visible spectrum. Infrared lies below the threshold of visibility, while ultraviolet shines above it. Unfortunately, both photo emulsion and video image chips pick up ultraviolet light, requiring a UV blocking filter at all times.

In white balancing a camcorder, you adjust its electronics to treat a particular light source as if it were white. This makes human flesh come out true to life. Film emulsions don't offer a white balance control, so an image shot under non-standard light must be color corrected to render colors truly. Professional video cameras feature built-in color correction filters to maintain white balance under different lighting conditions. Colors remain consistent from location to location.

On consumer camcorders, filters can be attached to the lens itself. The most common filter is #85 orange; it converts daylight, with its heavy blue content, to match the high orange content of tungsten. Like most filters, the #85 is usually lens-mounted, converting all light entering the camera. It allows shooting in daylight with a tungsten white setting.

The fluorescent conversion filter will correct an image shot under fluorescent light to, say, 3,200 degrees Kelvin. It's of limited use unless you know what type of tube is in use. Even then, the gas discharge tube's broken spectrum can make for a sickly greenish cast. The videographer should white balance under fluorescent light, but is helpless if the space contains an assortment of tubes.

Light Mixing

In both film and video, adding 3,200 degrees Kelvin movie lighting to an interior scene already lit by daylight means trouble. You are shooting under mixed color temperatures; they'll probably appear as strange orange-covered shadow areas on a face otherwise nicely color-balanced. Or you'll display a normal foreground with a lurid blue world out the window.

When you need to boost light levels in a daylit room, filter the window so incoming daylight matches the 3,200 degrees Kelvin of the supplementary lighting. Location film units generally tape large sheets of #85 gel to the windows, usually on the inside so air movement doesn't cause the gel to waver.

Another approach to color correction uses blue #80A heatproof filters over tungsten light to produce 5,400 degrees Kelvin light matching incoming daylight. This is less practical because of "filter factor" loss—too much precious light gets lost in the filter itself. The #80A's filter factor is two stops, meaning only one fourth of the light's output gets through. You need to open your camera's iris two additional stops to achieve the same exposure.

The #80A and #85 are just two of a number of color conversion filters allowing savvy videographers to unify diverse lighting sources.

Color, Contrast and Fog

If you want to shoot video with subtle and consistent scene coloration, your best bet is to balance the camera, then use a weak blue or yellow lens filter. Remember to set your white balance control to manual, or the auto white circuitry will sabotage your efforts.

Sunrise filters can enhance nature; a blue filter can simulate nighttime shooting, a process called day for night. Shoot either late or early in the day when there's sunlight and long shadows, and underexpose.

Remember to turn on the car headlights and streetlights and put lights in windows. Or just shoot at night.

UV filters screen out ultraviolet tight, invisible to the human eye but recorded on video as haze. UV filters also serve as good protection for the front of your lens. It's cheap and easy to replace a UV filter compared to lens repair.

A neutral density (ND) filter, like gray sunglasses, reduces all colors of light equally. A filter with a factor of .3 reduces light transmission by one stop; .6 reduces transmission two stops. ND filters usefully cut a len's light intake when the scene is very bright or you want to force the lens to work at a wider aperture to produce a restricted depth of field. (See Figure 8.1.)

Low contrast filters use very fine etchings on the glass to create light dispersal within the filter itself. White light redistributed from highlights is scattered throughout the image. This raises light levels in shadows and lowers the overall contrast between highlight and shadow, at small cost to picture resolution.

The low contrast filter reduces the characteristic look of video—hard contrast and saturated colors—and produces a softer "film" look with de-saturated pastel colors.

A diffusion filter softens the image, giving it a soft, dreamlike look to your scene. Fog filters are strong diffusion filters. They make the image look as though shot through mist or fog. (See Figure 8.2.)

Figure 8.1 By reducing the amount of light that reaches your lens, a neutral density filter can change the depth of field in your shot.

However, when something moves nearer the camera in genuine fog, the image clears—not so when using a filter.

Nylon Glass

An inexpensive and extremely reliable diffusion filter is a nylon stocking. Just be sure to empty the leg out first. My father, a makeup man often hard-pressed to generate glamour in superannuated actresses, used to speak dryly of close-ups "shot through a sock."

Another easily produced filter is a sheet of thin optical glass smeared with petroleum jelly. This produces a misty image with flares around highlights known as halations. You can limit the effect by keeping the center clear and lightly treating the edges of the frame only.

A softnet filter—fine netting laminated between clear glass—creates soft diffusion

Figure 8.2 Diffusion filters can add a "dreamy" look to your shot.

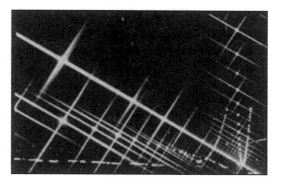

Figure 8.3 A star filter puts stars into your shot wherever there's a point of light.

Graduated, Spot and Split

Graduated filters are half clear, with a soft transition between. A graduated neutral density filter lined up on the horizon can cool a hot sky. The clear lower half leaves the land unfiltered, so the filter functions like a tinted-top car windshield. A graduated color filter used on a static shot can make the sky a rich violet. Of course, you can't tilt the shot up or down without giving the game away.

Graduated filters can also operate vertically. You might line the filter so its dark half reduces the light entering through a doorway, creating consistent lighting throughout the whole scene.

A center spot is a heavy diffusion filter with a clear spot in the middle. This effect is useful for nostalgia shots or drawing attention to the spy in the cafe.

Split field filters are those lenses that divide the field of view into two separate focal lengths, like bifocal glasses. This enables deep focus shots by dividing and thus extending the effective depth of field. You can use the fields horizontally or vertically by rotating the lens. Disguise the telltale dividing lines with a horizon, doorjamb or other eye-distracting compositional factor.

The polarizing filter (Figure 8.4) is another axis-sensitive filter particularly useful for landscape shots. It can reduce the light-polarized glare thrown off by water, plastic and glass surfaces—but not

and lowered resolution without highlight halations or lightened shadows. Softnets come in black, red, and skintone for enhanced effects. A white softnet acts much like a low contrast filter.

Star filters, which are pronounced diffusion filters, produce the four or six-point highlight star effects so dear to glass and jewelry advertisers. (See Figure 8.3.) Star filters are ineffective in panning shots unless you're a fan of alarming psychedelic effects. And you can't rotate the filter unless prepared not only for stars, but rotating stars.

Figure 8.4 *A polarizing filter allows you to control bright reflections.*

metal. It consists of a light-polarizing material that rotates until its polarity opposes the incoming reflection.

The polarizing filter can also effectively darken a blue sky by tuning out much of the blue light refracted from skylight moisture droplets. It works best when the lens-to-subject axis is about ninety degrees to the sun.

Mounting Filters

We arrive now at a major problem in consumer video—the mounting of filters.

Professional cameras use a matte box, an adjustable filter holder with an extendible lens hood bellows. The device holds square or round filters securely in front of the lens. No matter what lens you use or how much it rotates or extends, the standard filter adjusts and remains solidly in position. This allows rotation of axis-determined filters like stars.

The dedicated do-it-yourself type can of course improvise something. Tiffen makes square filters that fit the Cokin "P Series" filter holder, but this range of pro filters can cost the proverbial arm and a leg.

A holder can also grab custom vignette slides, such as keyhole or binocular shapes for what-the-butler-saw movies, and gunsight or periscope masks for those with warfare in mind.

In most stores, only circular screw-in filters are available to videographers, and must be ordered for a specific lens diameter. Changing is slow and fiddly. If you acquire a wide-angle lens adapter, you'll require a whole new set of larger filters.

You'll handle your filters quite a lot, so consider durability. Gelatin is optically the best material—thin and inexpensive—but it scratches and buckles easily, ruined by a single fingerprint.

Be aware that if you sandwich filters together, you tend to produce rainbow refraction circles called Newton's Rings. Manufacturers make the most common combinations. Gel laminated inside glass is durable and easy to clean, but can be susceptible to moisture. Dyed-in-the-mass glass filters vary in consistency and are expensive; semi-rigid thermosetting resin is a light and scratch-resistant material and optically as good as glass.

In Conclusion

Filters are an easy and inexpensive way to improve your camcorder footage. As such, they're the perfect upgrade for camcorder owners who want to improve their work without emptying their bank account.

One final note of caution: filters come in a variety of price ranges; don't assume that a cheaper one is necessarily a bargain. As with most videography gear, you generally get what you pay for. Caveat emptor!

9

Dissecting a Video Editing Computer

Joe McCleskey

Ever wonder what exactly makes a video editing computer work? Ever want to know what separates the ordinary, game-playing, document-creating PC from the kind that can easily pump out hour-long, professional-looking home videos? No matter if you already own a video editing computer or plan to buy one—it still pays to know exactly what makes this special breed of machine tick. We'll discuss PCs here, since they are much more dissectible than Macs, but the concepts are the same.

In this article, we'll take apart a typical video-editing computer piece by piece, much the same way you might have taken apart a hapless frog in junior high science class. Why? To help you troubleshoot problems, increase performance, and make more informed purchasing decisions.

So without further introduction, let's put on our rubber gloves, grab our scalpels, and get busy (see page 44).

Software

Editing software is the interface between your ideas and a finished product. Software used in video editing covers a wide range of different types and capabilities, including nonlinear editing, photo and graphics manipulation, audio editing and special effects creation, to name just a few. Once you've got the basic system together, the software provides the means to make your video dreams a reality. It's what you'll spend the most time learning to operate—and the most time blaming when things don't work properly—so don't skimp here; be sure to find the software that works best for your needs.

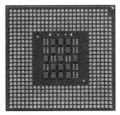

CPU

The CPU (central processing unit) is the heart of any computer. A computer can really do only two things: 1) perform calculations and 2) move or copy information. The CPU does these things; in essence, it is the computer itself on a single chip. A video editing computer needs the fastest CPU available for rendering. Some use two or more CPUs; video editing machines greatly benefit from an added CPU to share the task of rendering video files, even if the software doesn't explicitly support multiple CPUs.

Motherboard

The motherboard holds the CPU, connecting it to the other parts of the machine. The part of the motherboard that ships info back and forth between the components is called the bus. Video editing machines require motherboards with fast bus speeds in order to handle the immense flow of information that takes place while editing. Faster bus speeds result in faster rendering times. Also located on the motherboard are places to connect peripheral devices—hard drives, video capture cards, FireWire cards and memory. In video editing machines, the motherboard should have a number of open PCI slots for peripheral devices; lots of room to expand RAM; connections for high-speed hard drives; and a bus speed of at least 100 MHz.

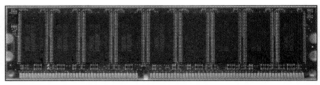

RAM

RAM (random access memory) is a computer's temporary storage place for information. It's the place where the software stores and moves pieces of information for processing. A video-editing computer typically has lots of high-speed RAM available—at least 256 MB for starters, but often more than a gigabyte. Both speed and quantity of RAM will have an effect on the rendering speed of your computer: The more, and the faster, the better.

Hard Drives

The hard drive of a computer is the place where information gets stored in the long term. (Contrast this with RAM, which stores information only until you turn off the computer). When you capture a clip, it writes onto the hard drive. Note that editing computers should have two hard drives—one for the operating system and software, and another solely for video and audio capture and storage. The separate video/audio drive should be the largest, fastest drive you can afford, should spin at 7,200 RPM and should minimally support a true sustained data transfer rate of at least 5 MB per second in order to handle the rigors of video editing. And always remember: the amount of storage space on the video capture drive directly relates to the length of video clips you can work on at any one time. You can never have too much space and good drives can be found for as little as $1 per gigabyte.

Video Capture/Fire Wire Card

To edit video on a computer, you need some way to get the video from the camera or VCR onto the hard drive. This is the role of the video capture card (or, more commonly, the FireWire or IEEE 1394 card). A digitizer card can take an ordinary analog video signal and digitize it (change it to a series of ones and zeroes). A FireWire card allows transfer of digital video from a digital camcorder or VCR to the hard drive. Video capture cards vary widely in price and performance, but the only real concern with a FireWire card is whether or not it works and continues working—the resulting video will look exactly the same as it did when you shot it, regardless of the quality of the FireWire card. Some capture cards have special hardware that improves rendering speed and performance during editing.

10
Editing Appliances:
Cracking the Case

Charles Bloodworth

Editing Appliance. Its name evokes images of refrigerators, dish washers, microwaves and toasters. Turn it on, stick in some video, set the timer and wait for a finished project. Well, almost. While they are relatively easy to use, these boxes are anything but simple. Inside they are more like high-powered computers than kitchen gadgets.

What exactly is an editing appliance? If you're a regular reader, you'll probably recognize names like Casablanca and Avio from Draco Systems and Screenplay and Sequel from Applied Magic. With the entry-level prices for these devices now below the $1,500, editing appliances have become extremely attractive to first-time editors and budget minded pros. Many people are still confused about just what appliances are and how they do what they do. In this article, you'll get to know the anatomy of an editing appliance as we perform an appliance dissection.

Pull the lid off any editing appliance and you'll find some pretty ordinary computer parts, a hard drive and some specialized software. Like computers that can process video, editing appliances have CPUs, memory, capture/compression hardware, one or more large, fast, hard drives and editing software. They also have connectors for input and output devices. Some have "slots" for smart media cards, some have CD-ROM drives and others rely on floppy disk drives to allow software updates and effects plug-ins. Let's take a look at each of the major pieces one at a time and see how they work together to make an editing appliance tick (see Figure 10.1).

Processor

The CPU, or Central Processing Unit, is the heart of any computer system. Many of the editing appliances use processors that may seem rather slow compared to the state-of-the-art CPU technology in your home computer. Not to worry though the CPUs that come in editing appliances are more than sufficient for the task at hand. Remember, unlike a PC or Mac,

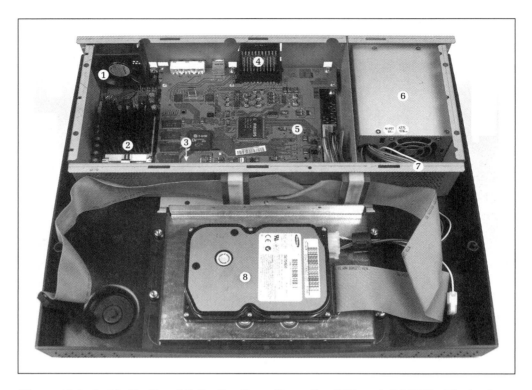

Figure 10.1. *Inside the Box: (1) Cooling Fan—Keeps the CPU cool; (2) CPU—The brains that make the box work; (3) RAM—Short term storage of operating system programs; (4) A/V Inputs/Outputs—Ports for getting video in and out of the editor; (5) Main Board— The "central nervous system" connecting all the components; (6) Power Supply— Harnesses juice to power the box; (7) Chasis—The frame in which it all resides; (8) Hard Drive—Stores digital video for random access editing.*

which must do everything for everyone (including running Windows, creating spreadsheets, word processing, playing games, balancing checkbooks and accessing the Internet), an editing appliance only has to do one job: edit video. Editing appliance manufacturers strike a balance between the CPU's cost and performance. And while the CPU speed can factor in on the rendering times of transitions or special effects, many editing appliances now provide real-time or near-real-time rendering that works independently from the CPU.

Memory

Memory comes in many forms and is just what its name implies. An editing appliance

stores its programs, data and video in various types of memory, including both volatile and non-volatile memory. Volatile, like its name suggests, is not stable. You lose its content when you turn off your computer. Random access memory (RAM) would be one example of volatile memory. Non-volatile memory usually resides on a disk or hard drive and you retain its content even when you power down your computer. The storage capacity of a computer's hard drive would be an example of non-volatile memory. A PC running Windows, for example, requires tens of megabytes of RAM to function smoothly, but an editing appliance needs only a few megabytes of memory. Some use as little as four megabytes of RAM. But, as we've already seen with the CPU, what might be inadequate for a

PC may be more than enough for an editing appliance.

Hard Drive

Unlike most general-purpose computers, appliances use hard drives primarily to store the compressed digital video. With a PC, the hard drive quickly fills with applications and data that have little or nothing to do with your video editing tasks. Windows and the Mac OS both consume huge amounts of disk space. Video editing and special effects software also eat up large amounts of storage space. Most editing appliances conserve valuable space by storing their operating system and editing software in one form or another of ROM (Read Only Memory) and by only storing data related to the user's preferences and projects on the hard drive. This not only allows the system to maximize the performance from the drives, but it also allows the operating system and application software to be available almost instantly when you turn on the appliance. One notable exception to this is the original Casablanca, which holds its operating system on the removable hard drive.

Capture and Compression

Capture and compression hardware is essential for any form of digital video processing. Capturing video in a digital format is the first step to working with it in the digital domain. All current consumer editing appliances require compression hardware because of the huge amount of space that video storage requires. Uncompressed video can take from anywhere between 2-to-100 times the storage space that compressed video would. Codecs (compressor/decompressors) solve this storage limitation. There are a variety of different Codecs that work in different ways. But all of them essentially squeeze the incoming digital video data into a more compact form so the hard drives can keep up.

Inputs/Outputs

All of the appliances on the market accept analog audio and video inputs. RCA and S-video video connections are standard issue. If you use a Mini DV or Digital8 camcorder, you can get an optional IEEE 1394 DV input on a Avio, Casablanca, or Sequel or Screenplay, to allow you to transfer the digital video from your camcorder to the appliance in its native DV form. Although they Sequel and Avio also offer optional DV inputs, but they do not store and manipulate the video in the DV format. Instead they "transcode" the data into their own native format. This allows more storage space for high resolution DV video, but compromises image quality slightly. That's not to say that the images look bad by any means. Many viewers won't be able to detect a difference. Those who examine each frame closely may see a digital artifact or two.

Draco's Avio uses MPEG-2 compression while Applied Magic's Sequel uses Wavelet compression technology. The details of the two compression methods are beyond the scope of this article. It's the high quality video and manageable data rates that concern us here. You won't get the same quality of transfers you get with a higher-end system like Draco's Casablanca or Applied Magic's Screenplay, but the images created by the Avio and Sequel will look provided they are shot well.

Editing Software

Each appliance comes with its own editing program that is made and installed by the manufacturer (see Figure 10.2). Proprietary software sets appliances apart from PCs. While computers can run a wide variety of software applications, editing appliances run only the editing program installed at the factory. You won't be installing Adobe Premiere or Apple's Final Cut Pro on one of these babies. As such, the interface and its ease-of-use are

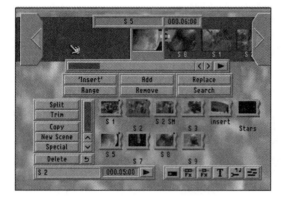

Figure 10.2 *The proprietary editing interfaces are designed to be user friendly like Applied Magic's Sequel (above) and Draco's Avio (below).*

Figure 10.3 *Disc Us— Applied Magic's Sequel has a CD-Rom drive for installing software upgrades.*

key factors for anyone considering an editing appliance.

What is the advantage? Because the appliance's operating system runs only a single program, it yields a system that can render effects and transitions in real or near-real time, using much less expensive hardware than a PC that has similar capabilities.

Other Inputs

An appliance isn't a sealed black box, however. While each model has its own method, they all offer some procedure for upgrading the on-board software and adding additional effects and transitions. Methods vary from CD-ROM drives to floppy drives to SmartMedia slots (see Figure 10.3). As appliances gain popularity, the number of available add-ons and plug-ins will likely increase. The software upgrade process could hardly be easier. With the Avio, for example, you simply plug in the SmartMedia card before you turn the unit on, and when you apply power the updates are implemented automatically. It's hard to imagine anything much easier than this.

Last Look

And so, you have had a peek inside the typical editing appliance. While its parts are similar to those inside a high-tech computer, you cannot think of editing appliances as computers in the sense that you have become accustomed. Essentially, an editing appliance is a computer with a single purpose: editing video. And while it performs just one function, it does its job extremely well.

11
6 Ways to Optimize Your Computer for Video Editing

Joe McCleskey

Computers that are capable of editing video are quite common in today's marketplace, so much so that one entire computer platform—the Apple Macintosh—has made video editing a prominent feature on all of its computers. Affordable desktop video has become almost as common as the word processor or spreadsheet.

Even so, there are a number of tweaks you can perform on today's off-the-shelf video-editing computer that can greatly enhance the performance of your machine, resulting in fewer crashes, faster rendering and smoother video playback. Though developed over the years by experts in the computer editing field out of necessity, these system tweaks are very easy for novice video editors to perform using today's operating systems.

In this article, we'll look at a number of simple things you can do to your computer to change it from a typical workaday desktop computer into a lean, mean video editing machine. We'll cover simple, no-cost performance tweaks as well as some more high-end, cost-intensive solutions for creating a high-performance video editing machine that professionals would be proud to own.

Dedicate Your System to Video

Dedicating your computer to video-only is probably the most important piece of advice we can offer, because a computer system dedicated to video editing will have far fewer problems and conflicts. It's also the most difficult to achieve, because not everyone has the money to invest in a separate computer system just for editing video. If you must use the computer for other tasks, or if it's a shared computer, you should set yourself up as the computer's administrator, if you can, and enforce healthy rules and permissions on other users—or even on yourself, if need be. The goal is to keep the computer from acquiring all of the random junk it tends to acquire when people aren't paying attention to keeping it error-free. It is possible to run a healthy computer for both video editing and other purposes, but it requires more forethought and care.

Install a Video Capture Drive

The hard drive that came with your computer may be able to store 80 GB or more. Even so, your system will be much happier if you invest in a hard drive that's dedicated to video storage. A separate video drive affords the luxury of regular formatting, defragging, and all-around housecleaning between projects, which will greatly improve performance by providing a clean slate to work on each time. Also, keeping your system files and software installations separate from your video capture drive will help keep your software and operating system running smoothly. And finally, can you ever really have too much storage space?

If you can afford it, consider getting a RAID for your video editing computer. They're not cheap, to be sure, but they can solve problems of massive storage size and performance all at once. Caution: though many newer operating systems offer a simple way to create a software RAID, this solution is not what video editors are

after. To get the added performance that video editing machines love, go all the way and purchase a hardware RAID.

Buy more RAM

Unless your system has the maximum amount of RAM you can put into it—and if it's a newer system, that's a lot of RAM—consider purchasing more. Video editing can potentially make use of about as much RAM as you can install, and both system performance and system reliability are enhanced when you install more. It's one of the least expensive ways to upgrade your system and see very real results in terms of performance. Today's video editing computers often have 1 GB or more, but 256 MB is often sufficient.

Perform Regular System Maintenance

System maintenance is a simple way to keep your system running smoothly. Start by defragmenting your dedicated video hard drive between projects (see Figure 11.1). Watch for critical software and driver

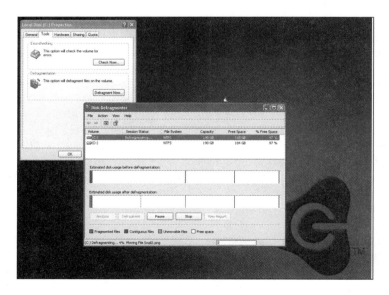

Figure 11.1 *Defrag—Monthly defragmenting of your media hard disks is an easy way to maximize performance.*

patches and updates online. You might even consider completely re-installing the operating system once a year or so. In both the Windows and the Mac world, it's a good idea to make use of a drive maintenance utility, such as Tech Tools or Drive 10. These offer simple diagnostic and maintenance utilities that can tell you if a drive has a problem, as well as help you fix problems with performance or reliability.

Enable Write Cache on Your Capture Drive

Capture drives provide better performance if you enable Write Caching (see Figure 11.2). This can provide a smoother flow of information from the video capture device (FireWire or digitizer card) to the hard drive. In Windows, you can often locate the drive's Device Properties in the Control Panel's Device Manager and enable Write Caching. Unfortunately, this is not universally true or even a possibility on all drives or systems.

Disable Unnecessary Programs

Whether you have a Mac or a Windows machine, your computer automatically runs a number of programs when it starts up, and keeps those programs running in the background. As you install more and more software on your computer, there's a likelihood that you'll have more of those little programs running in the background. Each one takes up a little bit of system resources and compromises performance (see Figure 11.3). Virus checkers are a good example. They do provide a much-needed service, but if you can keep your computer off a network and off the Internet, and keep from installing any questionable software, you may not need a virus checker on your video-editing computer. Other programs that run in the background that are often overlooked include instant messaging applications and file sharing software. Bottom line: keep only those programs running that are necessary for keeping your operating system running smoothly and disable all others.

Figure 11.2 Write Caching—Write Caching provides a smooth, uninterrupted flow of information from the video capture device (FireWire or capture card) to the hard drive.

Figure 11.3 Task Manager—Keep only those programs running that are necessary for keeping your operating systems running smoothly and disable all others.

Determine Your Needs

If you primarily edit home videos, you'll probably only want to worry about optimizing system performance on an as-needed basis. In other words, if it isn't broken, you probably don't need to fix it. If, on the other hand, you intend to pursue videography as a business, you'll undoubtedly want to keep your machinery in excellent working order, optimized and maximized in performance in every way that your budget will allow. This will not only save you heartache and frustration, it'll save you time and money and could make the difference between success and failure.

Sidebar 1

Making the Most out of Mac OS X

Does OS X really offer the stability and power of Unix with a friendly Mac interface? Many video editors applaud the OS X solution, especially now that Apple ships all of its Macintosh desktop computers with dual processors (that's "faster render times" in English). Even so, there are a few things every OS X user should know in order to get things running as smoothly as possible.

- Don't set up your system to dual-boot with OS 9.X. This is probably the hardest pill to swallow, because not every piece of hardware and software has caught up with OS X. We are confident, however, that all of the major players will soon be on board. Consider building a new, sleek system from the ground up, software and all, and make it 100 per cent OS X compliant.

- Turn off animations. Perhaps the most obvious of these is the Dock animation, which makes program icons appear larger as you move the mouse pointer over the Dock. Turn this and other animations off using the System Preferences application.

- Select programs that address dual processors. Apple's Final Cut Pro software will make use of both processors in a new desktop Macintosh, but not all software will. Check to make sure yours does before you make a purchase. This will make the extra money you pay for a dual-processor Mac worth the investment.

Sidebar 2

Making the Most out of Windows XP

It's a great new look and feel for Windows, but is it right for video editors? The answer is "it depends." XP is a major improvement over Windows 98 (or 95), but you are probably OK if you are running 2000. If you keep the following pointers in mind, you'll have much better success at creating a finely-tuned computer for video:

- Upgrade all of your drivers to the XP-compatible version. This includes drivers for your motherboard, peripherals, monitors, video display adapters and video capture cards. Many manufacturers have now released XP-specific drivers, but if you have hardware from a company that hasn't done so, consider taking the opportunity to upgrade that piece of hardware.

- Give your video editing software priority. XP allows you to give certain software applications priority for processor and memory usage. Doing this for your video editing programs may speed up rendering time and minimize crashes.

- Turn off visual effects. XP makes use of enhanced animation effects for such mundane operations as opening and closing a window. Turning these off will make more system resources available for video editing and playback.

12
Sound Track:
Microphone Types

Robert G. Nulph

Has the selection of microphones offered by your favorite electronics store ever overwhelmed you? Have you stared in awe at the vast array of silver or black, big or small, expensive or cheap microphones available to you? Have you wondered about HiZ versus LowZ, dynamic versus condenser, cardioid versus omni-directional or shotguns and lavaliers versus handheld and boundary mikes? Throughout this column, we will take a look at impedance, the two major ways microphones work, microphone pickup patterns and microphone styles. So sit back, relax and proceed through this quick look into the sometimes confusing world of microphone choice.

HiZ and LowZ

Before you choose the style of microphone you'd like to use, you have to know what impedance of microphone is compatible with your camcorder. Your system might require a HiZ microphone input.

Impedance is the resistance to the flow of electrical current in a circuit or element. We measure impedance in ohms, a unit of resistance to current flow. The lower the impedance, the better the microphone or recording device.

Most older consumer camcorders have a high impedance (HiZ) microphone jack meant to be used with high impedance microphones. These microphones range in impedance from 600–1400 ohms. HiZ microphones are very sensitive and require very little amplification, which is why less sophisticated consumer equipment is designed for them. They are, however, susceptible to hum and electronic noise and can be used only with a very short microphone cable.

Low impedance microphones, with an impedance level of 100–600 ohms, have become the norm in video production. Even much of today's consumer equipment now has low impedance inputs to allow you to use professional microphones. Using these professional microphones with low impedance gives you two advantages: (1) They are not as affected by electronic hums and noises that can be caused by fluorescent lighting or electric motors and (2) you can use long cables without worrying about outside interference.

If you buy a microphone and plug its cable into your camcorder and nothing happens, it may be due to an impedance mismatch. If your camcorder requires a HiZ microphone and all you have are professional mikes, don't despair. You can purchase an inexpensive LowZ to HiZ transformer. Plug your microphone cable into the transformer and the transformer into your camcorder. You should now be able to use any professional microphone with your system. Now that we've gotten impedance choice out of the way, we can move on to the other mike variables.

Inner Workings

Most microphones fall within one of the two major families: dynamic or capacitor (condenser) microphones. The dynamic microphone has a fixed magnet, a diaphragm that moves when sound hits it, and a coil attached to the diaphragm. When the diaphragm moves, the coil moves, making changes in the magnetic field. These changes generate voltage through the microphone cable to the recorder, amplifier or speakers (see Figure 12.1).

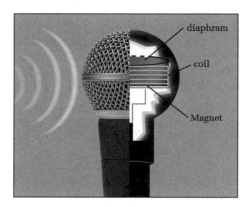

Figure 12.1 *Dynamic Mike—In a dynamic mike, a vibrating diaphram moves a magnet and coil past one another to create an electrical signal.*

The dynamic microphone has a number of attributes that you need to take into account when deciding on the type of microphone you need. This type of microphone is extremely durable. Dynamic mikes can tolerate wide temperature ranges and humidity as well as take a great deal of abuse. I have seen them dropped, banged around, used in the dead of winter, in the high heat of a tropical rain forest and even (believe it or not) used as a hammer (not recommended), all without affecting the mike's ability to record high quality audio. Dynamic mikes are also fairly inexpensive. Good quality dynamic microphones like the Shure SM58 costs around $200. Lower quality dynamics run as low as $77. Even the extremely good dynamics rarely cost more than $350.

Another attribute of the dynamic mike is its ability to provide a warm, rounded sound for vocals and yet take the abuse of recording high impact sounds such as drums and screaming voices. Many lead singers in rock bands use the hand held dynamic because of its ruggedness and its ability to pick up a wide range of sounds from screams to whispers. However, the dynamic microphone has a less accurate sound reproduction than the condenser.

A final advantage of the dynamic is that it requires no outside power. Plug it into your recorder or sound system and go. No batteries or power supplies needed. In video work, the dynamic microphone is ideal for on-camera interviews, recording very loud sound sources and crawling around the toughest terrain.

The capacitor or condenser microphone uses variations in voltage within a capacitor. The capacitor, which is capable of holding an electrical charge, is made up of two parallel plates, one fixed and one moving, separated by a small space. When sound waves hit the movable plate, it vibrates and causes a change in the amount of voltage held by the capacitor. This change in voltage is sent down the wires to be recorded or amplified through speakers (see Figure 12.2).

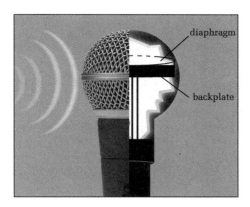

Figure 12.2 *Condenser Mike—A condenser mike uses changes in capacitance in the element to turn soundwaves into an electrical signal.*

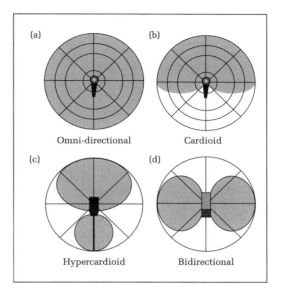

Figure 12.3 *Pick it Up—Microphones come with various pick-up patterns. You need to know how to use the one you have.*

The condenser microphone has a number of attributes that are important for the videographer to consider. The condenser mike is not so rugged as the dynamic, and the more expensive models are downright delicate. They range in price from around $100 for a basic condenser to well over $5,000 for a high-end studio mike. Although the condenser is usually more expensive, its frequency response and true sound rendering make it ideal for the videographer seeking the best fidelity.

You will have to consider one other attribute when purchasing a condenser microphone: its need for an additional power source. A battery, or AC power source can provide this additional "phantom" power. If you have a mixing board with phantom power built into the inputs, it will supply power to any mike you plug in. You can purchase a condenser microphone and begin using it right away. However, if you plan to plug a phantom-powered microphone into your camcorder, you'll need to purchase a phantom power unit to supply juice for your mike. Fortunately, most microphones that you would use for field production have a battery space built-in. You just have to remember the batteries.

Pickup Patterns

Whether you choose either a dynamic or condenser microphone, you must also decide the best pickup pattern for your production. There are four primary pickup patterns to choose from: omnidirectional, cardioid (or unidirectional), hypercardioid (or shotgun) and bidirectional (see Figure 12.3).

The omnidirectional microphone picks up sound in every directionfront, back and sides (see Figure 12.3a). This microphone is good if the sound source comes from a wide variety of directions and is moving from one side to another in front of the mike.

The cardioid or unidirectional microphone picks up sound primarily in a heart shape from the front of the microphone, including a little from the sides, but does not pick up from the back (see Figure 12.3b). This pickup pattern is excellent for voice mikes and miking musical instruments.

The hypercardioid microphone picks up only sound from the front and is very directional (see Figure 12.3c). You must point it at the sound source to get a good pickup. This type of pick-up pattern is excellent for isolating sound sources like bird calls, individual actors talking in a drama, or isolating one voice in a sea of voices.

The bidirectional microphone picks up sound from two distinct sides of the mike (Figure 12.3d). You would use a mike with this pickup pattern primarily to record two voices talking into the same microphone. You can also use it as part of the MS Stereo Miking Pattern discussed in last month's Sound Track column.

You can find all of these pickup patterns in a variety of microphone styles. Some of the more expensive microphones even have switches that enable you to choose multiple patterns from a single mike.

Styles of Microphones

After you make the choice between dynamic and condenser, and select an appropriate pickup pattern, you have to choose what style of microphone to use. This choice is entirely dependent on the type of production you are doing and whether or not you want to see the mike on screen. The major types of microphone styles are: handheld, shotgun, lavalier or lapel mike, boundary or PZM (Pressure Zone Microphone) mike and parabolic mike.

The handheld microphone is just that, a microphone that you hold in your hand. This mike is usually flat black or metallic and generally has either an omni-directional or cardioid pickup pattern. It is ideal for direct addresses to the camera by your talent. It looks good and the talent can handle it quite easily. It is the mike of choice for TV news reporters, singers, politicians and talk-show hosts.

The shotgun microphone is a long slender mike that usually has a hypercardioid or even a supercardioid (extremely focused) pickup pattern. You would primarily use this microphone in field production, mounted on a suspension mount

at the end of a long fishpole. The boom operator that manipulates the fishpole keeps the microphone out of the frame about 18" from the talents mouth so that they can pick up a consistent voice level. You can use this mike to record sound effects and other sound sources because it picks up sound only from the direction it is pointing, cutting most of the sound from its sides and back.

The lavalier or lapel microphone is a very small microphone that the talent can wear on his or her lapel or some place near his or her mouth. You can hide these microphones in costumes or weave them into an actor's hair. If you ever get bored during a live play or musical, try to find the mikes on the main actors. Costume designers and makeup artists are very ingenious in finding places to hide the mikes and power packs. Lavaliere microphones usually have an omni-directional or cardioid pickup pattern and closely mike a single talent. You can also use the omni-directional lavalier to mike various acting areas by hiding them in plants, furniture and other set pieces. Just be careful that the talent doesn't touch or bang into their hiding place. You will definitely hear it.

The boundary microphone is a fairly new style of mike that has really made a name for itself lately. This mike is mounted on a flat surface and usually has an omni-directional pickup pattern. These are great for miking conferences where you have a flat table with people sitting all around. You can use them extensively as stage mikes (not placed directly on the stage where footfalls would create heavy interference) to enhance theatre sound levels; or use them to record a group of people in a closed environment like a class or seminar.

The parabolic microphone is for long-distance audio pickup. This extremely directional microphone looks like a small handheld satellite dish which reflects all of the sound to a center-mounted microphone. This mike is primarily used to record the sound at sporting events or to

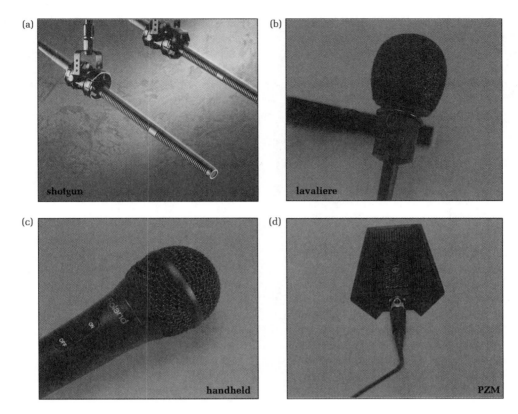

Figure 12.4 *Mike Types—Different mikes work better in different shooting situations, you may need more than one in your kit.*

pick up the sounds of wild animals. Both this microphone and the shotgun microphone are ideal for picking up middle to high frequency ranges but are not suitable for high quality, total range sound recording.

Microphone Accessories

As with all equipment, once you find the microphone you want to use, you have to accessorize. A friend of mine who runs a recording studio is constantly explaining the need for the strange looking ring with what looks like panty hose stretched over it. This is an extremely important microphone accessory called a windscreen or more precisely, a pop filter. He places the mesh surface in front of the microphone so that the talents' breath does not pop the

microphone when they say words with hard "P"s and "B"s (see Figure 12.5).

Windscreens come in a variety of shapes and surfaces. If you ever see a microphone with a gray or other colored foam ball covering its end, you are seeing one type of windscreen. Another popular windscreen used with shotgun microphones is a zeppelin or blimp (these names coming from their resemblance to the early 1900s aircraft). These windscreens completely enclose the microphone and are attached directly to the fishpole or mike stand. If you see someone using a big hairy microphone outdoors, he is using a blimp with a windjammer cover. This cover is extremely effective when you are shooting in windy conditions.

Shock mounts or suspension mounts, are another extremely valuable microphone

Figure 12.5 *Things That Go Pop–A pop filter reduces the intensity of popping Ps and Bs in narration.*

accessory. Suspension mounts prevent sounds traveling through the mike stand or fishpole from being picked up by the microphone. Soft elastic materials like rubber or nylon suspend the mike so that the sounds created by your hands rubbing the fishpole or something hitting the mike stand are not heard. It is extremely important that you use a suspension mount when using a shotgun on a fishpole.

Mike Check

When buying microphones and accessories, the kind of equipment you buy will depend on the type of production you do. Look at your needs and compare them with the instruments described above. There is a microphone designed for every type of production. It is up to you to decide what your production requirements are and the microphone that will best fit your audio needs.

13
Putting Radio to Work:
The Low-Down on Wireless Mikes

Larry Lemm

A wireless microphone system can be a videographer's best friend or worst enemy. Learn a how wireless microphone systems work and you'll be able to choose and use the best system for your needs, so you can get the best audio possible.

The Basics

There are a few different types of wireless microphone system setups. They all require three separate parts to make them all work as one: a microphone, a radio transmitter and a radio receiver (see Figure 13.1).

Some wireless systems have hand-held microphones with built-in transmitters. Others use lavalier microphones with small transmitter packs strapped to a person's belt. These are very popular and provide a discrete method of miking a subject. It is important to note that a moderately priced wireless microphone often won't have the same frequency response range as a moderately priced wired microphone. Some of the frequency range is

sacrificed in the transmission from transmitter to receiver. This signal loss may not be noticed when miking a person speaking, however, because the human

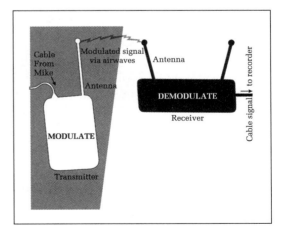

Figure 13.1 *The transmitter modulates the signal coming from the microphone onto a radio frequency carrier wave and transmits it through the air. The receiver demodulates this signal back into a form your camcorder can record.*

voice falls in the middle of the frequency range.

Wireless microphone systems operate in two different radio frequency ranges. These acronyms, also used in TV, will probably seem familiar. The FCC licenses wireless mikes to operate between 150 to 216 MHz in the VHF (Very High Frequency) spectrum. It also licenses operation between 400 and 470 MHz and again between 900 and 950 MHz in the UHF (Ultra High Frequency) spectrum. Much lower frequency, and usually much cheaper, mikes, operate between 41 and 49 MHz where they are subject to interference from all kinds of other devices.

VHF wireless microphone systems are generally less expensive than UHF systems. Much like VHF TV stations, VHF wireless mikes have less range and power than their UHF counterparts.

Your Own Tiny Radio Station

A wireless microphone system's transmitter pack is essentially a tiny radio station. The mike attaches to a tiny transmitter, which has a tiny antenna and a tiny power supply (in the form of a battery). This usually means tiny signal strength too, which is why your signal won't stretch across town like a high-powered radio signal. Instead of calculating your range in miles, the range of the tiny radio station within your wireless mike is measured in feet. And it's usually less than a few hundred feet for VHF and less than 1,000 feet for UHF.

On the other end of this cozy little microphone system is the receiver. It works much like a car radio, except it only tunes into the channels that your transmitter uses. For most videographers, wireless systems that use small battery-powered receivers are often favored over larger table-top systems that cannot attach to a camcorder.

Breaking Up is Easy to Do

Using a wireless microphone system presents some potential dangers. On a densely-populated shoot, where several other videographers are using wireless mikes, you may encounter interference with another mike operating on the same radio frequency. With more and more radio devices in use, it's more and more likely for that to happen. Most wireless systems, however, offer a few different channels to work with, so hopefully you'll notice that type of interference before you roll tape.

The next type of interference, multipath interference, is an inherent flaw of using radio frequencies (especially indoors), and often requires wireless microphone manufacturers to double-up on the electronics in a system (see Figure 13.2).

Multipath interference occurs after a transmitter sends out a radio signal. Some of the signal goes directly to the receiver, but other parts of it bounce around and sometimes hit the receiving antenna with just enough delay to cancel out the signal or cause interference. Multipath interference is the reason developers had to come up with diversity and true-diversity wireless systems.

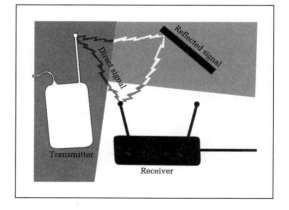

Figure 13.2 *Multipath interference results from the transmitter's signal bouncing off objects in the environment. When a signal and its delayed reflection enter the receiver, they may be recorded at a reduced quality- or may result in no signal getting recorded at all.*

Truly Diverse

What's diversity to a wireless microphone? Well, there are two answers, and both are aimed at eliminating the effects of multipath interference.

A true diversity system has two antennas, each leading to a separate receiver. A kind of switcher monitors these two for signal strength and makes sure the strongest of the two is sent out to the recorder on a moment-by-moment basis (see Figure 13.3). A good diversity system does this quickly and seamlessly, introducing no static or switching noise into the signal.

On the other hand, we have "ersatz" diversity mikes. From the outside these look like the true variety, as their receivers also have two antennas. The difference, however, lies within. If you cracked one open, instead of finding two receivers and a switcher, you'd find that both antenna wires lead to the same receiver (see Figure 13.4). The single receiver receives the signals from both antennas all the time. This type of system is not as effective as the true diversity type at eliminating the effects of multipath interference.

On the Level

The last thing you should understand about a wireless microphone system is the receiver's output. There are three types of outputs: mike level, consumer line level and professional line level.

Small, portable systems that attach onto your camcorder and plug into its microphone jack use mike-level outputs. The output of consumer line-level units, however, measures −10 dB and the output of professional line-level receivers measures +4 dB. Be sure to add the correct attenuation and adaptation to either of the latter before trying to plug the output into your camcorder's mike jack.

Consider a wireless system that has mike-level inputs that you can strap onto your camcorder and go to town. You may consider a more expensive wireless microphone system, designed with musicians in mind. But you may also need a soundboard to use one of these to best results. No matter what type of video you make, understanding how wireless mikes work will help you be a better shopper and a better video producer.

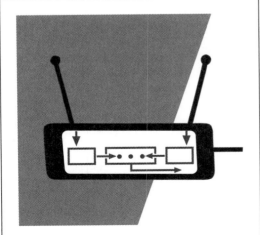

Figure 13.3 A true diversity receiver contains two antennas, two receivers and a switcher.

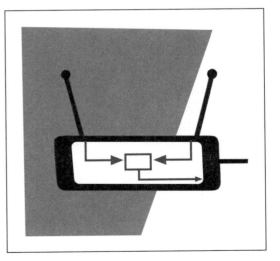

Figure 13.4 An "ersatz" diversity system has two antennas, but only a single receiver.

Sidebar

Wireless Audio Advice

Here are several tips for getting the best sound from any wireless microphone system:

• Keep it close. Keep the distance between transmitter and receiver as short as possible. Every wireless system has its limits. The shorter the transmission, the stronger the signal.

• Don't stray too far. The goal of a wireless microphone is usually to unhook your talent from cables. You may be able to accomplish this with an extremely short distance between microphone and receiver. Try putting the receiver near the talent, just out of the camera's view, and run a longer cable to the camcorder (wherever it may be).

• Reposition the receiver. If you just can't get a clean signal, especially indoors, try moving the receiver. RF signals bounce around in strange ways, and a movement of just three or four feet could make a huge difference.

• Reorient antennas. Sometimes, simply cocking an antenna can reduce dropouts (that's why antennas are usually hinged). Try laying the receiver's antenna horizontal instead of vertical, try a 45-degree angle or try spinning the receiver itself 90 degrees.

• Watch those batteries. Wireless systems eat batteries quickly, and can get rather flaky as the battery voltage drops. If all else fails, try new batteries.

• Try a different environment. If all else fails, you may need to try a completely different shooting location. Some locations are not friendly to wireless systems, while the room down the hall may pose no problems. As a rule, wireless microphones fare better outdoors than in.

14
Blending a Sweet Sound:
Audio Mixers

Jim Stinson

You've got your camcorder; you've got your VCR. What you might want next is an audio mixer. That's because a good soundtrack is crucial to quality video, and an audio mixer gives you greater control over the soundtrack. The trick is to get the right one.

In this chapter, we'll review what a mixer does and how to choose the best mixer for your particular needs. You'll learn how to find the unit that delivers the features you want at a price you can afford.

Audio Mixer Basics

Though a big professional unit comes with more intimidating knobs, sliders, buttons and displays than the cockpit of a 747, audio mixers are really straightforward critters that perform two basic tasks:

1. They balance the volume of sound elements—camera sound, music and narration—coming in from several different sources and blend them into a single audio program.

2. They process sound elements by adjusting their volume, timbre and perceived location.

Why bother to balance and process sound? First, because effective sound editing contributes powerfully to any video program. (Hollywood's known that for over 60 years; that's why they give Oscars for sound.) Audio mixing improves sound clarity by balancing elements so that the important sounds dominate the track. The process can intensify the drama of your images with realistic effects, and enhance the mood of your images with music.

Another reason for building creative audio is that the process itself is so satisfying. Enhance your video with a sophisticated audio track, and you'll fall in love with the creative challenge that is audio editing. In short, audio editing is fun.

Audio mixers come in a wide variety of flavors and prices. You can work with two mono channels or with 48 stereo channels—or more. You can pick up a simple box for 50 bucks or shell out the price of a Mercedes for a unit as big as a pool table—or spend any amount in between. You can twiddle a couple of simple knobs or play arpeggios on an instrument with more bells and whistles than the collected works of Spike Jones. But mixers with eight channels or fewer are most likely to meet the needs (and the budgets) of prosumer videographers.

Mixers fall into four different classes: production, DJ, studio and audio/video. Each class includes a number of units with a range of features and prices.

On-Site Production

Production mixers are different from the rest in one crucial way: they're designed to mix sound elements during the actual videotaping rather than during post-production. In other words, they record mixed sound on the original camera tape, not the edited assembly tape. (All professional video crews use production mixers—usually run by the person who wields the mike boom.)

You can use all production mixers during the editing phase; just remember that many of them offer fewer features than those units made expressly for post-production use.

Disco Meets Video

A number of vendors offer audio mixers designed primarily for the disc jockeys hosting most contemporary parties, banquets and balls.

These hard-working artists have special needs. A disc jockey wants to:

- Fade from one music source to another one in real time, using a cross-fader control.

- Prepare the next piece of music privately by listening to it through headphones patched to the cue channel.

- Detonate soothing and tasteful sound effects like machine guns and sirens, either with built-in digital effects or with a pre-programmed sampler.

- Dip the levels of music and machine guns together while performing voice-over announcements via the mixer's talk-over feature.

What's any of this got to do with video post-production? Lots, when you think about it. Like running a disco, video sound editing is often a real-time operation. Since you must record your final composite audio in a single pass, you are often juggling several sound sources at once. You may want to mix from one sound source to another, so a cross-fader control would simplify the task. You may need to locate the next sound effect or piece of music while recording, so a cue channel would let you audition a source without recording it. You may want to lay down perfectly synchronized sound effects, so a sampler that stores effects and puts them at your fingertips would sure help.

And if you're adding narration, it would be great to have a talk-over function that would consistently dip both music and ambient sound to a preset level whenever you began speaking.

With all that said, however, a DJ audio mixer can work beautifully in video production—if you already have one. But if you're buying a new, full-featured mixer, a studio unit might be preferable.

In the Studio Audio

In general, studio mixers tend to offer more versatility in input/output functions and signal processing.

Those mixers tend to cost more than the others discussed in this chapter do, but as with most audio equipment, you get what you pay for.

The most basic advantage of these mixers is simply better sound. They are designed for audio alone, so they offer the most in audio quality. The manufacturers of these units tend to be more careful about such considerations as audio noise and shielding.

They also offer more in the way of versatility—stereo line inputs, mike and phono inputs, analog or digital VU meters, equalizers, cueing channels, cross-faders, and so on.

Still, you may prefer to trade some advanced features for convenience and lower cost. Maybe you should check out an audio/video mixer.

Audio/Video Processing

Audio/video mixers combine video and audio processing functions in one piece of hardware. In the video department, they mix A and B rolls and often supply special effects ranging from simple color wipes to elaborate digital processing. If you can live with their usually limited audio processing abilities, A/V mixers offer two big benefits:

- They put both audio and video functions under your fingertips in the same place and using the same style controls.

- Some compare in price to stand-alone audio mixers with similar features.

For example, some A/V mixers include two audio inputs for line and mike signals. That means you can mix original camera sound with music and narration— which is as much as many videographers need to do.

Some even offer video fades and wipes—something you can't expect from any audio mixer, no matter how expensive.

And if you want to go upscale a bit, you can get fancier audio/video features, such as stereo inputs and cross-fade controls between A and B rolls.

Two Sound Tricks

Many audio mixers have few channels and even fewer sound processing features.

Here are two simple ideas for getting around these limitations.

FIRST TRICK: Premix unsynchronized tracks. Audio tracks fall into three types:

1. Those you must perfectly synchronize, such as original camera sound with dialogue,

2. those that should be closely but not perfectly synchronized, such as narration and music and

3. those that are unsynchronized, such as atmospheric background tracks including surf, traffic and restaurant chatter.

If you have four tracks—camera, narration, music and background—but only three audio inputs, you can premix all but the camera audio to make an audio subassembly tape, and then make a final mix of this tape and the camera.

This is a practical solution, because the generation-to-generation quality loss in audio signals proves much less obvious than in video.

SECOND TRICK: Daisy chain processors. If your mixer does not have a built-in equalizer or limiter, and it also lacks a send/return capability, simply patch your signal processor between the source and the mixer.

For example, background traffic noise can often ruin your on-camera interviews. To reduce that noise without affecting your narration or music channels, connect your video source's Audio Out to a graphic equalizer and then patch the equalizer's Line Out to your mixer's Source In.

Or, if you want to equalize the entire audio program, connect the graphic equalizer between the mixer and the assembly record deck.

Decision Time

As you can see, choosing the right audio mixer for you means deciding what you want to do with it, how you want to do it and what you want to pay. To help make those decisions, here are some general suggestions.

- If you have not yet performed much sound mixing, start with a simple, inexpensive unit. Then, if you enjoy the process of audio editing and feel the results are worth your effort, you can move up to more versatile equipment.

- If you are an experienced sound editor and know your current and future audio needs, get the best and most versatile mixer that will meet those needs and still suit your budget. One more time: high-quality sound is well worth the investment.

And whichever route you take, remember that sound is not a post-production chore but one of the most creative aspects of video production.

Give it the care and imagination it deserves. You won't be sorry.

15

Tape Truths:
All Exciting Overview of
the Making of Videotape

Loren Alldrin

Ask any videographer about the craft of video, and you'll likely get an earful. Try it sometime—grab any videographer and ask about the topic of your choice. Be it lighting scenes with glowbugs, shooting from atop a moving train or even audio production with 8-track cartridges, chances are you'll find you have an expert on your hands.

Then, slyly, slip in a question about videotape. Don't make it too hard. Start with something simple like, "What is the difference between grades of videotape?" or "How is videotape made?" You'll probably get a different response altogether.

You'll probably get silence.

Surprisingly few videographers know what separates one brand or grade of tape from another. This is largely the fault of tape manufacturers, who've introduced a slew of confusing buzzwords and acronyms in an attempt to create some distinction for themselves within the market. The result is that videotape, the very medium of our visual expression, has for many years been the victim of numerous half-truths and marketing ploys.

Fortunately, the essential nature of that thin black ribbon is not hard to comprehend. The more videographers know about the materials and manufacturing of videotape, the better informed their buying decisions will be.

Advances and Variations

On a basic level, all magnetic tape is the same. Whether audio, video or computer data tape, there's still that thin layer of magnetic particles covering a flexible mylar backing. By passing this thin ribbon over an electromagnet, information is stored and retrieved.

A tape's magnetic particles number billions per square inch and function like tiny bar magnets. Though each particle is physically anchored in the tape's coating, its magnetic polarity is free to change and swivel when a magnetic force is applied.

Before recording, the particles are oriented randomly. During recording, the video heads arrange the particles into patterns dictated by the changing voltage of the video signal. These patterns are then picked up by a playback head; amplified and processed to become the video image.

Improvements in videotape over the years have been dramatic, keeping pace with advances in hardware. Today's tape offers frequency response and noise levels that match or exceed the decks and camcorders they enter.

This doesn't mean further advances in tape manufacturing are impossible. On the contrary. The closer tape manufacturers come to the perfect tape, the closer we get to realizing the full potential of video gear.

There are many variations in the tape manufacturing process, because there are many different manufacturers. Each puts a personal twist on methods and materials, hoping to achieve an edge in the market. Considerable research and development is invested in tape manufacturing, with special attention directed toward high performance—and high priced—formulations. Capturing the dollar of the uncompromising video purist is quite the competitive industry.

Secret Formulas

While videotape may appear simple, it's actually the culmination of years of audio and video research.

From the early days of magnetic audio recording on thin metal wire to the first rust-covered tape with paper backing, magnetic recording technology has steadily advanced. Today's manufacturing techniques benefit from the latest research in physics, chemistry and electronics, yet the basic methods resemble those of yesteryear.

The actual magnetic medium in videotape starts out suspended in a liquid known as a binder. Where binders were once simple glue holding the magnetic particles in suspension, today they've become a complex molten brew of adhesives, lubricants, cleaners, solvents, dispersion agents and static-controlling compounds. Each manufacturer has its own blend of binder

ingredients, and jealously guards the details of its exclusive mixture.

To this hi-tech soup are added the actual magnetic particles. Mixed in liquid form in large sealed vats, the binder and magnetic particles are computer-monitored for temperature, humidity, pressure and time. When conditions are perfect, the binder is applied to the tape's base film, bonded by chemical action. The tape is then passed through large ovens where the binder is dried and hardened, the magnetic particles suspended and dispersed evenly on the surface of the tape.

Initially, the magnetic particles are oriented randomly in the binder, scattered through the liquid like pigment in paint. Yet the physical alignment of the particles is crucial to efficient magnetic recording. To orient the particles in the same direction, the tape is passed through strong magnetic fields as the binder hardens. The more uniform the dispersion and orientation of the particles, the better the tape performance. Early techniques used a single magnetic field; today manufacturers achieve improved uniformity by passing the tape through two or more fields.

A smooth finish on both surfaces of the tape is crucial. This is accomplished by compressing the tape through large, polished rollers under extreme pressure. Called "calendaring," this deceptively simple process affects the noise level, friction and overall stability of the tape.

At this point the tape is still in large rolls, each many feet wide and weighing thousands of pounds. Before being loaded into cassettes, it must be slit to the desired width and wound onto large "pancake rolls." These are then placed in automatic tape loaders, which add a small section of leader and wind the desired amount of tape into the cassette. Pancakes are also sold to cassette duplicators, who load the precise length needed into shells before duplication.

A high degree of precision and cleanliness is necessary throughout the entire manufacturing process. The tape must be slit within microns of the desired width to insure smooth operation in VCR or camcorder. It must be properly loaded into a well-designed cassette, or jamming and breakage will occur. Specks of dust or backing material picked up at this stage will manifest as dropouts or clogged video heads.

Making the Grade

The star of every tape is the tiny magnetic particle, solely responsible for picking up and carrying the video signal. Particle size, composition, density and distribution play a large part in determining a tape's performance, and these are the areas where tape manufacturers concentrate most of their efforts.

Early videotapes used magnetic particles that were relatively large. They were easier to formulate, disperse in the binder and distribute evenly along the tape. But the size and relatively sparse distribution delivered limited frequency response and high noise levels.

In the old days, ferric oxide was the most common magnetic material used; cobalt was added to the particles to stabilize and improve their magnetic properties. Chromium dioxide—chrome—was employed by some manufacturers.

Early research was devoted to reducing size and increasing particle density. Particle size decreased steadily, but manufacturers soon discovered smaller particles were more difficult to disperse evenly in the binder. New binder formulations and application techniques were then developed in response, causing videotape performance to improve dramatically. Longer, elliptical particles were created for even greater magnetic densities.

Today's formulations benefit from smaller, needle-shaped magnetic particles that can be packed incredibly tight on the surface of the tape. New production technologies allow particle orientation to be controlled with a high degree of precision.

Greater magnetic density is one of the major differences between the different grades of videotape. High-grade tapes use smaller particles in a greater concentration than normal-grade cassettes. This results in improved S/N ratios, better frequency response and a greater amount of magnetic retention. High-grade tapes cost more, as they require more expensive materials and stricter manufacturing methods. Extremely high-grade cassettes are usually manufactured in much smaller quantity, a factor contributing to their cost.

The difference in performance between normal and high-grade tapes is often dramatic, with the latter delivering greater detail, truer colors and less noise. Some high-grade tapes, when recorded in the slower EP speed, will outperform normal tapes recorded in SP. Multiple generations hold up better on high-grade tapes: third-generation high-grade tapes may look better than first-generation normal-grade.

Super-VHS formulations take high-grade even higher, using even smaller and more densely packed particles. More magnetic energy can be stored at a higher frequency, as required by the format. Manufacturing tolerances are even more stringent than for high-grade cassettes, with quantities considerably lower. S-VHS tapes command the highest price of any half-inch format; they also deliver the best performance.

Some videotapes are labeled "hi-fi," promising increased audio performance. In reality, most manufacturers feel the relatively few hi-fi tapes purchased don't justify producing a special hi-fi formulation. Instead, manufacturers may use a different sort of selection process for determining tapes with optimum noise and dropout figures. Other manufacturers simply adorn a high-grade tape with the "hi-fi" logo to increase sales. According to tape manufacturer Scotch 3M, virtually all high-grade tapes deliver excellent hi-fi performance.

Heavy Metal

In the '90s, a slightly different particle formulation appeared under the aegis of VHS tape manufacturers JVC and Maxell. Called magnetite, this cobalt-doped material offers a 20 percent increase in magnetic potential over standard cobalt ferric oxide. Magnetite was first researched over a hundred years ago, but found to be too unstable for magnetic recording. JVC and Maxell have succeeded in encasing volatile magnetite in a sheath of stabilizing material, and have begun using it in all grades of VHS videotape.

Metal particle tape (MP), common in consumer-level 8mm formats, uses normal manufacturing methods with magnetic particles of a different composition. Based on an iron molecule, MP formulations deliver dramatically higher performance than standard cobalt ferric oxide tapes. This allows high quality pictures to be recorded on tape with significantly less surface area than half-inch formats. While MP formulations could conceivably be used in VHS and S-VHS formats, the magnetic powders involved cost quite a bit more than cobalt ferric oxide. Whether the resulting difference in quality would justify the cost to consumers is questionable. Many professional formats, including digital video systems, use MP formulations.

A more recent advance in videotape technology, metal evaporated tape (ME), uses a different manufacturing method to deposit magnetic particles. Instead of being carried in a binder and painted onto the tape, ME magnetic particles are vaporized from a solid and deposited onto base film. Inside a vacuum chamber, an electron beam heats metal to thousands of degrees. Inside the chamber the metal vaporizes, adhering in an extremely fine layer to the specially prepared base film. A protective coating is then applied to the magnetic layer. The result is a smooth, thin, densely-packed film of pure magnetic particles.

Due to the extreme purity of the magnetic layer, ME tapes deliver performance many times that of standard VHS formulations. No binder is used, allowing the individual particles to mesh with a density approaching solid metal. While early ME tapes were known to suffer from dropout problems, newer methods have reportedly reduced dropouts to levels comparable to other formats. ME tapes therefore represent the pinnacle of consumer tape manufacturing, and it is the technology used by the various DV formats.

Advances in tape manufacturing have affected all grades of tape, with today's least expensive name-brand VHS tapes offering much higher performance than normal-grade tapes of the past. Ultrahigh-grade tapes available today deliver video quality unobtainable even a few years ago (see Figure 15.1).

Frequency Response

As with most forms of manufacturing, making videotape involves tradeoffs and compromises. Advances in one area create challenges in another. But tape manufacturers continue to believe videographers will choose whoever promises a better videotape.

One area of tape performance caught in compromise is frequency response—the range of frequencies a tape is capable of capturing and reproducing at the same signal level. Wide frequency response guarantees the tape will accurately reproduce the entire spectrum of video information. This characteristic relies in large part on the size of the magnetic particles, with smaller particles generating better luminance detail through extended high-frequency response.

Unfortunately, such small particles don't do as well with the lower frequency color information. The result is a crisp, detailed image with compromised color accuracy.

Using larger particles extends low frequency response and delivers better color reproduction, but high-frequency detail suffers. One solution involves using two different magnetic layers, the lower using larger particles for optimum low-frequency response, the upper incorporating smaller particles for optimum luminance detail. This method, used in Fuji's Double

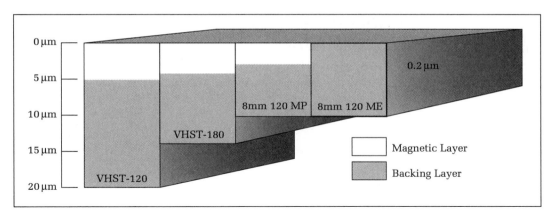

Figure 15.1 *Videotape thickness.*

Coating videotape line, is said to offer broad frequency response and reduced noise levels.

An ultra-smooth magnetic surface provides better signal-to-noise ratio by improving the contact between video heads and magnetic media. At the same time, a smoother surface also increases friction between tape and head/transport assembly. The solution lies in integrating advanced lubricants into the binder to reduce friction, insuring the heads enjoy an easy trip over the tape's surface.

A completely different challenge arises at the back of the tape. Here, friction is actually an ally to smooth, consistent movement of the tape through the transport. Coating the backing with layers of carbon increases friction and makes it more uniform, insuring the transport drive surfaces get a good bite on the tape. The carbon also serves to control static buildup, an enemy of any kind of recording.

Tape Strength

Binder composition presents tradeoffs as well. It needs to be solid enough to hold the magnetic particles in proper alignment but flexible enough to not impede tape travel or shed oxide. Early binders were deficient in preventing magnetic particles from flaking off in the transport,

which reduced the life of the tape as well as the hardware. Modern binders are considerably more durable and flexible, some nearly eliminating oxide shedding completely. A number of manufacturers use a multi-layer binder, with a slightly different composition on each layer. This allows a more rigid binder to be used on one level, with a more flexible composition above or below it.

One of the most obvious tradeoffs in videotape manufacturing is the relationship between tape thickness and durability. Longer record/playback time is a significant purchase point for many videographers; manufacturers have scrambled to be accommodating by fitting more tape into cassettes. The convenience, however, comes at a price.

A videotape's tensile strength is determined by the thickness and composition of the base film. Longer tapes require a thinner backing, which can compromise tape resistance to breaking and stretching. Temperature extremes, poorly designed or maintained tape transports, even frequent play/rewind cycles can put significant mechanical stress on a videotape. Even though some manufacturers claim to have developed stronger, thinner backing layers, shorter tapes still have a better chance of surviving such rigors.

In addition to snapping or stretching the tape, mechanical stresses can also cause small sections of magnetic material to shed off the backing. Visible as fleeting white lines knifing through the video image, dropouts spell disaster—or at least frustration—for the video producer. An otherwise perfect shot can be rendered useless by just one poorly-timed dropout.

Selection Confusion

The actual performance difference between brands of tape within the same grade may be hard to measure and even harder to see. All tape manufacturers face the same trade-offs and compromises, and all have experienced advances and setbacks at roughly the same pace. Unless scrutinized in a side-by-side comparison, with all other variables eliminated, it's hard to determine one tape's superiority over another.

Other factors add to the confusion. There is no industry-wide standard for judging tape performance; instead, each manufacturer measures videotape against its own "reference" tape. Most manufacturers use a high-grade tape, but each reference is a little bit different.

The bottom line is this: when comparing tapes between manufacturers, the numbers mean very little.

Comparing different grades of videotape requires hardware up to the task. If you expect to see a dramatic difference between normal and extra-high-grade tape on your $189 VCR and twenty-year-old TV set, you're dreaming. The hardware is simply not capable of tapping the increased potential of the higher-grade tape. Perform the same comparison on a high-end VCR and monitor and the differences will become obvious.

Sometimes, differences between batches from the same manufacturer are greater than those between brands. Computer-assisted quality control has helped eliminate inconsistencies between manufacturing runs, but there's still some variation. Batches of binder and magnetic material may differ slightly; the large sheets of base film may possess slight surface deviations. Fortunately finding yourself the victim of a "bad batch" is becoming a rare phenomenon.

The key to avoiding substandard videotape is to find a brand that offers consistent results and stick with it. Many videographers swear by a given brand of tape, touting its merits with almost religious fervor. The more you understand about the materials and techniques that go into tape manufacturing, the less you'll feel at the mercy of chance when selecting videotape stock. For every pound of advertising jargon, it's the ounce of fact that should guide your decision-making.

If a manufacturer comes out with a promising new development, don't be afraid to give it a try. Remember that most manufacturers offer a free replacement policy if you're not completely satisfied with the videotape. Don't be afraid to return a tape riddled with dropouts, offering poor video performance or emitting questionable noises.

Lastly, use your new knowledge of videotape to turn a critical eye to manufacturer claims. Analyze cassette boxes, brochures and advertisements with an eye to gleaning fact from fiction. Beware of "breakthroughs" that are nothing more than marketing hype. Yet be ready for legitimate advances that could have a real impact on the quality of your video productions. They do happen.

16
Resolution Lines

Bill Rood

With video equipment manufacturers increasingly engaged in spec wars over lines of resolution it seems appropriate to investigate those figures, what they mean and why they're so often misleading. Knowing how to measure resolution will help you make a smart purchase the next time you look for a camcorder, VCR or monitor.

Much of the confusion centers around the use of the term "lines." Lines of horizontal resolution should not be confused with scan lines. In America, the National Television Standards Committee (or NTSC) television system mandates that the television picture will consist of 525 vertical scan lines, each scanning from left to right on the screen. This fact does not change, no matter how sophisticated the video gear.

So when a manufacturer boasts that a device features "400 lines of resolution," the reference is not to vertical resolution, or the number of scan lines. What's under discussion is horizontal resolution, or, more specifically, horizontal luminance resolution. The chroma resolution in the NTSC system is as little as one tenth that of the luminance, depending on the particular hue. So for our purposes, I'll discuss only luminance resolution.

When a Line Is Not a Line

While the number of scan lines is fixed and can be counted, the number of "lines" in the term "lines of horizontal resolution" is in fact strictly a unit of measurement. There are no actual lines you can count, except with a special test chart (see Figure 16.1). You can put your face right up to the picture tube and see the scan lines, but you can't see lines of resolution.

We should actually refer to horizontal luminance resolution as "video frequency response." It's expressed in megahertz (MHz), usually with a tolerance, just as with audio equipment. Unfortunately, consumer video equipment manufacturers apparently believe this too complicated for the average consumer to understand, so they use the questionable lines method instead.

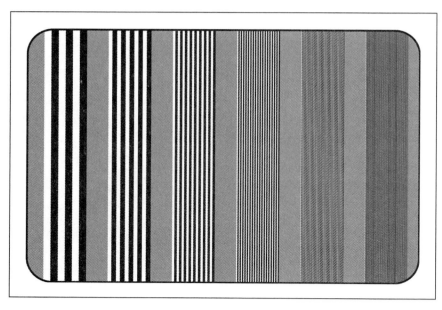

Figure 16.1 *Horizontal resolution test chart.*
Credit: Thomas Fjallstam.

Measurements stated in lines also sound more impressive than those expressed in megahertz. Three hundred lines sounds better than three-and-a-half megahertz.

So how does this frequency response differ from vertical resolution? You can measure video frequency response by examining just one of the 525 scan lines, provided you are displaying a test signal of vertical bars. The frequency response of the entire picture should be the same on every line.

As an example, let's examine one scan line of a black-and-white picture. As the scan line traces from left to right, we'd see that the brightness of the line at any given point is a function of the picture content at that point. If the picture consists of a white picket fence against a dark background, the line would start off dim, then brighten as it reproduced one of the pickets. It would go dark as it passed between pickets, then brighten again when it hit the next one. And so on. This sequence would continue until the end of the line.

What happens if we make the pickets on the fence closer together? The line still

must switch between light and dark, but faster. In effect, we've upped the frequency of the input signal we're trying to reproduce. At some point, a given piece of gear cannot make the changes fast enough; thus, we arrive at the limits of its resolution. As the pickets got closer, they would begin to appear less bright. Finally, you would no longer distinguish a picket from its neighbor. The black and white pattern will melt into a neutral gray.

Specs Game

So how do we measure video frequency response, or obtain horizontal resolution specifications?

For equipment handling video signals in a purely electronic form, use a test signal known as "multiburst". This signal contains a series of bursts, nothing more than white/black/white transitions. Tiny picket fences, if you will, each higher in frequency than the one previous. When viewed on an oscilloscope, each burst should offer the same amplitude.

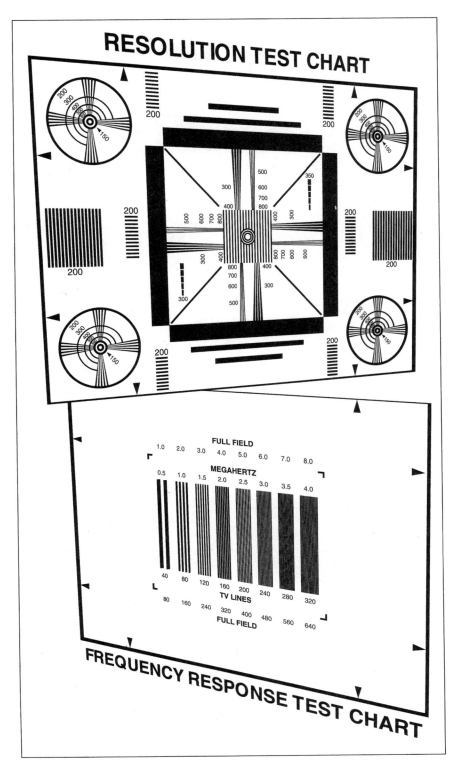

Figure 16.2 *Resolution and frequency response test charts.*
Credit: Earl Talken.

If the signal drops off as the frequency rises, you know you're seeing high-frequency response roll-off. The frequency of each burst is fairly standard; usually 0.5 MHz, 1 MHz, 2 MHz, 3 MHz, 3.58 MHz and 4.2 MHz. The beauty of this method is its extreme precision, with no sloppy guesswork.

For devices which pick up or display images, like cameras and monitors, virtually the only way to determine horizontal resolution is to display a special resolution chart (see Figure 16.2). This chart features little wedges: a series of converging black lines on a white background. As the lines come closer together, you again begin to encounter a point where the change from black to white to black occurs so quickly the lines become indistinct.

Along the outer edge of the wedge at regular intervals are line numbers, reading 200, 250, 300, 350, 400 and so on. This is where "lines of resolution" comes from. As you might guess, it's a rather inexact method at best; the scale is quite coarse, and open to interpretation as to where exactly the lines blur together. It also doesn't take into account the fact that while black/white/black transitions may be visible, they may appear at a substantially reduced level, indicating high-frequency roll-off.

Unfortunately, this method is used to spec virtually every piece of consumer video gear, be it camera, VCR, disc player or whatever. This means you should take any stated resolution spec with a grain of salt the size of Nebraska. There's much room for error, interpretation and fudging.

Lines to Megahertz

Approximately 80 TV lines equals 1 MHz of video bandwidth. So a piece of equipment rated at 300 lines would feature a video frequency response of roughly 3.75 MHz. This is all well and good, except the 300 lines figure most likely came from observing the wedge pattern, and may be less than accurate. Also, it's impossible to tell by this method if the response is flat at 3.75 MHz, or even if there's any response at all.

With an off-air broadcast, video frequency response cannot rise above 4.2 MHz. Using the above formula, we could then say that TV broadcasts feature 336 lines of resolution. The reason for the limit? The design of the television transmission system from way back when. It places the audio carrier at 4.5 MHz; picture information must vanish by that point.

Most TV broadcasts originate from digital video, stored either on hard drives or from digital videotape, such as D-1. These machines also master virtually everything seen on pre-recorded home video, from VHS, to DVDs. These digital masters are a "full" 480 lines of resolution, or 6 MHz of "flat" video frequency response. Unfortunately, the best resolution figure you can hope to see from broadcast is 360 lines—80 "lines" × 4.5 MHz.

Until all manufacturers come clean and start stating horizontal resolution in terms of megahertz, and within a certain tolerance, we'll never have a reasonable standard with which to compare products.

Until then, read the specs if you will, but don't make judgments based upon them alone.

17
An Inside Look at Cables and Connectors

Joe McCleskey

Visit any place where video editors work and you'll likely find more than your share of cables: S-video cables, audio cables, power cables, composite cables, headphone cables, microphone cables and cables for cable TV reception, among others. And if the cables aren't confusing enough for you, there's a whole host of connectors to go with them, with names like BNC, DIN, RCA, phone, phono, XLR and stereo mini-plug.

In this chapter, we're going to take an in-depth look at some of the cables commonly used for video. We'll take a look inside the four main cable types that home video producers deal with: composite (RCA-style) cables, S-video cables, RF cables and DV (IEEE 1394) cables.

Composite Cables

Composite cables are perhaps the most commonly encountered cable type in consumer video. They often come in the box with home VCRs and camcorders.

Sometimes, they come in groups of three attached cables—one with yellow RCA-style connectors for video and two with red and white connectors for stereo audio. Also included in this category are those cables that have yellow, red and white plugs on one end and a mini-plug connector on the other end. This type of cable often comes packaged with miniature camcorders that make use of the single connector on the camera body. (See Figure 17.1.)

Often, video gear (especially professional video gear) will have BNC (bayonet nut coupling) connectors for composite video. The chief advantage of the BNC connector is its ability to lock in place with a push and a twist; this prevents connections from wiggling loose, a common problem with the typical RCA-style connectors.

On the video side, these cables carry composite signals, so called because the signal is a composite (or mixture) of all black-and-white and color information contained in the video signal. They

Figure 17.1 *Composite cable and composite input.*

To send both chrominance and luminance information together on the same cable, the two signals must be mixed together in a process known as modulation. The modulation of the signals—and subsequent de-modulation at the other end—is what makes the composite video signal highly susceptible to generation loss (the tendency of a signal to degrade whenever you make copies of it). The only type of video cables that are more susceptible to generation loss are the RF cables used for cable television and antenna hook-up.

RF Cables

RF cables gave cable television its name. The ubiquitous RF cable can be found mostly on television sets and VCRs, as well as a few old-school camcorders. RF stands for radio frequency. The name is appropriate because this is the cable most commonly used to transfer radio-frequency signals from an antenna to the VCR or TV set—or even from the cable TV station to your house.

RF cables are generally made of coaxial cable, a cable that carries two metal leads, one inside the other. The two wires do not carry two different signals; instead, they carry the power and ground for a single signal, with the ground (outside) cable providing limited shielding from radio interference. (See Figure 17.2.)

The RF cable (sometimes referred to as an F cable) provides the best means of long-distance signal transfer. This is why it's most commonly used to connect cable TV stations to clients; with a heavily shielded cable and amplifiers in far-away neighborhoods, it's possible to send an RF signal miles and miles without serious degradation. However, it is the worst solution for making copies or editing. Here's why: remember how we told you that composite video signals mix the color and black-and-white signals into one? Well, the RF cable does this one better: it carries audio along with the mixed

usually consist of two wires running parallel to one another down the cable; one wire (power) corresponding to the tip of the connector and the other wire (ground) corresponding to the outside ring portion of the connector.

Why aren't these cables just called video cables? Because they actually carry two separate signals that are composited into one. Inside your camcorder and/or VCR, the black and white (luminance) information is dealt with separately from the color (chrominance) information. Back when television technology was black and white only, the only type of video signal a television had to cope with was a black and white signal. When color came along later, it was dealt with as another layer of information on top of the black and white signal, in order to make color TV signals compatible with existing black and white televisions.

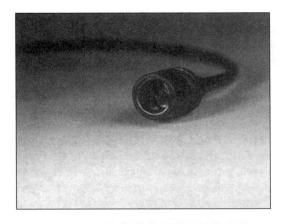

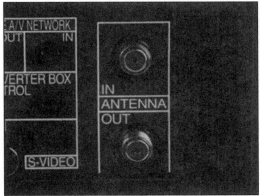

Figure 17.2 *RF cable and RF input.*

color/black-and-white video signal. This means that problems arising from modulation/demodulation of the signal are multiplied in RF cables. Generation loss accures at a much faster rate and even second-generation copies tend to have an abundance of video noise, audio noise and bleeding colors.

Camcorder enthusiasts who have television sets without composite video inputs (yes, they do still exist) must find some way to connect the video outputs of their camcorder to the RF-style connectors of their TV. VCRs usually provide the needed connections, but for some who still have older VCRs without video connectors, the RF-to-composite connection may require a separate inexpensive device called a modulator, readily available at consumer electronics outlets.

Unfortunately, you can't just whip up an adapter to connect composite cables directly to RF cables without a modulator, because RF cables transmit signals differently than composite cables.

In short, you should only use RF cables for viewing video and use some other type of cable for copying and editing.

S-Video

One obvious way to solve the modulation problem that composite video and RF cables present is to leave the color and black-and-white information separate and send them down a pair of wires in the cable. That's what S-video or Y/C, cables accomplish. (In video technical parlance, Y is the symbol for luminance and C is the symbol for chrominance.) Because S-video cables do not carry two signals modulated into one, they provide a very robust means of editing and copying video.

Looking at the end of an S-video connector (See Figure 17.3), it's easy to see that it consists of two pairs of wires instead of a single pair. One pair of wires (power and ground) carries the color information, while another carries the black-and-white information.

S-video connectors are found only on high-bandwidth cameras and VCRs. You'll find them on S-VHS, Hi8 and DV equipment, but not on 8mm or VHS gear. More and more televisions are coming equipped with S-video connectors, but they are far from universal.

S-video cables do have some minor limitations. The most prominent is perhaps the length issue: when the cable goes beyond twenty-five or thirty feet, you notice significant degradation of the signal. For this reason, they are not the best solution for long-distance cable throws. There are devices (called line amplifiers) that can solve this problem, but they usually add a significant amount of noise to the signal.

There are adapters that convert Y/C signals to composite, but beware: because

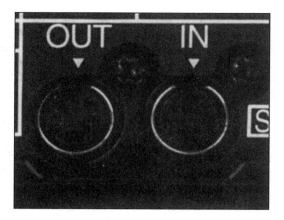

Figure 17.3 *S-Video input.*

composite signals are modulated, the use of such an adapter negates the benefits of the S-video connection. In fact, it may make the problem worse. Inside these adapters is a small ceramic filter that de-modulates the composite signal before sending it down the S-video cable. This demodulation is the same sort of thing that adds noise to a composite signal. The use of an S-video-to-composite adapter just adds one more place where the signal can degrade when it's copied.

S-video connections work best when used throughout your entire system. In other words, you won't get all the benefits of S-video technology if you use composite video cables between, say, your special effects generator and your record VCR, with S-video cables everywhere else. It is possible to safely connect a monitor to the output of your record VCR with composite or even RF cables. Because they sit outside the main signal stream, these cables won't affect the quality of your final product one bit.

FireWire

The cable types we've dealt with so far are all similar in that they're designed to carry analog signals. IEEE 1394 or Fire-Wire or i.LINK, is special because its main purpose is to carry digital signals. Thus,

you'll find FireWire connectors only on equipment that's designed to handle digital signals. In the consumer video market, this equates to Digital8 and Mini DV camcorders and VCRs.

Briefly, the difference between analog and digital signals is this: analog signals carry a continuously varying voltage, which corresponds directly to the type of signal that analog VCRs and televisions were designed to interpret. Digital signals, on the other hand, consist of long strings of numbers in binary notation (zeros and ones). Because digital signals only consist of two values—zero and one—they're much more resistant to noise and other forms of signal degradation. This means that it's possible to copy, say, twenty generations of DV or Digital8 footage without noticing the slightest loss of picture quality.

It's important to remember that although the DV and Digital8 formats are the most prominent applications of FireWire technology to date, in essence FireWire technology has nothing to do with digital video. It's just a way of transferring digital data from one location to another at a high rate of speed. FireWire is a serial data protocol, number 1394, approved by the IEEE (Institute of Electricians and Electronics Engineers).

FireWire connectors come in two basic types: the six-pin connector, agreed upon as a standard in the mid '90s, and the smaller four-pin connector, which has become most prominent on digital camcorders and VCRs. While one connector type will not fit the other, both are interchangeable for all other purposes, which means it's possible to have a FireWire cable with both types of connectors, one at either end. (See Figure 17.4.)

Like S-video, FireWire connections must remain throughout the signal stream for users to reap all its benefits. In order to get copies or edits without a hint of generation loss, you must use FireWire connections throughout your system. Unfortunately, there are currently no titlers with FireWire connections, and only one special effects generator (Videonics' MXPro DV). FireWire connectors are

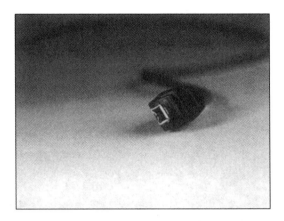

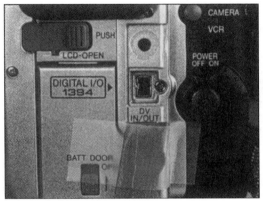

Figure 17.4 *FireWire cable and FireWire input.*

becoming quite popular on home computers, which have reached a point where they have plenty of muscle for video editing.

FireWire's primary drawback: cable lengths are limited to 15 meters (about 45 feet).

Making the Connection

One final note about cables: in general, it's best to buy the highest quality you can afford, to insure the stability of your system and keep generation loss at bay. When purchasing cables, video editors are faced with a wide array of options. Even if you just want a simple yellow-tipped composite video cable, you still find yourself faced with a plethora of types from which to choose. Some boast greater shielding; some even come with built-in hook-and-loop cable ties to help you organize your workspace; some add gold tips. While gold certainly is an excellent conductor, it's usually the case that a gold-tipped connector is an expensive and unnecessary addition to a quality cable. More often than not, an ordinary nickel-plated connector will perform identically to its gold-plated brethren and gold plating has a tendency to flake off in time.

To summarize: whenever you're making analog video connections, use S-video cables if at all possible to minimize generation loss. If you can't use S-video cables, use high-quality composite cables. Avoid using RF cables for anything but viewing video on a monitor. And if you have two or more pieces of video equipment with FireWire connectors, then by all means use FireWire and avoid the ill effects of generation loss entirely. With all this in mind, go forth and cable your system with confidence.

18
Try a Tripod:
Some Valuable Features
in the Three-Legged Race

William Ronat

Few pieces of video support equipment are as useful as the tripod. Simple in concept, elegant in function, the tripod has a long history of bringing needed stability to the world of photography.

In pre-video days, tripods served still and motion picture cameras. As far back as the 1860s, people like Matthew Brady were lugging tripods onto battlefields to help steady huge still camera equipment.

And before tripods became popular for image gathering, they supported the surveyors' levels used to map out the countryside.

Why, you may wonder, a *tri*pod? Why not a monopod, or a quadrapod, or an octopod? This question doesn't require an Einstein to answer. One leg: camera falls down. Two legs: camera falls down. Three legs: camera stands up. Four legs: one more leg than you need.

The triangle is one of the most stable configurations for a support device. Ask a karate expert, or an offensive lineman. Or, for that matter, a tree.

Why a Tripod?

I know what you're thinking. "What do I need with a tripod? It's just one more thing to tote around."

Maybe you're right. If you have a steady hand, and/or a lens stabilizer, you may never encounter a situation requiring a tripod. But if you shoot professional video and work with heavy equipment, you know that working hand-held for any length of time can get darned uncomfortable. Just try holding your hand on top of your head for a couple of hours to simulate the experience.

Aside from avoiding pain, tripods are handy if you want to be in your own shot.

Say you're shooting a news story for a cable access show and you want to do a stand up. This is the shot where you appear on camera, looking solemn, finishing up with, "for Cable Access, this is John Smith, reporting from Bosnia."

Using a tripod, you can stop somebody passing by, make him or her stand in the spot where you'll be standing when you talk to the camera. You can then compose the shot using this surrogate John Smith. Lock down the tripod. Take the passerby's place and say your piece.

Three S Theory

A tripod's purpose can be described in the famous Three S Theory, which I just made up. Tripods keep it *Steady*, keep it *Straight* and keep it *Smooth*.

Put a camera on a tripod and it will be steady. It won't bob, wave or float, assuming it's locked down. It will sit there like a rock until you get ready to move it. That's steady.

Keeping your shot straight is a little trickier. Let's say you've set your camera on the tripod so your shot is looking out across a flat desert. The horizon is that line where the sky meets the earth. In a standard shot, the horizon should be kept parallel to the top and bottom of your frame. Cancel this if you're trying for the Dutch angle so popular in the old Batman TV shows, where everything is tilted. It's possible for a shot to start out looking straight, horizon parallel to the top of the frame. But when you pan, the horizon will start to go downhill.

This happens because your tripod legs stand in such a way the camera isn't level to the horizon. Your tripod is sitting with two legs on either side of the front of the camera; the third leg points behind the camera, and is shorter than the front two legs. Even though your shot looks level when the camera's pointed straight ahead, when you pan, the camera begins to lean in the direction of the third leg.

Or, as I like to put it: look out, the world's tilting.

On the Level

Some tripods come with a leveling bubble, a handy gizmo that is nothing but a bubble floating in liquid.

You position the bubble either inside a circle or between two lines on a tube. By moving the bubble to its correct position your camera becomes perpendicular, relative, I think, to the gravitational pull of the Earth (but don't hold me to this). The result: you can pan your camera 360 degrees, the horizon staying straight in the frame.

You can position the bubble by raising or lowering the tripod legs or by adjusting the tripod's head—if the head attaches to the tripod with a claw ball. The latter allows you to loosen the head and position the leveling bubble without touching the legs. A nice feature.

The last S in the Three S Theory is keep it Smooth. The part of the tripod responsible for this action is the head. Some tripods don't have heads: cameras attach directly to the tripod. But on more sophisticated tripods the camera attaches to a plate, the plate attaches to a head and the head attaches to the tripod.

Using smooth resistance, a head helps make camera movement smoother. This resistance, known as drag, is usually adjustable. With a small amount of drag the camera pans or tilts easily. Add more drag and moving the camera becomes more difficult.

If you don't want the camera to move at all, you engage the locks. There are separate drags and locks for both the pan and tilt functions of the head. If you want a pan but no tilt, you can lock the tilt control and the camera will only pan. And vice versa.

Heads and Legs

Heads come in two flavors: fluid head and friction head.

A friction head creates resistance by pushing metal against metal. A fluid head floats on a bed of oil or some other viscous fluid. Friction heads aren't as smooth as fluid heads, but they're also cheaper, which is the way things usually work in this world.

Tripod legs generally extend by telescoping. This is necessary to position a tripod level on a hill or stairs. With tripods that extend you can get your camera high up in the air, useful when you must ascend to eye-level with NBA players. Some tripods have a center column that cranks even higher.

A word of caution here, if you get up too high, your camera, tripod and everything else can tip over. So put a sandbag in the center of the tripod to make it more stable.

Some tripods allow the legs to straighten out until the head is resting almost on the ground. Good for low shots. Good angle for your remake of *Attack of the Fifty Foot Female Mud Wrestler*, featuring a point of view shot from the terrified town's perspective. Coming soon to a theater near you.

Wheels

With a nice smooth floor you may be interested in tripod dolly wheels.

What's a dolly? That's a movement of the camera and tripod. These moves can take the camera around the subject, or the camera can follow people at the same speed as they move. They require your tripod to have wheels or they require you to place your tripod on a wheeled device. These shots are very pretty, but they're also very difficult. If you don't have a smooth even surface every little dolly bump will translate into a very big video bump.

Wheels are handy, however, as transportation. Just leave your camera, extension cords, a grip bag and a light attached to the tripod and roll on to the next location. Sure beats carrying them.

Another feature you may want is quick release; a plate or shoe attached to the bottom of the camera. The plate fits into the head to secure the camera. But if you want to go hand-held in a hurry, you flip a switch or push a button to immediately release the camera.

If the head screws into the bottom of the camera, it will obviously take a lot longer to turn, turn, turn the knob to get it off again. Most professional model tripods feature quick release.

The Envelope, Please

Before leaving the subject of tripods, we should explore the Steadicam™. You may say, "Say, that's not a tripod!" And you'd be right. But it performs some of the same jobs, so we'll give it a glance.

The Steadicam JR™ is a system that balances your camera so completely the image seems to float on air. It eliminates shakiness, allowing a camera operator to walk up stairs or run along the ground without applying objectionable jiggle to the image. It's a slick little system, creating videos that look like feature film.

But a Steadicam™ is not the same as a tripod. Although it has a stand, you can't lock it down on a shot. Also, some people think a Steadicam™ is like a gyroscope, forcing your shot to remain horizontal. Wrong. There's a bubble level on the monitor to show the operators when the shot is level, but it's up to the operator to keep it there. My conclusion: Steadicams™ are great tools, but should supplement a tripod, not replace it.

If you're in the market for a tripod, shop around. Try the model before you buy. As you test drive the tripod think about the three Ss: keep it Steady, keep it Straight, keep it Smooth. If you watch your Ss, you should be O.K. And if at first you don't succeed, try another tripod.

PART II
Production Planning

Every minute spent in planning saves ten in execution. Here's help in getting yourself organized.

19
Honing Your Ideas: From Concept to Finished Treatment

Stray Wynn Ponder

See video clips at www.videomaker.com/hanbook

If you're like most videographers you probably have more project ideas than you can shake a camcorder at. So with a little talent and the right equipment, you should be able to produce top quality video work, right?

Right. Then why do so many great ideas fizzle out somewhere between that first blinding spark of inspiration and the final credit roll?

The answer is simple: before the lights come up, before the cameras roll, even before you write the script, you must take two essential steps if your video is to find and follow its true course:

Step One: clearly define your concept.

Step Two: write a concise treatment.

A concept nails down your program's primary message, and the manner in which you will deliver it to your primary audience. Later, as you navigate the winding curves of production, you'll think of the concept as your destination. A treatment is a written summary of the video's purpose, storyline and style. It will become your road map. These tools will help you maintain solid and continuous contact with the video's intended direction every step of the way.

These are probably the most overlooked steps of pre-production, but if you conscientiously pursue them on every project—no matter how simple—you'll save time and add polish, propelling your work to new horizons of quality.

Developing the Concept

How does a concept differ from a raw idea? Let's look at a couple of ideas and watch how they change as we develop them into concepts:

1. *The Trees of New England*; and

2. *Car Repair*.

Each of these has possibilities as a video project; but if we were to pick up a camera, or to start writing a script at this point, we'd suffer a false start. Before we can set out on our creative journey, we need a clear understanding of our destination.

Admittedly, many ideas don't deserve to survive. Who among us hasn't pulled the car off a crowded freeway to jot down a "great idea"—only to read it later and find that great idea somewhat less than overwhelming.

Take our first idea: *The Trees of New England*. This sleeper might die right on the drawing board. Why? Because, for the videographer trying to earn a buck, it lacks profitability. And for most hobbyists, it involves too much time and effort. The visual effect could no doubt be stunning, but who would purchase (or finance) a video about trees when public television carries a variety of nature shows that feature similar subjects every week?

To succeed in the marketplace, your work must effectively deliver a primary message to a primary audience. To prove worth the effort, *The Trees of New England* would have to distinguish itself from similar programming through style or content to appeal to existing markets. Another option: *The Trees of New England* could deliver its message in a way that would captivate audiences in a new market niche. *Note*: if you can see a way to make money with this tree idea, please feel free to run with it.

You may find yourself shelving many ideas that survive this kind of initial scrutiny; these ideas typically lack some element necessary to a profitable video, such as reasonable production costs or a viable market. Or through research you may discover that someone else has already produced your idea. That's okay; you can always generate more ideas. Don't get too caught up in creative decisions during these first stages of exploration. In the process of transforming a germ of an idea into a viable concept, necessity will make many decisions about a project's direction for you.

How about our second wannabe video—*Car Repair*? This one offers a multitude of development possibilities. But remember, you can't please all of the people all the time. Avoid the temptation to create a "do-all" video. As producers, we always want the largest audience we can get—up to a point. Create a repair program that appeals equally to master mechanics and interior designers, and you'll get a show without a specific destination. In other words, your project could end up running out of gas in the wrong town.

Your first move: define the audience. Let's find a target group who could use some information about car repair.

Brainstorm A-comin'

Here's where brainstorming becomes indispensable. There are as many ways to brainstorm an idea, as there are people, so there are no hard and fast rules. Basically, you need to distract the left (logical) side of your brain so that the right (creative) side can come out to play.

Here's what works for me: I speak my thoughts aloud, no matter how silly they sound, while bouncing a rubber ball off the concrete walls of my basement office. This technique gets the creative hemisphere of my brain churning; my subconscious coughs up ideas from a well much deeper than the one serving my logical hemisphere. I write down the more coherent mutterings on a dry erase board as they erupt. All in all, it's probably not a pretty sight, but you're welcome to adapt this method to your own brainstorming technique.

Here's a condensed version of my brainstorming session for the car repair idea. I flip the ball. It hits the floor, the wall and then slaps back into my hand.

"Repair," I say to myself, as I continue to bounce the ball. "Maintenance ... mechanics ... men ... women ... children ... women ... smart women ... independent women ... car maintenance ... where's the need? ... when would they have the need? ... college! ... BINGO!

When young women go away to college, they no longer have Mom or Dad around to watch the oil level and check the belts. The same is surely true of young men, but I decide to target women as the larger of the two potential audiences. Should I go after both in hopes of selling more tapes? Absolutely not. Since the buying characteristics of the two groups will be different, I must tailor the style of the production to one audience or the other.

Through brainstorming, the original idea "car repair" has now become its simpler cousin, "car maintenance." Do we have a real concept now? Not yet, but we're getting there; we know our target market and our message. Still to be considered: the production's style, or the best manner in which to convey our message. This will eventually encompass shooting style, lighting style, acting, wardrobe, makeup and dozens of other factors. For now, however, we'll break style down into two parts: 1) getting the viewer's attention; and 2) keeping it.

Hook, Line and Profit

A hook is the attention-getting element that yanks viewers away from their busy day, and into our product. The need for a good hook is the same in every communication medium, whether it's an advertisement, a popular song or a training video. Human beings are frenetically busy creatures; you must seduce them into giving their attention away. After delivering this interesting hook and convincing them to look our way, we must follow through and give them a storyline that will hold their interest for the duration of the program. There are a number of ways to engage and keep the viewers' attention:

- Shock value
- Self-interest
- Visual stimulation
- Glitz and glamour
- Comedy

To decide which combination of elements will work best for our car maintenance video, we need a better understanding of our target market: 18 to 22-year-old females needing to perform simple car maintenance themselves. As with many aspects of concept development, most of our decisions are made for us as we discard what will not work—which leaves us with what will.

My gut says to skip shock value in a program that deals with cars. Self-interest is definitely an important consideration for a young lady who is both: 1) trying to assert her independence for the first time (ego self-interest); and 2) living on a budget (financial self-interest).

Visual stimulation? Our target group comes from a generation accustomed to the kaleidoscopic imagery and lightning fast cuts of beer commercials and music videos. Let's use this one.

Glitz and glamour are obvious shoo-ins for this age and gender. Comedy can be an excellent tool for communicating many subjects, as long as you execute it well. Let's keep humor in mind, too.

Simply being aware of these tools is not enough. More important is an understanding of the ways they will impact our target audience. If we can effectively use one or more of them in our production (and our marketing package), we may just have a moneymaking project on our hands.

To recap: we need an eye-catching (visually stimulating) presentation that offers college-aged females something they clearly need (self-interest) in a manner consistent with their accepted versions of self-image (glitz and glamour). If we can discover ways to enliven this delivery through the use of comedy, all the better.

Even if we are unable to meet all these criteria, we must be aware of them, so at the very least we avoid working against the psychology of our target audience.

More ball bouncing is probably called for at this point to help us predict how we'll apply these general ideas to our intended audience. But rather than put you through that again, I'll just tell you what I came up with for our sample project: *A Young Woman's Guide to Minor Car Maintenance*. The package resembles that of a concert video or a compact disc more than an instructional videotape jacket. Lots of neon colors surround a snazzily dressed college-aged woman, who leans confidently over the open hood of a small automobile. Her posture says, "I have the world by the tail, and so can you if you take a closer look at this."

The back of the jacket explains that you'll need no tools to perform most of the tasks covered in the program. These tasks are simpler than you ever thought possible, even fun once you give them a chance. Best of all, you'll feel an exhilarating new sense of independence after you master these simple skills.

Writing the Treatment

We've come a long way from the original idea. By asking the right questions, we've developed a potentially viable concept. We understand it in terms of:

- to whom the video speaks,
- how the video will speak to them and
- what the video will say.

Now we can write a treatment, which will help us pursue our project without losing sight of our concept. By clearly defining our direction in this way, we can hold true to our original vision for the project.

Depending on the complexity of a production, its treatment may be long or short. Some in-depth treatments resemble scripts; others simply document mood changes and/or visual effects, with technical annotations along the way. Regardless, the treatment should always move the reader chronologically from the beginning to the end of the program.

There's no established manuscript format for a treatment. Just try to tell a story in as readable a way as possible. The

treatment for our car maintenance video might begin like this:

Project Name: A Young Women's Guide to Minor Car Maintenance

Statement of Purpose: The main goal of this project is to provide information about basic car maintenance to female college students under the age of twenty. These young women face the full responsibilities of car care for the first time in their lives.

In the interest of hooking and keeping the attention of the target audience, we'll present this information in a series of three music videos. Cuts will be as short as possible. A different actor/musician with a distinct personality will demonstrate each automotive maintenance task.

Most important, the tasks will not be overly technical in nature. Our audience needs to understand only the basics of car care: how to check belts, check the oil and other fluid levels, change a tire, fill the radiator, replace a burned-out fuse and so on. The frequent use of common-sense metaphors will remove any feelings of intimidation this subject may arouse in viewers.

The video jacket layout resembles that of an album cover rather than an instructional videotape. The songs contained in the program will be remakes of popular rock-and-roll songs, with lyrics pertinent to the mechanical tasks.

Summary

The opening credits emulate the digital-animated effects common to music video TV stations. These lively visual effects are choreographed to heavy guitar and powerful drums. The monolithic CTV (Car Television) logo vibrates in time with the music.

Cut to a perky female vee-jay who says, as if continuing a thought from before the latest station break, "We'll hear more of the latest tour information soon, but first let's take a look at this new release from Jeena and the Jalopies..."

Cut to close-up of female lead singer in the middle of a concert. We hear the giddy cheering of a large crowd as she introduces the next song. Her tormented expression prepares us for a tale of love's cruelty; but when she speaks, it's about how her car has done her wrong. The hand-held cameras circle like vultures on the fog-drenched stage. Her dead-earnest performance mocks the lyrics, which seem comically out of place.

Cut to a dressing room interview with Jeena. "Yeah," she says, "almost every song I write is taken from my own life. I hated that car. (She takes a drag from her cigarette.) "And I loved it. Know what I mean?" Music from Jeena's live performance fades up as the camera holds on her face.

(Music continues.) Cut to Jeena standing next to her car, a late model import. She wears the demeanor of a child instructed to shake hands with an enemy, but stubbornly refuses to do so. She casts occasional guilty glances at the camera, but refuses to look at the car, with which she is obviously quite angry. "My old car wasn't like this," she claims, shaking her head. "I could see the dip stick—easy. Check the oil and be done with it. So, you know, easy." Video dissolves to a memory sequence of Jeena opening the hood of an older automobile.

That gives you an idea of how the beginning of our treatment might read. It paints a much more complete picture than the words Car Repair. This video will probably be around 30 minutes in length; its treatment will run about ten pages, typewritten and double-spaced. If that sounds like a lot of writing, compare it to the amount of money and work required to reshoot even one minute of video.

More Treatment Tips & Tricks

Some productions, like our car maintenance video, will involve fairly hefty budgets financed by outside investors. The treatment then becomes a sales tool for communicating the project's value to potential investors.

Depending on the type of video you're producing, other uses for a treatment include:

- Seeking client approval,

- giving a "big picture" of the program to the technical and creative staffs and

- making sure that you can arrive at your destination.

Perhaps the most important benefit of writing a treatment comes as a result of the writing itself. In moving from the general concept to the specific steps to develop that concept, your treatment will pass through many incarnations. Problems will crop up at this stage of the video's development; you'll solve them by revising the treatment. In overcoming each of these obstacles on paper, you will save yourself from facing them later on the shoot itself.

Production Planning Tools

Videographers have traditionally used several tools to help them navigate the circuitous pathways of production. In filmmaking, there's the storyboard, a comic book style layout of sequential drawings that tell the visual story of a movie. Some videographers use storyboards as well; but for many low-budget productions storyboards prove too expensive a luxury.

This is certainly true for our car repair video. For this production, our treatment must do the storyboard's job—by creating compelling, descriptive images with words. The treatment must clearly map out the avenues we'll travel without necessarily describing every fire hydrant and blade of grass along the way.

A general rule of thumb: gear the sophistication of your treatment to the purposes it must serve. If you need to impress the board of trustees at a major cable network and feel you are out of your league in terms of writing skills, hire a freelance writer to prepare the treatment. The earlier in the creative process you bring this person in, the more benefit you can gain from his or her experience.

Don't sell yourself short, though. If you feel reasonably sure that you can tell your video's story from the beginning to the end, in a readable way that your colleagues will understand, do it.

Planning Counts

The worst mistake: skipping these crucial planning steps altogether.

Even the simplest video can flounder if you neglect the proper planning process. The meticulous development of concept and treatment allows you to cut and polish your rough project. The goal is to move into the later phases of the work with a crisply faceted jewel that will withstand the rigors of scripting and production.

20
Budgeting Time

William Ronat

Let's say that you've planned a location shoot at a restaurant so you can get some shots for a production. You told the owner you would be there at 3 p.m. Suppose you have some other shots to do in the morning at several locations. If you didn't prepare a schedule, you have no idea how long any of them will take. Each shot will undoubtedly take longer than anticipated, you forgot to allow for travel time, the crew is hungry (don't forget time for lunch!) and when you finally get to the restaurant, you are two hours late. The owner now has to take care of the dinner crowd and you're out of luck.

You didn't get into video to become a bureaucrat. You bought your camcorder and gear to watch your visions materialize, to breathe life into ideas, to create a piece of truth where moments before there was merely air. These are laudable goals. The problem, however, is actually achieving them. And that takes planning.

Your time is valuable. Spend it like you would spend money. To make sure you get the most value from your effort, you have to do some preparatory work before your finger hits the Record button. There is a saying in the biz, "Everything takes longer than it takes." That means that no matter how well you plan, something will happen that you didn't anticipate.

You can minimize the pain by doing your homework. Many professionals spend as much as 90 percent of production time in the planning process. Alfred Hitchcock was famous for planning his films in such minute detail that he found the shooting process dull. He had already seen the movie in his head and the rest was mere mechanics. You may say, "Hey, I don't want to be bored when I'm shooting," to which I say, "Is your name Hitchcock?" All right, then.

In the Beginning

If you're serious about choreographing a video production from start to finish, you will need a script. It doesn't have to be an elaborate document. In fact, it can be an outline scribbled on a napkin (although they have a habit of disappearing during lunch). Just make sure that the script helps you understand what needs to be shot and it will do the job.

Work with "split-format" (audio/video) scripts and "film-style" scripts. Split-format scripts are ideal for short projects, like 30-second commercials or industrial videos, while film-style scripts lend themselves to dramatic productions. You can easily use your word-processing program to set up a table and create a script that looks like Figure 20.1a. The same script done film-style would look like Figure 20.1b.

If you plan to write for the film industry, this format must be absolutely perfect or your manuscript will be tossed without a second look. There are software programs available that can make this process easier (See the *Film Script Software* sidebar).

Shot by Shot

Once you've written your script, you can begin to plan like a pro. First, break the script down into shots. In our example, we have three shots: one, a mailman walks up; two, close-up of a dog, and three, the dog attacks the mailman. Now it's time to create the next document in our bureaucracy of video, the production schedule.

Using the schedule will help you during planning in many ways. You will know approximately how long it will take to shoot shot sequences, what props and equipment you will need, how many crew members to bring and when to break for lunch (see Figure 20.2).

It can be helpful to take the split-format script table we illustrated earlier and add some more columns to it. As you can see, planning is all about detail. The script should tell you everything about each

Figure 20.1 *Shot lists can be formatted in any word processing program. The top example is typical of a video production, while the bottom is more commonly used for film.*

Figure 20.2 *While you shoot, keep your shooting schedule with you (along with the script). And stick to it.*

shot. Using this information, you can create a production schedule to illustrate how much time it will take to achieve the script's needs. The far-right column indicates times for each shot. Here are some rules of thumb to help you put numbers like this to your own schedule.

- The first shot of the day always takes the longest to set up. People need to get into the rhythm of the shoot, people are still groggy and equipment needs to be checked and prepared. Because of this, try to schedule your most difficult shot first. The rest of the day becomes is a downhill slide.

- The first shot in a new location takes longer than the rest of the shots in the same location. If you use lighting gear or other special equipment such as wireless microphones, you probably pack them away carefully as you move from place to place. This means unpacking them at each new location. But after you are set up, each shot will take less time, because you are ready to go.

- Complex shots take longer than easy shots do. This is common sense, which does, occasionally, have a place in video production. If you set up a shot that involves moving the camera, changing the focus and having the talent juggle bowling balls all at the same time, it will take longer than a static shot of a flower. Don't ask why, it's a mystery.

- Wide shots take longer than closeups. This is true, because there is usually more going on in a wide shot. Not always, but it's a good rule of thumb.

- It takes time to change locations. Besides tearing down and setting up equipment, you have to move it to the next shooting location. If this is across the county, you have to allow for the time that it will take to get there.

- Shots either take 30 minutes or 15 minutes to capture. For scheduling purposes, you can usually assign these times to

your shots. Some shots take longer and some are done in a heartbeat. But by consistently using 30/15, your schedule will even out by the end of the day.

Stop or I'll Shoot

Once you have a script and production schedule, you're ready to shoot, right? Nope. You need to create a shooting schedule.

Shooting schedules look a lot like production schedules except for one crucial difference. All shots from one location are grouped together. This simple phase can potentially save you more time than anything else in this article. Why is grouping shots so important? Because returning to a location not only wastes time, it also sends a signal to your crew that you are not in control. And that's a real confidence buster. Let's say you are shooting at a location and trying to remember all the shots you need in your head. You finish, strike the equipment, get in the vehicle and start to drive away. Then it hits you. You didn't get the closeup. Arrrgh! Turn around, unload everything, set up the gear and get the shot. Now look at your crew's faces. Do they love you for the extra effort that you have just caused them to endure? Or are their faces black with smoldering hatred? If this scene is repeated over and over, a volunteer crew will probably not return for more. And a professional crew will not trust your judgement on other aspects of the production.

Now you have a script, a production schedule and a shooting schedule. Keep a copy of each of these documents in a single notebook when you go into the field (see Figure 20.3). You will probably work mainly from the shooting schedule. Cross-off shots as you finish them and keep track of the best ones by writing down the time-code number next to the shot on the shooting schedule. This will help you find the shot when you sit down to edit. If your recording device doesn't have time

Figure 20.3 *Electronic PDAs can also help you manage your time and take notes.*

code, you can note which tape (or digital media) the shot is on and the amount of time that has been used on that media. This is not as precise as time code (where each frame has a unique number) but can be helpful.

Keep a copy of your script with you in the field; just carrying the shooting schedule is not enough. On the shooting schedule, the shot's location is the most important element, but you often need to know how the shots are going to work together in the real script. This way, you won't shoot two shots that are too similar to each other (a head-to-waist shot of the talent, for example) and try to edit them together later. Such an edit can make the talent appear to jump from place to place (which was fine on *Bewitched*, but might not be the effect you're looking for).

Put it All Together

If you have done your homework and kept good notes during shooting, your editing process should go much more smoothly (see Figure 20.4). This is harder than it sounds, because working in the field can be like being in battle, with problems and unforeseen obstacles flying like bullets. (You're trying to get audio while in the flight path of the airport; or you need blue skies and it's starting to rain.) However, let's pretend we live in a perfect world and all has gone well.

Figure 20.4 *Better planning of your shoots will ultimately save time in post-production editing.*

Editing is like putting together a jigsaw puzzle. If you know where all the pieces are before you start, you will save yourself a lot of trouble, which translates into time. If you create a simple show with straight cut edits, you can figure that each minute of finished program will take you about an hour of editing time. If you plan to use wipes and special effects, double the estimate. If you want to experiment while editing, triple it.

Make sure you have everything you need when you go into an edit. Will you use a voice talent to narrate the show? Have it done before you start. Are you identifying on-camera interviewees with titles? Make sure that you know how to spell their names.

Taking a video from start to finish is a big undertaking. It's best to know what you're getting into before you invest your money and time. With a good plan, you will not only have more fun during the process, you will have a good chance of actually getting the darn thing done—and that's the best plan you can make.

Sidebar 1

Quick Tips

To plan effectively, you need to create the following:

• Script — Put on paper what you are trying to achieve.

• Production Schedule—Break the script down into shots and plan what props, talent and time each shot will need.

• Shooting Schedule—Similar to the production schedule, but with the shots grouped by location.

Sidebar 2

Film Script Software

Software programs are available to help you create film-style scripts. (Scriptware also does split-format.) These programs automatically format the page and can even help break the script down into a shooting schedule. Here's a sampling of some of these programs.

Final Draft
16000 Ventura Boulevard, Suite 800, Encino, CA 91436
(818) 995-8995
www.finaldraft.com
$299

Movie Magic Screenwriter 2000
Screenplay Systems
150 East Olive Avenue, Suite 203, Burbank, CA 91502
(800) 847-8679
www.screenplay.com
$299

Page 2 Stage
Windward Studios
1127 Barberry Court, Boulder, CO 80303
(303) 499-2544
www.page2stage.com
$80

Scriptware
Cinovation Inc.
1750 30th Street, Suite 360, Boulder, CO 80301-1005
(800) 788-7090
www.scriptware.com
$300

21
It's all in the Approach:
Creative Approaches for Video Productions

Jim Stinson

Some informational programs use gimmicks like butter on popcorn, to hide the bland taste of the subject matter: "Hi! I'm Percy Peatmoss, and we're gonna meet some exciting lichens!" (Suuure, we are!) Though spokes-mosses like Percy went out with 16 mm projectors, promotional, training and educational programs still need what you might call a *presentation method*.

As the term implies, this is a systematic approach to laying out the content of a program. Mr. Announcer on the sound track, Julia Child behind the cooktop, the talking head in the interview—each of these is a presentation method, deliberately selected because it's well-suited to the program's subject. What are some of these presentation methods and how do you select the right one(s) for your show? Step right this way, folks; the tour starts here.

When you come right down to it, there're only a few basic presentation methods: documentary, interview, expert presenter and full script. As we look at each method in turn, remember that most informational videos use them in various combinations.

Documentary

A documentary purports to capture and display a subject as it really is, allowing viewers to draw their own conclusions from their impressions of the material. In some programs, they're assisted by narration or commentary, while in others the edited footage appears to speak for itself. (We say "purports" and "appears" because no documentary is a truly passive, neutral pipeline of information. For more on this, see *Liar, Liar!* in the October 2000 issue of **Videomaker** or at www. videomaker.com).

The documentary method works well where you want to convey a free-form impression of your subject. *Beautiful Downtown Burbank, Recreation in Bigfoot County, Where your Sales Tax Goes*—these are good subjects for documentary programs.

The most rigorous documentary form (represented by the films of Frederick Wiseman) uses no verbal commentary to organize the presentation and point the message. The entire effect comes from the selection and juxtaposition of shots. To the newbie, this may seem like the easiest form of program ("Hey kids, let's showcase Fillmore High!") but it is in fact, the hardest to do successfully. Without the guidance of voiceovers and titles, the result is often an inexpressive jumble of footage.

That's why many professional documentarians (notably Ken Burns) use multiple voices on the sound track—often a mix of narration, dramatized voices and interview quotes. This method is easier because it allows you to comment on the footage as you display it. However, juggling multiple audio sources is a sophisticated process.

For fail-safe simplicity, try mating documentary footage to voice over narration. By scripting a single stream of commentary, you can control your presentation more precisely.

Figure 21.1 *Single & Dual Interviews— Single interviews, the most popular form in professional TV show, look spontaneous, but dual interviews are easier to manage.*

Interview

Interviews offer ways to get variety into your presentation, especially if you include several people. Interviews are great for subjects that are essentially verbal and require some expert input.

As the sidebar, *Pictures, Words or Titles?* explains, some topics are difficult to visualize. No matter how many photo albums you have, they don't display family history, but only *moments from* that history. For the actual narrative, nothing beats Great Grandmother on the sound track. Other good interview subjects include *Our Corporate Five Year Plan* (interview with the CEO) and *Coping with Depression* (interviews with sufferers and therapists). As these examples suggests, interview programs come in different flavors: single, dual and multiple.

The single interview doesn't look like a Q&A session, but like spontaneous conversation by the subject (see Figure 21.1).

The interviewer is never seen or heard, and the questions (dropped on the cutting room floor) are phrased to elicit statements rather than answers ("Tell us about the Boston branch of the family"). Because they omit the overhead of questions, single interviews are the most popular form in professional programs.

However, the dual interview is easier to manage. In this form, viewers see the interviewer and hear the questions. Replies can be free-form in this approach. For example, "Where were you born?" "Cleveland." is fine in a dual interview, but the answer would be meaningless in a single interview. Two-person interviews also offer built-in cutaway material in the form of the interviewer.

A more complex interview form is multiple voice. Using man-on-the-street vignettes or short sessions with the many people connected with the topic, you weave together a composite audio track that adds richness and variety as well as information. If people you know have some performing ability, you might try dramatized "interviews" with historic figures or people otherwise unavailable. Be cautious, however, because voice-only acting is a highly specialized skill and amateurish results sound frankly embarrassing.

Expert Presenter

If you've watched a David Attenborough nature video ("The vegetation [*wheeze*] here at 15,000 feet [*gasp*] is, understandably [*rattle*] sparse.") then you've seen an expert presenter. This method has many things going for it. First, the expertise of the spokesperson lends authority to the whole enterprise. Secondly, he or she can often be relied on to flesh out a skeletal content outline by ad-libbing material (see Figure 21.2).

The expert is best in the field—whether that field is a studio cooking show kitchen or a construction site or the Sonoran desert. If that isn't possible, you can establish the expert on camera in interview mode and then shift his or her remarks to voiceover narration.

The simplest approach is commentary: the experts react to whatever is presented to them. At its best, this method elicits priceless observations that would never occur to a script writer. At worst, it delivers the DVD prattle of movie directors reacting off-the-cuff to screenings of their films.

One step more formal is the demonstration, anything from a construction project to a science experiment to a cooking show. A demo is more clearly sequenced (by the steps in the project or recipe) but it still offers ample opportunity for ad-lib expert commentary. A demonstration format works best when the project can be completed at a single place in real time (except for the 45 minute baking period) and when the personality of the presenter adds interest to the show.

A popular variation seen on home repair, gardening and cooking shows is the dual (and sometimes dueling) expert format pioneered by Siskel and Ebert. This approach combines the virtues of the expert and interview methods, especially if one of the presenters serves as prompter/straight man to the other.

The next level up is a full-fledged lecture, either scripted or ad-lib. Since even the most dynamic expert is still just a talking head, it's good to cut away as much as possible to visuals of the subject matter. In fact, a project like this often starts with the taped lecture; then appropriate visuals are scripted and shot after the fact.

Sometimes, the effect of a lecture can be created by a skillful one-person interview. The questions select and sequence the material, and then drop away, leaving a seamless narrative.

Figure 21.2 *Expert presenter—the expert presenter lends authority to your subject and can ad-lib to expand on outlined program material.*

Full Script

An expert isn't necessary when reading narration that's been fully scripted. There are several reasons for going to the trouble of a wall-to-wall script. In some cases there are issues of legal or technical accuracy. You don't want to misrepresent details of *Employee Benefit Packages* or *Self Administration of Insulin*, and the best way to avoid doing so is by writing down (and getting approval for) every image and word.

In training and similar how-to programs, you want the clearest camera angles and the simplest language possible. In highly controlled situations like this, you'll want every sentence written and every setup storyboarded (see Figure 21.3).

A scripted program can use any mixture of presentation forms, including an on-camera spokesperson, a voiceover narrator and superimposed title buildups. You can even use interviews if the questions are closely coordinated with the script. (In real world situations, the script is often revised *after* the interviews are completed, in order to bring it into line with whatever was said.)

Full scripts and/or storyboards are almost always prepared for professional commercials, infomercials, video press releases and training programs, for one

Figure 21.3 *In some situations you may want to script the narration for your talent in clear simple language.*

overwhelming reason: the client. Most people and organizations are reluctant to spend good money unless they can see (or at least *think* they can see) what they're getting.

As we've seen, the presentation method chosen depends first of all on the nature of the topic. But real-world constraints also play a large role. What if you don't have an expert? Worse, what if you do have an expert who's a droning bore but still wants to be in the program? In situations like this, you need to know the alternative methods available to you and their suitability to your topic. We hope this little survey has helped.

Sidebar 1

Pictures, Words or Titles?

Different types of information want different presentation media. Some things are impossible to describe but easy to show; others are the opposite. Here's a quick rundown on choosing the best medium for each type of content.

- *Pictures.* If you can show it, do so. Images should always be your first choice, when appropriate, because video is inherently a visual medium. Through slow or fast motion, split screen shots and other formal devices, the medium can also display things in ways that can't be seen in real life.

- *Words.* If it's an abstraction, then talk about it. "Good citizenship" can be shown by examples (voting, picking up litter) but the concept itself is impossible to visualize. That's where narration does its best work.

Words also work well for summarizing because they deliver meaning so efficiently. "Your one-stop transmission and tire service since 1966" takes five seconds to say. You could show transmission work, tire installation and maybe a wall plaque proclaiming "Founded 1966" but these visuals would be time-consuming and lame.

- *Titles*. Titles make wonderful labels and organizers. *Cliche* that it is, a bulleted agenda that builds up line by line (via PowerPoint or titling software) is still the best way to orient (and periodically re-orient) viewers to the content of the program.

If the list is short, you can also display all the lines at once, color-highlighting whichever one is the current topic.

Combo Platters

Different viewers have different learning styles, visual, aural or textual; so try to deliver important points in at least two ways, or even three if necessary. For example, you could cover one step in a construction project like this:

- *Visual*: big CU of tab A inserted into slot B.

- *Aural*: NARRATOR (V.O.) Now insert tab A into slot B.

- *Textual*: Subtitle supered over the shot: "Insert Tab A in Slot B."

When delivering information redundantly, avoid varying its form. If the narrator says, "Now complete the assembly of the sub-widgit," viewers have to make a mental connection between this line and Tab A and Slot B. This effort can be distracting or even confusing.

22
Script Right:
Video Screenwriting Tips

Stephen Jacobs

See video clips at www.videomaker.com/handbook.

Even the best videographers often balk at writing scripts. Take my friend Mike Axelrod. A video computer programmer since graduating from college, Mike recently quit work to return to school.

As a film buff who's created a few videos with friends, he decided to combine his two interests and major in computer animation. He signed up for a required screenwriting course and experienced no difficulty in writing individual scenes three to five pages long.

Then he learned the second half of the course required completion of a screenplay for a fifteen-minute film, fifteen to twenty pages in length. The news left him pale.

"Fifteen to twenty pages! I'll never write something that long," he howled. "I'm not a writer!"

Well, maybe not. But good video begins with good writing. In this chapter, we'll show how even non-writers like Mike can put together a serviceable screenplay.

Videographers as Storytellers

Some people think writing is a talent reserved for those lucky enough to be born with it. This is not necessarily so. Writers who seem to have come from the womb pen in hand are the exception, not the rule. Most have to work at it. In many ways, writers are no different from videographers. Both are people trying to communicate specific information, a story, a particular point of view.

When you pick up that camcorder and press the little red button, you start to tell a story. Whether you're shooting the science fiction epic of your dreams, documenting a wedding for the 300th time or producing a thirty-second public service announcement for the local Red Cross, you're still telling a story.

So before you begin you should first consider what message you are trying to convey, and to what sort of audience. If you don't know what you're trying to say or whom you're trying to reach, you'll have a hard time getting your message across.

You may begin with the goal of writing a screenplay for an introductory videotape on washing machine maintenance; suddenly you find yourself showing the viewer how to make a washing machine from scratch. Or you write something for an experienced group of professionals, then find yourself explaining the basics.

In fiction, the routine Hollywood script features an easily identifiable protagonist, the hero; and an equally transparent antagonist, the villain. The hero confronts a problem and spends much of the film working toward a solution. The antagonist seeks to block this progress. Along the way the hero inevitably undergoes a change in character.

Some films slightly alter this formula. Director Barry Levinson has said his film *Rain Man* was a real challenge because the protagonist of the story, the autistic Raymond, by definition couldn't experience a change in character. It's his brother who must change.

Outline and Outpouring

For some people, outlining is extremely beneficial. Others find it gets in the way of the actual writing, another little task aiding and abetting procrastination. Some projects are more conducive to outlining than others. The larger the project, the more likely it will benefit from some pre-scribble structuring.

Beginners should definitely outline. It helps you understand where the story's heading. Does outlining mean the formal, Roman numeral structuring they taught you in elementary school? No. Think of it as simply jotting down a temporary table of contents. Once that's complete, you're ready to start writing.

As a videographer, you try to avoid situations where you must edit in-camera. You know the more footage you shoot, the more you repeat shots and obtain different angles, the more you'll have to work with during editing. It's not unusual to read about professional film directors with raw footage ratios of 20 to 1.

As a writer, you should give yourself the same freedom. Begin by throwing anything and everything down on paper. This isn't always easy to do. But if you criticize every sentence as you write it, you may not finish the first paragraph. Let it all out first; you can edit and revise later.

Show, Don't Tell

Writing for video is different from other types of writing in two important ways:

1. The lengthy description and dialogue that distinguish some writing is notably absent here. When writing for video, you need to show things, not talk about them. So skip those long passages of narration. Instead, use different camera angles and shots of the same scene to highlight the features of the landscape you wish to emphasize. Don't use long sections of dialogue to explain anything. Show it.

2. Screenplays happen in the here and now. They describe the action as the viewer will see it unrolling across the screen. Use active voice and present tense. For example, write, "John looks into the mirror, then does a double take. There's a second head growing out of his neck. He screams in terror and blacks out…"

Don't write, "John looked in the mirror, then did a double take. He saw a second head growing out of his neck. He screamed in terror and blacked out…"

Or, "We see our John look into the mirror and do a double take. His reflection shows a second head growing out of his neck. We hear him scream and see him slump to the floor. He's blacked out…"

NOTE: These examples are based on an actual film, *How to Get Ahead in Advertising*, in which the main character does indeed wake up one morning to find a second head growing out from the side of his neck. As they say in Hollywood, you can make a movie about darn near anything.

Relevant Questions

As your script nears completion, ask yourself the following important questions:

Does every single scene in the script a) advance the action and/or b) develop the character?

Do all scenes, dialogue and narration serve a legitimate purpose? Does the third scene featuring John arguing with his new head show us anything new about them, or did you just like the dialogue?

If you've shown the viewer how to remove the left front tire of a '58 Thunderbird, do you really need to show removal of the right front? Where else can you cut? Where should you expand?

Remember: you want your dialogue or narration to sound natural. That's a hard one. A good way to check your writing for a natural feel is to put it away for a few days, then reread it. Does it still sound right? Read it aloud. Do you stumble, fumble, fall? Then your actors or narrators will as well.

Finally, ask a few trustworthy and literate friends to read your work with a kind and constructive critical eye. You don't have to take their advice, but you should at least consider it, especially when the same problem is identified by more than one critic.

Writing is rewriting. Put your ego aside and polish your work. Once you're satisfied that it's as good as you can make it, it's probably ready to go.

Script Requirements

It's not enough to write a good script. You also have to format it according to screenwriting conventions. There are two main scriptwriting formats. Fictional scripts, or scripts with a lot of dialogue, use a format that evolved from the theater. Documentaries, industrials and other productions which match narration to the visuals typically use a split page, two-column format.

There are a number of variations within these two categories (see Figure 22.1), but all will fall under one type or another.

In the theatrical format, scenes are numbered; it's best not to number your scenes until you complete your final draft. Manually renumbering scenes can grow tiresome.

Number the pages in the upper right hand corner. When a scene crosses over from one page to the next, place the notation "continued" at the bottom right corner of the first page. Mark the top of the second page with the scene number and a "continued" notation.

It's important that the finished screenplay follow the general visual format, allowing for simple identification of scene location, direction and dialogue. For example, the first time Dan's name appears in the script his name is set in capital letters. The second time it isn't. This makes it easy for the reader to keep track of new characters. When indicating dialogue, character names always appear in caps.

Technically, each time the camera moves it inaugurates a new scene; we have three scenes now, rather than just the one. Some screenwriters also capitalize all audio cues—TYPING, TICKING—for easy identification.

With documentary and industrial video, you are frequently more interested in matching certain visual information with spoken word audio. That's why it's easier to format this type of script in two columns. The description of the visual information goes in the left column and the audio information goes in the right.

As with the dramatic screenplay, these types of formats vary slightly from script to script. In some, a thin third column to the left indicates shot numbers. Other variations use an abbreviation for the shot as part of the description.

It's a Wrap

Yes, learning to write can pose a challenge, but take a look at Mike. He gritted his teeth, put his stuff down on paper, and found he actually enjoyed himself.

The fifteen-minute film he was assigned to write turned into three five-minute

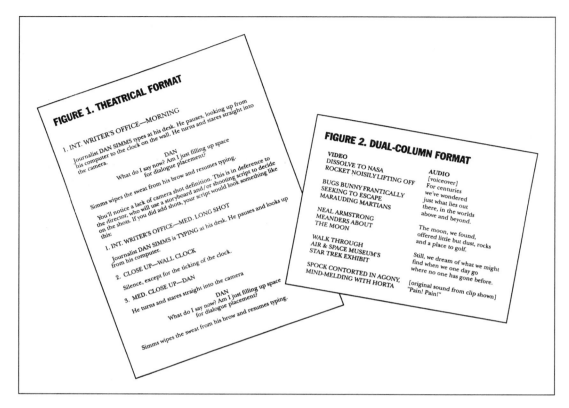

Figure 22.1 *Samples of theatrical and dual-column scriptwriting formats.*

sections for a feature film script he vows someday to complete. He scored himself an "A" in the course. Most important, he engaged in work he felt good about, and gained a new perspective on his capabilities. Now it's your turn.

Writing Tools for Videographer:

There's a wealth of help out there for script writers, from how-to books to formatting software. Below we list some of the most popular writing tools. For more, contact The Writer's Computer Store 1-800-272-8927 (www.writerscomputer.com).

How-To Books

Screenplay: The Foundations of Screenwriting by Syd Field, ISBN: 0440576474, Dell Publishing, $13.95.

The Complete Guide to Standard Script Formats: The Screenplay by Cole and Haag, ISBN: 0929583000, CMC Publishing Inc., $18.95.

The Elements of Screenwriting by Irwin R. Blacker, ISBN: 002861450X, MacMillan Distribution, $9.95.

The TV Scriptwriter's Handbook by Alfred Brenner, ISBN: 187950510X, Sicman James Press, $15.95.

Scriptwriting Tutorial

WritePro; for DOS, Windows or Mac, eight lessons, $199.

Script Formatting Programs

Final Draft, for Mac or Windows, $249.
Screen Writer 2000, for Mac or Windows, $299.

23

Look Who's Talking:
How to Create Effective, Believable Dialogue for Your Video Productions

John K. Waters

A script is a story told with pictures—but silent pictures they're not. Since 1927, when the debut of *The Jazz Singer* transformed "moving pictures" into "talkies," dialogue has played a crucial role in making successful films and videos.

But with everything else you worry about as an independent videographer—maintaining your equipment, getting the shot, getting paid—dialogue may be low on your list of concerns. Still, you don't want to underestimate its power.

Good dialogue works hard. It keeps things moving, ties individual segments together and unifies your piece. On the other hand, bad dialogue discredits your work, destroying your credibility and ultimately costing you your audience.

Whether you're shooting independent features, corporate image spots, local TV commercials or your sister's wedding, what your subjects say can make the difference between an amateur show and a powerful piece of professional videography.

Here's how to make sure what they say works.

What is Dialogue?

Any time you put words into the mouths of your on-camera subjects, you are writing dialogue. That definition includes hosts, commentators and spokespersons, as well as actors playing parts.

The primary purpose of dialogue is to move your story forward. It accomplishes this by revealing character, communicating information and establishing relationships between characters. It can also foreshadow events, comment on the action and connect scenes.

For example: in my script *Sleeping Dogs Lie*, the hero, Ray Sobczak, is a reporter working on a story that is annoying some very important citizens. Here, a local politico delivers a veiled warning.

JAMIE

What happened to you?

SOBOZAK

Zigged when I shoulda zagged. How's the campaign going?

JAMIE

Oh, I just love spending obscene amounts of my mother's money—and what your paper charges for ad space is truly obscene.

SOBOZAK

Something tells me your mother can afford it, Mr. Bockman.

JAMIE

My father, who could also afford it when he was alive, was Mr. Bockman. Call me Jamie.

SOBOZAK

Okay, Jamie. Think she'll win?

JAMIE

(ignoring him) How's the story coming?

SOBOZAK

Which story is that? (Jamie gazes out at the cluster of downtown buildings and the hills rising behind them.)

JAMIE

Salinas is growing, Ray. Over a hundred thousand at last count. But, underneath, it's still a small town.

This exchange probably won't go down in history as the most memorable in films, but it has many earmarks of good dialogue. It tells us something about the characters: Jamie is rich, has an ambiguous attitude toward his mother's campaign for mayor and has well-informed connections; Sobczak is tough, and won't let a bump on the noggin keep him from getting the story.

It foreshadows future events: people are watching. And it moves the story forward: this encounter gives Sobczak an idea, which leads him—and the story—in a new direction.

Keep It Lean

The above example also demonstrates another important quality of good dialogue: brevity. Good dialogue is a lean

exchange between people, composed of short phrases. On paper, it looks like lots of white space; big blocks of type are definite warning sign that you are overwriting your dialogue.

"The good stuff is a dance of two and three-liners between characters," says scriptwriter Madeline DiMaggio. "It's a bouncing ball that keeps your audience riveted."

When it comes to writing dialogue, DiMaggio knows what she's talking about. She has written over 35 hours of episodic television for shows ranging from Kojak to The Bob Newhart Show to ABC's After School Special. A former staff writer for the daytime soap opera Santa Barbara, she is also a teacher and the author of *How to Write for Television*.

DiMaggio says the kind of close-to-the-bone dialogue you want for your videos comes only through rewriting (See Figure 23.1.), "It doesn't happen on the first pass," she says. "At first your dialogue is cardboard—and that's the way it should be. It's only later, when you go back and take five lines down to two-and-a-half, and then two-and-a-half lines down to one, that you find the real gems."

DiMaggio says she plays a game with herself during her rewriting process: if she can whittle a piece of dialogue down to four lines, can she cut it to two? If she can chop it to two, how about one?

"If script writers were doctors," she says, the best ones would be surgeons. "Cut, cut, cut!"

Make It Sound Real

A tried and true technique for developing your ear for natural-sounding dialogue is to surreptitiously tape conversations and then transcribe them later.

I do this especially when I'm writing about types of people I don't know well. Ethical questions aside, this has worked well to awaken my sense of how people talk.

Figure 23.1 *Rewriting and rewriting and rewriting again is key when writing dialog.*

The first thing I noticed when I began doing this was how fragmented conversations are. The following is an example from my files.

MAN #1

Hey, what's up?

MAN #2

I dropped by the place. Thought I'd say hi, but nobody was, you know...

MAN #1

I was over there yesterday and...

MAN #2

... home. You know?

MAN #1

Nobody? Man, I...

MAN #2

That's because of the, you know, holiday 'n stuff, and her car was there and everything, but...

MAN #1

What a piece of *#@*!, man, that car...

MAN #2

Yeah, and, you know,
I left like, a note.

MAN #1

NO WAY!

On paper, this conversation looks like an exchange between two orangutans, but they sounded perfectly normal. That's why, unless you're making a documentary, you can't just transcribe tapes of real conversations and use them raw in your scripts. And even documentaries require judicious editing.

"If you went out to a coffee shop with a tape recorder," DiMaggio says, "and went home and put what you recorded into a script, it wouldn't work. Good dialogue isn't actually real. It just gives the illusion of reality."

DiMaggio says one of the best ways to learn how dialogue sounds is to record dialogue.

"That's how I got to know Santa Barbara," she says. "There were so many characters, and they all had their own voices! I would audiotape the show and then listen whenever I was driving. When you cut off the other senses, your ear becomes much stronger."

DiMaggio also recommends audiotaping shows to develop an ear for genre dialogue.

"Comedies, mysteries, dramas—it's an incredible way to learn," she says.

Good dialogue also has a spontaneous quality, as if your characters were speaking their lines for the first time.

"When the dialogue is stilted or too formal," says corporate video writer/producer Susan O'Connor Fraser, "the audience just laughs at it. When they start doing that, you've lost them."

O'Connor Fraser is the creative director for Tam Communications in San Jose, California. She's been writing and producing videos for Fortune 500 companies for the past 15 years. Her company produced a reality-based show on paramedics in San Jose, which aired on the local ABC affiliate.

"I don't think corporate video is that much different from features," O'Connor Fraser says. "Dialogue is dialogue, and every story has its own reality. Star Wars has a reality, and so does a corporate sales presentation. Everything must play and be believable within its own reality."

According to O'Connor Fraser, one of the most common dialogue errors she sees is characters addressing each other by name too often.

"I've seen it done in every passage," she says. "It's, 'Well, John … Well, Lisa… What do you think, John…I'm not sure, Lisa.' It's just not real."

She says reading your script aloud is one of the easiest ways to spot dialogue errors. (See Figure 23.2.)

"You're writing for the ear. So you need to find out how it sounds. You don't need actors, though they are a wonderful luxury. Just read it out loud with a friend, or by yourself while you're sitting at your computer. You'll hear many of the problems right away."

Stay in Character

When I write, I become the characters I'm writing about. This is pretty easy when I'm writing about thirtysomething white guys from the Midwest. But what about when the character I'm writing dialogue for is a New York cop, or a Southern doctor, or a black female Vietnam veteran with a Harvard MBA, two grown children and a neurotic obsession with alien abductions?

You simply cannot write dialogue that rings true unless you acquaint yourself with the kind of people appearing in your video. This is where real world research is essential. I'm talking about stuff you can't find in the library. But that doesn't mean that you have to spend a week on a fishing boat in Alaska or infiltrate the local Jaycees to get the right slang and jargon for your script, though those are tried and true approaches.

"If I don't have any personal experiences in my own life I can draw on," says O'Connor Fraser, "I track down the kind of person I'm writing about and take them to lunch." In her corporate work, she tends to deal with a limited number of "types," mostly from the high tech world; after 15 years she knows them well. But she still checks her "voice" with face-to-face interviews—especially when she's writing a script for an on-camera presentation by a company executive.

Figure 23.2 *Read your script aloud to make sure it sounds natural.*

"When I go out and interview a president or vice president who will be on camera," she says, "I listen very carefully, so I'm really hearing them talk. I don't want them to sound like they're reading from the inside cover of an annual report. I want them to sound very natural and comfortable, as though they were talking across the table from someone.

"Interviewing your clients is also one of the best ways to pick up the buzz words of their professions. Listen closely and make a list of unfamiliar words or phrases. Ask for clarification so you understand them in context. When you sit down to write your script, your list will prove invaluable."

Many writers just write the dialogue as best they can and then give it to someone from that character's walk of life to read. DiMaggio says she works on her dialogue,

"until I'm not ashamed of it," and then turns it over to a person with whatever special knowledge her characters would have. In her TV movie script, *Belly Up*, for example, one of her characters was a man who gambled on the golf course.

"I wasn't about to take up golf to hear how guys gamble on the golf course," says DiMaggio. "So I sent the script to my brother. He gambles on the golf course all the time. In five minutes he told me things I couldn't possibly know unless I was out there. I made some changes in the script and all of a sudden it sounded absolutely real. One producer told me I wrote like a man, which, under the circumstances, I took as a compliment."

In one of my own scripts I created a character who was a professional crop duster, but I had never met a crop duster in my life. So I picked up the Yellow

Pages, and a few lunches later I knew everything I needed to know to create a believable character. (And I now know to call them agricultural aviators.)

Go for Subtext

Syd Field, author of several well-known books on scriptwriting, including the now classic *Screenplay: The Foundations of Screenwriting*, calls dialogue one of the "tools of character." That's because what people say says a great deal about them. But what they don't say often says more. The best dialogue is not only about what your characters are saying, it's also about what they're not saying. This is subtext.

"Subtext is what's happening beneath the surface," says DiMaggio. "It's the key to truly great dialogue."

Examples of subtext abound in films like the 1944 film noir classic, *Double Indemnity*. One scene in particular comes to mind, in which insurance salesman Walter Neff (Fred MacMurray) puts the make on a client's wife (Barbara Stanwyck). They fence back and forth in a conversation about cars and speeding, but driving is the last thing on their minds.

Subtext enlivens good writing everywhere—even commercials. We've watched that couple in the Taster's Choice commercials meet, woo and bed in Paris—all while talking about coffee.

Subtext probably isn't as important in most corporate video situations; still, you ignore it at your peril. Human beings talk around things. Dialogue that's too "on the nose" won't sound natural. Even the dialogue in infomercials has subtext.

Figure 23.3 *Congratulations! It's a script!*

Write the Right Voice Over

Voice-over narration isn't really dialogue, but many of the same principles still apply. This is especially true if the narrator is a particular character, as in the case of a host, or one of the actors, such as the Holly Hunter character in *The Piano* or Walter Neff, who narrates *Double Indemnity*.

You write voice-over narration like you write dialogue—for the ear. It should sound conversational. Even if your narrator is an omniscient voice, that voice must conform to your audience's expectations of human communication.

"When I'm doing voice overs," says O'Connor Fraser, "I still get a character in mind and write for him or her. Of course this is really important if the narrator will ever appear on-camera, but I do it even if they won't. That way, the voice is consistent throughout."

Voice-over narration can be even harder to write than dialogue. "If you think dialogue has to be lean," DiMaggio says, "voice overs have to be the best of the best. It has to be very, very thrifty. The real gems. Otherwise it turns into an excuse for failing to write good exposition."

Practice, Practice, Practice

Writing authentic, believable dialogue is a special skill; it takes practice. But with some effort and more than a little patience, you'll get it. (Figure 23.3)

"You have to realize that the script you write today won't be as good as the script you write next year," says O'Connor Fraser. "And that's okay. I'm a much better writer now than I was a year ago. I learn something with every script I write."

"We're all students, really," says DiMaggio. "No matter how long you do this, there's always something to learn. I think that's the good news. It's one of the things that keeps this work interesting."

In the end, creating good dialogue is more about listening than it is about writing. Once you begin to hear the rhythms of human conversation, the dialogue you write for your videos will improve dramatically.

So keep your ears open.

24
Storyboards and Shot Lists

Jim Stinson

Some DVDs (*Shrek* and *The Matrix*, for example) now include sample storyboards—shot-by-shot sketches drawn to visualize the action of key sequences—as bonus material. As you study these slick drawings, you'll notice that most frames are remarkably close to the actual shots they predict. Back in Hollywood's glory days, most directors (with Hitchcock a notable exception) rarely worked with storyboards; today, however, they're everywhere. Should you be using them too? That's what we're here to discover. We'll start with a look at what storyboards do.

Storyboards Visualize

Basically, pre-designed storyboards in pencil or marker predict what shots will look like. Why not just invent shots as you actually shoot? Here are three reasons.

First, storyboards let you test complicated setups cheaply on paper instead of expensively on location. Suppose your script says, "He unrolls the treasure map

before him and she gasps as she sees where the gold is buried." But when you draw a high-angle insert of the unfolding map, you realize there's no way to get "she" into the frame (see Figure 24.1a). So you try a new angle: over her shoulder (see Figure 24.1b). By moving the camcorder to center her face and refocusing as she turns into profile, you can get both her relation to the map and her reaction to it; and you haven't wasted half an hour on a setup you'd eventually discard.

Secondly, you can check your coverage of a sequence and preplan your video camera angles for variety, continuity and rhythm. Suppose you sketch three shots of the male talent digging up the treasure chest (see Figure 24.2a). Hmmm: though the sketches are from different viewpoints, they're all neutral-height medium shots and are too repetitive. OK, substitute a point-of-view (POV) closeup of the emerging chest (Figure 24.2b) and change the last shot to a low-angle closeup of his greedy expression as he reacts to the chest (Figure 24.2c). In 10 minutes of doodling,

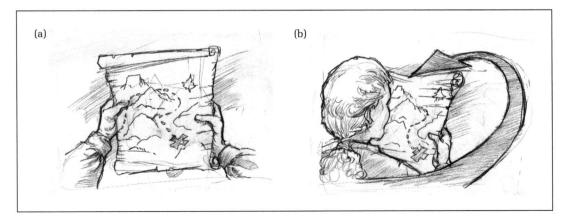

(a)   (b)

Figure 24.1

you've improved a sequence from ho-hum to dynamic.

Finally, storyboarding is essential for planning special effects. Say you want to establish a "pirate ship" by compositing stock footage of a three-master riding offshore with our hero in the foreground (see Figure 24.3). A sketch will guide your placement of the camera and the actor so that he'll relate properly to the scene.

Storyboard Vision

So far, you've been created storyboards for your own use, but storyboards also communicate your vision to others. Verbalizing image ideas is always chancy, so it's better to show what you have in mind visually.

In the professional world, storyboards are essential for communicating with clients, first to pitch concepts and then to preview the live action. Never forget that visual imagination is like a sense of humor: many people lack it, but no one will ever admit it. The client may nod and smile as you verbalize your vision, but yelp, "You never said you'd do that!" upon seeing the footage, even if that was precisely what you promised. Prevent that scenario—put that promise in sketches instead of words.

Incidentally, you should have a professional artist draw storyboards for clients. Even though you were hired to shoot, not draw, your amateur scribbles will likely cast doubts on your professionalism. (Hey, whoever said it was fair?) If you don't have a client to impress, don't worry about the quality of your thumbnail sketches. As long as they communicate to yourself and your crew, they do the job. There are two ways to do storyboarding nowadays, either draw them on paper or build them on a computer.

Paper and Pencil

To make a board from scratch, draw between six and 12 rectangles on a virtual sheet of paper (any word processor or paint program'll do it for you). Make the horizontal/vertical ratio 4 to 3 (4:3) for conventional video or 16:9 for wide screen. Leave enough space to write under each frame. Some people pre-print "Frame #," "action," "audio," etc., but you don't have to be that formal. Print out a large quantity of these blank boards.

Using simple lines and stick-figure subjects, sketch each setup in a frame, observing just a few conventions. Indicate subject movement with arrows in the

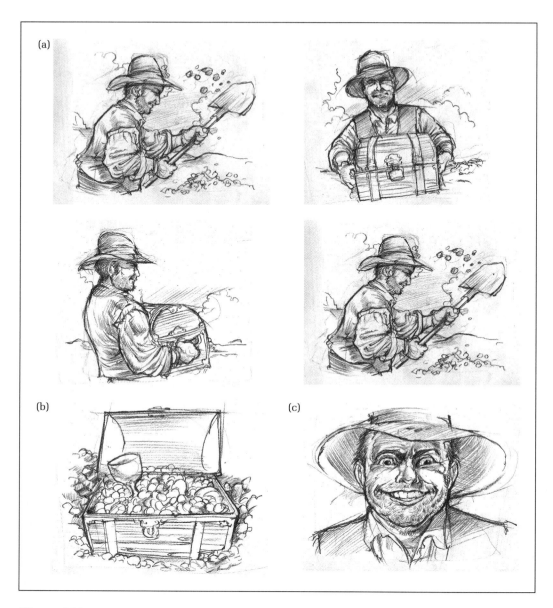

Figure 24.2

frame. Show zooms by sketching the wide-angle position, drawing a box around the telephoto position within it and adding diagonal arrows to show whether the movement is in or out. For pans or tilts between two distinct compositions, show each one as a separate frame, with an arrow between frames to link them.

The notes written below each frame should contain some or all of the following:

- Frame number
- Sequence ("27") or sequence/shot ("27B")
- Action ("John runs past; exits frame right")

Figure 24.3

- Camera instructions: ("No pan")
- Dialogue: ("JOHN: Come back here with that map!")
- Other audio: ("SFX: bullet ricochet")
- Visual effects: ("Bluescreen for ship composite")

Computer Boards

If you're deft with a mouse (or are fortunate enough to own a pad and stylus), you can sketch boards directly on your screen. Perhaps the easiest way to do this is with the draw tools in Corel Presentations or Microsoft PowerPoint. This approach makes frames easy to add, insert, delete or modify (see Figure 24.4).

A second method is to make individual sketches in the draw/paint software you favor, then use a graphics organizer to print them as sequential thumbnails. The ThumbsPlus software lets you add extensive notes under each image.

A third route is a publishing package like Adobe PageMaker. You can build a template page of blank frames, then either draw in each one or import an outside graphic or even location photo.

This brings us to commercial storyboard packages. As the sidebar suggests, they can make wonderful organizers for production

Figure 24.4 *You don't need to be an artist. Use a simple paint program to convey your ideas.*

planning, because you can import digital photos and write extensive commentaries. However, they can be cranky and limited in drawing the shots of your particular show. Though they might seem to allow non-artists to build presentation-quality boards, the skill needed to customize their generic components is substantial.

Shot Lists

Think of a shot list as the writing on a storyboard, without the pictures (see Figure 24.5). Though simple lists of shots don't let you pre-test potential setups, they do allow you to systematically verify that you are covering every angle you need.

Often shot lists are just quick and dirty notes that help you remember everything you need in a particular sequence. You can also cull a shot list from a fully-written script if you separate video into separate columns (or paragraphs). Just build a word processor macro that will strip out everything but the scene number and the visual description.

On the other hand, a shot list built in a database program (such as File Maker Pro) can be the most versatile production tool in your kit. Design a database using some or all of the fields suggested in the sidebar, using each shot as a separate record. By creating report forms with different fields and sorts, you can build a working document for everyone from the director to the wardrobe person.

Figure 24.5 *A coordinated shot list that matches your storyboard will make your job much easier.*

Sidebar 1

Storyboard Software

Commercial software is available for storyboarding but it suffers from problems that are very hard to overcome.

Most packages work by supplying a pre-drawn set of backgrounds, a grab bag of props (guns, flower pots, cars), and a repertory of characters. By selecting, placing, rotating and scaling these components, you can make very professional looking frames.

The trouble is, they can almost never illustrate your video. The script may say, "The old duchess sweeps into the palace banquet hall." but the software inventory lacks both an old woman (let alone a duchess) and a palace hall; and the drawing tools for building same are rudimentary, to put it kindly.

True, you can import custom backgrounds from programs like Bryce and characters from 3D modeling software, but expect to spend at least an hour per frame building these hybrid images. Do the math on a three-page board of 12 frames each and decide if this method is really time-effective for your project.

On the other hand, these packages can be useful in production planning if you import digital stills from location scouting and make notes in the fields provided. Shotmaster from the Badham Company (www.badhamcompany.com) is particularly versatile this way.

Bottom line: Storyboard packages have their uses, but don't expect them to draw what you can't draw for yourself.

Sidebar 2

A Shot List Database

Start your database by treating each shot as a separate record. Then add fields for every important aspect of production planning.

An Extensive List

A fairly complete set of fields might include the following (separate but related fields are grouped together):

- sequence, shot number and take
- interior/exterior and day/night
- camera setup
- audio (production, reference track, special effects)
- special equipment (like a dolly)
- shot content
- notes
- location
- talent 1, talent 2, talent 3 (etc., for as many actors as will ever appear together in a single shot)
- key prop (such as a rented vehicle), other props
- costumes
- day, date and start time

Plus any other production details you want to keep track of.

A Director's List

To create a director's shot list, build a report containing these fields:

- sequence, shot number and take.
- camera setup
- shot content
- notes

Then sort the list by sequence, setup and only then shot number. You'll get a sequence-by-sequence list of every shot organized by setup.

25

Budget Details: Successful Video Projects Stick to Budgets

Mark Steven Bosko

Creating and adhering to a realistic budget is important to the success of any videographer's project.

But just how do you compute that magical figure, arrive at an amount low enough to attract investors but large enough to get the job done? It's not easy. Thousands of people labor in Hollywood as budget wizards; not even they get it right always. So many variables and details can go wrong or astray; it's impossible to plan for every contingency. Most often, you just have to guess.

Still, in this chapter we'll offer a number of useful guidelines vital for budget preparation. Videographers who absorb these lessons will at least have a reasonable grasp of the basics of financial planning.

Reasons for Budgets

Video budgets both attract investors and allow you to exercise control over a production.

Since the budget is the foundation of any presentation to investors, it should be specific and accurate.

Realism is also a good idea. It's an admirable goal, applying LucasFilm-like effects to a dry-cleaning commercial, but hardly feasible when the video must come in at $499.

Most projects begin under-budgeted and under-scheduled. It's easy to understand why. A project will certainly seem more attractive to investors if you can convince them you'll finish the video for less money in less time than the competition.

But this shortsighted method of easy financing will eventually cause you suffering.

Projects under-scheduled and under-budgeted leave you with only two options once the show begins 1) the project goes over budget, or 2) the quality goes into the dumpster.

Say you tell a client $300 will do to create a training video. Then, during shooting, rain pours down; you must shut down the shoot and pay talent for a second day.

You've now spent an extra $50, money intended for post-production. So will you skip the original scoring, budgeted at $50, choosing instead to give the client canned tunes? Or jettison the spiffy title effects for hand-lettered cards?

Sticking adamantly to an unrealistic budget forces you to continually compromise. This leads to a loss of quality.

There's a minimum budget for every project, a certain amount necessary to produce a video meeting reasonable standards of quality. Determine your video's destination, then calculate the smallest amount of money needed to reach it. If the available financing is less than this figure, change the project.

Keep budgeting until you have a video you can afford to make.

Step by Step

It's important to give equal emphasis to all stages of production, from writing and principal photography to music and editing.

It's easy to get excited about the shooting stage of a video project. Here is the place for lights, camera, action. Just don't make the mistake of creating an excruciatingly detailed budget for production only to carelessly slop but a few dollars to post production. You'll pay dearly.

Become familiar with the functions and costs associated with every step of the production process. Talk to the people responsible for the script, the shooting and the effects. Without such intense research, you may neglect such costs as B-roll tape, music copyright fees and catering charges.

Actual working budgets vary in size. Major Hollywood studio budgets may end up as two-inch-thick tomes, while an independent thirty-second cable spot can come in a tiny one-pager.

Regardless of size, most every budget consists of two sections: costs above-the-line and below-the-line. The former includes cash for producer, writer, director and talent. These costs are usually fixed, set amounts. Below-the-line costs include everything else associated with production. Each line item contains many separate details contributing to the total cost. I'll examine each in an attempt to explain what makes building a budget so tricky.

Over the Line

The first above-the-line item concerns screenplay and story rights (see Figure 25.1). If your production uses an adaptation of existing work, you'll have to purchase the rights. These can be costly for a known, popular author's work, or nonexistent if the story comes from a rookie simply seeking screen credit.

Unless you come up with it yourself, you will have to pay someone some amount for either an idea or an actual screenplay. Even for thirty-second commercials, people get paid to write scripts.

Hidden above-the-line costs can include photocopying, script breakdowns and rewrites, copyright registration and legal fees associated with purchasing work.

The producer is the one who generally runs the show; and, yep, often expects payment, too. A producer is responsible for finding story, actors, crew, equipment, locations, props, wardrobe and investors. This requires an enormous amount of time, even for a small, one-day shoot. A producer's talent lies in the ability to make and keep contacts; that's what they're paid for. Obvious expenses include phone charges, travel expenses, lunches, postage, contracts and legal fees.

In Hollywood, the director is paid for overall vision. On smaller productions, the director may be you, the camera operator or even the client. With very low budgets, you can skip this item; there isn't enough discretionary cash available to afford a director.

Talent includes lead actors, supporting cast, stunt people, voice-over artists and models. In budgeting talent, keep in mind

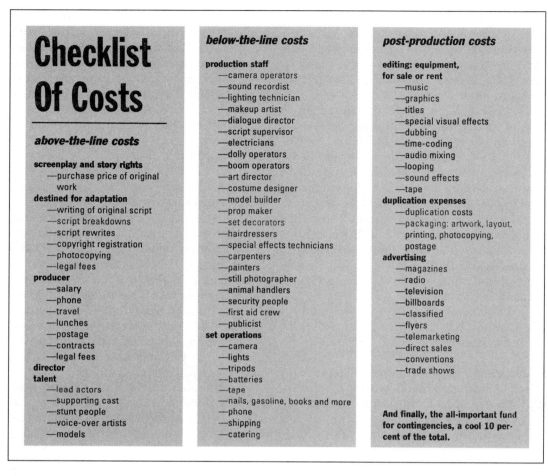

Figure 25.1 *Checklist of costs.*

daily or hourly rates. These usually vary according to how often the person works.

As an example, you might hire talent from the local actors' union for $200 a day, $150 for two days or more. Read the small print; often contracts demand that two or more days be worked consecutively. If you work your talent on Monday and Wednesday, you'll spend $400, not the planned two-day rate of $300.

For details on this intricate subject, consult Ralph Singleton's indispensable book, *Film Scheduling*.

Under the Rainbow

In an ultra-low budget affair you may spend little or no money above the line.

But every production—large or small—incurs production expenses.

Depending on circumstances, production staff may or may not require significant expenditures. When the local car dealer hires you to shoot a thirty-second spot, you discover the script calls for a night shoot requiring a two-camera setup and live sound. What began simply now demands additional camera operators, lighting people, sound recorders and probably three or four grips to jockey cables and equipment.

On the other hand, your sixty-minute documentary on the mating habits of waterfowl requires only you and your camera.

Obviously, a project's length bears little relation to total costs. It's the script details that matter.

On most projects, regardless of size, the key staff members are the camera operator, sound recordist, lighting technician and makeup artist.

Support positions include dialogue director, script supervisor, electricians, dolly operators, boom operators, art director, costume designer, model builder, prop maker, set decorator, hair dresser, special effects technician, carpenter, painter, still photographer, animal handler, security, first-aid crew and publicist (see Figure 25.1).

Set operations, like staff, can demand either a large or small chunk of cash, again depending on the project. If you already own a camera, lights and sound equipment and all your locations currently exist; operation costs may be few. No need to buy or rent gear or build sets.

If your video seeks to portray a sci-fi world, get ready to dole out the dollars. The set builder needs wood, the wardrobe manager gold *lamé*, the makeup artist latex and the gaffer colored gels. The set operations segment of this budget requires great detail; include every imaginable associated cost.

It's not neurotic to include such costs as the tissues actors will need for their noses during chilly outdoor shoots. It's these little things that throw a project into disarray. Don't overlook such "obvious" items as nails, screws, bolts and glue; gasoline for automobiles and generators; rentals and permits; duplicate sets of clothing; bottles, cans, books and plants; and, of course, tape.

Again, talk to your people; learn what they require. Sometimes it's not a bad idea to ask your support staff to create their own budgets; these you can incorporate into your final estimate.

Postage and telephone fees can add up quickly. It's amazing how many long-distance calls people make in the middle of a production. And if you're on the road with a cellular, cash outflow can grow quite frightening. Same for postage and shipping expenses. If your client lives in another town and insists on dailies, you'll go broke if you haven't budgeted properly.

To cast and crew, the most important cost is catering. Believe me, you don't want to face down fifteen hungry people with nothing but a jar of peanut butter and a loaf of bread.

Post-production Funds

The last formal segment of the budget concerns post-production audio and video editing.

Those who own their own editing equipment will find costs fairly minimal. If forced to rent, the prices can get steep. Don't underestimate the amount of editing time. This will depend on such variables as length of script, timing, client approval and number of effects.

If you've shot footage for a thirty-second spot requiring only five or six edits, an hour may be enough. If that same spot requires a rapid assault of images and sounds, you may spend two or three days in the edit bay.

You usually reserve editing time by the hour, day or week, with price breaks for longer periods. Other post production costs include music, graphics and titles creation, special visual effects, dubbing, time coding, audio mixing, looping, sound effects and extra tape.

A final cost to consider is the promotional expense associated with selling and marketing. Final product should be presented in a professional form. All videos properly labeled and packaged. You don't want to hand a client a VHS copy in a cardboard sleeve with masking tape crookedly proclaiming the title on the spine. A nice hard-shell package with a printed label is the only way to go; include these costs in your budget.

If you want your production to reach the masses, think about full-color packaging costs like artwork, layout and printing. Any worthwhile marketing effort includes mailing promotional copies to potential distributors and buyers. Estimate photocopying, postage and duplication costs.

Don't forget advertising. Magazines, radio, TV, billboards, classifieds, flyers, telemarketing, direct sales, door-to-door, conventions and trade shows whatever form you plan requires cash. Obtain quotes for ad rates during the time your ad will appear. Remember, your commercials will probably air more than a year after you've assembled the budget.

Because so much can go wrong, add a 10 percent contingency amount. This allows for unpredictable events, and lets investors know you're handling the project in a professional manner.

It's not easy to create budgets. It's harder yet to stick to them. But with a little preparation, forethought and diligence throughout the production, you could still find change in your pockets when the credits roll.

26
A Modest Proposal

William Ronat

Your phone rings. On the other end is a potential client. You like potential clients, as they represent potential profits. (Okay, so maybe you're not a professional videographer at this point. Stick with us anyway; as your skills and your reputation grow, you just might get such a call one day.)

The conversation is pleasant enough, with the potential client giving you a nebulous description of his potential video project. Then it's your turn. "What's it going to cost?" asks the potential client pleasantly.

That's the problem with some potential clients. They want to know exactly what you are going to do before you do it. And they want to know exactly what it will cost before they even know *what* they want to do.

Here's how I handle such a question. "Look," I say, "every video project is different. It's like asking how much a house is going to cost before you tell me what kind of a house you want to build. How many rooms does the house have, does it

have a water view, how many acres of land? Ceramic tile? A swimming pool? You see?"

"Ah, of course, I see perfectly," says the potential client pleasantly, "But *how much is it going to cost?*"

"A million dollars," I reply.

Learn to Earn

This is the time to get some details on paper, usually in the form of a proposal. A proposal is simply a document that outlines what the video is going to accomplish. How you plan to make it happen, and an estimate of what it's all going to cost. Ahhh—we're back to the cost issue.

How can you come up with an accurate estimate of a "potential" video? By learning everything you can about the project. Who will be watching the final video— CEOs of corporations or first graders at the local elementary school? How long is the video? Will you need to shoot on Digital Betacam or is S-VHS acceptable?

Are you and your crew going to have to travel to Istanbul or will everything be shot locally?

Be sure the client understands what he or she is getting. If your price is for shooting and editing, then let the client know that scriptwriting will be an additional expense. Or if you do take the job from start to finish, then outline all the steps (selecting talent, scouting locations, production scheduling, shooting, editing, and dubs). Make sure the client understands that your price includes these items only.

Before you state a price for the project, see if you can find out what the client's budget is. It may be more than you thought, which gives you the freedom to add more elements to the production. On the other end of the spectrum, the budget may be so small that it's not even possible to accomplish what the client wants. It's better to learn this sad fact early, before you invest your valuable time.

Set the Parameters

Once you state a price, the client will try to hold you to it. Client-human nature is to lock you into a price and then add complexity that will cost *you* more money. "Did I forget to mention that you could shoot on the warehouse floor only between 3 a.m. and 5 a.m.? Must've slipped my mind."

This is why you want to be specific in the cost estimating process of your proposal. If you tell them exactly what they are getting for the price you are quoting, the client won't be able to add on more complexity without that price going up.

On simple jobs, I usually break my estimate down into two parts: 1) the Treatment and 2) the Estimate and Authorization.

Earlier, we looked at how you should ask questions to learn about the client's project. With the information you learned through your questions, a natural method of creating the video will probably pop into your head.

For example, a client might be a builder of million-dollar homes. The client wants

to show off the many features of the different models. Your treatment might look like this:

Classical music plays as the camera floats past the house with a breathtaking wide shot. The scene dissolves to a closer shot of the front of the house. As the camera floats forward, the front door opens and the camera (who is the viewer,) is greeted by a butler. This butler (a professional actor) proceeds to give the viewer a full tour of the house.

The treatment can be as simple or as complex as you like, as long as it serves the purpose of telling your client what the show is going to look like. If the client likes the concept and agrees on the price, you are ready to move into scripting. If there is something the client doesn't agree with, you know it before you discuss money.

Also, if the clients love your idea, they're more likely to go with you than one of your competitors. Of course, the client can always steal your idea and use another company, anyway. The unfortunate fact is you can't copyright an idea.

Author, Author

The second part of the proposal I send to clients is the *Estimate and Authorization*. On this sheet, I try to be as complete as possible, putting down my best guesses on what each part of the video will cost. There are two schools of thought on this. A buddy of mine, who also produces video, only tells his clients what the total cost of the production will be. He has found that some clients try to lower the price by eliminating parts of the video ("Look, we can save $200 if we re-use a stack of VHS tapes from home…).

Whatever method you choose, the important item is the last line on the page. This is where it says:

Authorization: _____

Date: _____

Have the client sign and date your document and you can get started.

Does this document protect you from a client who wants to rip you off? Nope. But neither do multi-page contracts. I know of a disreputable fellow who has run up thousands of dollars worth of video production bills (though not with me, thank goodness), refused to pay, been taken to court, ordered to pay by the judge, and still refused to pay. The last I heard, he had left town—without paying.

If you don't have a good feeling in your gut about potential clients and you think they might be in the sleazy category, back off. Talk to other people in the community who have worked with these people. Are your fears legitimate? A little homework can help you avoid major headaches.

So why get a signature? Honest people (the ones you *want* to work with) stand by their promises. But even these folks sometimes have short memories. ("I never agreed to that." "But you signed this document saying you did." "I did? I'll be darned.") Leaving a paper trail helps everyone remember these little details.

What Do You Propose?

Often, a proposal is much more than just a few descriptive paragraphs with a cost figure attached.

A proposal may become a long, involved chunk of paperwork, which explains in detail how you will create a specific video project. It is sometimes written in response to a *Request for Proposal (RFP)*. Government agencies and other large corporations often send out RFPs when they need specific services, be they video production or bomb shelter construction. What they get back from an RFP is a mountain of proposals, each explaining why the proposer is the best choice to provide that service.

How can you get in on the fun of responding to an RFP? One way is to team up with a larger company which is responding to an RFP that calls for a video as a part of a larger contract.

For example, I once worked on a project where a company was creating a simulator

for the Navy to train catapult officers on aircraft carriers. These officers stood on a simulated deck and looked at a large screen television showing F-14s, A-6s and other aircraft preparing to take off. The production company I worked for was the subcontractor responsible for capturing the aircraft on videotape.

As a subcontractor, the video company was only responsible for responding to a small part of the RFP. But it was important that the Navy was as comfortable with the information presented in the video portion of the proposal as the rest. If you can convince large companies in your area that you are the person to handle its video requirements, they might call you when they need a video subcontractor.

If the RFP is for the production of a video program, you could respond as the primary contractor on the job. But be aware that these RFPs go out to dozens of companies at the same time. If you don't feel that yours is the right company to do the work outlined in the RFP, you may want to save your energy for a project you *can* handle.

Why not respond to every RFP you can find? Because creating a proposal is a lot of work. You could conceivably spend all your time writing proposals and never win any of them.

For Example

What kind of information do most agencies expect to see in a proposal? The following is the actual wording of the proposal format from an RFP from the State of Florida.

1. Table of Contents.

2. Tab 1. Executive Summary—Include a synopsis of the proposal prepared in a manner that is easily understood by non-technical personnel.

3. Tab 2. Certification and References— the proposer shall provide a list of not less than three (3) nor more than five (5) different previous clients during

the past 3 years as references. This part shall include the dates of the previous projects and the name, title and telephone number of a responsible employee of the previous client who is familiar with the project. The proposer must include a certification that in the previous project it was the original provider of the services.

4. Tab 3. Resumes of Individuals Proposed to Work on this Contract—the proposer shall include resumes of the individual it proposes to assign to this project, specifying relevant educational and work experiences, and shall designate which individual will be the producer/director responsible for the coordination of work efforts of the other personnel assigned to the project. Availability of each individual shall be described, as well as the estimated number of workdays of commitment from each.

5. Tab 4. Description of Creative and Technical Approach—The proposer must provide a description of how it will produce the video programs. This description shall include the proposed production schedule of the estimated working days required to complete each part of each program, the degree of involvement by the Division, and the geographic location where the production will take place. It should also include general information about the talent (estimated number of professionals, semiprofessionals, and extras) and a general description of the proposed use of narrative, dramatics, animation and graphics.

6. Tab 5. Description of Video Equipment—The proposer must supply a list of production and post-production equipment intended for producing these programs.

7. Tab 6. Work Sample—The proposer must supply a sample in VHS format era previous instructional or training video program with production values similar to those offered in response to the RFP.

The work sample will be evaluated for both production quality and creative treatment of the subject matter.

You Get the Idea

Also requested by the RFP were a Cost Proposal Form, a proposal Acknowledgment List and a Sworn Statement on Public Entity Crimes. If you think filling out one of these puppies sounds like more work than you are now putting into entire video projects—you may be right. This is why you should feel you have a pretty good shot at getting a contract before you go after it.

The sample above, from the State of Florida, was an extremely well written RFP. A video expert was called in to give the writer advice on how a video is put together. But sometimes an RFP is written requesting strange or unworkable video solutions. It doesn't matter. You must respond to these requests as they are, even if they are bizarre.

Responding to request for proposals is a skill. You have to answer every question, dot every i, cross every t. If you don't, your proposal can be thrown out for non-compliance. It's harsh, but true.

If you can find someone who has dealt with RFPs before, it might be worth it to "partner" with them. It doesn't really matter if this person knows anything about video; that's your job, as long as they understand the language of responding to proposals.

Check with local business groups to see if they know of any retirees who used to work for a corporation. These people might have been exposed to proposal writing and they might be willing to help you learn how. They might be happy to pass on their knowledge to a new generation. If you can't find a real human to give you advice, check your public library for books on proposal writing.

Is responding to an RFP worth the trouble? Winning a contract can be extremely lucrative. But it isn't easy. If you think you can fill the requirements, I propose you give it a try.

27
A Word From Your Sponsor

William Ronat

You have a great idea for a TV Show. Now all you have to do is produce it and wait for the accolades and money to roll in. Right? If only it worked that way.

Unfortunately, it takes money to put a show on the air. It takes money to shoot and edit a show and it takes money to buy the airtime so that the audience can receive it on their TV sets.

We can assume, then, that to go through this process you need... money. You can supply this money yourself if you have it, or you can find benefactors, patrons, or as we often call them, *sponsors*.

Sponsors might fund you for several reasons. They might take this step 1) because you look like a nice person who needs help, 2) to make money as a result of good publicity or the advertising value they receive from your show, or 3) because they're relatives and have more money than sense.

Addled relatives may be the best solution, but if you come from a family of poorly financed underachievers you will probably opt for an individual or business looking to make a buck. This is best. If a sponsor fails to prosper from your efforts, he will simply not fund your next project. A disgruntled family member may very well disinherit you.

On With the Show

You should pre-qualify potential sponsors before you contact them. What do I mean by pre-qualify? Find out the answers to questions such as these: will my potential sponsors be receptive to the idea of financing a TV show? Do they have the budget for such a project? Does the content of my show "fit" with the business of these sponsors?

The more you know about your sponsors, the better. If you approach a cigarette manufacturer to finance a show about lung cancer, you may not have much luck. Don't waste your time (or the time of the potential sponsor) by setting yourself up for failure. Rejections are mentally debilitating. Avoid them.

What kind of show might a sponsor pay to have produced? You can look to the television networks for the most prevalent type: one that attracts viewers who may buy the sponsor's product.

We call daytime dramas *soap operas* because companies like Proctor and Gamble—soap manufacturers—sponsor these shows. Traditionally, these shows were watched by the person in the household most likely to make the soap-buying decision.

Sporting events find sponsors in beer breweries, athletic shoe makers and car manufacturers, among others. Toy companies basically own Saturday morning children's programming. In fact, many of the shows have ties to specific toys and vice versa, an odd symbiosis. Think about who will want to watch your show and then match a business that has a product to sell to this audience.

Another type of show that a sponsor might pay for is the *infomercial*. Demonstrating a product can be an effective selling method. Door to door vacuum cleaner salesmen knew this technique. Throw some dirt on the floor and then use the product to clean it up while the customer watches.

Infomercials often go the same way. These shows are basically a long commercial for a product, but are disguised to look like a talk show or a news magazine format show. The channel-surfing viewer might get hooked before realizing he or she is being sold. If a sponsor can take direct orders (from an 800 number or through mail-ins) an infomercial might have appeal.

If one of your local stations is part of a home shopping club network you may be able to create a local version of their programming. Then, for X number of minutes (which you or your sponsor would buy) the station would be selling your sponsor's product instead of pots and pans or ceramic dolls.

If your goals include more intellectual pursuits, you may be able to get a sponsor for a drama or documentary if the quality of your show is superior. The leadership of a potential sponsor's company may understand that a fine drama adds to the quality of life of everyone. Or maybe they recognize that supporting a popular program could help change their "unpopular" status with a certain slice of the viewership.

Either way, the arts get funded. Without speculating on motive, here are two examples of corporations which sponsor artistic endeavors: the long-running series of dramas under the banner *The Hallmark Hall of Fame* and *Masterpiece Theater* sponsored in part by Mobil Corporation.

Psst, Buddy, Wanna Buy a TV Show?

How do you approach potential sponsors? First you have to find them. This means doing research to learn which companies in your area would even consider funding your show. But just because you have a great idea and your potential sponsors are the perfect candidates to benefit from it doesn't mean they will do so. You have to sell them on the idea.

Being in business, you have probably had to ask a bank for money. That's not an easy process, is it? You probably had to create a business plan and outline your life's history. Then you had to prove to the bank that you are a good risk and that the bank would get the money back that you wanted to borrow.

When you ask a sponsor for money, prepare your case as well as if you were asking a bank for a loan. You are asking a sponsor to risk capital without collateral or any guarantee that the sponsor will get the money back. How receptive will the potential sponsor be to such a plan? That depends on how good a plan it is.

It won't be easy to get an appointment to discuss a sponsorship. You will have to determine who the appropriate contact is. It may be a marketing person inside the company or the company may have an advertising agency, which would handle such a project. You may have to explain your way through several layers of people before finding the right contact. You may be ready to collapse by the time you reach the decision-maker, but this is the point where you must be your most convincing.

Be professional. You are conducting a business transaction. Dress and act appropriately. You may feel that you are an artist and should enjoy creative freedom—even in your choice of dress—but torn jeans and a ratty T-shirt may give a potential sponsor the wrong impression.

Prove the worth of the idea. You know your idea is a winner, but the decision-maker may not. Start at the beginning and take the potential sponsor through a step-by-step explanation of who the audience will be, what style you will use and why being associated with the show will be good for the sponsor. Don't try to do this off the top of your head. Make notes and *practice* in front of the mirror. If you lose the potential sponsor during the initial pitch they're probably gone for good.

Prove that the audience exists. If you plan to air the show on Channel X at 8 p.m. on Friday, get backup data from the television station that shows demographically who makes up the audience in this time period. Salespeople at the TV station need this information to sell commercials to their clients and will share it with you if you tell them your plan for purchasing a chunk of airtime.

Prove that the audience will watch. This is a tougher assignment. You can't really *prove* this point, but you can make a good argument if you do your homework. Show ratings for similar shows in similar time periods. Get as much hard data as you can. Facts often sell better than enthusiasm.

Prove to the sponsor that they will receive R.O.I. (Return On Investment). If 100,000 people watch your show and 1% of them buy the sponsor's product (a Rolls Royce Motorcar, for example) at an average price per car of $100,000, the sponsor will gross $10,000,000. (Actual numbers may vary.)

Prove that you can do the job. Have you ever done a TV show before? What was it? If not, have you ever done similar jobs before? Do you have a demo tape showing some samples? Can you give potential sponsors a *warm, fuzzy feeling*? You may have thought proving your competence in the video production field was the only step you needed in order to land a sponsor, but as you can see it is merely one of many important steps.

Because each show is different you will run into different obstacles for each of them, but if you can't go through the steps mentioned above with confidence, then you can go back to step 1. You remember step 1: look for a rich but not overly bright relative.

The acid test is this: is your idea good enough that you would use your own money to produce it and buy the air time if you had the money? If the answer is no, then why would you expect a sponsor to say yes?

Johnny on the Spot

Instead of finding one sponsor to fund your entire operation, you may instead want to sell pieces of time within your show. The sponsors can then use this time to run promotional spots about themselves. You've heard of these; we call them commercials.

You will still have to convince sponsors of the worthiness of your show, but because the amount they are spending is smaller, the decision may be easier for them to make. On the other hand, you will have to sell many different sponsors instead of one, which means your job will be more difficult.

There is also more risk for you because you will be buying the airtime and then recouping that money by selling commercials. Let's say you will run your show on cable.

The rate that a cable company can charge you for their airtime is based on a formula created by the FCC. The formula is tied to a cable company's markup and number of subscribers. For example, say your cable system buys HBO for $4.00 per month per subscriber and they turn around and sell it for $10.00 per month to their customers.

But only 25% of the potential subscribers actually order HBO, which has an effect on the formula:

```
 $10.00 subscriber fee
-$4.00 cost of programming
 ..............
 $6.00 mark up
 X.25 percent of subscribers purchasing
 a premium channel
 ..............
 $1.50 implicit value of the premium
 channel, per subscriber, per month
```

These numbers are for a premium channel. For a channel included in the basic package, the cost would probably be closer to $0.50 per subscriber. But remember, that's *for the whole month*. If you only want an hour of time, you would divide that by 720, the number of hours in a month. The answer is $.00069 per subscriber per hour. If your cable system reaches 100,000 households you would pay $69.00 per hour. The cable system can also add fees for billing and collection, marketing and studio services, so ask for an estimate to be sure you are getting a good deal.

On top of that cost is the money you spend on production, promotion of your show, etc. If the total expenditure is $1,000 per week and you have room for 20 commercials, you would sell each commercial for $50 to break even. But you want to make a profit, and there will be times when you won't be able to sell all the commercials in a show. So you need to charge enough to make up for this shortfall. Supply and demand will have an effect on how much you can get for your spots. If the sponsor's target market loves your show and you can prove it, the sponsor will pay more. If nobody watches your show, you won't be able to give your commercial space away. But, hey, that's business.

Landing sponsors can give you the opportunity to create some great television. But before you start knocking on doors, be sure that your idea is as great as you think it is. Do your homework, back up your theories with facts and get your ducks in a row. Then, assume your best professional demeanor and go get 'em. It's not an easy gig, but you should be used to that by now. As you know, in video, nothing is ever easy. And that's the way we like it.

28
Finding Talent for Videos

Randal K. West

As you increase the production level of your videos, you will arrive at a brand-new challenge—acquiring talent. How do you identify potential personnel for your videos and how do you evaluate those people to ensure they are the correct choices for your projects?

For the purpose of this article, let's group talent into two general groups: models and actors. We'll define a model, not as a person with the potential to appear on the cover of *Vogue*, but as someone who will appear in your video. An actor, on the other hand, will probably have a limited acting requirement and will appear to either deliver dialogue or at least convey some type of emotion.

Securing a model merely involves finding someone who has the appropriate look for your piece and is willing to be shot. Many times, the best way to cast a "young mom" model, for example, is to just go find a genuine young mother and convince her to appear in your project. Locating and evaluating an actor who will actually need to deliver lines and convey some emotion is a little trickier.

The Project

Let's suppose that you, as the member of your local service organization who owns a Mini DV camcorder and a computer-based editing system, have been asked to create a video that publicizes your upcoming club-sponsored Kids Day. The purpose of the video is to highlight what will take place on Kids Day and to encourage local businesses to get involved. You need to script this project and then secure a host or hostess to be the on-camera talent and to lead the interviews. Then, find a couple of older folks, a young couple, a high-school student and a few kids to enact short scenarios depicting what will happen during Kids Day. These scenarios will be loosely scripted, but you'll probably let the actors create some of their own dialogue to try to keep it sounding more authentic and less scripted.

Finding the Talent

Talent can be uncovered in a variety of different locations. A local community theater is an obvious choice, but local choirs, churches, community organizations, service clubs, high schools and community colleges also can provide potential thespians (see Figure 28.1). You can also post a message on an appropriate bulletin board, but actually contacting someone with some authority and explaining what your project involves is a better approach. Perhaps that person could solicit volunteers or, better yet, allow you to visit the group and create some enthusiasm for the project to actually get some people to commit to an audition.

The local newspaper may also be a good resource: perhaps a columnist will put a mention in the paper that you have a project and are looking for talent. Many schools have video classes and clubs, and you may also be able to locate a few videographers-in-training to help you as crewmembers for your shoot. Of course the classifieds are a very direct way to get the word out. Announce your auditions about two weeks before the actual audition date and either have everyone arrive at a given time, (a cattle-call audition) or provide a phone number and have the individuals call and then assign each of them an audition slot. I prefer the latter approach.

Organizing the Audition

I was once asked by Hal Prince, the well-known Broadway director, how I held my auditions, and I told him that I executed a very formal, "Go stand on the white mark and await instructions" audition. After the talent approached the mark, a stage

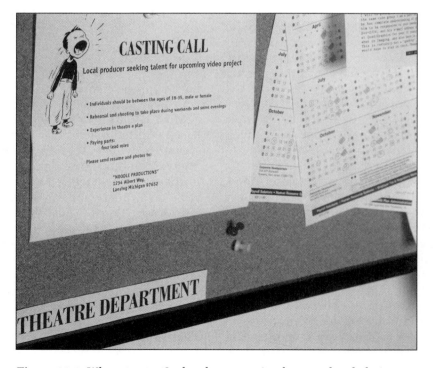

Figure 28.1 *Where to start?—local community theaters, local choirs, community organizations, service clubs, schools, community colleges, churches.*

manager would tell them to begin. Two minutes later, unless I indicated otherwise, the stage manager would say, "Thank you very much," and off they went.

"Why do you audition that way?" Mr. Prince asked. "Well, because that's how I've always been auditioned," I answered. He went on to explain that he didn't agree with establishing an even more terrifying environment than was already created by the act of having to audition. He explained that when folks auditioned for him, it was in a room where he greeted and spoke with the people, putting them at ease before they ever read. This strategy gives you a better chance of seeing what they might actually bring to your project, he explained. I have held informal auditions ever since, and I think it has much more effectively allowed me to gauge how well someone will perform (see Figure 28.2). So, when you hold an audition, find a comfortable room where you can meet each person and keep it casual (see Figure 28.3).

Videotape your auditions to gain more insight into your applicants, but talk with them first (see Figure 28.4). Tell them all about the project, find out about their experience and then shoot the audition. Auditions should last about 10 minutes per person, but if this is your first set of auditions, allow 15 minutes so you don't feel rushed.

Evaluating Potential

How do you determine whether your church pastor or your bank president will be a better host for your program? And what should you look for in a host, anyway? Well, an ideal candidate would be someone who has a pleasant voice, good

Figure 28.2 Initial comfort—keep the atmosphere warm and relaxed for that important initial interview.

Figure 28.3 Scripted interview—script reading is important, but actors can reveal a lot in the interview process as well.

Figure 28.4 Taped auditions—playing back recorded auditions will refresh your memory and help with deliberations.

Figure 28.5 Wide and tight—shoot both wide shots and closeups during the audition.

timbre, good diction and has a certain vocal presence or command. Someone who possesses an interesting or unique-but-pleasant appearance is also a consideration. You can make these initial evaluations before ever deciding to audition the applicants. If they meet these criteria, bring them in. If your project has a script, have them read from it, but shoot part of an informal interview as well. When actors read, their attention focuses down and they concentrate on just reading the material. When you interview them, you get much more of a sense of how they will shoot (how comfortable they appear on camera), as well as a clearer example of their personalities.

When actors are on stage, they act with their body, but when actors act on television, they act with their eyes. So, shoot parts of the interview close enough to really capture the actor's eyes. Shoot part of it wide enough to see the whole body, too, so you can evaluate whether the person shows any overt signs of stress, such as tearing at cuticles or a consistently twitching foot (see Figure 28.5).

Hopefully, you will find people who put more into their auditions than just proving they have mastered the ability to read. They should seem to "own" the verbiage and make it their own. A more experienced applicant will adopt a plan of attack with your material and immediately identify any humor or any point resembling a climax or a twist in the script.

Considering our example, producing a video about Kids Day, the chance for these types of more sophisticated acting moments are probably limited, but an actor may well ask you what type of tone or style you are looking for in the read. An easy way to place the read in the more low-key category is to tell the talent you want more of an FM-radio sound. An AM-radio sound is more energetic. If you want them to go way over the top, just tell them you are looking for a "used car" or a "monster truck" read, which tells them you want all the shouting and yelling they can muster.

If you are having them perform a "dry-read," and they ask for a few moments with the material, give it to them. Anytime you can provide the written material to actors before their appointments, you will likely get better reads from them. In addition to actual excerpts from the script, you should also include a short description of the project and the purpose of the role for which they will read.

If your video involves performing a demonstration, (cooking pancakes or making balloon animals might be two key components of Kids Day), determine whether just inquiring about ability or actually requiring the actor to perform the demonstration is appropriate. For example, if you are looking for someone to cook pancakes in your video, simply asking whether they have ever flipped a pancake is probably enough. If you want to know if they can actually make animals out of balloons, (a bit more of a refined skill), you should have some appropriate balloons available and just let them make you a puppy or a hat.

If you are filling roles of a couple (husband and wife, mother and son), it's a good idea to have them read together to see how they interact.

If you plan to use a teleprompter, have the talent actually read the material off the prompter. Some actors are very good at not looking like they are reading. But teleprompters throw some actors for a loop and they not only look like they are reading, but they just look uncomfortable. The best protection against getting a day-of-the-shoot surprise is to have them read off a prompter at the audition.

Paying the Talent

Do you need to pay your talent? Maybe. If you expect the host of your program to memorize the script and perform it on-camera, offer this person a small token payment for the time they will have to spend memorizing the material. They may tell you that they are doing it for the experience, but a small payment on your part puts you in a better position. You can expect the material to be correctly memorized.

If your project is for a non-profit cause, such as Kids Day, people will probably volunteer. If your actors will wear standard street clothes, ask them to provide their own. If the clothing involves any special attire, (a uniform, a tuxedo, a formal dress), plan to provide it. Ask women to wear regular daytime make-up and not evening make-up, (unless you want them to appear "made-up"). Have powder available at the shoot to powder the bright spot off a bald head or a sweaty brow, but men don't usually need to wear any make-up aside from clear powder you apply to reduce shine. Promise all the people who are cast that they will get a copy of the end product and, if the project has credits, that they will appear in them. If the shooting requires people to miss a meal, you should feed them and provide some light snacks, water and juice for the talent during the shoot.

Giving Talent a Try

Now that you have thought though the process of putting talent into your next video, it's time to go cast your Kids Day project. Remember, most of your talent will be doing their first video work, so be patient and sensitive to their needs and you'll do fine.

The only way to get comfortable coaching performances from actors is to do it, and then keep doing it. Just jump in, and you may find that recruiting and shooting experienced actors to serve as talent greatly improves the quality of your videos.

Sidebar 1

Where to start? Local community theaters, local choirs, community organizations, service clubs, schools, community colleges, churches.

Sidebar 2

Directing Tips

1. Keep it simple. Don't tell actors more than they need to know. Communicate succinctly and give them specific suggestions.

2. Reassure your actors. Explain that this is not live television and that you will simply shoot until you get takes that work for everybody. Nobody will ever see the takes that don't work.

3. Don't act like Cecil B. Demille. Don't get caught in the trappings of video and start making a big fuss about shooting. Keep the environment non-intimidating and friendly.

4. Put the actors at ease and keep the set warm and a little loose and you'll probably get stronger performances.

29
Location Scouting:
Be Prepared

Bill Fisher

We've all had that unforgettably disastrous shoot, where the tape ran out or the battery died at exactly the wrong moment, and we vowed never to let it happen again. But there's one kind of readiness you might not have thought of, and it's as essential as spare tapes and batteries. We're talking about scouting locations, a vital pre-production step that will help you meet almost any challenge when you shoot video in the field. Here are several tips that will help you as you scope out potential video shooting locations.

1. *Know your script.* Choose a site that matches the setting of your story. This is the first rule of location scouting. As you set out to evaluate locations, you'll likely face countless possibilities: natural areas, historic sites, distinctive buildings, urban landscapes and waterfront settings, to name a few. Remember, above all, that you have a story to tell. Choose a location that lends itself to the story you want to produce. You should never be bound by your locations. Locations are simply raw materials. You

need to know what the script demands before you can select a suitable location.

2. *Scout at the right time.* Be aware that locations can change. It's wise to check your spot on the day of the week and the time of day that you'll be taping: these factors can produce surprisingly large changes on the suitability of a location (see Figure 29.1).

Figure 29.1 *Synchronized light—when scouting an outdoor location visit the site the same time of day as the scheduled shoot in order to monitor the angles of the sun.*

Automobile traffic and noise, visitors to recreation and entertainment spots, and tourists at scenic or historic areas (to name just a few examples) all come in waves that vary dramatically based on the time of day, the day of the week and the season.

3. *Look at light.* Churches, ballrooms, restaurants, auditoriums and homes generally feature low amounts of available lighting. Check light levels by shooting a few seconds of test footage with your camcorder.

Solutions for poor lighting might be as simple as scouting out window blinds and curtains that can be opened to add daylight. In some cases you may wish to bring in lights or ask permission to replace the bulbs in accessible light fixtures with brighter-burning units.

4. *Follow the sun.* Outdoor lighting conditions can be as challenging as those indoors; exterior illumination changes all day long. As you're scouting locations, pay attention to whether a given spot is in full sun, partial sun or full shade. Bright sun can be harsh on people's faces, and light-colored surfaces can blow out in full sunlight, causing automatic camcorder lenses to underexpose shots. Partial sun can be tricky, as well; today's camcorders, though sophisticated, can have trouble handling the high contrast in this situation. Ultimately, you may find that fully shaded locations or overcast days produce the most consistent results (see Figure 29.2).

5. *Check for power supplies.* Many outdoor locations are far from power sources and even some indoor locations can pose AC challenges, so multiple camera batteries are always a good idea. But you'll still need to evaluate your power options at any location.

How will you power your lights? What if you do end up draining all your batteries? Is there anywhere to plug in the charger? Is the spot remote enough to make a car-lighter AC adapter a good idea? In a location that does have power, you may be able

Figure 29.2 *Examine exposure—pay attention to whether a given spot is in full sun, partial sun or full shade. Bright sun can be harsh on faces, and light surfaces can blow out in full sunlight.*

to plug in, but you'll still need to think about the system's pre-existing load and whether or not you can get to the fuse (breaker) box in case something blows.

6. *Listen.* Clean, high-quality sound is critical in making a video that rises above the ordinary, and it's silence that ensures you get the location sound that you came for.

The whooshing of traffic, the white noise of moving water, and the echoes of voices and movements can all get in the way of high-quality audio. As you scout a location, check for any of these conditions by listening to your camcorder's microphone pickup through headphones. Test your wireless mike at the site as well, listening closely for interference.

7. *Examine the elements.* Sun, rain, wind, snow, heat, cold—all can help or hurt, depending on what you're hoping to capture on tape. So, it's critical to check the forecast as you're scouting.

Video cameras don't like rain, salty beach air or moisture from waterfalls. Smeared lenses and water or salt inside the tape transport can spell disaster. Bright, hot locations with lots of sunlight can also be a problem: black and gray camcorder bodies absorb the sun's rays and can cause overheating when left exposed. A beach or patio umbrella can help protect your gear from the elements in both sun and rain.

Cold temperatures can drain batteries and make you and your helpers uncomfortable very quickly. Plan to keep equipment warm by storing it inside a coat or car until you're ready to shoot, and by wrapping it in a spare scarf or jacket while taping. And watch out when bringing cameras back into warm interiors from the frigid outdoors: this can cause significant amounts of moisture to condense inside both optics and electronics.

8. *Decide where to set up.* Make sure that there's adequate space for you to set up all of your gear, so that you're able to get the shots you have in mind. A small shed may seem like the perfect location for a shoot, until you realize that there isn't enough room to position your gear. You may have plenty of room in a large space like a church or an auditorium, but you may not be able to roam freely. As you scout your locations, verify that you can physically get to the spots you intend to shoot from.

9. *Get permission.* Be aware that you'll need to secure permits and other legal permissions to shoot at certain locations. As you're looking at a location, do a legal reality check. Have you chosen a street or sidewalk location that will impede traffic? Do you plan to shoot on someone else's property? Cemeteries, malls, grocery stores, corporations and businesses are all private property. Many owners will be happy to accommodate you if you ask, but if not, you'll need to choose another

location. It's better to get permission in advance than to have a shoot interrupted by the authorities (see Figure 29.3).

10. *Evaluate the area.* Check on communications: Is there cell phone reception in the area you've chosen to shoot? How about a nearby pay phone? If you're driving a long way, have you planned for a breakdown?

Search the area for quick food stops to satisfy you and your crew in the midst of a busy schedule and double-check the address of a local electronics store, just in case you need to replace a cable or adapter.

One day, something will go wrong; it's inevitable. But when you've scouted out the backup possibilities at a location, you can take most obstacles in stride.

Figure 29.3 *Take heed—don't trespass or otherwise overstep your bounds. Pre-arrange permission to shoot before you show up with your crew.*

Figure 29.4 *Note it—carry a pen and paper with you, and take notes on each location you scout.*

11. *And finally, take notes!* When you sit down to evaluate a location after a day of exploring, you'll be glad you have scouting reports to refer to (see Figure 29.4). In your scouting expeditions for a shoot, in your daily travels, on your family vacations, and in your mind's eye, you'll come across countless locations and changing conditions, each of which will be unique and potentially important to you. Write them down, take still photos or shoot a little video with a running audio commentary. Note the time of day, the quality of the light, the sounds in the air, and the things you felt. One day you might return.

Sidebar 1

Location Scouting Kit

Be sure to remember the priceless places you've found with this list for a location scouting kit:

- Notebook (or PDA) with writing implement for field notes
- Still camera for creating location archive photos
- Camcorder with headphones for recording test video and audio
- Compass for checking sunrise/sunset, wind direction, etc.
- Watch for time-sensitive observations
- Maps especially for remote locations
- Cell phone just in case

Sidebar 2

Top Locations and Their Quirks

You're practically guaranteed to visit one of these locations sooner or later. Here is a list of things to look out for.

School auditoriums: poor audio, large space, hard to get close to action

Churches: low lighting, echoing sound, hard to be unobtrusive

Parks and natural areas: changing weather, difficult gear transport

Urban centers: background noise, high traffic and pedestrian presence

Beaches: wind noise, salt air, sand contamination, direct sun

Outdoor events: competition for space, poor audio, crowd noise

30
Copyright:
Legal Issues You
Need to Know

Mark Levy

That diminutive encircled c symbol © can be a powerful force for you—friendly or frustrating. The people who create copyrighted works that you may want to use in your own productions include performers, composers, movie makers, still photographers, writers and artists. To understand the limits of your rights and the rights of others, you should know at least a bit about the copyright law.

What is a Copyright?

United States Copyright Law has its origins in the Constitution, which secures exclusive rights to authors for their writings for a limited time. People who create works that we all enjoy and appreciate should be compensated for their talent and hard work. The copyright law, officially known as the Copyright Act, ensures that we all do the right thing: respect the effort, as well as the intellectual property, of others.

The copyright law has been updated over the years to reflect new technology.

The updates or revisions to the law expand the definition of "authors" and "writings," among other things. Nowadays, an "author" can still be a writer, but an author can also be the person who creates works that our Founding Fathers could never have envisioned. Here are just a few developments that didn't exist in 1790, when the Copyright Office was established: photographs, sound recordings (from Edison wax cylinders to vinyl LPs to 8-track tapes to audio cassettes to CDs to MP3s), movies, soundtracks, software, and, of course, video productions on tape, laser disc, DVD or streaming Internet video.

Over the years, Congress also expanded the term of copyright enforceability. At the turn of the last century, you could secure copyright protection for 28 years and you could renew it for another 28 years. After that, your work entered the public domain, so anyone could copy or modify your work without your permission. As of 1978, however, law protects your work for 70 years after your demise. Until recently, the term was actually your

Figure 30.1 You're covered—copyright law provides copyright protection for any completed work.

A good, conservative rule of thumb is that you should assume that a work is protected by copyright if it had been created after 1922, as all works created before that are now in the public domain. For example, older photographs, paintings, books and sheet music are available for your use without permission from the author. Copyright law protects a musical performance recorded after 1922, even if the score was composed before 1922. You can contact the U.S. Copyright Office to find registered material. Copyright Office personnel can conduct a search, for a modest fee.

life plus 50 years, but when Sonny Bono served in the House of Representatives, he helped extend copyright protection for "I Got You Babe" (as well as all other works, of course) for an 20 additional years.

Another major and relatively recent (1978) development in the copyright law provides copyright protection for any completed work (see Figure 30.1). The copyright notice (© + your name + year of creation) was required on all works and it is still recommended, but not mandatory. You are also strongly encouraged to register your work in the Copyright Office, but that action is also not required, unless you intend to enforce your rights in court. For information about copyright registration, access the Library of Congress and the Copyright Office Web site www.lcweb.loc.gov/copyright or contact an intellectual property attorney.

Exclusively Yours

A copyright is an exclusive right. That means you have the right to exclude all others from copying your work or from making works derived from your work. The other side of the coin, of course, is that you do not have the right to copy another person's work (music, screenplay, images) without permission, unless the work is in the public domain.

Wedding Bells

What do you do if you wish to use a copyrighted work? Producing a wedding video is one typical situation. Frequently, the couple may want you to include copyrighted material, often a favorite song performed by a favorite artist. As the producer, you can be liable for the copyright infringement. In fact, the copyright owner can bring a legal action against you, personally. If you do decide to go ahead anyway, you may need an agreement with your client (who should be wealthy enough to survive such a lawsuit) to indemnify you for a copyright infringement action. Clients would be foolish to enter into such an agreement, and you would be foolish to obey the client's instructions if you don't get indemnification. Indemnity does not free you from responsibility or liability, however.

The Risk of Infringement

The law is specific about what constitutes copyright infringement. Except for unusual and egregious situations, the government doesn't normally police and enforce copyright law. It is up to the copyright holder to find copyright violations and bring a lawsuit against the infringers. Songwriters routinely use certain societies

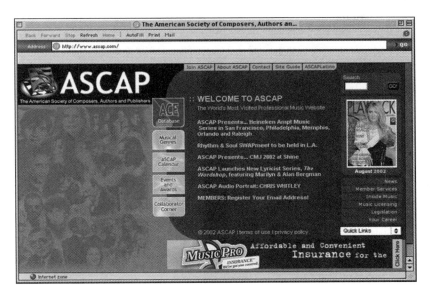

Figure 30.2 *Who to ask—societies or guilds such as ASCAP and BMI can help you get permission to use a copyrighted song in your production.*

or guilds, such as ASCAP and BMI, to find violations. These organizations send undercover representatives to random nightclubs, restaurants and catering halls to police their members' works. If the establishment does not have a license to play or broadcast the musical work, it may be fined or it may become the defendant in a lawsuit. As a videographer, you may need to get copyright permission even for live or recorded music played at an event you videotape. Ask the musicians or disc jockeys whether they obtained a license to play such music at the event (see Figure 30.2).

If found guilty of copyright infringement, under the criminal portion of the law, or liable, under the civil portion, you may face a penalty of five years imprisonment and up to $250,000 in damages. Willful infringement is clearly more serious than unintentional infringement. Once again, as video producers, even if the law weren't so serious, we have an ethical duty to respect people who create original works. Stealing another artist's work is tantamount to stealing their car, their instruments and, literally, their livelihood.

What is the likelihood of being caught using someone else's copyrighted work? Generally, not very high. In the real world, professional wedding videographers often use copyrighted music without permission. One important aspect of prosecution is the demonstration of real commercial harm to the copyright owner as a result of the infringement, which is likely to be miniscule in the case of a wedding tape distributed to 10–50 people. But every once in a while, someone in the music or publishing or movie industry decides to make an example out of a low profile person or non-profit organization. Don't let it happen to you.

Cheap and Easy

You may find that getting copyright permission is cheaper and easier than you'd thought. In fact, it might be as simple as asking for it (in writing) (see Figure 30.3). Explain why you need the material and how you will be using it. (See the *Sample Request* sidebar.) The difficulty arises where the respective rights of a bewildering array of people and organizations overlap.

Figure 30.3 *Put it in writing—you may find that getting copyright permission is cheaper and easier than you'd thought. In fact, it might be as simple as asking for it.*

For example, in order to obtain permission to use all or part of a top 40 record, you may have to contact the composer, the performer, the publisher, or the professional association(s) representing any or all of them. You may need performance rights, publishing rights, reproduction rights, mechanical rights (for copying and using audio/visual works), film rights, electronic rights (for use on computers or the Internet), translation rights, adaptation rights for altering the work or making instrumental arrangements, or even broadcast rights.

Of course, you may obtain the right to use the work, but only if you pay a substantial fee. In general, unless you are making a major motion picture, attempting to obtain a license to use copyrighted materials might not be worth the effort.

Do the Right Thing

Creating your video productions is stressful enough without having to worry about copyright infringement and the penalties associated with it. Choose to do the right thing: a) avoid potential problems by using works that are out of copyright or create original works by yourself or with friends and relatives; or b) belly up to the bar and obtain permission from the copyright holder to use the work. It might be less expensive and easier than you think.

Sidebar 1

Sample Request for Permission to Use Copyrighted Material

Dear [Mr./Ms. Copyright Holder]:

   I am producing a 30-minute wedding video for the family of a bride and groom and wish to include in the video your song, "Fools Rush In." Your song is the bride's favorite song and has great sentimental meaning for her. I will distribute the video only to a handful of friends and relatives, and will not offer it for sale or broadcast.

I respectfully request permission to use your song or parts of it in my video production, on a non-exclusive, royalty-free basis. If you agree to this request, kindly sign and date the enclosed duplicate of this letter and return it to me in the self-addressed, stamped envelope, also enclosed.

If you have any questions about my use of your song or would like a copy of the finished video, please let me know. My clients and I greatly appreciate your cooperation.

Sincerely,   AGREED:

_____   _____
John Smith, video producer   Sal Songbird, songwriter

                                          Date: _____

Sidebar 2

License to Use Music from Composer/Performer

I, _____ [insert composer's name], hereby grant a non-exclusive, worldwide, fully paid-up, irrevocable license to _____ [insert video producer's name] to use my song, "[song title]" or portions thereof in his/her video production, entitled, "[video title]," which may be sold, leased, displayed or broadcast by _____ [video producer] with no further accounting to me.

_____
Signature of composer   Date: _____

PART III
Production Techniques

Tips for capturing the highest quality video and sound.

31
Framing Good Shots

Brian Pogue

The images you record are the building blocks and foundation of your video productions. As your foundation, some thought and planning should go into how your shots are composed. A well-composed shot grabs and holds your viewer's attention. It also influences the mood of the scene or the comfort level of the audience.

When done right, the composition will not draw attention to itself. Instead, it will instill a sense of normalcy and stability. On the other hand, a poorly composed shot will have the opposite effect. It will distract the audience, or worse, make a scene entirely unwatchable.

In this article we'll give you some basic composition guidelines that experts use as their foundation, as well as some common pitfalls you should try to avoid.

The Rule of Thirds

A basic rule of composition is the rule of thirds. This guideline gives you ideas on where to place your subject within the frame. Though your tendency may be to position your subject dead center on the screen, the rule of thirds will give you a more compelling picture.

First, imagine that two vertical and two horizontal lines divide your viewfinder into thirds. (Think of a slightly elongated tic-tac-toe board). The rule of thirds suggests that the main subject in your shot should fall on one of the points where these imaginary lines intersect. The resulting image will be much stronger than if you simply place your subject in the crosshairs (see Figure 31.1).

When videotaping a person, that person's eyes are your main focal point. Whether using a wide shot or a close up, compose the shot so that the person's eyes fall on one of the uppermost imaginary intersections. The intersection you choose depends on which direction the person is looking. Frame someone looking screen left on the right third of the screen. This places the subject slightly off center and builds in another element of composition called "look room."

Figure 31.1 *Eye liner—keep the eyes on the upper-third line, even if you loose the top of the head or hair.*

Figure 31.2 *Look room—the top image doesn't leave any look room. The framing in the bottom image is much better.*

Look Room, Lead Room and Head Room

Look room is the space that you leave in front of someone's face on the screen. This space gives the person room to breathe, as well as gives the impression that the person is looking at or talking to someone just off screen. If you don't leave enough look room, your subject will appear boxed-in and confined (see Figure 31.2).

Be aware that the amount of look room necessary is dependent upon the angle of the subject to the camera. A person looking directly toward the camera will require less look room than someone shot in full profile.

Moving objects such as cars require a similar buffer called "lead room." Allow extra space in front of a moving car so that the viewer can see that it has someplace to go. Without this visual padding, the car's progress will seem impeded.

Head room is another element you should consider when framing your subject. Headroom is the amount of space between the top of someone's head and the top of the frame. If you leave too much space, the person will appear as if sinking in quicksand. If you don't leave enough room, the person will seem in danger of bumping his head. By positioning the subject's eyes on the top third imaginary line, you will be building in the proper amount of headroom.

When considering head room, be sure the shot is loose enough so that you see part of the subject's neck or the top of the shoulders. If not, you'll end up with what looks like a severed head on a platter. However, don't be as concerned with cutting off the top of someone's head. Viewers do not perceive this as abnormal as long as you frame the actor's eyes where they should be.

The Background

Many composition pitfalls lie in the subject's environment. Trees and phone poles, vases or pictures on walls may all cause problems.

Be aware of lampposts, trees or other such objects that are directly behind your subject. A flagpole protruding from the top of an actor's head looks ridiculous, as does a vase that may seem balanced on someone's shoulder. Likewise, a power line running through the frame may appear to be going in one of your subject's ears, and out the other. Steer clear of any such visual distractions (Figure 31.3).

Even if these objects are not directly behind your subject, they can still cause problems. A lamppost running vertically through the middle of the frame will not only disrupt the balance achieved by the Rule of Thirds, it can also isolate or box-in the subject. It may also take away the look room that you've built into the shot. Be aware of these background objects, and work to avoid them whenever possible.

Framing Using Objects

While objects in the background can cause problems, objects placed in the foreground can lend a hand. This technique can add depth and character to your shot.

Try using something in the environment to obstructed part of your shot (see Figure 31.4). Place a piece of furniture in your foreground and shoot past it by framing it to the extreme right or left. You can shoot through open doors, where the doorjamb frames the edges of the screen.

Be careful, however, not to over-do it. Using the environment to frame your

Figure 31.3 Watch the background—poles protruding from your subject's head can be distracting. The receding lines in the shot on the right add depth.

Figure 31.4 Natural frames—look for object (natural or artificial) in the environment that act as natural frames.

shots should not be so blatant as to distract from what is happening in the scene.

The Ultimate Goal

Good composition is a means to an end. When it's done well, the audience should not notice it. Instead it should help create a mood, or at the very least, a sense of normalcy and stability. The next time you watch a movie, pay attention to how the cinematographer frames the shots. You'll notice that they use the rule of thirds as their foundation, and build from there.

32
Shooting Steady

Dr. Robert G. Nulph

Shooting steady video is perhaps one of the most fundamental skills of good video production. If your camera isn't steady, your shots will be difficult to watch (unless you provide a healthy dose of seasick pills). In this column we will take a look at various ways you can shoot good solid video every time, no matter the subject or the situation. We'll start out with the fundamentals of shooting handheld video and move towards more sophisticated electronically-aided methods for keeping your video smooth and steady.

Shooting Fundamentals

Shooting handheld video is perhaps the most difficult way to capture images on tape. No matter how steady you think you are, even your breathing can make the camera move and shake. If you find yourself in a situation where you must shoot handheld, there are a few things to keep in mind.

One of the most important things to remember about camcorders and their lenses is that zooming emphasizes movement. The closer you zoom, the more your movement is magnified. Because of this, when you are shooting handheld video, you should get as physically close to your subject as you possibly can and zoom out as far (wide) as the camcorder's lens will allow. This will give you the steadiest shot possible.

The second step towards good handheld shots is maintaining good posture. Keep your back straight; legs shoulder width apart; knees slightly bent and your elbows close to your body. If you are handholding a small camcorder with an LCD screen, hold the camera with both hands in front of your body, elbows tucked into your sides. If shooting from the shoulder, tuck your elbow into your side and use your right hand and arm for support, while your left hand controls the focus and iris.

If you have to move while actively shooting, do so slowly and as smoothly as possible, keeping your subject composed well in the shot and maintaining good solid posture throughout the move.

Figure 32.1 *Rock stable—if you find yourself in a situation where you don't have a tripod, any solid surface can act as a camera platform. Set your camera on a rock, fence post or parked car, or lean up against a tree or the edge of a building.*

Figure 32.2 *Required equipment—every videographer should own a good tripod. A tripod lets you shoot solid, steady video with little effort.*

The World Around You

If you find yourself in a situation where you don't have a tripod, any solid surface can act as a camera platform. Set your camera on a rock, fence post or parked car, or lean up against a tree or the edge of a building (see Figure 32.1). Use a table or chair to steady your shot. If shooting on the beach, lay some plastic down and steady the camera on the sand, or set the camera up on the steps of the lifeguard tower.

When using a solid platform to shoot from, you will most likely have to tilt the camera to get the best shot. Once again, objects around you might be useful: credit cards, cardboard, newspapers, pencils, even gum wrappers can be used to stabilize your shot. Once you compose your shot, press the record button and take your hands away.

Tripods

Every videographer should own a good tripod (see Figure 32.2). A tripod lets you shoot solid, steady video with little effort. There are, however some things you need to keep in mind when using a tripod. Always set your tripod and camera up so that one of the three legs is pointing towards your subject. This will create a

space for you to stand in between the other two legs. If you know you are going to pan in one particular direction a lot, point the front leg of the tripod halfway between the farthest left and farthest right your subject will move so you won't have to walk around or step over one of the back legs.

When adjusting the height of your tripod, use your subject as your guide, instead of setting it at a level that makes you feel comfortable. Set your tripod up so that the camera, when completely horizontal, is pointing at the neck of your subject. Unfortunately, this might mean that you will find yourself in some uncomfortable shooting positions, but that's a small price to pay for better-looking video.

If you do not have to move the shot and the subject will not be moving, lock down the tripod, press the record button and let go. If you do need to move, position yourself with the camcorder so that you are as solid and comfortable as possible and slowly move in the direction you have planned. Always plan and rehearse camera movements before making them.

Monopods

A monopod is like a hiking stick with a camera mount at the top (see Figure 32.3). Monopods are primarily still-camera tools, but can be quite handy when you must be

Figure 32.3 *Fly right—handheld counter-balanced supports allow you to move freely while shooting and produce gliding, shake-free video.*

mobile and you still need to shoot steady video. You will often see camera operators on the sidelines at football games or other sporting events using monopods. The monopod is lighter and more manageable than a tripod. While the monopod prevents vertical movement of the camcorder, it does nothing to stop the horizontal or tilting movement.

Flying Supports

If you have a little extra cash in your pocket, you might want to check out one of the many types of flying camera supports on the market. These handheld counterbalanced supports allow you to move freely while shooting and produce gliding, shake-free video. The most famous flying camera support is the Steadicam and the brand name has become a shorthand for the entire class of products. Beyond simple handheld devices, you can get complex vests and harnesses that will help you hold the camera during long shoots. The professional gliding camera

stabilizers are so smooth you can barely tell the camera is not sitting on a tripod. One note of caution: if you are considering buying one, try it out first to see if it will work with your camcorder.

You can create a flying camera support of sorts by mounting your camcorder onto your tripod or monopod and lifting it off the ground, using the weight of the legs to act as a counterbalance for the camcorder to keep it upright. This will not produce anything close to the results you'd get from a precisely engineered and finely balanced flying camcorder support, but you may be pleasantly surprised at the look of the shots.

Image Stabilization

Image stabilization is the video engineers gift to amateur videographers. Your camcorder's built-in image stabilizer seeks to smooth out handheld video, minimizing camera shake. Image stabilizers are found in most camcorders today. There are two types: electronic and optical. Optical is generally better, and is typically found on higher-end camcorders. Although they can be quite handy if you find yourself in a situation where you must shoot handheld, they do have a couple of limitations. First, electronic image stabilization can reduce the overall number of pixels on the CCD that are used to capture an image. This can result in a general softening of the picture (see Figure 32.4). Second, when the stabilizer is used during a pan, the smooth pan might jump slightly from one point to the next as the stabilizer tries to correct your intentional movement. Still, image stabilization, both electronic and optical, can be a shotsaver when shooting handheld.

Keep It Steady

There are times to move the camera and times to hold it still, but, unless you are trying to create an earthquake effect, there are seldom times when shaky video is good video.

Figure 32.4 *Oversized CCD—electronic image stabilization can reduce the overall number of pixels on the CCD that are used to capture an image. This can result in a general softening of the picture.*

Sidebar 1

Time is of the Essence!

You should never handhold shots that demand rock solid video. Long interviews, cutaways of objects with vertical or horizontal surfaces, and steady landscapes should never be handheld. Moving subjects, shots with camera movement already built into them, such as pans and tilts and shots where the camera physically moves from one place to another can easily be handheld. Always plan your movement and move steadily and in one direction.

33
Make Your Move

Michael Hammond

Unlike our counterparts in still photography, those of us shooting video have a wonderful advantage—motion. With some imagination, a steady hand and a good tripod, you can take your viewers on a great visual ride. Let's review a few creative moves that you can all use to add interest in your videos. Keep these in mind as you plan your next project and work them in where they seem to fit.

Movin' on Up: The Pedestal

The pedestal move is a great way to add some vertical action to a scene. It allows you to create some anticipation with a viewer, to add a greater sense of height and importance to a subject and to link more than one subject in a single shot.

A pedestal move involves moving the entire camera vertically (see Figure 33.1). The move is named for the adjustable center post found on many tripods. Unlocking this center post allows you to raise the camera while the tripod legs remain in a fixed position. Not all tripods have a pedestal that allows you to make a nice, smooth move. In some cases a tripod isn't practical, so you may make this move as a handheld shot.

The trick is to keep the vertical movement as steady as possible and to set your viewfinder before you start shooting. If you're working with a camcorder that has a flip-out LCD screen, by all means use it. Try to position the screen so that you can keep the framing in sight throughout the entire shot. If, for example, you're shooting a person's foot and moving up the body to end on the face, here's how to approach it. Frame up a nicely composed shot to start and check for clear focus. Since you're starting at almost ground level in this example, begin from a bended knee position with the camera directly in front of you, albows resting just above your knees. Slowly life the camera with your arms and then begin to stand as you rise up through the shot. Keep your elbows tucked in as close to your body as possible, and practical, to help keep things steady until you reach your end position.

Figure 33.1 Pedestal- a
pedestal move involves
moving the entire camera
vertically.

This move could be great at a wedding to reveal a bride's dress. An example of linking subjects with this move might be starting on a full-screen shot of a house For Sale sign and then doing a pedestal up to reveal the home behind it.

Keep on Truckin': The Truck Move

In a trucking move, you, the tripod and the camera pick up and move to the left or right. This move is great for following, or creating a stronger sense of action. Let's say you're shooting someone jogging. If you just pan the camera to follow the runner, you'd need to be on a pretty wide shot and there would be a pretty significant change in the backgrounds and perspective as you follow the subject left or right. It also isn't as dramatic. Set up a trucking shot and you'll see the difference. Choose a distance from the runner, let's say you want to keep him full-body throughout the shot, and set up alongside of them with good focus. Unless you've rented or purchased a Steadicam or some other kind of stabilizing gear, if you actually jog beside the subject yourself the video will likely be unusable. You need some wheels! Without going to great expense, you can use an automobile, a wheelchair or a child's wagon to provide your motion (see Figure 33.2). Whatever you choose, be sure you have a partner to get you moving and keep you safe and stable while you're shooting. If possible, start moving the camera first, then cue your subject to start running. Settle on a comfortable speed and nice framing. Lead room is important in trucking shots. Give the subject some space between his or her nose and the edge of your frame so it looks like you're leading them and not trying to play catch-up. If you don't like the profile you get from trucking right alongside the subject, pick up some speed and get ahead a bit. This allows you to see more of the runners face and changes up the background for some interest.

Figure 33.2 *Truckin'—in a trucking move, you, the tripod and the camera pick up and move to the left or right. Without going to great expense, you can use an automobile, a wheelchair or a child's wagon to provide your motion.*

Taking Flight: The Flying Camera

The flying camera move gives you an opportunity to take your viewer on a ride. Think of this as taking on the point of view of an insect moving in and around subjects. I started using this type of move when my oldest child was a toddler. Fly around at kid-level to make the viewer more an active part of the child's world. Of course, it works for shooting adults, too.

Let's say you want to capture some treasured moments of a child eating in a highchair. You might hold your camera at your waist with arms tucked into your stomach for stability. Begin the shot from behind the child, showing someone feeding the little one, then arc around the chair to the front. For more action, you could begin with the camera held high, coming down and around the chair. The opportunities with this one are endless. Picture a table with a great spread of food. The camera starts high, taking in most of the table from above, then sweeps camera down and runs the length of the table, flying past all of the treats. For a smooth move and good focus throughout the move, it works best with the lens zoomed out wide.

Guud Eeevening: The Hitchcock Zoom

This move is one of the most dramatic, and it requires a bit of practice. Alfred Hitchcock made use of this camera move, and the film *Jaws* used a similar version of it. When done well, this move gives the appearance that the main subject is stationary as the background crashes in or flies away. Set the shot up by framing the subject with the lens zoomed out wide (see Figure 33.3). Begin to dolly away from the subject as you simultaneously zoom in to keep the subject the same size in the frame. The optics of the lens provide a unique look. Timing is important here in matching the dolly speed with the zoom, but when it all works it leaves a very dramatic impression with a viewer. Try the reverse, as well, by dollying in while zooming out. Great moves with powerful results.

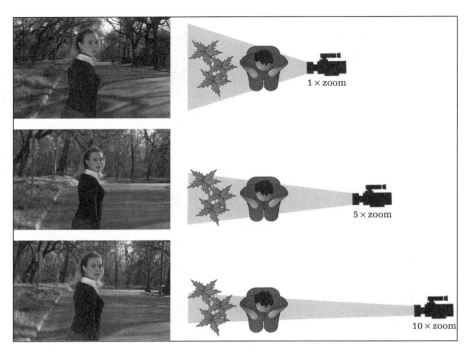

Figure 33.3 *Hitchcock Style— dolly away from the subject as you simultaneously zoom in to keep the subject the same size in the frame. This move gives the appearance that the main subject is stationary as the background crashes in or flies away.*

Walkin' the Walk: The Walking Shot

This is a favorite of mine because it's easy to execute and adds zip to a normally dry shot. Rather than a static shot of your subjects walking, move with them. For a shot of two people passing by from behind, hold your camera about waist-level with a wide lens and begin to walk ahead of your subjects. Cue your subjects to start walking and overtake you, entering the frame from behind, one on either side, and continue walking away (see Figure 33.4). The reverse of this would be for you to begin walking backwards, cueing your subjects to walk toward you, passing you on either side as they exit your shot. You can give this last one an even more interesting perspective by zooming out as you walk backward.

Figure 33.4 *Walking on by—begin walking backwards, cueing your subjects to walk toward you, passing you on either side as they exit your shot.*

Sidebar 1

Easy as 1-2-3

Unlike still photographers, videographers can move their cameras to create action or cover several focal points in a single shot. This means your composition—what you choose to include in a shot and where you choose to put it—will change as you move. It may help to think of every move that you make in three distinct parts.

  1. *Beginning composition.* This is where the shot begins. Choose carefully what to include in your scene and how to arrange it all for good balance. Identify this composition before rolling tape.

  2. *End composition.* This is where the camera comes to rest. Again, identify this composition before you start recording and try to achieve a good overall balance in the shot.

  3. *The bridge.* This is the camera move that connects the beginning shot with the end position. Practice the moves you intend to do as much as possible. Work to make the move smooth, maintaining good composition and focus. You may shoot a move several times adjusting the speed of the bridge for editing options.

Sidebar 2

Shoot Like an Editor

This old adage is good to remember while shooting. It'll be of great help during editing if you think through all of the possible uses of what you record as you plan your shots. This means if you're doing a camera move, record it several times at several speeds. If you've recorded some fast moves and a few slower versions, you've covered your needs for whatever pace you use in the final production. It's always a good idea to record a version of the shot without a camera move, just in case. You may find when editing that you don't have time for a camera move after all, and trying to freeze a shot—extracting a still frame from a moving shot—may not provide the quality you're looking for.

34
Use Reflectors Like a Pro

Jim Stinson

Reflectors are so versatile, useful and simple that professional videographers deploy them even in high-rent productions. Advanced amateurs may know how to use reflectors for outdoor fill light, but that's only their most obvious application. So let's conduct a quick flyover of professional reflector techniques, both outdoors and in.

First, lets take a quick taxonomy of reflector species. Reflectors are either rigid or flexible. Rigid reflectors may be faced (in order, from brightest to softest) with shiny aluminum, matte aluminum, wrinkled aluminum or white paper. Paper-faced reflectors are usually foamcore: rigid Styrofoam sandwiched between paper surfaces and available at any art or craft store. (Tip: pay the modest premium for one-inch-thick boards. They far outlast thinner ones.)

Flexible reflectors are usually cloth spread across thin metal hoops that can be folded for storage. Fabrics may be metallic for greater reflectivity or plain for a soft, diffuse effect. They come in white or sometimes gold, for reasons detailed in the sidebar.

Which to choose? Flexible reflectors are light and easily stored, but they're unstable in any breeze, making their light waver visibly on-screen. Hard reflectors are cheap to buy (or easy to make for almost nothing) but they're bulky and rigid, making them difficult to transport and store away.

Since these critters are most often used in wide open spaces, let's see how to employ reflectors outdoors as key, fill, rim or background lights. (NOTE: For simplicity, we'll describe everything via a clock face metaphor, with the subject at the center and the camcorder at six o'clock.)

Reflector Key Light

With the sun shining, why make your primary light a reflector? Often the sun's in the wrong position or the subject's standing in adjacent shade. In fact, the sun can become a gorgeous rim light, outlining the

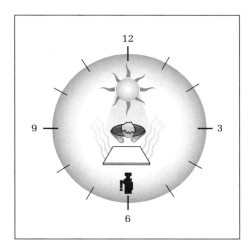

Figure 34.1 *Below the shot—start by placing your subject with the sun behind them (between ten and two o'clock). Then use a white reflector placed between four and eight o'clock, close to the subject and just below eye level, to fill in nose and chin shadows.*

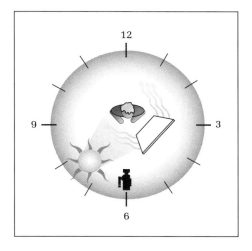

Figure 34.2 *Key reflector—more often, we'll use the sun as the key and the reflector for the fill, with each light source placed between three and nine o'clock, though I personally limit the arc to four to eight on our clock face.*

subject's head and shoulders and separating them from the background.

Start by placing your subject with the sun behind them (between ten and two o'clock). Then use a white reflector placed between four and eight o'clock, close to the subject and just below eye level, to fill in nose and chin shadows (see Figure 34.1). If you want to get fancy, use a reflector on either side, with the key unit closer, so the subject is lighter on that side.

A reflector key light also works well when the subject is in the shade. Bounce the light in, moving the reflector in or out until it is two to three times as bright as the ambient shade light creating the fill.

Reflector Fill Light

More often, we'll use the sun as the key and the reflector for the fill, with each light source placed between three and nine o'clock, though I personally limit the arc to four to eight on our clock face (see Figure 34.2). As always, place the reflector just slightly below the subject's eye level

to fill nose and chin shadows. Too high a position delivers a Hitler moustache effect and too low creates a vampire. If the sun is at seven to eight o'clock, you can often get a nice effect with the reflector all the way around to three o'clock, filling the subject's profile.

Every type of reflector can and should be used for fill. For closeups, a diffuse white card looks most natural, but its intensity is too low for the throws required in longer shots. If you're shorthanded, have subjects aim a white card, held below the frame line, up at themselves for their closeups. It often works great.

When higher intensity is needed, bring in the aluminum or metallic fabric models. They have enough punch to keep the reflector out of camera range and still work effectively. Always try to use the softest version that will deliver enough fill, starting with a metallic fabric model.

Using aluminum reflectors for key or fill light requires care, because they throw a hard, narrow beam and they can make subjects squint unattractively. Make sure you place them far enough away to reduce their intensity.

Reflector Rim Light

Those hard aluminum surfaces are perfect for rim-lighting the subject, especially when the sun is between four and eight o'clock. Place the reflector very high and opposite the sun or as nearly opposite as possible while staying out of frame.

Rim lighting works best when a second reflector is delivering fill light, as described in the previous section. If the sun is close enough to six o'clock and low enough in the sky, fill light may be unnecessary, but the golden glow of rim light might look wonderful.

When the subject is in shade, rim lighting doesn't work, unless the protected spot is just outside a sunny area. A hard aluminum unit in the sun can often bounce light off a second hard unit in the shade and back onto the subject's hair and

Figure 34.3 *Versatile sun—the sun produces plenty of light for a reflector to be used as a fill or light.*

shoulders. That's what bright aluminum reflectors are for: very long throws of relatively narrow light beams. In bright sunlight, I've seen hard aluminum units set as far as 100 feet away, from which position they can spread a broad, diffuse light on subjects without hurting their eyes (see Figure 34.3).

Reflector Background Light

Suppose you have a subject in the sun with, say, a shaded building wall as background. That makes for great facial exposure, but often a boring background. To spark it up, fill in the backing with one or more hard aluminum reflectors (softer models are too low-intensity to work) (Figure 34.4a).

Here, the keys to success are angle and distance. If the wall is parallel to 12 o'clock, behind the subject, try to get the reflector as close as 11 o'clock (sun angle permitting) to rake the background with an oblique wash of light (Figure 34.4b).

If you have the resources, aim multiple reflectors at different areas of the background (I've used three or four). With care, you can produce a variegated and interesting wash of light that looks quite natural.

Or you can go a step further and use an improvised cookie. A cookie, short for "cukaloris" (a word lost in the mists of theatrical history), is a stencil pattern of leaves, bars or whatever you like that is placed between a spotlight and a surface. Cookies create interesting light and shadow patterns.

Hard aluminum reflectors throw a concentrated light beam that you can place cookies in front of them to create surface patterns. To control the effect, move the cookie closer to the reflector for softer edges or farther away for harder ones. Because of the large surface areas of reflectors, the cookies must be much larger than those used indoors with spotlights. Outdoors, I sometimes improvise

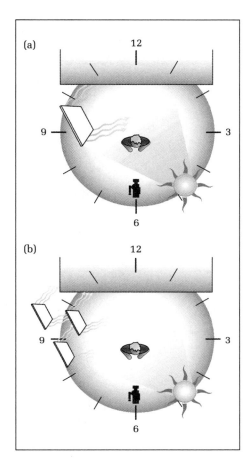

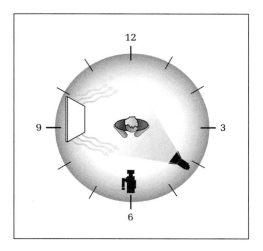

Figure 34.4 *Background—suppose you have a subject in the sun with, say, a building wall as background. That makes for great facial exposure, but often a boring background. To spark it up, fill in the backing with one or more hard aluminum reflectors (softer models are too low-intensity to work).*

Figure 34.5 *Indoors—if you're working with just one spotlight, use it as a key light and place a large, white card out of frame on the opposite side. The result is a very soft natural looking fill light.*

and use a dead branch with leaves still on it. Even if the leaves move in the wind, the effect on the background is quite natural.

Reflectors Indoors

Reflectors are not as versatile indoors because the light sources they depend on aren't as powerful as sunlight. Even so, you can easily use them to make one light do the work of two.

If you're working with just one spotlight, use it as a key light and place a large, white card out of frame on the opposite side (see Figure 34.5). The result is a very soft, natural looking fill light. You can even soften the naturally hard spot beam a bit with spun glass diffusion (e.g. a furnace filter) and still put out enough light for the reflector.

Even if you have more spotlights, you may want a softer look to your lighting design. To achieve it, turn the lights away from the subject and bounce them back in with reflectors. In this application, metallic cloth or crinkled aluminum types work better than ultra-soft white cards. Carrying this to its logical conclusion, I've seen studios with 8×8 foot white walls on roll-around stands that make jumbo-sized reflectors delivering window light quality soft illumination.

So there's a quick rundown on reflectors. Once you see how versatile they are, you'll realize that reflectors aren't lights for poverty-stricken productions: they're versatile tools that pros use all the time.

Sidebar 1

Going for Gold

Foamcore, cloth and even some hard reflectors can be colored gold instead of white. Hoop-and-fabric units are sometimes two-sided, with one side gold and one side silver.

Gold reflectors are very useful for warming up the light they throw. Here are just a few ways to use them:

- To simulate the magic hour look of sunset.

- To counteract the naturally bluish cast of open shade.

- To warm up one light source (also useful in creating day-for-night effects).

- To add glamour to closeups, either as fill light or as a warm rim light on hair and shoulders.

The most economical way to acquire a warm reflector is by buying a piece of tinted foamcore. Instead of true gold, try a lighter yellow color to start, then experiment until you find what suits your needs.

Sidebar 2

Zoom In

A telephoto lens is excellent for closeups. Not only does it flatter human faces, but it includes less background, letting you sneak reflectors as close as even the eleven o'clock position.

35
Three-Point Lighting in the Real World

Dr. Robert G. Nulph

Three-point lighting is familiar to anyone who has been reading **Videomaker** for a while. You've read about it, seen pictures and understand it—in theory. In this months column I'll take you with me on a typical location shoot, from the time I choose my equipment until shooting begins.

The Situation

I was recently called to do an interview featuring a corporate CEO who worked in a big, beautiful corner office with huge windows and a desk large enough to field a pee wee football team. Behind the desk was a long shelf that ran under the windows and was full of awards, family pictures and knick-knacks. The CEO was a personable guy with large glasses and shiny bald head. I had one hour to setup and complete the interview.

Preparation

Preparation always begins at home. I started with my favorite interview key light, a large soft light. This light is a fluorescent soft light that has the capability to change out lamps so that you can light for an indoor or outdoor color temperature.

Since I would utilize three-point lighting techniques, I'd need a backlight and a light to fill in the shadows. For the backlight, I chose a Lowel Tota. This small light, as well as its tripod and other mounting equipment, easily fits in the Caselite's carrying case. I also tossed in some blue gels and a gel frame just in case I wanted to change the light's color temperature, a couple of diffusion gels to add some softness to the light and some neutral density gels to reduce the intensity of the light if needed.

To my accessory bag I added some gaffer's tape, a piece of foam core, some clothes pins, a few scissors clamps, an extra light stand, extra lamps (bulbs), an extension cord, a couple three-to-two prong electrical outlet adapters and a small compact with neutral colored face powder and some handkerchiefs (see Figure 35.1).

Figure 35.1 *Pack, man—I packed gaffer's tape, foam core, clothes pins, scissors, clamps, an extension cord, electrical outlet adapters and a small compact with face powder.*

Figure 35.2 *Light 1—I positioned my soft light as the key light, to the right of my camera about three feet away.*

On Location

When I got to the office, my first concern was deciding where to put the camera and dealing with the windows. I decided to close the vertical blinds that covered the window behind his desk and partially close the blinds on the window to the left of his desk. I did this for two reasons. First, the window behind the desk provided an interesting blue striped background behind the CEO during the interview. With the blinds completely shut, the outside light shaded the seams between the blinds with a light blue, adding a nice touch of color to the scene. Second, the light coming through the partially closed blinds at the side of the office provided a subtle blue tint to the fill light on the left side of the CEO, again adding a bit of soft, dramatic color. Closing the blinds let me control the light as well as the overall color temperature of the light in the room.

The physical space was my next concern. Because the desk was so massive, I decided to use just a corner of it, providing a surface for the CEO to rest his hands if needed, but not showing enough of the desk to create too big a separation between the CEO and the audience. I also made sure that the camera could see a group of family pictures behind and to the side of the CEO's chair, adding a personal touch to the scene.

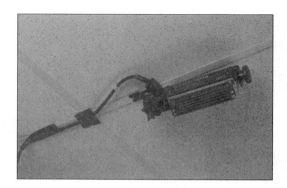

Figure 35.3 *Light 2—I clamped the small Tota light onto one of the metal strips to hold up suspended ceilings.*

Light 1: The Key

I used my soft light as the key light, positioned to the right of my camera about three feet away (see Figure 35.2). I then raised the light so that it was at about a forty-five degree angle above his head pointing directly at him. The soft key light cast a smooth, even glow on the CEO and the set.

Light 2: The Back

I then set up my back light directly across from the key light, behind the CEO's chair (see Figure 35.3). Using a scissors clamp, I clamped the small Tota light onto one of the metal strips used to hold up suspended ceilings. I then ran the cable along the ceiling, fastening it in place with some gaffer's tape. This light, positioned about forty-five degrees above and behind the CEO, provided a light on the back of his head and shoulders to separate him from the background.

Light 3: The Fill

It was now time to consider the fill. At this point, I asked the CEO to take his place in his chair so that I could see the effects of the two lights I had already placed. After adjusting the back light so that no light was shining on the top of his head, I looked through the camera's viewfinder to see what I had accomplished. The light coming from the side window was adding a little too much blue to the scene so I decided to fill in the left side of his face with light reflected from the backlight with a three by four piece of foam core (see Figure 35.4). This light diluted the blue from the window and filled in some of the shadows created by the key light. If I had wanted to create really dramatic lighting, I would have moved my key light further to the side and reduced the intensity of my fill light, making the

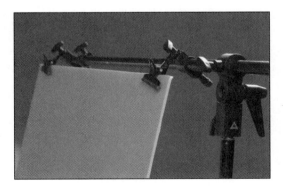

Figure 35.4 *Light 3—I decided to fill in the left side of his face with light reflected with a piece of foam core.*

camera-left side of his face darker than the right.

Taking Care of Small Problems

Looking through the viewfinder, I immediately saw the two problems I knew I was going to have to contend with: glasses and a bald head. The head was no problem. I pulled out the makeup powder and after a few jokes, I patted down his forehead and the top of his head, reducing the glare tremendously. The powder not only absorbs any perspiration there may be, it also gives the skin a matte finish. The glasses are a bigger problem. I first had him tilt the glasses down by slightly lifting the back of the earpieces. This helped a great deal. I then moved my key light a bit further to the side and a bit higher, watching the glare on the glasses until it disappeared. Some might ask, "Why go through all of this trouble? Just have him take his glasses off." Most people that wear glasses all of the time just don't look like themselves if they take them off. If a CEO is making an address to the troops, he wants to look relaxed, comfortable and like himself. It's worth the effort.

Once I fixed the glare, positioned the family pictures perfectly in the viewfinder (also checking for glare in their frames) and checked my talent one more time, I positioned myself to the left of the camera so that my eyes were at the level of the lens and began the interview, having the CEO look at me instead of the lens.

A Few Notes About the Overall Experience

Remember, three-point lighting will make them look good, but it is your attitude and how you work with them will make them feel comfortable. In the end, the better they look, the better you look.

Sidebar 1

Dramatic Intensity

Keep in mind that when doing interviews, you want to use a soft light as your primary light source, unless you are trying to create a very dramatic look and want to see every wrinkle in your talent's face. In that case, you would use a small, intense light to create a hard light with sharp shadows.

Sidebar 2

Peripherally

Any time you find yourself shooting an interview in someone's office or home, use the time while you set up wisely. Engage your subject in conversation. Tell them what you are doing and how you will conduct the interview. Go over the first few questions with them as you position your camera and hang your lights. I really try to get to know my subjects in the time that I am setting up. I find it makes the interview process go a lot easier.

   Don't be afraid to ask your subject if you can move things around. I have yet to ever come across someone who wouldn't let me rearrange their office. Explain to them what you are doing and why. Most of all engage them and make them feel like the whole interview process is fairly pain free and fun.

36
A Dose of Reality:
Lighting Effects

Robert Nulph

See video clips at www.videomaker.com/handbook

The firelight flickered against the cabin wall, warming the cool blue light of the full moon filtering through the tattered curtains. Suddenly the ominous blue then red flash of police lights filled the small room and Carson knew his game was up.

Suddenly the director yells "Cut!" and the camera pulls back to reveal two Hollywood flats painted to look like cabin walls and a squadron of techies moving a myriad of lights and other equipment to new locations. Nowhere in sight in the cavernous sound stage is there a squad car, a full moon or a flickering fire.

For years Hollywood and independent filmmakers as well as corporate video producers have used lighting techniques to make us believe things exist that aren't really there. You can too! It is all a matter of collecting the right lighting instruments and accessories and adding a large dose of imagination. Mix them all together to give your scene a large dose of reality. Throughout this chapter, we'll look at a variety of ways to bring reality to your scenes. It is all in the power of lighting.

Mr. Sun and Mr. Moon

It's a good idea to always plan the outdoor and daylight shots first for your productions, because you have more control of indoor lighting than you do over the weather. All you need to make sunshine or moonbeams is a small, powerful light source and some colored gel. You can create sunshine, even at night, by placing a powerful light (1000 watts or so) outside your window. (It is not advisable to do this if it is raining.) Make sure you place it at an angle similar to that of the sun at the time your scene takes place and is out of the camera shot. It works best if you use a small, intense light to create the light of the sun or moon because you want to imitate their qualities. If you think about it, the sun and moon are very small intense lights that throw very hard shadows. A big soft light will not do the trick.

To recreate the sun, you have to determine what time of day your scene is taking place. If your scene is in the early morning, you may want to place a single blue

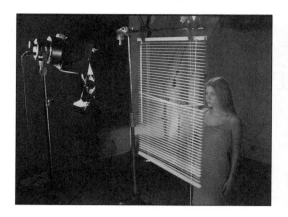

Figure 36.1 *Shine a light through a set of mini blinds to imply the existence of a window.*

gel in front of the light. For midday, use no gel and for evening, use a yellow/gold, orange or red/orange gel, going towards the red as the day progresses. A light shining into a hard gold reflector and reflected through the window makes a fabulous evening light.

To recreate the moon, place two Color Temperature Blue (CTB) gels together in front of your light. Dim the lighting in the room to pick up the color of the moonlight and create the feeling of nighttime.

If you are creating the sun or the moon on a sound stage or other big room, you can also create windows through which they can shine. Place a window frame just out of camera shot so that its shadow falls across the floor and the background wall. Set up window blinds (Figure 36.1) and let the light filter through the slats. You instantly have a wall with a window.

Cars and Cops

With a little mechanical skill and a good sense of pacing, you can easily imitate car headlights, city streetlights, the flashing lights of a squad car or a searchlight being used to find the bad guy. You'll also need a couple of small, focusable lights that you can gel.

One of the easiest, yet most effective lighting effects you can use is the imitation of a car's headlights. Using a four-foot long

2 × 4, mount two narrow beam lights about two feet apart. Slowly sweep the beams of light at an angle across the darkened back wall of your set. Instant car lights. If you are shooting a scene in a car at night, you can use the same technique both for cars passing you from the other direction as well as those coming up from behind.

In the same driving scene, you can imitate the passing of city streetlights, by rhythmically passing the beam of a powerful flashlight over the hood of the car, avoiding the camera lens. A flashlight works well because its lamp has a yellow color temperature and should look different from the lights you are using for headlights.

If your characters get in trouble with the law, you can fill the car or house with flashing blue and red lights by rhythmically passing a double or triple blue gelled light then heavily gelled red light past the background or interior of the car. The Lowel Omni light has a comfortable soft rubber grip that allows you to move it around without being burnt. Focus your light's beam to the tightest setting possible and pass first the red then the blue past the set. You can flash the set, tilt the beam to the floor and pass it again. With two people, it is a bit easier, but one person can handle it. Take the gels off one of the lights, put on a yellow gel, widen the focus on the beam and you have just created a searchlight.

If your scene occurs on a city street or in a seedy motel room, you can add the pulse of a red neon light. Reflect a diffused red-gelled light onto the background or into the interior of your car. By turning the light off and on or moving a flag to cover the light occasionally, you can imitate the stuttering of an old neon sign. Add a few sound effects and your characters are in for a long and dramatic night.

Living Rooms

Fireplaces, televisions and lamps that you see used in video and movie scenes more often than not, don't really work the way we think they do. You can create it all through the magic of lighting.

If your character is supposed to be watching television yet you don't see the front of the set, you can create a very believable TV light. Get an old TV set, remove the picture tube and tack a double CTB gel to the front. Inside, place a lighting instrument that has a good quality switch on its cord. Quickly turn the light off and on; pausing at times for longer lengths of both light and dark. A television is never always bright so the flickering makes it look more realistic. Of course, you could always plug in an actual TV set, but hey, that would be too easy.

If your character is sitting before a warm fire, you can create the effect by setting up a small, diffused light, angled up from floor level. In front of the light, hang inch wide strips of red, yellow and orange gels on a broomstick. Gently shake the gels in front of the light to create the feeling of firelight movement, as in Figure 36.2. Another method uses a round wheel (like an old bicycle wheel) covered with various orange, red and yellow gels cut with holes and layered to provide a variety of combinations and the occasional flash of real light. Turn the wheel slowly in front of the light to create the movement of the flame. Again, add sound effects and bake to perfection.

For lamps that you will see on the screen, the first thing you need to do is

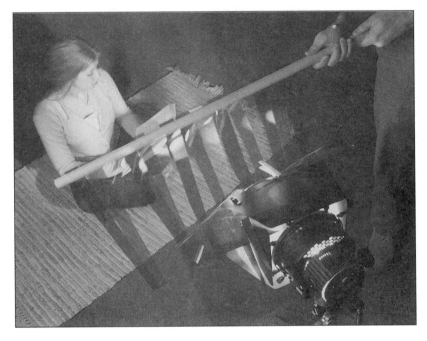

Figure 36.2 Red and yellow gel strips waving in front of an orange-gelled light create the illusion of firelight.

remove the regular bulb. A sixty-watt bulb will cause the lamp to glow on camera and look much brighter than it should. Place a 15-watt bulb in the lamp to provide a soft internal glow and supplement the light with a diffused 600-watt or more lighting instrument. Be sure to flag the light so that its beam does not fall on the lampshade of the light you are trying to use. If you place the lighting instrument just off-line from the real light, you can light your character in a warm glow that will look like it is coming from the lamp beside them.

Water Water Everywhere

Sometimes, the script calls for water ripples reflecting in your characters eyes or on her face. Often, it just isn't very convenient to set up lighting to get this effect using a real water source like a creek or lake. Don't worry, it is really a quite simple effect to recreate. All you need is a deep pan like a roaster or a painters roller pan. Carefully break up a mirror into two to three inch pieces and place them in the bottom of the pan, face up. Cover the mirrors with about three inches of water. Shine a small, intense light into the water so that the light reflected from it falls onto the face of your character. (See Figure 36.3.) Gently lift one end of the pan up and down to create a soft ripple effect. You should see

Figure 36.3 *Light reflected off of water and broken pieces of mirror create a shimmering pool side effect.*

water ripples in your characters eyes. If your scene occurs at night, add a CTB gel to your light. Add a few seagulls, some water sounds and your ready for a day or night in paradise.

Reality

Always be aware of the world around you. Look at the light that makes up our world, its reflections its colors and the shadows it casts. If it occurs in the real world, you should be able to re-create it for the camera. A bit of knowledge, a dose of imagination, and a touch of lighting magic can create any reality you wish.

37
Outdoor Lighting: What you Need to Know to Shoot Great Footage Outdoors

Michael Loehr

How do you light the outdoor scenes in your videos? Do you plan and stage each shot carefully to make the most of the sun's glow? Or do you just switch to outdoor white balance, call out "Action!" and roll tape?

Even if you choose the latter, chances are your videos still look pretty good. Today's camcorders work well enough in daylight to make very acceptable pictures, even with no attention to lighting.

Maybe that's why videographers don't worry too much about outdoor lighting. Perhaps they think making the best use of sunlight requires expensive instruments and tools they can't afford. Perhaps they just never learned the tricks of managing sunlight in a video project.

That's where this guide can help. In this chapter are some of the popular outdoor lighting techniques. They can help subjects look more natural on video, and improve the overall look of your projects.

You'll learn what tools and gadgets you need to make the most of sunlight. You can build many of them with inexpensive

stuff from art supply and hardware stores. We'll even teach you how to create the illusion of a dark night in the middle of the afternoon.

So start taking advantage of what may be your greatest asset as a videographer: the sun.

Principles of Light

The fundamental principles of good lighting apply whether you shoot video indoors or out. However, sunlight presents unique challenges to videographers. On almost any given day, there is more than enough light outside to shoot a scene. At first, an abundance of light seems like an asset. However the hundreds and thousands of lumens cast by the sun can actually cause problems for your camcorder. Not technical problems, but aesthetic ones.

At its brightest, the sun can shed more than 10 times the light of one typical indoor instrument. When it shines brightly, it also casts very dark shadows.

In video lingo, the difference between these light and dark areas is commonly called the contrast ratio, or *contrast range*.

Our eyes can compensate for the high contrast range of a bright day. Our camcorders, however, don't react as well. They require a much lower contrast range, especially to capture detail accurately. (Of course, our eyes also see better when we lower the contrast range, which is why we often wear sunglasses on sunny days.)

On bright days, the contrast range is usually too high for your camcorder to make good pictures. If you shoot without any lighting equipment or assistance, the sunlight won't flatter your subjects. Dark shadows may leave unpleasant or unnatural accents on facial features. Your images may also look washed out.

A high contrast ratio also affects your camera's automatic iris feature. You may have noticed that when the auto iris is on, its position changes constantly while you shoot.

As you move into a shadowed area, the iris opens to allow more light into the lens. As you move back to the bright areas, it closes again to avoid overexposure. That means you might get even, natural lighting from one angle, and harsh, overexposed lighting from another. The constant movement of the iris makes maintaining continuity between different camera angles difficult. It's also very distracting mid-shot.

The goal of outdoor lighting design is to lower the contrast range without damaging the natural look of the subjects and the outdoor setting. You want a lighting setup that looks the same to your camcorder, no matter where you put it. To do this, you need to brighten the dark, shadowed areas, and perhaps even lower the overall light level, depending on how brightly the sun shines.

Tools and Tricks

If you're shooting indoors and need more light, the standard practice is to plug in a

light and point toward the dark areas. Outside, you do practically the same thing, only with different tools.

You only have one light source—the sun. It doesn't need extension cords or power outlets. Even better, it will usually give you more than enough light to work with.

All you must do is redirect some of that excess light toward the shadowed areas of your set and your subjects. The best, most affordable tools for redirecting light are reflectors and diffusers; they will point light in different directions, and alter the way it falls on a subject. Light will bounce off a reflector, and pass through a diffuser.

Learning to use reflectors is easy. Their behavior is somewhat constant, given the fact that light bounces in predictable angles.

Reflectors vary, however, in three ways: 1) how much light they reflect, 2) how large an area their reflection covers and 3) the color of light they reflect.

Foil or mirrored surfaces reflect the most light over a small area. Pure white surfaces usually cover larger areas, but with less light. Some reflectors have a gold foil surface; these bounce light with a warm, rich quality that really flatters skin tones.

Diffusers filter direct beams of sunlight, spreading them evenly over a large area. Like reflectors, they're easy to use and fairly predictable.

A material's porosity and transparency determine its diffusion characteristics. Dense or very cloudy materials allow less light to fall onto the subject. Highly porous materials allow more.

Diffusing sunlight is probably the most effective technique for taming unpleasant shadows and reducing contrast. It does an excellent job of brightening dark areas, while retaining much of the outline and contour.

To use a diffuser, simply suspend or position the material between your subject and the sun. Where you place the material and how you angle it depends on the look you want. To create shadows on the face, place the diffuser close to the subject and off to one side. To spread light

Figure 37.1 *To control excessive contrast from the sun (a) use an overhead canopy of diffusion material (b).*

overhead. This lighting tends to be flat—some subjects may look bland under diffused light.

One solution: bounce more sunlight toward the subject. This highlights the subject and slightly increases the contrast range.

Or you can abandon diffusion altogether and bounce light around the scene with reflectors instead. By using reflectors, you can maintain the look of a summer day and still reduce contrast.

Position the reflector to bounce excess sunlight toward shadowed areas, as in Figure 37.2. This lets your camcorder use more incoming sunlight without washing out your subjects.

If you're shooting at midday, unpleasant shadows may appear on your subject's face. The simplest solution is to move your subject out of the direct sun, if possible. (See Figure 37.3.)

Another solution is to use a reflector. Try putting the reflector below the subject's face; this should help eliminate the shadow. Be careful to avoid the "monster look," however. Strong light from below the face is a classic horror film technique, hence the name. Unless you want your subject to look frightening, make sure the reflected light flatters the face. Reposition the reflector as necessary to eliminate the monster look.

One last tip: videographers on the go may prefer reflectors to diffusers. Diffusers can sometimes be cumbersome to set up. Reflectors offer better portability, and still solve many outdoor lighting problems.

Simple Solutions

Other very effective and inexpensive outdoor lighting techniques involve simply staging a scene in the proper place with respect to the sun.

You've heard the saying that the sun should always be behind the camera when you shoot. True enough, but it doesn't tell you whether the sun should be to the left, the right or directly behind the camera.

evenly and minimize shadows, place the diffuser above and away from the subject, angled down slightly as in Figure 37.1.

Experiment with the diffuser to determine the most effective position for your particular scene. No matter where you put it, your camcorder will make better pictures with diffused light.

There are, however, a few drawbacks to using diffusion. It simulates the light you might see on a slightly overcast day, especially when you suspend the diffuser

(a)

(a)

(b)

(b)

Figure 37.2 *When shooting in direct sunlight (a) a simple reflector can bounce light back into dark areas to improve contrast (b).*

Many videographers default to the center position, where the sun sits directly behind the camera. This is a bad idea for two reasons:

1. It puts the sun in the subject's face, which almost guarantees squinting eyes in the shot (See Figure 37.4) and

2. the shadow that you and your camcorder cast is likely to wind up in the shot.

You can avoid these rookie moves by adopting an outdoor version of the classic

(c)

Figure 37.3 *If you must shoot during the day, try to get your subject out of the sun (a) and into the shade of a building (b) or a tree (c).*

Figure 37.4 *Direct sunlight hitting your subject from the front causes squinting eyes.*

three-point lighting setup, which is used to add more light to indoor shooting situations.

In the three-point setup, one light serves as the main or "key" light. It provides most of the light for a scene. It's positioned to light one side of the subject, angled approximately 45 degrees horizontally from the subject.

A second, less intense light shines on the opposite side of the subject. Called a "fill" light, it balances the shadows that define contour and shape. It's often somewhere between one half and two thirds as bright as the key light.

Sometimes a third light adds backlight. A *backlight* separates the subject from what's behind it, and provides shoulder and hair highlights on people.

Here's how you can adapt this three-point setup to outdoor lighting situations. Instead of standing with the sun directly behind you, change your position so that the sun shines from behind you over either your left or right shoulder. In this position the sun becomes a key light, shining light on one side of the subject's face.

This takes the light out of your subject's eyes and lowers the chance of your shadow appearing in the shot. When the sun shines at an angle similar to a key light, the shadows will fall away from you and the subject, and hopefully out of the shot.

You can also add a very inexpensive fill light by just using another reflector. Once you've established the sun as the key light, either clip a reflector to a spare light stand, or have an assistant hold a reflector near the subject on the side opposite the sun. Rotate the reflector back and forth to bounce light onto the "dark" side of the subject. Move away to lessen the intensity, closer to raise it.

If you have another spare reflector, particularly one with a foil surface, you can simulate a backlight. Stand just off camera behind your subject, on the side with the key light. Point the foil side toward the sun and rotate it until the reflection lights up the back of your subject. Presto! Instant backlight.

Occasionally you will encounter outdoor settings where the background is as brightly lit as the subject. This is another aesthetically unpleasant situation.

When the subject and background are both very bright, they conflict with each other, creating an image viewers will find difficult to watch for very long. To solve this problem, you must highlight the foreground subject. Instead of trying to reflect more light onto the foreground, try shadowing all or part of the background.

The technique is subtractive lighting, or "flagging." It involves using a card called a "flag" to block sunlight from hitting certain areas. You can buy ready-made flags from video stores, or build your own from black foam boards. In a pinch, a reflector will work as a flag, but black foam board is better. The reflector's white surface sometimes bounces light where you don't want it.

To shadow the background, position the flag behind the subject, just off camera on the key light side. Angle it so that it casts

a shadow on the background. You may
need to move the subjects away from the
background to avoid casting a shadow on
them as well.

Position Problems

Because the earth rotates in space, the
sun's position, intensity and color balance
change through the course of a day. This
can create problems for uninitiated videographers. Understand these changes, however, and they can become tremendous
assets.

If you shoot a series of scenes during an
entire day, you'll notice the lighting
changes from scene to scene. Shadows
gradually change position, density and
direction, and the contrast range changes.
Color temperature also changes throughout the day.

For example: a scene shot very early in
the morning will have long horizontal
shadows, a slightly orange glow and a
lower contrast range. A scene shot in the
same location at midday will have dark
vertical shadows and a much higher contrast range.

You will experience difficulty when
you try to edit these scenes together.
Differences in shadow placement and
color balance will reveal that you shot the
scenes at different times. (See Figure 37.5)

A diffuser is an excellent way to prevent such problems. Diffusing sunlight
hides the movement of the sun across the
sky, and disguises the time of day. Sometimes the earth's atmosphere provides its
own diffusion in the form of cloud cover.
If the forecast says the clouds will hang
around all day, you may not need to set
up a diffuser at all.

Many projects call for dramatic use of
light and shadow to convey specific
moods or emotions. If yours is such a project, avoid using diffusion; it lessens the
impact of shadows. Also avoid shooting
in the middle of the day, when shadows
make subjects look less than their best.
Instead, shoot your footage either late in

(a)

(b)

Figure 37.5 *Shooting in the evening or early*
morning results in a soft light (a). Mid-day
sun is brighter and harsher (b).

the day or early in the morning, when the
shadows are most flattering.

When the sun is near the horizon, its
color temperature is different from when
it's high in the sky. At noon it casts a
white light high in color temperature,
usually around 5,600 K (Kelvin). Your
camcorder's outdoor filter works best with
this type of sunlight.

At dawn and dusk, however, the sun is
lower in the sky, and its glow is a warm,
golden-orange color. Videographers often
call this period the "golden hour," since

it usually lasts right around an hour. Its color registers much lower than the 5,600 K light of midday—usually around 3,100 K.

Consequently, your camera may react differently when switched to the outdoor setting. If you white balanced early in the day under regular 5,600 K light, the video will turn more and more orange as the evening progresses. If you don't want this look, simply white balance your camera at the beginning of every shot.

While this change in color temperature may prove inappropriate, it can also be perfect for certain types of shots. The golden hour's long shadows and warm lighting make it an ideal time to shoot dramatic or romantic scenes.

Be aware that the moment only lasts a short time. You can extend the golden hour a little by reflecting sunlight off a gold-surfaced reflector. However, once the sun either disappears in the evening, or reaches a 45 degree angle above the horizon in the morning, the golden look will be difficult to maintain. If you know exactly when the golden hour will happen, you can plan to take advantage of it on your next project.

On very rare occasions you may need to add artificial light to make an outdoor scene suitable for shooting. This is most common when shooting under either very dark clouds or heavy shadows. In these cases it may be appropriate to use your indoor lighting instruments instead of reflectors to light a scene.

Remember, the color temperature of sunlight is much higher than that of indoor studio lights. To use indoor lights outdoors, you must put a blue gel in front of them. Also be aware that indoor lights shine a very small amount of light when compared to the sun. You may need two or even three instruments to light a subject adequately outside.

Night Lights

Shooting outdoors at night can be trouble for professional and amateur videographers alike. Even with low-light camcorders, it's still very difficult to get good pictures without adding artificial light.

To solve this problem, use a technique called day-for-night shooting. It involves shooting a carefully staged and controlled scene during the day, making it look as if it were shot at night.

Day-for-night shooting isn't easy, and it isn't always effective. To make it work, you must create an illusion of nighttime that will fool your audience. To do this, pay close attention to how your eyes see at night.

Pay close attention to colors. At night our eyes don't see colors as well because of the lower light level. The same is true for our camcorders. Dress your subjects in muted colors to keep the color intensity down.

If your camcorder has a monochrome mode, consider using it instead of the color mode; this will help reduce the amount of color in the scene. Some editing VCRs have chroma controls or monochrome switches, which can also mute color intensity.

Consider buying a blue filter for your camcorder. This helps create the illusion of moonlight by turning sunlight blue. Most video stores carry a selection of filters to fit your camcorder. Be sure to get one that fits your model's lens.

When combined with the other techniques, the blue filter greatly enhances the nighttime look.

If there are any ordinary lights in your scene—car headlights, porch lights, window lights—switch them on. Indeed, before you shoot you should turn on any and all lights normally on at night.

You also must know how to disable your camcorder's auto iris and auto white balance circuits—if it has them. When activated, an auto iris circuit lets the optimal amount of light into the lens to make pictures.

With day-for-night shots, you want to limit the light entering the lens. You can only do this when you turn off the auto iris.

The same applies to auto white balance. If active, the feature will try to get an accurate white balance, even with the blue filter on the lens. The goal is to fool the camera and ultimately the audience, so switch off the auto white balance.

With the circuits off, white balance the camera without the blue filter. Place the filter on the lens, and manually close the iris until a small amount of light enters the lens. Let enough light through to distinguish your subjects, but not any more than that.

The result is the nighttime look: a grainy bluish image with muted colors and contrast. If your editing VCRs allow it, try lowering the black level and raising the luminance during post production.

This increases the contrast enough to match what our eyes typically see at nighttime.

Wrap It Up

Enhancing your outdoor shoots with reflectors and diffusers is more art than science. The techniques reflect personal preference as much as rigid rules.

So use reflectors and diffusers to express your own visual ideas more effectively. The best way to learn is to experiment with them.

Stage a simple scene outside, and then create four or five different moods by just changing the lighting design. This'll teach you how sunlight works, how to make the most of your tools and how your camcorder reacts to sunlight.

Experiment, too, with different materials and techniques. You may discover a style that becomes the signature element in your videos.

38
Audio For Video:
Getting it Right
From the Start

Hal Robertson

So, you've bought a shiny new digital video recorder and you're blown away by the image quality. But what about the audio? Audio is possibly the most overlooked element in video production. That's too bad because audio quality can make or break any video project, regardless of budget.

You may be able to fix some things in post-production, but why go to all the trouble when you can get it right the first time? This article explores 10 tips for gathering the best possible audio on your next shoot. Some are common sense tips, but many are hard-earned lessons from the field.

Plan Ahead

When shooting on location, a smart videographer scouts the site before the shoot, looking for ideal lighting and backgrounds to produce the best image possible. For your next shoot, scout with your ears too. Listen for traffic noises, machinery, animals and aircraft—anything that might ruin the audio during the

shoot. Depending on your topic, some background noise may be acceptable or even desirable. Just make sure you can hear your subject over the ruckus.

Use an External Microphone

Unless you have a high-end professional camera, your built-in microphone is absolutely worthless for anything more than your 3-year-old's birthday party. First, the microphone is built into the camera's body, and is very sensitive to noise from zoom, focus and tape drive motors. The second problem is a matter of distance. Even though you can zoom in on a subject from across the room, the microphone is stuck 20 feet away. Trust me, you need an external microphone.

Choose the Right Microphone
for the Job

OK, I've convinced you to use an external mike, but what kind? There are four basic types: handheld, lapel, shotgun and boundary (see Figure 38.1).

Handheld mikes, typically used by news reporters, add a newsy feel to your video. Directional handheld mikes minimize background noise while non-directional mikes collect the audio flavor of the scene.

News anchors and sit-down interview participants often use lapel, or lavaliere microphones. They are useful anytime you want to get close to the source, but minimize visual impact.

Shotgun microphones, highly directional and often used on TV shows and movie sets, usually suspend from a boom or "fishpole." Shotgun mikes typically hover just out of the video frame and point directly at the subject.

If you shoot legal or corporate video, the boundary microphone could be your new best friend. Boundary mikes turn an entire table, wall or floor into a pickup surface. Unfortunately, their incredible sensitivity is a double-edged sword. They clearly pick up voices from every direction but also amplify shuffling papers and air conditioner noise equally.

Use a Windscreen

You're familiar with the effect of wind blowing into a microphone. The resulting rumble masks all but the loudest sounds, making the audio useless. Subjects speaking close to a microphone also produce small blasts of wind from their mouths. One of three basic windscreens will minimize or eliminate these problems altogether.

Foam windscreens are the most common since they are inexpensive, and work great for both handheld and lapel microphones (see Figure 38.2). Although shotgun mikes also use foam windscreens, the pros usually use a special type called a zeppelin. This special-purpose windscreen gets its name from its shape. It looks like a long, skinny blimp. Porous cloth or fur typically covers the mike and blocks the wind, while letting sound through unharmed. A shotgun microphone mounts inside the zeppelin where the entire mike is protected from audio-wrecking wind noises.

When you record the narration for your next video, consider using a hoop-style windscreen to improve the sound quality. Hoop screens are usually about six inches

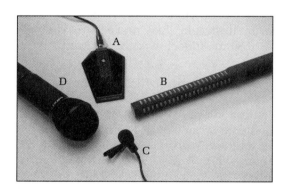

Figure 38.1   A. Boundary Mike—also PZM, lies, flat on a table or surface and is typically used for miking people sitting around a table.
B. Shotgun Mike—Usually has a highly-focused pickup pattern and best at gathering sound at a distance or in a noisy environment.
C. Lapel Mike—is very small and can be hidden on or around the subject to completely conceal its presence.
D. Handheld Mike—comfortable to hold in the hand, it is commonly used by television newscasters, singers, public speakers and talk-show hosts. It's ideal when you want the talent to directly address the camera.

Figure 38.2   Screen test—a simple foam windscreen can do wonders to minimize outdoor gusts and plosives in the voice.

in diameter and covered with one or two layers of fine mesh cloth. Recording studios worldwide use this type of windscreen on critical vocals, and you can too.

Position Microphones Properly

Some simple attention to microphone placement can make a dramatic improvement in sound quality. Take the shotgun mike, for example. Its extreme directional characteristics and high sensitivity make it great for picking up audio from a distance. But point a shotgun up at your subject from the ground (instead of overhead), and you might pick up birds singing in the trees or the 3:30 flight to Albuquerque.

Misuse of lapel microphones is just as easy. Ideally, they are worn on the outside of clothing, attached to a lapel, tie or shirt. However, hiding lapel mikes under clothes minimizes wind noise and visual distractions (see Figure 38.3). This location guarantees a muffled sound and the sound of cloth rubbing on the microphone. If wind is the problem, try positioning your subject with their back to the wind. If cosmetics are the issue, try a smaller microphone, a less distracting location or a shotgun mike.

Learn to Deal With AGC

Automatic gain control, or AGC, is built into virtually every camera on the market. This seemingly magic circuit constantly monitors your incoming audio, then keeps the loud sounds from getting too loud and the soft sounds from getting too soft. Sounds like a great idea, doesn't it? It's not a bad idea, but problems crop up later during editing when you try to match clips from different takes. One take will be loud and strong, but another will be softer with more background noise. Now what are you going to do?

There are a couple of solutions. First, have your talent re-take the material, starting before the break point. This will

get the AGC working in a similar range to the previous take, making your edit point more consistent. The second method is to turn the AGC off. This only works on certain camcorders, but if yours has this feature, use it. You can adjust the audio level manually for consistent sound, take after take.

Monitor With Headphones

If your camera has a headphone jack, buy a pair of good headphones and keep them in your camera case (see Figure 38.4). The next time you shoot, you will hear exactly what the microphone hears, making mike positioning easier. You will also catch bad connections, dead batteries and background noise before you commit it to tape. This is an absolute must and will save you much frustration and embarrassment.

Figure 38.3 In or out?—it may be tempting to conceal a lapel mike in the clothing; however, it will cause the audio to be muffled and the sound of rubbing cloth to be picked up.

Figure 38.4 Listen in—always use headphones when using an external mike.

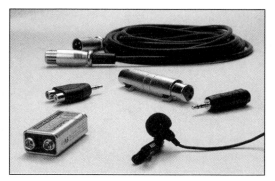

Figure 38.5 Hooking up—with a variety of cables, adapters, and spare batteries you'll be prepared for every audio occasion.

Get Connected

Audio cables and adapters are a necessity for the videographer—just make sure you have the right ones before you shoot (see Figure 38.5). Wireless mikes often need jumper wires to connect the receiver to the camera. Professional microphones use three-pin XLR connectors that won't plug into most consumer and prosumer cameras. For these mikes string together several adapters or, buy an interface box. If you're connecting to a sound system or other audio equipment, bring every adapter you own to the shoot. You'll need them.

Get In Close

Regardless of your microphone choice, the closer you get it to the subject, the cleaner your audio will sound. Position the handheld or lapel mike a little closer than you previously had. Boom in as close as possible with the shotgun. This technique also reduces background noise and further improves your audio.

Bring Spares

Spare cables, spare adapters, spare microphones and spare batteries. This tip will save your skin in an emergency and give you some creative freedom. Perhaps you get to the shoot and discover your single lapel microphone won't work because there are two subjects speaking. Your spare shotgun or handheld microphone will work even better and you'll look like a very smart cookie.

Take these ideas to heart and your next video production can sound match the sound of a professional studio. In a future article, we will explore how to create professional sounding audio in the edit suite.

Sidebar 1

An Audio Horror Story

Last year I shot a video for my church in a city park. I scouted the site and found a great location for audio and video. What I failed to notice was the railroad behind a wall of trees on the east side of the park.

The day of the shoot threatened rain, so we had to work quickly. Unfortunately, we had to stop shooting twice for a passing train—destroying 20 precious minutes of clear sky. We got the video done, but we also got wet packing the equipment back to the car. Lesson learned.

Sidebar 2

Watch With Your Ears (or Listen With Your Eyes)

Still not sure what type of microphone is best for your next shoot? Broadcast TV shows offer a valuable and free resource of audio examples to help you decide what microphone to use.

News broadcasts provide the perfect opportunity to listen to the differences between lapel mikes (anchors) and handheld mikes (field reporters). Close your eyes and carefully listen to the variety of audio sources.

Most sitcoms and dramas offer a chance to examine the sound of a shotgun microphone in action. If you listen closely, you'll begin to notice when the mike isn't pointed exactly at the subject.

39
Outdoor Audio

Hal Robertson

Ah, the great outdoors. It's a video shooter's dream come true. Loads of free lighting, gorgeous backgrounds and breathtaking scenery—what more could you want? At least visually, shooting outdoors is a wonderful idea. For audio, however, an outdoor shoot presents a new set of challenges. Learning to deal with these challenges is a combination of the right tools and a knowledge of all the variables. Grab your walking stick and camcorder and join us on a hike through the backwoods of outdoor audio.

It's Not Nice to Fool Mother Nature

If you plan to shoot outdoors, rest assured you'll have to deal with less than ideal weather conditions from time to time. Of particular concern are the detrimental effects of rain and snow on your precious (i.e. expensive) audio and video equipment. Wet weather and electronic gear mix like oil and water, so you'll do well to prepare for the worst.

First, and most important, is to keep the water out of your camera. Surely you've seen the advertisements in the back of **Videomaker** for rain slickers made specifically for cameras. These are excellent accessories for those who shoot outdoors on a regular basis. The occasional outdoor videographer, however, can make due with a simple plastic trash bag. Cut a hole for your lens in one corner of the bag and a hole for the viewfinder in the other corner. You'll still have easy access to the controls from underneath, although it will be difficult to use a flip-out LCD and certain viewfinders. It's not as waterproof as the rain capes with watertight lens holes, but a trash bag might be sufficient in a light mist.

Zipper sandwich bags come in handy with your audio equipment (see Figure 39.1). A wireless microphone transmitter pack doesn't like the wetness any more than your camera, so keep it dry too. You'll need a knife and some gaffer's tape to complete the task, but the finished project will keep your transmitter dry and

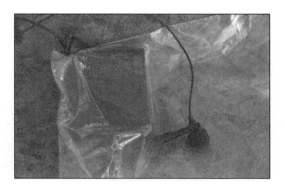

Figure 39.1 *Bag it—zip up the delicate electronics in a sandwich baggie in extreme environs.*

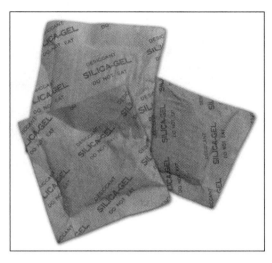

Figure 39.2 *Do not eat—silica gel packs in your camera bag can absorb moisture.*

away from the repair bench. Wired microphones fare better in the elements, but it's still a good idea to keep the connectors dry with a simple wrap of electrical tape. The same applies for battery doors.

Exposed microphones—whether hand-held, shotgun or lapel—are more of a sticking point. It's never a good idea to get a microphone wet, regardless of type or application. For a quick outdoor shoot, a simple foam windscreen will keep the microphone dry enough, but extended shoots require measures that are more drastic. While you can cover your microphone with the same bag as your camera, the audio will suffer. Not only will you hear the drops of rain falling on the plastic, the covering will dramatically change the quality of the sound. Honestly, there isn't a simple fix for this problem. There are professional windscreens that make notable improvements, but the price may be out of reach for many casual shooters. If you're using a lapel microphone, it's possible to secure the element under your talent's clothing or even under the brim of a hat. These are extreme measures and will negatively affect the sound quality, but it's a reasonable tradeoff if the alternative is to abort the shoot.

Although not specifically audio related, it's a good idea to avoid rapid shifts in temperature and humidity—your audio and video gear won't like these changes and

may rebel. Condensation (when moving from cold to warm environs) will produce everything from random glitches to a complete shutdown to fried circuitry. You can minimize these effects with two simple techniques. First, place several packs of silica gel in your camera case to absorb excess humidity (see Figure 39.2). Second, when moving from a cool environment to a warm one, give the equipment several minutes to acclimate. You'll eliminate the embarrassment of an equipment failure and save wear-and-tear on your gear too.

The Windscreen is Your Friend

Whether you shoot in wetness or not, every outdoor shooter has to deal with wind noise. Uncontrolled, wind noise can render your audio useless and there is no way to repair the damage in post-production. Regardless of the audio you capture outside, your microphone needs a windscreen.

The most common type of windscreen is made from open-cell urethane foam (see Figure 39.3). Although available as an accessory for virtually every type of microphone, some microphones come with the windscreen permanently installed. The

Figure 39.3 *Foam fun—cheap foam covers can help eliminate wind noise.*

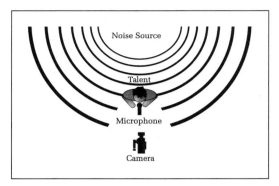

Figure 39.4 *Block it—if you're shooting a subject using a handheld or lapel microphone, position him with his back to the noise. His body will block a great deal of noise and can make an impractical set-up feasible.*

Figure 39.5 *Aim for the mouth—it is important to point directional microphones correctly.*

windscreen's task is simple—keep the wind out of the microphone. Foam windscreens vary in their ability to accomplish this mission, but they're inexpensive, readily available and work well in many situations.

In more extreme conditions, you'll need a professional windscreen—often called a windsock or zeppelin. These windscreens differ in size and construction, but most often use a special cloth stretched over an open frame. The microphone is enclosed inside the frame and the cloth blocks the wind from entering. The completed assembly looks something like a blimp, hence the zeppelin reference. The windsock is effective at eliminating wind noise, but costs a good deal more than the common foam windscreen. In addition, the length and diameter of your microphone factor into the design of the enclosure. For shooters in brutal wind conditions, the addition of a fuzzy fur cover to the windsock can eliminate the detrimental effects of wind noise up to 60 miles per hour.

Dealing With Background Noise

Whether outdoors means mountain streams or traffic jams, you have to deal with unwanted noises in your audio. These may manifest themselves as simple, random interruptions or as a constant roar that all but obscures the sound you *want* to record. In any case, there are weapons at your disposal to minimize these effects.

The simplest technique is to use natural barriers to block the noise. If you're shooting a subject wearing a lapel microphone, position him with his back to the noise. His body will block a great deal of noise and can make an impractical setup feasible (see Figure 39.4). You can exploit other barriers such as buildings, rocks and trees to similar effect. When using directional handheld or shotgun microphones, utilize the built-in null points to your advantage (see Figure 39.5). You can leverage this knowledge of pickup patterns by placing the microphone where it will pick up the maximum amount of sound you want and a minimum of the sound you don't.

On the other hand, you *are* shooting outdoors and your viewers associate certain sounds with being outside. If the area you're featuring contains colorful audio, capture several minutes of sound on tape after the shoot. Back in post-production, you'll have a way to cover abrupt edits and scenic shots that don't have acceptable audio. Properly blended, these patches will sound perfectly natural, plus you'll have another soundscape for your audio effects library. It is better to have the option to add ambient noise back into the mix in post than to try and remove it.

Shooting in the great outdoors can be challenging, but some preparation and practice will have you ready to tackle those projects, and you'll have some impressive audio to show for your efforts.

Sidebar 1

DIY Windsock

Professional microphone zeppelins or windsocks can cost several hundred dollars and aren't worth the cost for casual use. A few dollars and a trip to the fabric store will supply most of what you need to build a simple windsock. First, pick up a small roll of fiber batting—the type used to fill quilts and blankets. Next, buy some costume fur with a nap of one inch or longer. Installation is simple. First, wrap some batting around your microphone, securing it with rubber bands. Then, do the same with the fur if you're shooting in strong winds. This setup will likely thin out the sound, but wind noise won't be as much of an issue.

Sidebar 2

Listen Closely

Most shooters know to monitor their audio with a pair of headphones, but monitoring outdoors adds some complexity. Many camcorders offer skimpy headphone amplifiers, so you have to make the most of every milliwatt. Start with a pair of sealed-cup (circumaural) headphones. These will block outside sounds and allow you to concentrate on what's coming through the microphone. Several manufacturers offer excellent sealed-cup models, but try them with your camcorder before buying if possible. As you sample several brands, you'll discover that some headphones play much louder than others. Find the best tradeoff of sound quality versus volume and you'll have an audio reference that will serve you well in every circumstance.

40
Stealth Directing: Getting The Most Out of Real People

Michael J. Kelley

It must have been Take 30, but we weren't quite sure because we were no longer using a slate, nor did we stop tape in between takes, for fear of losing the little momentum we had gained. The talent was a beautiful young woman who had volunteered for the part. She was well-cast by the bank's producer. Her considerable knowledge of the subject matter meant that she had her lines down, but her lack of experience in front of the camera made this training video laborious to capture. Even worse: The experience was completely humiliating for her, the performance was indeed embarrassing and she would very likely never again volunteer for a shoot. It can be difficult to coax an agreeable performance out of an amateur, but it can be done.

Be Realistic

Professionals know that to deliver a compelling performance, the talent must be comfortable not only with the script, but also with being the center of attention, where lights, microphones, camera and production crew all hang on every move. This alone is a tall order for most people: Remembering lines is one thing, but putting it all together with eye lines (where the talent should direct their gaze), blocking (where the they should stand and move) and interacting with other players and props in a well-timed and natural way reminds us all why the really good actors deserve the big bucks. Even under the best of circumstances, it's not easy to deliver a believable performance.

Using real people is a calculated risk. The successful director manages an exercise in stealth, regardless of the size and scope of the production environment. Most of the management techniques that typically apply to pros can be tossed out from the beginning. From pre-production coaching to the first rehearsal, all the way to the last shot, the director of amateur talent is most successful when being downright sneaky.

Figure 40.1 *Ready off the set—ready the talent off of the set, preferably in an environment which is both familiar and relaxing.*

Tread Lightly

Standard techniques, such as on-camera rehearsals or calling for "places, lights, camera, action," just don't work. The pressure while waiting on the set is generally too much for amateur talent to bear, so much so that, while the shot is prepared technically, the stealthy director can best use the time to ready the talent off of the set, preferably in an environment which is both familiar and relaxing (see Figure 40.1).

Aside from any artistic or technical prowess, the director is equal parts coach, baby-sitter, mentor, friend, psychologist, boss and dentist (as some "teeth" can be extracted more painlessly than others). The director is also much like a valve, constantly bleeding off pressure while developing an acceptable flow. Finally and always, the director is also a good writer (able to adapt scripts in a heartbeat), editor (able to adapt to new sequences as they occur), and actor. You, as the director, must invisibly manage your own pressures sufficiently to give every attention to the fragile talent. Normalizing the talent's pressures is the your primary task,

for, without an acceptable performance, all of the rest is but a drill.

It's crucial that you be so well-organized that your manner is relaxed and friendly, stress-free and even playful. Much of this has to do with doing your homework and providing ample time for the scene to be captured. Advanced preparation really pays off here, and a flexible production timetable which is able to cope with surprises, delays and unanticipated bits of serendipity is a must.

For most people, being in front of a camera is an exciting experience, complete with ego attachments, unfounded expectations, vain fantasies and delusions of grandeur. Given a little extra time, a clever director can use all of that energy to great advantage.

Call Talent Last

It's best if the set is fully prepared before the talent ever arrives (see Figure 40.2). Stagger your call times, call the talent in as late as possible, and, by all means, do not over-rehearse your talent. Repeat your technical run-throughs separately until they are

Figure 40.2 *Last call—it's best if the set is fully prepared before the talent ever arrives.*

consistently on the mark. This is where the sneaky part starts: With the talent arriving fresh and full of anticipation, the director should focus all attention on the talent, perhaps assigning a production assistant specifically for the talent if possible. The whole crew should be welcoming and relaxed. This first impression cannot be over-estimated. Setting an inclusive stage makes every difference, so always provide the time for the talent to be fully introduced to the crew and the environment.

Prep Off the Set

Next, get the talent off the set. Applying makeup, tending to hair and wardrobe, or even wiring a concealed mike may make the talent feel important, but it also ups the pressure. These tasks are all best accomplished off-set. It's also a great time for the director to distract the talent by casually discussing the shot and how the talent will deliver their part (see Figure 40.3).

Show Time!

With the crew in position, the tape cued and everyone at the ready, escort the talent

to the fully-lighted set. As the director leads the talent through their blocking, perhaps even giving an example of how lines are to be delivered, the crew is on full alert, keenly watching for the roll cue which may be as subtle as a silent nod or a flick of the hand. With the talent slowly and carefully massaged into place, the director should casually call for a rehearsal; that's often the cue to roll tape too. No tally lights, no calls for "Action!", no extra pressure.

If all goes well, you may have your shot finished before the talent even knows you've started. Recording "rehearsals" sometimes yields the freshest, least self-conscious delivery. Of course, many performances improve with a little work and encouragement from you, but even when conducting interviews, you'll find that the best performances come from talent that is fully prepared in advance of ever reaching the set and is then gently coaxed through short segments with as little hoopla as possible.

After all, real people are often very talented, attractive and capable, if only the director and producer take the time to conceal the pressures of the process and prepare for what may be the performance of a lifetime.

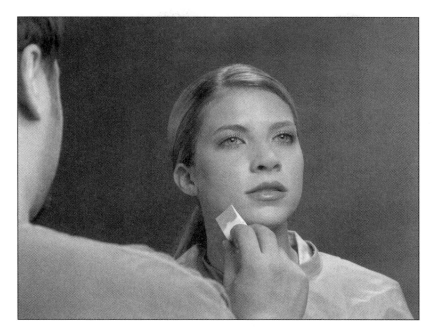

Figure 40.3 *Off-set application—applying makeup, tending to hair and wardrobe, or even wiring a concealed mike may make the talent feel important, but it also ups the pressure. These tasks are all best accomplished off-set.*

Sidebar 1

Craft-Services Prep Pays Off

A thoughtfully catered table can offer needed liquid refreshment and nourishment. Find out your talent's preferences ahead of time and provide meals which are appropriate for the time and length of the production day. The talent may be a strict vegan or allergic to the almond torte you specially prepared. You want to fuel the performance, while calming the performer, so have choices. Snacks of fresh fruit are always crowd pleasers. Carefully regulate the use of sugar and caffeine, and save the champagne for when the shot's in the can. Whatever you do, give the talent plenty of water, but don't let them use ice, as it may constrict the vocal chords.

Sidebar 2

It's in the Eyes

Interview subjects are usually experts in their fields, but most experts aren't performers, so it's up to you to give the talent every encouragement. Choose your questions carefully. Don't put your expert on the spot, and, if an answer is difficult, move along and come back to a rephrased version of the question later on. Your body language is very important: Attentive, upright posture and focused eye-contact, coupled with an open, pleasant smile and nods of encouragement, will all help your talent to feel relaxed and conversational. Have them tell their stories to you in their own words, and have the stealth camera crew there, almost invisibly capturing every nuance.

41
Sets, Lies and Videotape

Jim Stinson

When you think of movie sets you probably imagine structures built from scratch on Hollywood sound stages—structures that need too much big-time money, skill and space for most videographers.

True, full-scale sound stage sets can cost thousands or even millions of dollars, but professional videographers routinely "build" effective video sets that cost little or nothing in under an hour or even a very few minutes.

But wait, you say. I shoot weddings (or family events or vacations or training guides or business conferences), so I don't use sets.

Oh, yes you do. If you move a distracting picture, fill a dull corner with a ficus plant, pull a desk away from a wall to remove a shadow—in short, if you change the shooting environment to improve the look of your video, you're creating a set, however modest in scope. And if you know the tricks of the trade, you can make more elaborate sets—whole new environments, in fact—with a minimum of time, effort and expense. This chapter explores those tricks of the trade.

To show you what we mean by a "set," let's start with a quick review of the various types.

Types of Set

We begin, of course, with the classic built-from-scratch sets you find on a Hollywood sound stage. I don't recommend that you construct one of these, even if you do have some place to put it. Real sets are heavy, expensive and time-consuming to build. Interiors are generally finished in actual drywall (though it's much thinner than normal), complete with taped and "mudded" seams and full paint jobs. Windows, doors and moldings are real.

In short, a set requires all the building and finishing skills you need for a real room. A more practical alternative: a sort of location set—a part of an actual environment that you can customize for your video.

For instance, I once needed four offices for an industrial video I was directing. We couldn't work in the maze of cubicles where the client's actual personnel toiled without disrupting operations, so we commandeered a large conference room. Once emptied of furniture, what we had was a 25-foot square room with wood paneling on one wall, draped windows opposite it and neutral-toned painted walls at either end.

Perfect! By arranging furniture in one corner, I made an office with windows to the left and a painted wall at the rear. The opposite corner yielded the painted wall on the left (with different artwork) and the fancy paneling to the right. Upscale furnishings turned this corner into an executive office. The third office set used only the full expanse of the painted wall, again dressed with different artwork and a potted plant.

And the fourth? We obtained two panels of the modular office dividers used in the client's actual offices and set them up at right angles inside the conference room. By propping them up on wooden boxes (called "apple boxes"), we raised them high enough so that the camera could not see over their tops and reveal where they actually were. And since we videotaped the actors seated at their desks, the camera did not show that the divider tops were abnormally high.

Improving Reality

More often, you don't have to create a set from bare walls; you just want to customize an actual location to fit your needs.

A desk is a desk, after all. Put a "GO, PANTHERS!" poster on the wall behind it and you have a principal's office. A couple of medical school diplomas and it's a doctor's office. A performance chart for Acme Industries and it's an executive office.

The relatively low resolution of video makes improving reality all the easier. Countless sets have been constructed or enhanced with nothing but pieces of foam, glue and spray paint. A cheap poster hung behind a window in the set wall becomes

a beautiful view. Some TV news studios dot their sets with photo-copies of equipment to look more impressive. Our saving grace is that the video camera is not that discerning, particularly in the consumer realm, and especially from a distance.

Often you create a set by subtracting items as well as adding them; that is, you frame off unwanted elements so that they never appear on screen. Once, for example, I needed to shoot into the corner of a room with a door in one wall. The trouble was, the adjacent wall was actually an archway into a much larger room. But I had three feet of solid wall before the arch began, so I made sure that my camera never panned quite far enough left to reveal it. As a result, the background "became" two full walls of a small room.

Major Principles

This example demonstrates an important principle of set making: *if it's not in the frame, it doesn't exist.* Remember that the sets you build or the locations you use need only be finished as far as the camera will reveal.

The flip side of this principle is: *if you can't see it, you can't tell that it's not really there.* I once shot a scene in what seemed like a large and busy restaurant. It was actually a wall with a door in it—plus just three tables, three actors and video crewmembers as extras.

Imagine the door screen on the right and the three tables to the left of it, along the wall. We put upscale paintings on the wall, added the tables with snowy white linen and bentwood chairs, lit the area to simulate intimate down-lights and installed the crewmembers as patrons.

Action: over-the-shoulder of the maitre d' as two diners come in the door. He greets them, picks up two menus (from a tacky orange crate beside him but out of sight of the camera), gestures left and escorts them to the far left table as we dolly past the other "diners" to hold them. Add ambient restaurant sound in the editing process, and voila! a blank wall becomes a complete restaurant populated by scores of staff and customers.

As long as we're talking about principles, here's another biggie: *the world on the screen has no fixed geography.* For example, the two sides of a door are not always the same door. I taped my diners as they walked down an actual street, turned and entered an actual restaurant. In editing, I then cut from that exterior to the shot of the diners entering the restaurant set. By matching the action of the door opening—actually two different doors— I "attached" the set to the real exterior, which, in fact, was 10 miles away. In addition, the actual restaurant exterior helped sell the reality of the set.

For another video I zoomed in on a window high up on a great glass skyscraper. Then, in my location office set, I placed a pane of glass in front of the camera, deliberately lit to show light reflections. A piece of fabric hanging behind the glass on one side simulated office drapes.

Then my actor stood behind the glass, staring pensively down at the "city" below, then turned and walked away, revealing the office behind her.

When making a cut from the exterior zoom shot to this shot, I effectively placed the office inside the skyscraper.

Making Do With Less

Sometimes you can get away with a very small shooting area. In the video with the four offices, an actor in one of them makes a phone call. I placed the actor who answered that call in a swivel chair in front of a painted wall on which I'd hung a framed print. This wall was in a little-used office corridor.

I then framed loose head-and-shoulders profile shot of the actor as he answered the phone. There were no desks, no cabinets, no other decorations; the actor had to hold the telephone base on his unseen knees. But by rocking and swiveling gently as he talked, he sold the idea that he was sitting in a complete office.

You tend to think of a video set as falling behind the actors, but it can be very useful to place it in front of them instead. I once needed a shot in the stacks of a library, but it was impractical to create long rows of six-foot-high shelves full of books. Instead, I placed a three-by-four-foot open-backed bookcase on a table five feet out from a blank wall and filled most of it with books. The spines of the books faced the wall.

Next I positioned the camera on the far side of the bookshelves so that it faced the books, which filled the entire frame. Strategic gaps in the ranks of books let the audience see parts of the wall beyond.

The actor walked on-screen between the wall and the book case, paused with her face framed in one of the gaps between books, selected a book and walked out of the "library stacks." For that scene, three-by-four feet of set was all I built.

If you can, though, choose a room that gives your set the most "throw." Throw is the distance from your camera to your subject, and it's crucial for achieving certain visual effects. If you want the compressed, flat look of a long zoom setting, you need to get your camcorder back from your subject. A 10-by-10 room won't allow you this option.

Remember that you'll never be able to make a wide shot in a small room look like a wide shot in a large room, but it's easy to make a large room look small.

Moving Outdoors

We tend to think of sets as indoor critters, but you can make them outdoors as well. Just remember the two key principles: if it's not in the frame it doesn't exist, and in the world on the screen there is no fixed geography.

To illustrate the first principle, I once had to show a vigorous senior citizen playing golf. The trouble was, we had to videotape her at her home, far from any golf course.

Here's the sequence of shots I made on her front lawn, to solve the problem:

HIGH-ANGLE CLOSE-UP: a patch of cropped grass. A woman's hand enters the shot, deposits a golf ball on a tee and exits. CUT TO:

WORM'S EYE ANGLE (sky and tree branches fill the screen): the woman wearing a golf outfit, eye shades and golfing gloves, enters the shot and addresses the camera with a club, as if it were the ball on its tee. CUT TO:

CLOSE-UP (an out-of-focus hedge fills the background): The woman raises her look from the ball to the distant, off-camera green. She swings. CUT TO:

HIGH-ANGLE CLOSE-UP: the ball being whacked solidly out of the shot. CUT TO:

CLOSE-UP: The woman follows the ball (off-camera) as it sails (presumably) toward the green. She smiles at the result and walks out of frame.

See? Because the telltale details of her residential neighborhood were never in the frame, they didn't exist.

I warped screen geography to solve a problem in another program, in which a passing citizen comes upon a bank robbery.

As the bad guys rush out of the bank, the passerby looks around, spots a phone booth, runs to it and calls the police.

Just one hitch: there was no phone booth anywhere near the bank exterior. To solve the problem, I put the citizen in the foreground, watching the perps in the background.

He looks off-screen right, sees something and rushes out, screen right.

Pause, while the felons clear out of the shot; then the citizen runs back in from screen right. An hour later and three miles away, I centered a phone booth in full shot. The citizen rushes in from screen left, enters the booth and makes his call. Then he runs back out the way he entered, screen left.

In editing I inserted the phone booth sequence into the bank shot, between the point at which the man leaves and the later point at which he returns. The effect: to move the phone booth next door to the bank.

The Frankly Artificial Set

So far, we've talked about sets that work hard to convince you that they're actually offices or restaurants or golf courses. But other sets are just, well, sets. News, game show and talk show sets are examples of video environments that make no attempt to disguise themselves as something else.

Like other studio sets, these are probably too elaborate for modest productions. (Imagine trying to build the set for *Jeopardy!*) But you can use two simple alternatives to create "frankly studio" sets.

Your first option is a seamless paper backing. Available on rolls from photo supply houses, seamless paper comes in a wide range of sizes, colors and patterns.

Simply hang the roll high in the air and pull down as much as you need to create a "wall" behind your performers. If you select a chromakey blue color seamless, you can use properly equipped special effects generators or computer editing systems to replace the blue color with matted-in images (like the TV weather reporter's maps).

The simplest set of all is no set whatever. Instead, you create your set by lighting the actors and furniture in the foreground and leaving the background dark.

This works best when 1) you can exclude ambient light from the shooting area and 2) your camera permits manual exposure control.

For simplicity, we've discussed ideas for sets one at a time, but you can combine several of them.

For instance, one of my video students wanted to insert an actor into an actual event. Happening on a serious auto accident on a busy boulevard at night, he'd taped it with the Hi8 camcorder he carries everywhere.

It was perfect for the public service video he was making on safe driving. Now the trick was to place his on-camera narrator at the accident scene.

Here's how he did it. He took the actor to another busy boulevard, where the ambient background sound was similar, but shooting was safer because of wide sidewalks. He placed the actor under a streetlight so that the camcorder's auto exposure system would reduce the background to darkness.

Then he positioned an assistant just out of frame, holding a battery-powered revolving light. As the actor read his lines in medium shot (down to the waist), the revolving light splashed his face with an intermittent red glare. Intercut with shots of the real accident, the narrator seemed to be standing beside a police car at the scene.

In faking his narrator into the scene, the director used the following principles:

1. If it's not in the frame it doesn't exist (the technician holding the light),

2. if the videographer says it exists outside the frame, then it does exist (the police car) and

3. screen geography is not fixed (combining the accident and narrator locations).

If you keep these fundamental principles in mind as you plan and shoot your programs, you can put together almost any set you like.

42
Makeup and Wardrobe for Video

Carolyn Miller

Though many people equate makeup and wardrobe with high-budget Hollywood productions, even the most modest video can greatly benefit by simple, inexpensive attention in this area. Wardrobe and makeup (this includes hair, as well) are closely tied to the whole look and style of a piece. They help tell the story and offer important visual clues about the characters—whether they are actors, spokespersons or interview subjects. They can subtly but significantly enhance your presentation—or, if you haven't done your homework—seriously undermine it.

Even if you intend to shoot your subjects in all their raw, unblemished uniqueness, disregarding these "vanity" concerns can turn your searingly honest piece into an unintentional comedy. Do you really want your audience distracted by a bald head that gleams like a light beacon, by patterns on shirts that take on an animated life of their own, or by clanky jewelry, jarring color schemes, or faces that look like floating heads? If not, then you're going to have to devote some time to makeup and wardrobe.

Planning Ahead

Like every other aspect of making video, it's a good idea to think about wardrobe and makeup well in advance of production. As you envision your completed video, ask yourself what overall look you're striving for (for example, glamorous, upscale and sophisticated; or hip, young and wacky). Clothing style, colors, makeup and hair should all support this look. Susan Stroh, a Los Angeles based pro who over the years has worn many hats on industrials and documentaries (producer, director, script supervisor, writer), calls this "image positioning," a term that is borrowed from the world of corporate marketing.

Even if you're using real people in your video, as opposed to actors, you'll want to make sure they are dressed in a way that fits their role in the piece. You probably don't want your CEO to be wearing jeans, or your auto mechanic in a suit and tie. But then again, your concept may call for exactly that. Just make sure you convey your vision to your subjects.

Joan Owens, a veteran Hollywood documentary producer, director and writer (TV's "Hunt for Amazing Treasures" and "ZooLife with Jack Hanna") feels the goal of documentaries is to capture people as they usually are, in clothing that reflects the flavor of their specific world. "Sometimes people want to make a good impression for the camera," she notes, "and dress more elegantly than they normally would."

Joan encourages her subjects to wear appropriate clothing, and also makes sure they have wardrobe changes for all the scenes they'll be in. For instance, while making a documentary about the recovery of a Civil War submarine, one of her subjects needed an outfit for an on-camera interview and a very different type of outfit for a scene on a fishing boat to re-create an event from the past—and both scenes were to be shot on the same day. Sometimes, though, you'll want one of your performers to wear the same outfit throughout the shoot. Joan points out that Jack Hanna, as host of his wildlife series, always wore a safari jacket. It not only clearly reflected the theme of the series, but also made it easier to mix and match scenes in the editing room.

Special Considerations

One important wardrobe consideration is whether or not you'll be shooting chroma-key scenes, to electronically "transport" your talent to a different set. If your chroma-key background is blue or green (sometimes called "shooting bluescreen" or "shooting greenscreen") you want to make sure your talent is not wearing the same color garment. Otherwise, there will be a gaping hole in the talent's clothing, filled in electronically by the chroma-key set.

You should also scout your locations in terms of your overall wardrobe approach.

You'll want your talent to be dressed in colors that will harmonize with the set and not clash with it. And outfits should be thematically appropriate to the environment, too. For instance, if one of your locations is a rough-hewn hunting lodge, your talent will look better in a casual suede jacket than in a tailored business suit.

During the planning stage, also give some thought to the physical appearance of your on-screen personalities. If you're aware of facial features that may present special problems—acne scars, closely set eyes, a very round face—you'll want to make sure you've got items in your kit that can handle this. It doesn't mean, though, that you should attempt to turn them into something they're not.

Greg Braun, a Chicago-based Director of Photography who owns his business, G.B. Productions, specializes in high-end work for major corporations and has strong views on this subject. "I'm not trying to re-create the person in any way," he states emphatically. "But I do want to enhance their appearance—to make them look their best."

If you realize you're going to be faced with makeup challenges that are beyond your abilities, it may be necessary to call in a professional. This may be especially true if you're doing a fictional piece. Both makeup and wardrobe can be extremely demanding in fictional dramas, particularly stories set in a different era. In projects like this, specialists can be a big asset. This doesn't have to be as expensive as it sounds, as long as you're resourceful.

Producer-director David Phyfer, based in Geneva, IL., has a number of ideas about how to get assistance without spending a fortune. His company, Stage Fright Productions, makes educational and children's videos on less than lavish budgets. David suggests that community businesses might help out. A local store might offer clothing, costumes or shoes in return for a scene set in their shop; a beauty salon might provide hair or makeup services on the same basis. You might also be able to get wardrobe items in return for guaranteeing product placement in the video, or an on-screen credit.

Wardrobe Dos and Don'ts

Once you've decided on your wardrobe approach, you'll want to go over it with your talent, since in most cases they'll be using their own clothing. Here are a few examples of what your talent should not wear:

- fabrics that wrinkle easily, like linen

- baggy clothes (they make people look heavier than they really are)

- shiny or noisy jewelry; dangling earrings

- silk (it rustles, causing sound problems, and shows sweat stains quickly)

- hats, unless necessary for the identity of the character (they cast shadows)

- fabrics with tight patterns, like checks, stripes, herring bone and hounds tooth (they create an unstable, vibrating, jumpy effect called a moir' pattern)

- clothes and shoes that display brand names or commercial logos

- outfits in the latest style (fads will quickly date your video)

- deeply saturated colors, especially red (video doesn't handle them well and they tend to bleed when duplicated)

- bright white or extremely dark colors.

This last point deserves special attention. While it's true that video cameras are able to deal with sharp contrasts in tone better than formerly, it's still challenging to light someone wearing bright white or very dark clothes. White, for instance, picks up all the light, and to compensate, faces tend to be underexposed.

Joan Owens recounts an incident illustrating the problem with white. She was writing a documentary set in an exotic foreign locale, and the cameraman shot a great scene of the American ambassador riding a motorcycle through the city streets wearing a white tee-shirt—"a wonderful Marlon Brando image." But when the footage came back, everything was too dark, virtually unusable, to compensate for the white shirt.

Extremely dark colors are equally difficult, and sometimes create bizarre effects. Los Angeles producer-director Bob Silburg, who's done hundreds of PSAs (Public Service Announcements) and short videos, ran into this problem with a PSA featuring Jack Lemmon. The subject matter was quite serious, so he'd asked his star to wear a dignified navy blue blazer. Unfortunately, the office they were shooting in had dark walls, and as a result, Jack Lemmon "…looked like a floating head without a body." Luckily, Bob was able to solve the problem by tweaking the backlighting.

For wardrobe colors, David Phyfer recommends pastels and pale shades—light blue shirts and gray jackets, for instance. "Avoid sharp contrasts between dark and light," he advises, "and pull your colors together as much as possible."

When it comes to fabrics, natural materials like wool and cotton shoot much better than synthetics. Susan Stroh, for one, pays close attention to fabrics and textures, believing they help convey the message of the video—tweed and corduroy for an earthy look, for example, and damask for a luxurious look. She feels simple clothes work best for women, and are the least distracting. She prepares a detailed wardrobe checklist for her talent, and instructs them to bring duplicates, or near duplicates, of shirts and blouses, in case of spills or stains.

For most productions, it's a good idea to have talent bring three completely different outfits, including shoes and accessories, to provide ample choices. Men should bring a selection of ties, and women might be asked to bring some scarves.

On the Set

Most women in your cast will probably apply their own makeup and do their own hair. They should be encouraged to strive for a natural look, which works best for a video camera, unlike heavily exaggerated makeup, which works better for the stage. A good foundation is important, because it covers blemishes and evens out color. But if a woman is inexperienced in applying it, watch out for makeup lines around the eyes and jawline, where the foundation leaves off and the skin begins. You might also need to add some blush to emphasize her cheek bones or chin, or eyeliner to make her eyes look larger.

Though men need makeup, too, some are uncomfortable with the idea and even professional actors rarely apply their own. Greg Braun, who shoots many top executives, is careful to make sure none of their subordinates are nearby while he's doing their makeup—the last thing they want is an audience. And he jokes a little to put them at ease. "This is what made Charles Bronson so handsome," he might say as he dabs on the foundation. He works fast, completing the job in two to three minutes. Bald heads—"chrome domes"—are a common challenge. He uses a fat makeup brush and loose powder to remove the shine. Greg carries three different shades of powder and three shades of foundation to cover the range in skin tones.

Once your talent is made up, dressed and ready to go, don't forget to check them out in a color monitor before you shoot. You're sure to catch things you hadn't noticed with your naked eye—smudged mascara, a crooked collar, or a moir' effect on a tie. But after you've made the necessary adjustments, don't think your makeup and wardrobe duties are over. As you shoot, be alert for wrinkled shirts, bunched up jackets and faded lipstick. Fly-away hair and glint from buttons and eyeglasses are extremely common problems. And then, always, there is facial shine—oil and sweat brought on by the heat and tension. But before you add more makeup, blot off the moisture and oil with a tissue. Otherwise, you might get caking and streaks.

For fly-away hair, experts recommend spraying your hands with hair spray and lightly patting the hair, rather than spraying the hair directly, which can result in an unnatural "crispy" look. Shiny buttons and jewelry can be dealt with easily with dulling spray, although be cautious with costume jewelry, which could be damaged by. Eyeglasses are a tougher problem. Dulling spray could ruin them, and there aren't any other good substitutes. You might have to take care of the glint on glasses by lighting adjustments or re-positioning the talent.

Finally, pay close attention to continuity, making sure wardrobe and makeup and consistent from scene to scene. Carelessness here can give your video a sloppy look. If possible, have an assistant keep notes as you shoot. Is there always a hanky in that pocket? How is the scarf draped? Is there a lock of hair tucked behind the right ear?

Clearly, there's a great deal to consider in terms of makeup and wardrobe, and some of it is quite minute. But each detail contributes to the overall quality of your production. Yes, your mother may have tried to convince you that beauty is only skin deep. But when you're making videos, the visual appearance of your performers is hardly a superficial matter.

43
Time-Lapse Videography

Tim Cowan

If you've ever watched a scene on television or in the movies where clouds race overhead at a supernaturally fast rate, or where a flower appears to blossom in seconds, then you've witnessed a cinematic technique known as *time-lapse*. Often used to compress the apparent passage of time on film or video, time lapse consists of recording a few frames of film or tape, pausing for a certain amount of time, then recording a few more frames, and so on. When the sequence is played back, it appears that the action recorded is happening much faster than it does in real life.

In many ways, time lapse is similar to animation, using the technique of taking a succession of very brief shots to create the illusion of a steadily moving sequence. However, instead of fooling your mind's eye into thinking that a collection of still images are moving, time lapse compresses a lengthy event into a short span of time.

If you've ever wondered how you can perform this feat with your camcorder, wonder no more; this chapter will explain the process in detail, from setting up the shot to using the final footage in your existing video productions.

Before You Begin

There are several ways to achieve a time lapse effect with video, depending on how smooth you'd like the final product to be, what equipment you have and how much time and effort you're willing to put into it. However you choose to do it, there are a couple of constants you should be aware of.

For smooth recording, be sure your camcorder doesn't move at all during the sequence you're shooting. Otherwise, your footage will come out looking jumbled and unwatchable. This is best done by mounting your camcorder securely on your tripod and tightening the pan and tilt screws to make sure the camcorder doesn't move (known as a "locked down" tripod).

It's a good idea to switch the microphone off while recording a time lapse or animation sequence. If you don't, you'll end up with a quick snatch of many random noises on your soundtrack. Disabling the mike can be done fairly simply if your camcorder has an external microphone jack; simply stick an adapter that's not connected to anything into the socket and your camcorder mike will automatically switch itself off.

It's probably wise to switch over to manual focus while shooting a time-lapse or animation sequence. If you don't, your camcorder's autofocus will "hunt" for what it thinks to be the prominent feature in the shot to focus in on. If anything within range of the auto focus momentarily becomes more prominent than what you intended to shoot (i.e., a bird flying past while you're shooting the clouds), it could spoil the entire sequence.

If your camcorder can manually override its automatic light meter, you'll probably want to switch over to that as well. First make sure the manual level it's set on leaves enough light for your shot but not so much that it violently overexposes. It's also a good idea to make sure, before you even start shooting; that the light you're shooting with highlights what you're recording. After all, you wouldn't want your time-lapse sequence of a flower growing to be shot in silhouette, would you?

Most importantly, keep a close watch on your camcorder. If you're shooting out on the street, there's always the risk your camcorder could be stolen or damaged by someone passing by. Even if you're in your own backyard, there's a chance your camcorder could get jostled by a child or pet, or simply pitch over lens-first due to uneven weight distribution.

Calculating Time Lapse

Figuring out the length of time needed for either a time-lapse or animation sequence is pretty simple, once you know what you and your equipment are capable of. Since NTSC video always plays at 30 frames per second (fps), a single time lapse/animation

shot of, say, 1/5th of a second will go for six frames. Five of those shots will equal thirty frames—one second of your completed video.

Let's say you want a 30-second time lapse sequence of clouds going by, and you've decided that one shot every half-minute will give you the desired effect. Assuming the five shots a second mentioned above, that means that 5 (shots per second) times .5 (minutes of real time) per shot times 30 (seconds of video time for the sequence being shot) equals 75 minutes of shooting time.

Being able to calculate the amount of shooting time needed has a number of uses. If you're shooting outdoors with battery power, for instance, it's vital to know just how much time you'll need to get the sequence you want, or if it's even possible given your batteries. Even if you don't need to calculate for battery time, it's useful to know just how long it will take in real time to get the sequence you want.

Shots Per Second

You may have noticed that I've gone to some trouble to distinguish between "frames per second" and "shots per second" when talking about time-lapse and animation videography. That's because, as I said above, NTSC video always plays at 30 frames per second, no matter what images you may have playing during that time. Ideally, the closer you can come to 30 shots per second the better, since your results will look a lot less choppy.

While a second doesn't seem like much time, it plays havoc with the smoothness of a time-lapse or animation effect. This is because both video and film rely on something called "persistence of vision" to convince you that a long string of still pictures is moving. Since your mind can't assimilate a series of fast-moving still images, it assimilates them instead as one continuous moving picture. The instant this collection of images slows down to the point where you can mentally register each single picture as such, the illusion's blown.

If you're using time lapse simply to show the passage of time (for instance, a shot of people setting up before a play or concert), then one shot per second will probably work perfectly fine. On the other hand, if you're hoping to do a sequence where a smooth flowing of the shots is essential (as in an animated sequence) then you're probably not going to be satisfied with anything less than 10 shots per second, and 15 or even 30 shots per second would be even better.

In-Camera Time Lapse

The easiest way to perform time lapse or animation is by using a camcorder with an interval timer function built in. Using these camcorders is very easy—you simply mount them on a locked down tripod, switch the interval timer function on and the camcorder does the rest. Depending on which model camcorder you have, interval timers can record as little as 1/10th of a second (3 frames) or as much as a full second of video each time.

If your camcorder doesn't have an interval timer feature, you can still do a reasonably effective in-camera time lapse or animation sequence—provided your camcorder has flying erase heads (most models manufactured during the last five years do) and you've got the patience for it. Set up your camcorder on a tripod, engage and then immediately disengage the record feature, wait for the amount of time you want between shots, and then repeat the process until you have the sequence length you want. To ensure that the camcorder doesn't shake when you hit record, you might want to use your camcorder's remote if it has one.

Depending on how well your camcorder responds to your pushing the record button twice in rapid succession, and how fast you are on the trigger, you could get individual shots of as little as 10 frames (3 shots per second). While not as

smooth as 30 or even 15 shots per second, it's still surprisingly effective.

One last technique that may or may not work for you is to utilize your camcorder's edit search feature if it has one. What you do is record a couple seconds of video, utilize edit search to get to the beginning few frames of the last shot, and then repeat until you've gotten what you want. Keep in mind, though, that this is an extremely labor-intensive process, and difficult to do if your camcorder's edit search function can't jog search.

Post-Production Time Lapse

If you want a bit more control over what your final product looks like, you might choose not to record time lapse in real time; instead, you can attempt it in post-production instead. The advantage to this is that you can experiment with the time between shots to find what works best far more easily than you can "out in the field." The disadvantage is that for a decent sequence, this requires a great deal of time and some fairly high-end editing equipment.

First, you'll need some footage that you can edit your time-lapse sequence from. Place your camcorder on a locked down tripod, just as you'd do if you were shooting an in-camera time-lapse sequence, and roll tape normally for as long as you've calculated you'll need for your sequence.

Remember the technique utilizing edit search on camcorders mentioned above? Well, it also works if you're using a VCR with edit search; jog shuttle and flying erase heads as a record deck. What you do is record a couple of seconds of video, engage the edit search, then utilize the jog wheel to creep back to a few frames right after the first frame of the last shot. It'll require a little practice to figure out just how far you'll need to advance the tape to leave just one frame, and a great deal of patience, but you can get 30 shots per second time lapse or animation this way.

If you're using an edit controller to run your playback and record decks, how close you can get your cuts to each other will vary depending on the quality of your setup. Controllers that utilize LANC or Panasonic 5-pin edit control protocols for playback control and infrared remote for recorder control probably won't be able to get much better than one or two shots per second. This is due to these edit controllers' inability to respond quickly enough for the extremely short cut-ins and cut-outs that time lapse and animation require.

Controllers that use LANC or Panasonic 5-pin protocols to control both player and recorder can get much closer—10 shots per second, if your playback and record decks are calibrated properly. By contrast, a professional editing setup utilizing time code and frame-accurate decks can give you true 30-shot per second accuracy—if you're willing to pay for them.

So What Are You Gonna Do With It?

Okay, I've told you a couple ways to do time-lapse or animation recording, and I've even covered why the more shots you record per second, the better it'll look. But what's it really good for?

I've already mentioned the most popular use of time lapse, compressing a lengthy event like clouds rolling by or people setting something up. So what else can you do with this technique?

Stop Motion Animation. This is the sort of animated sequence where an object that doesn't normally move, like clay or an action figure, appears to be in motion.

You've seen this a lot on television and in the movies, like those "California Raisins" commercials where clay models of raisins dance around and sing, or the original *King Kong*, where Kong was an articulated doll that appeared to be a fully moving giant gorilla.

To perform stop motion animation, you'll first need to create a space where you can set up your lights, camcorder,

tripod and whatever you're going to animate. The advantage to this is that, once you've gotten everything set up, you can easily control the lighting and background so that all you need to worry about is animating your object.

Once you've gotten your object where you want it to start, turn on your camcorder and take your first shot. Remember that, for the animation to be smooth, you'll probably want to get at least 10 shots per second, and 15 or 30 would be even better. Then move your object slightly and take the next shot, and so on until you finish your sequence.

Keep in mind that for animation to look convincing, the audience has to get the impression that they're seeing the process of motion. For instance, if you're animating an action figure throwing a punch, you can't simply have your first shot with the figure's fist up, and the next with the punch fully thrown—you have to have the fist moving forward with each shot so it looks like it's getting there. To help you get some idea of how things move, it might be a good idea to watch a video of something you'd like to animate one frame at a time so you can see how it looks in real life before you try animating it.

Pixillation. A sort of variant version of both time lapse and stop-motion animation, pixillation is the process whereby a person seems to move in unusual ways. The music video *Sledgehammer* utilized pixillation so that Peter Gabriel appeared to slide around the room and even at one point seemed to be hovering above the ground.

To accomplish this, have your performer stand in one position while you take your first shot, then move forward slightly and stand still again while you take your next shot. If you continue this long enough, the person will appear to move across the room without walking. Make sure that whatever movements your performer makes from shot to shot aren't too radically different from each other, or the sequence won't look like a smooth movement.

Computerized Time Lapse

Performing time lapse or animation sequences utilizing a nonlinear editing system is surprisingly simple. Unlike videotape, digitized video can easily record one frame at a time. You simply lift the frame off your digitized video file, drop it onto the editing software's timeline, and look for the next frame you'd like to use. Once you're done, you save the results, turn your VCR on, and "print" your edited file to videotape.

Amazing as this nonlinear capability is, I think I'd better interject a few words of caution. First, the output quality of some older non-linear boards has often been described as "roughly VHS quality," which means that it isn't quite as good as VHS—you may notice some *artifacting*, which is what they call it when things that should be round seem to have little squares in them. Second, video files take up a lot of hard disk space—about 10–15 megabytes per minute of highly compressed video. Third, if you've got a lot of other boards or peripherals on your computer, there's a chance your computer will freeze up on you from time to time.

Of course, if you're one of the lucky ones with a miniDV camcorder, and a non-linear editor on your FireWire-equipped computer, you can create very high-quality time-lapse video.

You Could Always Cheat...

You might want to consider shooting a time lapse or animation sequence on an old Super-8 movie camera. Most Super-8 movie cameras have a single-frame option built in, which will guarantee a much smoother effect than you'd probably get with a camcorder or lower-end editing equipment. Some, like Minolta's better Super-8 cameras, even have an automatic interval timer.

To utilize a Super-8 movie camera for time-lapse photography, you once again set up your camera on a locked-down tripod, just like you would if you were using your camcorder. Take one frame using the single-frame option, wait for a specified period of time, and take another frame, continuing until you have enough footage for your needs. If your movie camera has the option of manual override of the automatic light meter, it's probably a good idea to utilize that so that your frames don't become darker or lighter abruptly. It's also a good idea to use Kodachrome 40 film instead of Ektachrome G, since the former is less grainy.

While it's harder than it used to be to process Super-8 movie film, Kodak can still do it. Your local camera store should have mailers for sale that cover the cost of processing and return postage in the purchase price, or check out Kodak's Web site. You simply stick the appropriate postage on the mailer, drop it in the mail, and wait for about two weeks. After you get the film back, you can either transfer it to video yourself if you still have your Super-8 movie projector and one of those film-to-tape transfer units, or you can have the job done professionally at your local camera or video store.

While this method requires both more money and a few more steps than any of the direct-to-video methods recommended in this article, it's worth considering if the effect is important to you; say, for a title sequence you intend to use more than once. It's obviously not to be used casually; still, you'll probably get smoother results this way.

All It Takes is Time

Once you've gotten the hang of time lapse and animation, you'll start to come up with a number of ideas on your own. The great thing about these techniques is that they don't require a lot of expensive equipment that you wouldn't use for anything else—even high-end editing equipment, should you choose the post-production option, will be useful for all your videos. All time lapse or animation takes, really, is time—and the results will certainly be worth it.

44

Move Over, MTV:
A Guide to Making
Music Videos

Norm Medoff

See video clips at www.videomaker.com/handbook.

On August 1, 1981, Music Television went on the air and changed the world of video forever. Now, years later, MTV—as Music Television is better known—has spawned several new music channels, and the making of music video has become an art form all its own.

On MTV networks, music videos are expensive Hollywood-style productions shot with multiple 35 mm film cameras and featuring snazzy special effects, big name bands and exotic locations. But you, too, can produce great music videos—right in your own hometown.

All you need is a little money and a lot of creativity.

Keeping Costs Down

If you find it hard to believe that you can make a quality music video on a small budget, consider the following points.

- Since you shoot music videos "film style," you can do it with only one camcorder. You just shoot many takes, which will provide different angles of the same action—as opposed to multi-camera shooting, which records several angles of the same action during one take.

- Big-budget music videos often use fancy—read costly—transitions requiring digital video effects generators and expensive editors. But you don't have to use such transitions; you can produce an excellent music video using cuts to connect shots.

- You don't have to pay a band to perform in your music video. No matter where you live, you should be able to find a local band interested in promotion. A music video gives a band valuable experience, both in making music videos and exposure to wider audiences. Your music video could also help the band of your choice secure concert dates or even a record contract.

- Shooting live performances is not as difficult or expensive as you might think.

Professionals employ a sophisticated and expensive camera dolly on a special track that allows the camera to move around performers; you can make do with an old wheelchair or shopping cart.

The good news is all you really need to make music video is a camcorder and the ability to perform insert edits. An insert edit allows you to add video to a sound track already on the tape. More on this later.

Getting Started

Before you do anything, determine how you'll exhibit your music video.

If you make it for private use only, you can select any music you want—no worrying about copyright and clearance. But if you plan to air your video on local cable or broadcast television, or even enter it in a contest, copyright becomes an issue. If you don't own the copyright on the music you use, you must obtain clearance.

This can be both time consuming and expensive. First, you have to contact the American Society of Composers, Authors and Publishers (ASCAP); the people there will direct you to the Harry Fox Agency in New York (212-370-5330). This agency will try to arrange clearance for you to use a particular song.

You can avoid this hassle altogether by using your own music or finding local talent to perform their own music. If you don't know any musicians, check out the local bars, which often feature up-and-coming bands and/or solo performers. These musicians can give you permission to use their music for your video.

Try to obtain recordings of potential performers. In most cities, you can buy CDs or cassette tapes featuring a sampling of local performers. Such recordings can help you choose both a group and a song for your music video.

HINT: when listening to the music, focus on the visual imagery that pops into your mind. Often the music you like does not conjure up any useful images. Don't be surprised if the song that inspires the best visual imagery is not the one you like most.

Pre-Production

Once you've selected your music and performers, you can begin the bulk of your work, pre-production. In this phase of the operation, you will do the following: devise a creative approach; write a treatment; make a storyboard; create a beat sheet; select a crew and record the song for lip sync purposes.

The creative approach. This is the fun part, where you generate the images for your video. There are three stylistic ways to proceed: illustrative, interpretive and performance. Illustrative video is the narrative approach that illustrates the story the song tells. Interpretive video uses the images you deem appropriate for the music, whether they relate to the lyrics or not. Performance video is just what the name implies—the musicians performing the song.

Many music videos combine all three styles of shots: illustrative, interpretive and performance. Resist the temptation to try one method and exclude the others. An all-performance video may rely too heavily on the musician's ability to be entertaining. An all-interpretive video may confuse viewers. And an all-illustrative video may tax both the resources of your performers—can they really act out the story?—and your budget.

Some music dictates the style. For example, instrumentals tell no specific story, so the most effective approach is often an interpretive one where the images create a mood or evoke an emotional response. Country songs often tell a straightforward story, facilitating an illustrative approach. Rock music gives you the most options; many rock videos are all attitude—with little or no regard for viewer orientation.

The treatment. Now that you've developed a creative approach, take the time to write a treatment or overview of your video. Simply describe in a few paragraphs what will happen in the video: the story, the characters, the mood. A treatment provides a convenient way of explaining the video to your performers and crew.

The storyboard. This step is crucial. The storyboard provides a visual record of the individual shots that will make up your video. Draw a series of rough sketches depicting the people, places and objects needed for these key shots. Put them in the order you intend to shoot them. Or use a Polaroid camera to snap the subjects and objects in the desired locations.

The beat sheet. Next, combine your storyboard with a beat sheet describing the music on paper. Match shots to appropriate sections of the music. Knowing what visuals you want and when you want them in your music video is the key to your pre-production planning. It's also the way the video professionals stay on target.

The crew. You may want to do all the work yourself. That's a lot of juggling: arranging lighting and special effects, directing talent and playing an audio version of the song while the performers lip sync. But you will be able to do a better job if you plan on a crew of at least two other people, one to act as a grip and audio assistant and one to shoot while you direct. If you don't know anybody, ask the band members if you can borrow their assistants or (known as *roadies*).

The recording. At this point, you should prepare a recording of the song you'll use as the sound track for your video. Not just any recording will do; you'll need an error-free version of the song on a safe and dependable recording medium. A CD is probably best, especially if you can take a CD boom box with you on location.

The next best sound source: a hi-fi version of the song—VHS hi-fi or Hi8 will do. This method creates some playback problems; you'll need an appropriate video playback machine and sound system.

A reasonable compromise: a good copy of the song on audio cassette to play while on location through a good quality boom box or a portable sound system.

Quality is critical, because the performers must lip sync to this version of the song.

Be wary of cheap audio cassette players suffering from speed variations or muffled sound. If you use battery power, keep plenty of fresh batteries on hand.

Slow audio recordings can adversely affect the band's performance—not to mention cause horrendous editing problems later on.

Shoot It Right

Now it's time to shoot the raw footage for your music video. There are two ways to accomplish this task.

The In-Camera Shoot

If your camcorder has a flying erase head, you can insert the visuals onto a videotape that already has a copy of the song.

To get the song on the videotape, you can record the song at a live performance using a microphone mixer.

Or, record the audio using line output from a CD or audio cassette player into the line input of your camcorder or VCR. At the time of this recording, you will also record video, so try capping the camcorder and letting the picture appear black. This *blackbursting* of the tape records the video control track you'll use to perform the insert edits later on.

The next step: record video over the audio track with a video insert. You can record the entire music video shot by shot. This "editing in the camera" technique gets the job done without extra equipment or editing systems.

WARNING: this technique is not as simple as it seems; only use it if you can't edit. It may not work with every camcorder. If your unit doesn't give the performers a few seconds of audible preroll at the beginning of a video insert, they won't be in sync with the music when the recording starts.

If your camcorder does not give an audible preroll, try to find a VCR that does. Plug your camcorder's video output into the VCR and do the inserts there.

If that doesn't work, you can always insert interpretive video segments over those out-of-sync parts at a later time.

Editing in the camera will also mean you continually record onto one tape: your master. One serious mistake—like rewinding too far before you reshoot a given scene—and you have to start all over.

Shooting For The Edit

If you have access to any kind of editing system, you should "shoot for the edit"— that is, plan your shots to provide plenty of material for the editing process.

Shoot scenes either in sequence or out of sequence, depending upon logistics. One easy way to organize your shoot: have the band perform the whole song in different locations or with different backgrounds and costumes. Tape three or four different versions of the song, and then mix and match shots from different versions. Shoot several takes of the lead singer singing the particularly dramatic parts of the lyric; be sure to get some extreme close-ups or unusual camera angles of the entire band. Keep close-up shots of the singers short; the lip sync may not be exact.

You can minimize time and travel for the band by cutting performance shots with location shots that help to emphasize the mood of the music, as in Figure 44.1.

Experiment. Rent a fog machine to create a dream-like setting. (Ask your local theatrical or video production house where you can rent one.) Try fog filters for your camera lens. Place your lights in unusual places, like lighting from the side or below the performers rather than from

above. Use colored gels over your lights or very narrow beam lights.

The shooting style of many music videos today incorporates vigorous camera movement and canted camera angles you may want to try yourself. Also common are combination shots taped while the camera is moving, i.e., zooming while dollying.

The usual rule of holding shots long enough for the audience to grasp what's going on also may not apply. Quick cuts— including cuts in the middle of pans, tilts and zooms—abound in music video. Most shots last two or three seconds.

Tracking your footage is the key to success when shooting for the edit. Keep a video footage log. By the end of the shoot, you should be able to consult your footage log to determine whether you've got the shots you need.

Don't leave the set/location until you're satisfied that you've shot it all. Check over your storyboard. Did you get every shot listed there? Review the key shots. Shoot them again if you're not satisfied.

Time to Edit

Once you have all the shots that you need, it's time to edit. If you have access to your own editor or one owned by a friend, go in with your storyboard, beat sheet, shot log and tapes and edit at your leisure.

If you plan to rent an editor or edit suite, the procedure is quite different. Here time is money, so plan all of your edits on paper before you enter the edit suite. Note: with the advance of nonlinear editing, you'll be able to experiment with more sophisticated editing techniques without paying an arm and a leg.

If you prepared a proper storyboard and beat sheet, you can review all of your raw footage, log it with your comments and your desired edit in and edit out points.

List the shots you want, the order you want them in and their exact location relative to the music. Such organization

Figure 44.1 Add cutaways to shots that match the feel of the song for a true music video look.

is particularly important for editing illustrative videos. Interpretive videos cut you much more slack; their looser flow allows you to put together seemingly unrelated shots without destroying the overall effect.

Be prepared to make 60 to 100 edits (or more!) for a four-minute rock or country video. Let the rhythm of the song suggest the pacing of your shot changes; shots and edits should match the tempo of the song. Try changing some shots on the beat of the music. You wouldn't want to do this on every beat, but it can prove effective, especially when it marks a noticeable change in tempo.

If your edit system includes a special effects generator or can perform some digital effects, experiment with transitions. Try some fancy wipes or digital effects like page peel or tumble.

Once your video is ready, make at least one copy of your edited master for viewing purposes. Keep the master in a safe place.

Break the Rules

Making music video is an art, not a science. Remember the conventions, but don't let them get in your way.

Go ahead and break framing, composition, exposure and transition rules—if it helps communicate your vision.

And by all means—have fun!

45
Practical Special Effects: A Baker's Ten to Improve Your Video Visions

Bernard Wilkie

See video clips at www.videomaker.com/handbook

Most videographers fall into one of two groups. First, the snapshotters—people who record scenes until their tapes are full, then view the disconnected events using the search button. Second, videographers and pros, who edit their tapes and employ all the techniques and processes necessary to obtain professional results.

It's not that people in the first group are unimaginative. They may not want to assemble their pictures or lay down soundtracks, but often they do wish to add variety to their videography. Thus this chapter can serve snapshotters as well as the more advanced. This list of special effects may also remind the experts that simple solutions can be the best.

Deep Water

Children mucking about in the pool occupy many tapes. However, all the action commonly occurs above water.

More exciting footage is possible with an underwater periscope, enabling videography beneath the surface. Camcorders become underwater cameras without the need for expensive blimps or aqualung equipment.

The *periscope* is simply a rectangular box with a sheet of glass cemented into the bottom of one side. It contains two mirrors, one at the bottom, one at the top. Surface-coated mirrors provide better pictures, but even ordinary mirrors will produce good results.

Set up the periscope poolside and record events above or below water while holding the camera and peering through the viewfinder in the usual manner. Weight the device to overcome its natural buoyancy. Clamp it to something solid, like the pool steps. Those going to sea can mount the periscope on a boat or sink it into the water for shots of marine life.

Another trick to improve waterside close-ups involves the simple trick of placing a shallow tray filled with water and broken pieces of mirror below the picture. Ensure that the sun's reflections fall on or around your subjects. Then tickle the surface of the water with your fingers. Voila! The ripple effect says your subjects are waterside though they may really be nowhere near water at all.

Sound Skills

Sound is perhaps the greatest special effect of all.

The videographer seeking to create the atmosphere of a shopping mall need only shoot characters looking into a store window. Sound effects added later will provide the essential ingredients—children calling, skateboards whirring, the voices of people walking by, a distant police siren.

For the best location atmosphere, shoot scenes where you can capture the best and most interesting off-camera sounds. When on vacation, don't always aim for peace and quiet. If you want footage of your family on a foreign railway station platform, wait for the moment the train pulls out.

When creating a drama, always think sound. Sound can often say more than pictures. Imagine a scene with two people watching TV. Suddenly they react to the sound of squealing tires on the road outside. The sound of the crash that follows has them leaping towards the window. The skillful use of sound effects has fooled viewers into believing something horrific really did occur.

Bet you didn't know you can create a simulated echo using a length of garden hose and a funnel. Just stick the funnel in one end of the hose. Place both ends close to the microphone of a cassette recorder. Then speak. The effect is certainly weird.

Different lengths of hose produce different delay times. This contraption is useful for adding echo or creating monstrous outer space voices.

An even better echo results from linking funnel, hose and mike to one input channel of a stereo recorder while using the other channel and a second mike straight.

Mirror Dimension

Video pictures are two-dimensional, with height and width but no depth. This fact is used repeatedly to fool viewers.

The scene outside a window may be only a painted backcloth, but who can tell? A photograph of an object can look the same as the real object. Use photos when you can't acquire the real thing—a priceless museum exhibit, for example. Photographs, or even photocopies, can simulate multiple items such as meter dials or control panels.

The fifty-fifty semi-coated mirror, or beam-splitter, is a most useful piece of videography equipment. Used to superimpose one picture over another, it works because half the light passes through the glass while the other half reflects back from the surface.

Often employed to produce ghostly apparitions, it also has other, less spectral, uses. For instance, superimposing captions over pictures. With the mirror placed at a forty-five degree angle to the lens, illuminate the words as they appear. This technique can create opening titles, or overlay words or arrows on a demonstration video.

Superimpose graphics with a box housing the mirror and shielding it from stray light. Stand the rig in front of the camera. Light the caption from front or back. If lit from the front, place the lamps to either side, To remain in focus, the superimposed material must lie approximately the same distance from the camera as the main subject.

Used with a spotlight, plain mirrors stuck to a revolving drum provide a strobe effect. Two stuck back to back simulate the flashing lights of emergency vehicles.

Gun Fun

It's not unusual to see a TV actor, chest riddled with bullets, stagger and fall to the ground. If he seems to move awkwardly it is probably due less to his supposed wounds than to the fact he's trying not to trip over the operating wires running up his trouser leg.

This effect, using small explosive squibs secreted under clothing, is too complex and dangerous to discuss here. But there do exist safe alternatives, which, if used imaginatively, can appear as convincing as those in the movies.

You can use a bicycle pump for bullets in the chest. Record as a separate closeup, for it works only with a short tube close to the pump.

Suck some fake blood into the tube and seal the end with a small piece of tightly stretched party balloon. Hold the balloon in position with several turns of a rubber band. Placed under thin cloth, the pump will rupture the diaphragm, flipping the cloth realistically and producing a spatter of gore.

For continuity, shoot the garment on a stuffed sack. Then remove and place on the actor. A limp balloon containing blood and worn under a garment will produce a spreading stain when punctured by a spike attached to a ring worn by an actor. The flow will increase by keeping the hand in place and pressing hard.

A rat-trap set up behind scenery can punch out a piece of wall or knock a hole in a door. The hole must be pre-made, filled with appropriate material to disguise its true nature. Insert a captive peg from behind. When struck by the trap the peg ejects the filling, leaving a hole.

Rat-traps can also simulate a bullet hitting a mirror. Protect the front with a sheet of rigid plastic and cover the back with self-adhesive vinyl. This is essential to produce a really good shattering effect; without it the glass just breaks.

A bicycle pump with some talcum powder in the barrel will produce a convincing spurt of dust from rocks or concrete. Use energetically and apply a good ricochet effect on the soundtrack.

No bullet effect will impress without realistic sound. Conversely, a poor effect can often pass with a professional soundtrack liberally sprinkled with gunshots.

Smoke and Flames

This can be a touchy area; as always, Videomaker does not recommend you endeavor to create sequences involving fire, smoke or explosions without assistance from experts.

Movie and TV producers often rent an empty house or store when they need to create an outdoor fire sequence. To record in a studio is too impractical and too expensive.

However, property is property, so these big fire scenes are rigidly controlled to ensure they don't get out of hand.

In many cases fire can be simulated without actual flames. At night, backlit smoke rising from behind a building suggests it's on fire. Rooms powerfully lit, with smoke pouring from the windows, imply a house afire. Stretch a clear plastic sheet behind the window and pump smoke up underneath it. This ensures maximum effect at the window while preventing too much smoke from filling the room.

But the fact there's no flame doesn't guarantee total safety. Always ensure crew and artists have a clear exit to the outside. No one should have to stumble around in thick smoke and darkness.

Smoke, of course, is essential for all fire sequences. Much depends on the sort of smoke used. In moviemaking there are two types: pyrotechnic, and machine-made. Of the two, only the smoke machine is controllable. Pyrotechnics, once lit, will burn to a finish.

You can rent smoke machines; those who don't know where to look should contact a local theater or TV studio.

Smoke from reputable machines should cause no breathing problems, even when discharged indoors. Pyrotechnic smoke is appropriate only for exterior work or in places where it won't be inhaled.

Movie studios produce controlled flames by igniting propane. The gear usually consists of a fireproof and crushproof hose with a shut-off valve and pressure reducer. At the business end is a length of copper tube terminating in a sort of flattened funnel.

You can smatter small areas of flame around a set by using absorbent material treated with a dash of kerosene, burned on metal sheets or fireproof board. With the appropriate amount of smoke this will simulate the aftermath of an explosion.

House Mess

Many videographers must shoot in their own homes, which can cause problems when trying to capture scenes of dirt and degradation. Fortunately, it's usually possible to obtain materials easily cleaned up at the end of the day.

Freely spread sawdust, dry peat, coconut fiber, Fullers Earth, rubber dust and torn-up paper; all will disappear beneath broom or vacuum at the end of the shoot.

It's not easy creating convincing scenes of mess and filth. The camera has a habit of prettifying even the nastiest setups. It's therefore often necessary to exaggerate the dirty scenes.

For oil, food or paint spills, pour liquid latex onto a sheet of glass or metal. When set, spray paint the mess with any color. Peel off to provide a movable puddle; place where required.

Dead and dried vegetation often complement this sort of scene. Torn plastic sheeting sprayed nasty colors and wrapped around pipes, faucets and radiators also looks good.

To make metal appear rusty, wipe with a smidgen of petroleum jelly. Then blow cocoa atop the grease.

Cobwebs are great for dirty scenes, produced by spinning liquid latex in a special device called a cobweb gun. These guns are for rent, the fluid available from TV and theatrical supply houses. Spin webs over a collection of objects bunched close together for the best effect. Cobwebs won't straddle open spaces; string thin cotton across voids. Blow talcum powder onto cobwebs to make them visible. Don't apply to absorbent surfaces.

Caption Making

Electronic devices to produce lettering for videos are now available, either as separate equipment or as integral camera circuitry. Stick-on or rubdown letters come cheap and offer a variety of typefaces. Even magazines and newspapers will produce usable opening titles.

No one wants to engage in the laborious chore of cutting round letters with a stencil knife. But if you cut the letters or words as rectangles from white paper you can stick them to a white backing, the joins between painted over with white artist's paint or typing correction fluid. Photocopied, the joins disappear.

You can apply rubdown lettering or reusable vinyl stick-ons to a sheet of glass and place over various fancy papers or illustrations. You can also place the glass in front of three-dimensional objects like flowers or coins. Tabletop captions are simple to produce and offer more variety than stereotypical electronic images.

A tracing paper screen and a slide projector are also useful for graphic backgrounds. You need not project slides onto a flat screen; you can project them onto textured surfaces like rumpled cloth, rough plaster or piles of snow.

Interesting animations can result by fixing the lighting, the camera and the lettering to a common mount in which loose objects such as marbles, sea shells, sand, sugar or liquids are free to move around. When you tilt the rig, the camera perceives no movement of the backing; meanwhile, the loose objects react strangely, defying gravity and moving in a random and seemingly unpremeditated fashion.

President Matte

Miniatures are models placed in front of a set to extend the scenery or provide an effect unobtainable by other means. Mattes perform a similar task, but are simply flat paintings on glass.

This is an over-simplification, because there also exist creatures like "hanging miniatures" and "traveling mattes." But these characters would take us into deep technical water, and we're interested here only in the simple stuff.

Say the action occurs in the oval office of the White House. They won't let you tape there, and a re-creation would eat up your entire budget. So go for the special effect.

You may have to hire a table and some chairs—pretty safe stuff, because who, after all, recalls exact details of the White House?

Sensibly, you'll video your fake president against an easily-obtainable neutral wall. But at some point you'll have to show the room, or at least a convincing recreation.

One option is a *matte*. If you can procure a talented artist, take a large pane of glass, mount it on legs and position it between Mr. P and the camera. With constant reference through the camera viewfinder the artist can paint the oval office, leaving a hole in the middle to perceive Mr. P, his desk and the back wall.

Suppose you don't have such an artist. So get a photo of the scene, blow it up, cut out an area where Mr. P will sit, and, if your photo is black-and-white, add some color washes. There. The White House.

Miniature Quixote

Let's try a second example: the story of Don Quixote, the man who tried to kill windmills.

Unable to take your unit to Spain, you'll use plaster-of-paris, sawdust, sand, cardboard and other materials to construct a *baseboard model* of a sandy plain. On the horizon position a model windmill with motor-driven sails. Finally, mount the model on a rig supported from one side only. Put in a sloping floor in the studio and cover it with sawdust and sand. At the back paint a ground row to provide the horizon.

Finish up with three components: the sky backing, the main scene on the floor and, sticking in from one side with its supporting leg out of vision, a model of a sandy plain and the windmill. Make sure everything lines up and adjust the lighting to insure a complete blend.

When using a miniature, join the model to the set along natural boundaries—hedges, woods, roads—where the foreground, which we see as the background, will blend unnoticed.

Don Quixote will stand on the opposite side of the set from the windmill, pointing towards the background and yelling, "Kill! Kill!" He'll look at the distant windmill, which in fact sits right in front of him. Keep him stationary: if he strolls across the set he'll pass behind the model and expose the trick.

If you'd like to try a matte shot, paint on a board a simple sky and set it up where it will cover a busy background. Make sure the bottom of the board lines up with the top of a wall or some similar feature. Shoot it. The effect can be quite extraordinary.

Cardtoon Creations

Children exposed to television since birth accept everything on the screen without question, and quite often without interest. So why not give them the chance to participate as creative artists?

A cardtoon is the electronic counterpart of the puppet theater, where little figures move around on sticks. Recording the cardtoon technique on video gives youngsters the opportunity to design their own characters and write their own scripts. After the show they can sit back and view the results.

Unfortunately, video cameras don't work in the same way as the movie cameras that film Disney cartoons, so the action and movement must take place in real time. This is accomplished by cutting characters from stiff card and articulating them with tiny rivets and paper hinges.

Animation comes from fixing the various parts to hidden sticks or incorporating cardboard levers hidden behind parts of the background.

A simple example involves a picture of the sea, drawn as repeating lines of stylized ripples. Suddenly, up leaps a fish, attached to a cardboard lever and rotated between two layers of the wave pattern.

Still at sea, imagine a pirate ship sailing across, pushed or pulled from one side. Or a diver surfacing from beneath the waves.

All videography is a combination of long shots and close-ups, so we'll have to see the faces of the pirates onboard ship. You can make them speak using a simple up-and-down movement of the jaw. It's the eyes moving that most give the characters expression.

A few versions of the same heads—left and right profile, large and small—will result in a really satisfying cardtoon.

You can usually manipulate the parts by hand, though certain creatures may have to move faster than your digits can. In these cases you can employ thin dressmaking elastic as pulling springs.

Trick of the Light

Light, like sound, is too often taken for granted. It can suggest things which aren't really there; backlit smoke that looks like fire is but one example.

Take a look at movie scenes set in the countryside. The trees and the dappled sunlight through the leaves say we're in a wood, but the effect is truly produced by shining a lamp through holes cut in thin plywood sheets.

Look at the two people in the front seat of a studio automobile. We know the vehicle is moving because the background is receding—achieved via chromakey—but the scene would look dead if it weren't for the fact that shadows continually sweep across the faces of the actors. A spotlight, some plywood, flags on broom handles and some keen staff to wave them about and we achieve the effect of an auto in motion.

For night shots sweep a hand-held lamp from front to rear.

The prison scene looks a lot more sinister if a spotlight, trained on the floor, shines through a cutout silhouette of iron bars.

Many of these effects cause the autofocus to hunt. Switch to manual whenever this occurs.

Give Them a Try

Does any of this sound like fun? It is. Just remember, you'll never know unless you get out your camcorder and do it yourself. All it takes is a little imagination.

PART IV

Post-Production Techniques

How to edit all that footage you've got "in the can" with precision and style.

46
Getting Started in Computer Video Editing

Jim Stinson

The best video editing programs bend over backward to help you learn them. You get paper manuals, digital references, CD-ROM tutorials, training videos, sample projects, and hot links to Web-based assistance. One or two fuddy-duddy companies even offer phone numbers answered by humans. Sooner or later, these helpers can teach you everything you need to know about operating their editing software. But not one of them teaches you how to make a video.

All those dandy training aids are like the book packed with your Acme Giant Carpentry Kit, which explains how to use every tool in your shiny new chest, but doesn't teach you to build so much as a breadboard, let alone a lawn chair or a house. The sad result is that too many folks who made boring incoherent video with their camcorders and VCRs now use editing software to keep right on making boring, incoherent programs. The only difference being that these are now *digital* boring, incoherent programs.

The cure? For starters, our Web site (www.videomaker.com) offers dozens of articles on video production techniques, with a lot of emphasis on editing, including [title] on basic techniques. To put these techniques into context, it helps to understand the basic principles that underlie them. With these fundamental principles and the editing techniques they support, you can tap the power of your computer-based editing system to make programs a pro would be proud of.

Cutting to the chase, here are those basic editing principles:

1. *Structure*. Without a coherent organization, a video is not a program but only a jumble of shots.

2. *Simplicity*. The better the content, the simpler its presentation tends to be and vice-versa.

3. *Brevity*. No matter how fine your program may be, no one else is as fascinated with it as you are.

4. *Pace*. Viewers can digest an image faster than you think. Throw them new ones frequently.

5. *Variety*. Even at a dizzy pace, too much of the same thing is deadly; and "too much" happens a lot sooner than you might expect.

With our list of principles in front of us, let's look a bit closer at each one in turn.

Structure

Your show is a failure if viewers respond, "And your point is ...?" Every video needs some form of organization to give it purpose and direction. Programs like training videos have their subjects, and often their structures, built right in; but what can you do to organize *Susie's 16th Birthday* or *Thanksgiving at Grandma's?*

One approach is to give the program a working title that announces a theme, like *The Great Driver's License Birthday* or *Grandma's Goes Vegetarian*. All of a sudden you have built in organizers to guide your shooting and editing.

Even if you don't think up a theme before you shoot, you can often find one when you edit. Were your vacation skies gloomy and gray? Call your video *A Good Trip in Bad Weather* and start each sequence with a visual reference to leaden skies or pouring rain. The repeated motif will help tie your show together (see Figure 46.1).

Editing a similar travel project, I noticed that, quite by chance, I kept appearing in different *chapeaux*: an Outback stockman's hat, a trucker's cap, a floppy fishing sun model, etc, etc. In the finished show, I made a freeze frame of the first appearance of each new headgear with a supered title like, *Hat Quest Continues* or *Is This Finally the One?* This corny running gag provided all the structure my modest family video required.

Simplicity

Digital newbies are subject to two fatal temptations. First, because they suddenly

Figure 46.1 *Structure—Make sure your videos have a clear purpose and direction.*

have the technical capacity to make a feature movie, they think they can make a feature movie. As a former high school teacher, I can't tell you how many student epics I've babysat that were planned to look like *Gladiator* and ended with amateur actors duking it out on a volleyball court.

Any video more ambitious than a weekend snapshoot is work. It can be fun, satisfying work like, say, a hot tennis game, but hard work nonetheless. If the projects you plan are too complex, the resulting videos will be disappointing or not even finished. So begin with simple program concepts and work your way toward more complex efforts.

The second digital tempters are bells and whistles: all the zippy transitions, whizzbang special effects and multiple video/audio tracks just begging to be played with. Resist their entreaties. Making digital whoopee may be a blast for the editor but the results are often confusing, irritating, boring or all three at once for the viewer. Instead of showing off your new digital

tricks, use formal elements strictly in support of content. After all, that content is the reason for your show's existence. Your audience can see better digital fireworks during breaks on the six o'clock news.

Brevity

Make it snappy. How snappy? As a rule of thumb, five minutes tops. For one thing, short plus simple equals practical: you're far more likely to finish shooting and editing short projects than long ones. For another thing, your viewers are more likely to remain alert and receptive, not to mention present.

What if you shot five hours of tape on your Hawaiian cruise? Sorry. No matter how much it kills you, cull it down to five minutes. All right, maybe ten, but no more than that because you may take it as an iron law that no one else on the planet is even ten percent as interested in your footage as you are. Give viewers only the very best of the very best of those

Figure 46.2 *Brevity—Keep it short. Short videos will be more satisfying to you and your viewers.*

five hours and they'll be pleasantly surprised and lavish in their praise. Force-feed them as much as you yourself want to see and you'll say *aloha* forever to that group of viewers (see Figure 46.2).

Pace

Even if your Hawaiian epic is as fast as a war canoe, it can still act like Novocain if it's nothing but, well, fast. Pace is not synonymous with speed. Pace concerns both the rate and the rhythm of your program material. Just as a succession of similar sentences grows boring, a string of similar shots feels dull and mechanical.

So if you assemble a lightning montage of Hilo shopping, follow up with a leisurely survey of lunch. Then perhaps a brisk anthology of the afternoon on a black sand beach and a languorous, tropical sunset. In this respect, a well-paced video is like a musical composition, constantly varying speed and energy.

But, you protest, we went wind surfing right after shopping; that's two fast sections in a row. Hey, who cares about when you did what. Move the wind surfing to after lunch, to provide a relief from the speed of the shopping sequence.

Variety

The virtues of variety go beyond pacing. It's good to shuffle subject matter as well as sequence intensity. Here again, the trick is to free your mind from the real-world chronology of the original events and re-sequence them to deliver a fresh topic every couple of minutes (see Figure 46.3).

That's right: every two minutes or even less. In a typical ten-minute program, I'd like to see between five and seven sequences. Does that seem way too short? Study commercials to see how much content can be delivered in 30 seconds.

By now, the underlying moral should be obvious: to keep your audiences interested in your shows and coming back for more, make your videos short, sharp and lively. And keep in mind that the awesome

Figure 46.3 *Variety—Divide and shuffle your subject matter to keep things interesting.*

capabilities of your new digital system should operate in support of not instead of solid content.

The Hawaiian vacation's easy because there's so much to do; but what if you've backpacked the Great Smoky Mountains instead? Hike, camp, hike, camp, hike. In fact, a hiking vacation offers an amazing variety of subjects, but it's up to the director to find and tape them.

Sidebar 1

Computer Editing: The Concepts Behind the Principles

This piece focuses on the principles behind all editing techniques, but don't forget that video editing is based on other concepts as well. Understanding these concepts can help you learn your new system more quickly and use it more productively.

- *Random Access.* You can instantly find, view and process anything at any time in both your source material and your program.

- *Computer Filing.* Because your materials are data files on a hard drive, they must be managed as systematically as any other computer files.

- *Multiple Display.* A project's ultimate display form (essentially, computer, TV or Web) has important effects on both its technology and its aesthetics.

- *Additive Editing.* Because your materials are in discrete pieces, you work by adding them to a project that begins as an empty page or timeline.

- *Multi-layer Audio.* Computer-based audio is such a powerful tool that it demands as much attention and creativity as video.

47
Computer Editing: 5 Phases of Editing

Jim Stinson

Computer-based video editing seems cursed with enough tools for a Sears hardware department and a learning curve steeper than Everest. To cope with this complexity, most of us plod through half a tutorial, read random bits of a manual, futz with a few simple projects, and basically fool around, while our expertise grows like moss on a tree trunk, though not quite that fast.

To speed things up, we need to cut our way out of the trees, climb that hill over there, and look down on the whole forest. From this perspective we can see that the tangled thickets of post production in fact have a design, an evident pattern of operations. Post production falls into five major phases: organizing, assembling, enhancing, synthesizing and archiving. By understanding this work flow, we can flatten the learning curve and get a grip on the whole post-production process.

As we do this, keep two major footnotes in mind:

- For simplicity, we'll pretend that you complete each phase in order, before progressing to the next one. In real-world editing, you may be working in several phases at once.

- Though the five phases of post production are more obvious in hard drive-based editing, they're relevant to tape-based linear cutting as well.

With the fine print out of the way, let's start with phase one: organizing.

Organizing

In an earlier sermon from this pulpit, we've harangued you on the importance of organizing your material before you start editing (see November 1999 issue or read the article online at www.videomaker.com) so let's just review the material in fast-forward.

Classify each and every piece of video and/or audio material.

- Identify it with a slate if it doesn't already have one. Slate with codes (like

"27A3" meaning sequence 27, shot A, take 3). Avoid descriptive slates ("helnngcu") because they won't make sense a week later.

- Log it in a shot database (typically part of editing software packages) with a description. A really big project might need fields for slate (27A3), angle (CU), content (Helen reacts to news), quality (ng), and notes (bad framing; 1st half OK). A short program might get away with a single field (27A3 CU Helen NG).

- Locate it by adding tape roll number, in/out-point (time code address or control track time), and file name (as stored on your hard drive).

- Stash it. For larger projects, establish a separate bin or folder for each sequence, plus bins for music, effects and other wild audio components. (Of course, this last step doesn't apply to linear editing.)

How compulsive should you be about organizing? In direct proportion to the complexity of your project. If you blew half a roll of tape on a family picnic, hey, go ahead and wing it. But if you're staring at ten, 60-minute cassettes on a feature intended for Sundance, you'd better classify every blessed shot (see Figure 47.1).

Figure 47.1 *Organize—Log each shot into a database and use coded file names for your clips.*

Assembling

With your building blocks labeled and stowed, the next step is to assemble them into a program for your video. Every single piece of your video must be selected, sequenced, timed and transferred to the master you're constructing.

In digital post especially, selecting shots is often a batch operation. It's easier to pick and mark all the shots you want transferred, and then let your software do the job for you.

Typically, sequencing, timing and transferring go together. Few editors will stick the unclipped shots in order on a timeline and then trim them all to length. Most people choose a shot, spec its in-point to match the previous shot, and lay it in. Personally, I like to leave the out-point open until I have the following shot roughed in. Then I experiment until I find the perfect cut point and set out-point 1 and in-point 2 at the same time.

In linear cutting, transferring is a discrete step because you have to determine in- and out-points before copying the source shot to the assembly tape.

Enhancing

Enhancing means touching up shots by improving, conforming, or downright redesigning them. I recommend that you do this after assembling the show. Otherwise, you might get so hung up on minute shot adjustments that you lose sight of the overall design.

Improving video usually involves exposure, contrast or color balance. There's not much you can do with grainy gain-up originals (though you can tweak the color saturation a skosh) but contrast is definitely tunable, especially with underexposure. Often those inky shadows do have details lurking in them. If your software permits, use a tone curve adjustment to boost dark areas without brightening highlights.

Even when a shot's quality is already good, it may not match the shots around it

Figure 47.2 *Enhance—Most editing programs let you adjust contrast and color balance to improve your shots.*

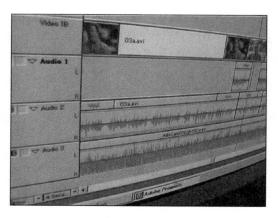

Figure 47.3 *Synthesize—Stack and blend audio and video layers to sweeten you production.*

because it was recorded at a different time you know: sunny one day and cloudy the next. That's where conforming comes in. (In film, it's called color timing.) Working shot by shot, you ensure that everything in a sequence looks the same (see Figure 47.2).

Redesigning means changing the basic character of a shot: turning straight color into a sunset glow or pure black and white, applying slo-mo or strobe effects, adding all kinds of digital filters, or flopping shots for screen direction.

If you're making a commercial or music video, you may stylize the color across the whole program to create a unique special effect.

And let's not forget audio. You improve it by optimizing volume and equalization, conform it by matching level and perspective from shot to shot, and redesign it by altering speed, pitch and presence. Inherently more plastic than video, audio can be molded into just about anything you want.

Synthesizing

Audio is also more susceptible to synthesizing: stacking multiple layers of material and blending them into a single program strand. In editing, it's common to have two tracks each of dialogue, effects,

background and music and double that number for stereo. Mixing audio to synthesize a final sound track is one of the most creative and satisfying jobs in the post production process (see Figure 47.3).

With digital post, the same flexibility has come to the visual tracks as well as audio. Multi-layer visuals include transitions, composites, superimpositions, multiple screens, graphics and titles.

All transitions (except for fades to/from a color) involve multiple images. Extend the middle of a dissolve and you have a superimposition, with two half-strength images sharing the entire screen. Place picture in picture and you get multiple screens (or carve the frame up into as many images as you like). Super a transparent bar or square and you're bringing graphics into play; and with text, you've got titles working as well. Finally, you can chromakey a new foreground into a background, or vice-versa; and with a good plug-in matting program you can combine all the elements seamlessly.

If this sounds like quite a list, consider a single moment that you might see on TV any time: as Mr. Announcer intones off screen, "Up next: today's weather on News at Six," the following things happen:

• A cube tumbles on screen to end as a 1/4-size window.

- The window shows the weather person in front of a chromakeyed map.

- A "smoked glass" rectangle fades on to fill most of the screen.

- A color bar sweeps in across the bottom of the screen.

- The numeral 6 pulsates in a square to the left of the bar.

- "Channel 6 Weather" fades up on the color bar.

- The whole schmeer fades to black for a commercial break.

Today, these multi-part syntheses are so ho-hum that we have to enumerate their parts to remind ourselves of how complex they really are.

Archiving

In linear editing, storing the finished program is automatic because the assembly tape is the archive (such as it is). In digital post, however, you have only a virtual video until you've output it in final form; and that final form may involve multiple decisions about recording methods, media, protocols and display standards (see Figure 47.4).

First decision: analog or digital? Digital storage wins hands-down if the only issue is permanence through perfect duplication. But for a short-term program that will need many copies (like a video press release) an analog master may offer easier mass duplication.

If you do go analog, what's your display standard? NTSC, PAL or SECAM? And don't forget that each standard has its subsets for different countries. If digital, which codec (compressor/decompressor): DV, MPEG, MJPEG, etc... and again, which flavor? If you're streaming to the Web, you also have to cope with screen size and frame rate.

Finally, what's your storage medium? Until recently, some kind of tape was the only answer. But with DVD-RAM burner's down to $300, maybe you want to choose a disc-based medium with its advantages of capacity, compactness and random

Figure 47.4 *Archive—Store your edited master on the best media you can to ensure the longest possible shelf life.*

access. The moral here is that the archiving process that was once automatic now requires a number of thoughtfully considered decisions.

Organizing, assembling, enhancing, synthesizing, archiving. Okay, fine; but what are these abstractions really good for? Basically, they take a complex and shapeless process and impose a kind of order on it an order that helps you keep it all straight. Obviously, no one is going to think, "Having duly organized and enhanced, I will now proceed to phase four: synthesize."

But as you edit, you can operate more confidently if you have an intuitive grasp of the organization that underlies the post-production process.

48
Overcoming Common Computer Editing Problems

Don Collins

Computer editing has become extremely popular. It provides flexible and powerful editing that lets anyone with an artistic eye create professional-quality video. You can undo, redo, add scenes, delete transitions, change titles and create nearly anything you can imagine, almost instantaneously. And it just keeps getting better as computer editing equipment becomes faster, more robust and easier to use.

However, there are still some pitfalls and hazards that every video editor will encounter that can make editing frustrating at best and a nightmare at worst. Luckily, for most of the irritating nuisances that crop up, there are solutions. Here are a few common problems that computer editors experience, and some suggestions for troubleshooting them. Although we use Adobe Premiere to illustrate the examples in this article, the principles taught here apply to most editing programs. If you're having trouble performing certain tasks in your editor, keep reading, this article just might have the answer you're looking for.

Reversed Transitions

You just placed a cool crossfade between a shot of the sunrise and a closeup of a frying egg, sunny-side up. You render the clip and when you preview it something weird happens: it shows a brief glimpse of the egg then it fades to an even briefer shot of the sun; then it cuts back to the rest of the egg clip. What happened?

You have inadvertently reversed the transition. In Adobe Premiere, and other timeline-based editing programs, you need to set the direction of each transition effect. For instance, if clip A precedes clip B, your transition effect must be set to start with clip A and end with clip B. If the effect is reversed, from B to A, the software will cut from clip A to clip B at the start of the effect, perform the fade from B to A, then cut back to clip B (see Figure 48.1a). It's a common error and one that is easily remedied.

To fix the problem, double click the transition on the timeline to open an options window. Once opened, you can

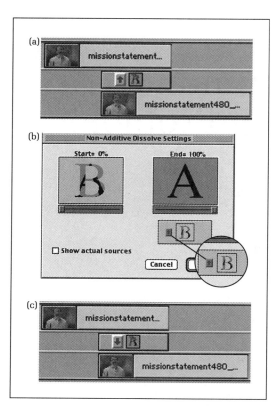

Figure 48.1 *Wrong Way!—A reversed transition effect (a) won't play properly (note that the arrow points the wrong direction). To fix it, double click the effect icon and edit the properties (b). When placed correctly, the arrow should show the signal flow from clip A to clip B (c).*

click on the arrow that reverses the order of the fade (see Figure 48.1b). Clip A should be on the left hand side and clip B on the right. You can also check the Show Actual Source box, which shows an icon of the actual clips to help you visualize the sequence.

Black Frames and Razor Remnants

A random black frame or single frame of video created by a razor tool can mar an otherwise perfect video. Black frames occur when two clips placed next to one another on the timeline are not pushed together all the way. The result is a flash frame of black between the two clips.

Razor remnants are single frames of video inadvertently created when using a razor tool. When using the razor tool to trim a clip, you may inadvertently leave a single frame of video on the timeline that cannot be seen. It is easy to unknowingly slice a single frame off the head or tail of a clip when using the razor. The single frame that is left can cause a few problems. It can create a flash frame that plays as a glitch, or, if you remove the larger portion of the clip without deleting the loose frame, it can prevent you from placing a clip on the timeline.

If there are only one or two frames of black or stray video, you may not detect them when you preview your project. One way to scan for random frames is to use the Zoom tool to change the time units on the Construction window to view single frame increments on the timeline. Then you can quickly scroll across your project to check for stray frames. Be careful though, if you view your project in increments as great as one second, extraneous black frames and razor remnants can go undetected.

If you do find any, zoom in to the 1-frame mode so you can delete the extraneous frame or extend a clip to bridge the black gap. You can also use the multitrack selection tool to move all of the subsequent clips to shore up a gap caused by a black frame.

Loss Due to Computer Crash

Without a doubt, frequent crashes are one of the most frustrating aspects of computer editing. Although they are becoming less frequent as both hardware and software improve, they still happen and they happen at the worst times. Our advice: save often. Preferably after each solidified edit or group of moves you make. That way, if (when) your program freezes, you'll be covered.

Some software have automatic save functions built in. If you choose to use the auto save, use it wisely, because with each save you forfeit all those handy levels of undo (32 max in Premiere). Many times retracing your editing steps with undos can unsnarl your production and help you learn from your mistakes. So in some situations you may want to hold off on saving until you have completed a task successfully. But once you have done that, save, save, save!

Mismatched Audio Levels

One of the most common causes for audio problems is assembling clips with different audio levels. This usually happens when you've shot in different locations. If you need to edit two people conversing in an airplane hangar, with footage shot outdoors on a mountaintop and an interview taped in a living room, you're going to have three different sound qualities and levels. It can also occur if you are editing footage shot in the same location on different camcorders using different microphones.

Editing software gives you control over audio as well as video. You can adjust the levels of an entire clip or segments within it. You can even add EQ and effects to your audio tracks (see Figure 48.2). When you place the mountain top clip next to the living room clip, you may need to adjust EQ and/or cross fade audio from the two scenes to make the change in the audio tone smoother for the viewer.

By clicking on the bottom of the audio track, you place handles that you can then raise or lower. To adjust the level of an entire clip, select the sound clip, go to the Clip menu, then select Gain and enter a value from 0 to 200%. Simply matching the lines that represent the audio levels of your clips is not enough. Because clip levels in your software are relative to the level at which each clip was captured, they are not reliable for balancing one clip with another.

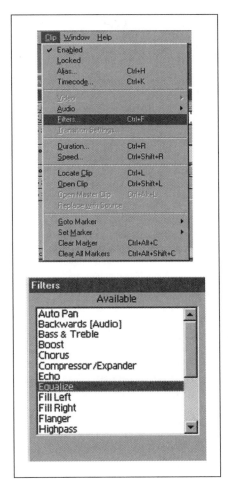

Figure 48.2 *Fine Tuning—There are many tools in the pull-down menus that give you control over your audio. You can equalize it, for example, by entering the clip menu, going to Filters and choosing Equalize.*

If all Else Fails . . .

Creating professional-quality video with a computer is becoming easier and more affordable than ever. Still, it's not automatic; we've covered just a few of the common errors inherent to computer video. Luckily, most of them are quickly overcome. For answers to more specific problems, consult your manual or contact tech support.

Sidebar 1

An Ounce of Prevention...

One of the best ways to avoid editing mistakes is to visualize your final edited video before you start shooting.

- See the big picture. Run through your video from opening to the final credits in your mind. Know what shots you are going to take and visualize the transitions between shots and scenes.

- Plan your shots. One of the best ways to prepare for your edit is to create a storyboard. It can be as simple or as detailed as you want. The important thing is to know where you're going so that when you're in the edit suite you aren't missing any key shots.

- Keep a shot log. By keeping a log of your shots, complete with time code in-and-out points and a comment area for grading each shot, you'll be way ahead of the game. That way, when you're capturing your footage to your hard drive, you will know which shots to keep and which shots to skip. Keeping a shot log not only saves a tremendous amount of time, but valuable hard drive space as well.

Sidebar 2

Managing Your Project Area

One of the most challenging aspects of editing is maintaining an organized workspace on your computer monitor. The most common editing errors occur because editors can't find a clip, don't see their transition or filter windows, miss an edit mark, confuse tracks, mistake clips and otherwise screw things up because the project area was cluttered. Here are some tips to help you keep it clean.

- Collapse the timeline to gain more horizontal space—especially if you're using only two tracks of video and two tracks of audio.

- Minimize seldom-used windows and adjust the size of those you do use regularly.

- Play with the timeline's measurement units. For precise editing, use the 1-frame mode. For rough edits and placement of clips, try the 1-second marker. And to gain a global view, use the 1-minute measure to view your entire project.

- Use short, descriptive file names for your clips.

- Adjust the size of the file icon on the timeline and clip bin.

49
Color Tweaking

Bill Davis

When we make video, our goal most of the time is to get lifelike images up on the screen. We chase natural skin tones, good exposure and proper white balance like racing dogs after mechanical bunnies.

But if you watch what's happening in the movies or on TV, you're probably already aware that sometimes, realistic just isn't good enough, particularly when it comes to color.

We accept daytime scenes awash in exaggerated hyper-golden sunlight and nighttime sequences bathed in green or blue. And we even see the use of hybrid scenes, where some of the footage is processed in black and white while other elements retain their colors.

The Countdown of Basics

The first thing to understand about the basics of video color is that at the base level, every television signal is actually a combination of two separate signal components—one for black and white information, the other for color.

In the beginning, all TV signals were exclusively black and white. It wasn't until years after TV sets started to appear in homes that engineers added a color component to the broadcast signal.

The black and white part of the signal is referred to as luminance and given the engineering shorthand, "Y," while the color signal is known as chrominance and given the designation "C."

The standard yellow RCA video plug mixes these signals together into a composite. S-video cables, on the other hand, are sometimes referred to as Y/C cables because they keep the luminance and chrominance signals separated. If you look at the end of an S-video connector, you can see a number of separate holes or pins used to carry the signals.

This split makes it a snap to take a color TV signal from your camcorder and translate it into black and white. All that your software has to accomplish is the elimination of the color portion of the signal.

Diminishing the chrominance signal relative to the luminance yields a reduction of color intensity and creates a muted pastel look. Many editing applications have basic chrominance or saturation controls to adjust this aspect of the video.

But to dive into the more exciting aspects of colorizing your video signal, we also need to break things down further and delve into the three primary components of your signal's color: red, green and blue.

Engineering RGB Space

Color television is said to reside in the RGB color space. It is this arrangement of mixing and matching three basic colors to create the entire pallet of colors the TV can display, that makes it a snap to manipulate the color of your video footage.

Most editing software programs allow you to change the balance of the three primary colors on a global, regional or even pixel-by-pixel basis.

Editing applications usually have some basic color manipulation tools, accessible through a panel in the main program or as a plug-in. As you manipulate the colors, you can increase or decrease parameters, such as the amount of red, green or blue applied to your selected part of a picture. You can also alter brightness and contrast, creating a washed-out feel of pastels, or a hyper-real environment, where you deliver suppressed midrange tones and the most extreme dark and light components of your original signals to the screen.

To Boldly Go

Normally, these controls need to be handled with a light touch, since they can dramatically alter the look of your video. Remember, the beauty of working in a non-destructive video-editing environment is that a return to reality is always as close as an "undo" command.

Special-effects filters and plug-ins can often modify colors in interesting ways. Just like the filters photographers have long attached to their lenses to change the image characteristics of their shots, the video filter is simply a way of changing one or more channels of information to create a different look for your video. In most situations, it is better to apply filters in post-production, since you cannot undo on-the-lens glass filters if you don't like the results.

Many filters have presets for popular color schemes such as sepia—a color effect that alters your footage with a yellowish-brown cast reminiscent of old-time photographs.

Beyond these kinds of simple presets are direct controls such as tint, which you can quickly apply as a global colorcast of your choosing to your footage. All those trendy colorized commercials, where the world is awash in a slightly green tint are examples of manipulating color information. You can simulate these effects with your color control tools.

But a note of caution. Look closely at the colorization examples in broadcast work. You'll notice that while the environment around that fancy sports car often looks surreal, the people still look pretty realistic. To achieve that kind of sophisticated colorized look, you need to be careful about maintaining healthy skin highlights and other reality checks rather than just slathering everyone and everything with a greenish wash.

That's where the power of channel-specific effects comes in. Look closely at your editing interface and you may discover that you can apply color corrections to narrowly-defined parts of your image.

Filters and Mattes

The real fun begins when you combine basic image manipulation with the power of masks, mattes and layers.

If you've ever watched a music video, where a brilliantly-colored character danced through an otherwise black and white world, you've seen the power of multi-layer mattes and filters at work.

Shots like these stack two or more synchronized layers of the same footage on multiple video tracks. Then, a moving matte applied to the dancing character isolates it from the rest of the scene. The layer with the foreground figure remains in color while a desaturate filter, which removes all the color information, applies to the background footage.

A word of warning: pulling a quality moving matte out of a single video clip without advance planning is just about impossible unless you are willing to go through and paint a matte for every frame of your video (30 of them for every second of footage). But if you have the time and patience (or a team of highly skilled animators), there's nothing to keep you from going in and isolating a character by re-shaping and moving a manually-created matte to follow the character. Don't forget to tweak the softness or blur the edges of the matte to make it appear more natural.

The Adventure Begins

There's literally no limit to this other than your creativity and imagination. So, the next time you're watching TV, pay special attention to how the producers use color tinting, layers and mattes to produce eye-catching images.

Then, consider that many of those same capabilities reside right in your own editing application, awaiting your exploration.

Sidebar 1

Alpha Channel

The separate RGB portions of video are referred to as channels. Some formats also have a fourth channel, called the Alpha Channel, used to specify transparency. If your editing application allows you to view the Alpha Channel, it usually appears in grayscale with black being 100 percent transparent and white being 100 percent opaque, although it is very easy to reverse this. The flexibility of editing software even allows you to select a specific color or range of colors to set as the Alpha Channel.

Sidebar 2

TV Can't Show it All

A typical computer monitor uses over 16 million colors to draw a picture on your screen. This includes the video-preview window in your editing application. The standard color television picture in the United States is composed of only about 2 million colors. This means that the wonderful color modifications you see on your computer monitor will likely not look the same on a television. When doing any computer generated modifications to your video, you must test your adjusted video on a television before declaring your movie complete.

50
Basic Compositing

Bill Davis

Compositing is the process of layering multiple on-screen elements—video, still images, text or graphical elements—into a single on-screen image.

A classic example of compositing that many people would instantly recognize is the title sequence for the nationally syndicated series *Baywatch*. The show's graphic designers specified that video clips and graphic elements be combined into multiple layers with images appearing behind, in front of and even within large block letters spelling out the show's title.

But a composite doesn't have to be anywhere near this complicated. In fact, many of the composites seen in video are really just two separate video images combined into a single screen presentation. These simple composites (and even some not-so-simple ones!) are well within the reach of anyone with even the most basic computer-based video production systems.

Before we look at ways to create your own simple composites, let's take a look at some basic compositing terminology.

Talkin' the Talk

In compositing, the term *layer* refers to a plane of video or graphics. A good way to visualize layers is to imagine them as pages stacked on top of each other on your computer desktop.

In most editing programs these layers correspond to the program's video *tracks*. The lower tracks appear further back on the screen, and each higher video track is stacked in front.

Another important concept to compositing is the use of *mattes* (pronounced "mats"). Mattes are the electronic equivalent of cutting a shape out of a piece of cardboard and holding the results over a picture. If you use the hole in the cardboard as the matte, the background image shows through the hole. If you use the cutout piece, you block the background picture with the shape of the cutout. Electronic mattes work the same way.

Most videographers are familiar with *wipes* as a way to replace one picture with another when editing between scenes. In compositing, a slowly or partially executed wipe can create the same effect as a matte.

Alpha channels are a way to make an image or an area of an image so that it is partially transparent. You can also use alpha channels to define picture borders so that they transition smoothly from opaque to transparent. An alpha channel matte uses shades of gray to represent the amount of transparency between the foreground and background images.

With *feathering*, an automated alpha channel process, the edges of an image are gently transitioned from opaque to transparent to avoid a hard line of transition between the image and content on an adjacent layer.

Okay, now that you've got some of the basic terminology down, let's look at some examples of simple composites.

Down to Basics

Sometimes beginners get confused when they try to execute a composite by simply stacking two scenes on top of one another in their timeline. The result is typically not a composite but a regular single image. The problem is that, if both scenes are "full screen," the picture on the highest track will totally block any scene behind it.

In order to create a composite, the picture closest to the screen must be manipulated to allow the scene (image) behind (or below) it to show through.

There are dozens of ways to do this. The foreground image can be moved partially aside, cropped, shrunk or made wholly or partially transparent. In one of the computer editing world's most useful tricks, you can create a matte that allows all or part of the background picture to peek through the foreground layer (see Figure 50.1).

Figure 50.1 *Blending scenes—by making the first layer of video semi-transparent, the second layer becomes visible.*

That's exactly why mattes are such an important part of compositing. They allow one track to show through to another in precisely the way you want.

Familiar Effect, New Twist

By using the same transitions you typically use between scenes, but freezing them in a state of partial completion, you can create simple video composites.

How many times have you seen the traditional split-screen used to bring together two sides of a telephone conversation in a classic movie? That's a basic composite. All that's needed to create this kind of scene is to set your transition controls to execute a common wipe and set the start and stop values to take place at the same physical location (see Figure 50.2). By the way, when you plan to do this kind of effect, it's important to pay close attention to the framing of your two shots when you shoot so that you leave plenty of negative space in the areas that will be covered by the other shot.

A cross-dissolve, stopped when half completed, is an equally effective form of simple composite. It results in a dreamlike combination of the entering and exiting scenes.

Again, you'll need to pay special attention to the framing of your picture when you record each scene. If you do, this simple type of composite can communicate some pretty powerful emotions.

Imagine an establishing shot of a woman washing dishes at the kitchen sink, then move to a head-and-shoulders shot framed with her looking out the window. Now partially dissolve in a scenic shot of a cruise ship sailing the blue waters of the Caribbean! The resulting composite clearly suggests that her thoughts are far away from getting the silverware clean.

Other classic "switcher effects" are equally composite-friendly. Take the picture-in-picture, for instance (see Figure 50.3).

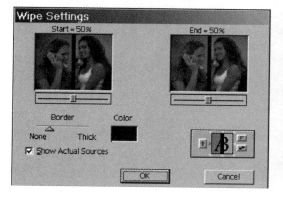

Figure 50.2 *Half-Wipe Composite-Programs like Adobe Premiere allow you to stop a half-completed wipe by setting start and stop values to take place at the same physical location.*

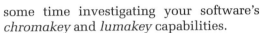

With multiple tracks easily accessible in most of today's editing software, it's a snap to composite two scaled-down pictures onto one master shot. If the master shot is a traditional head-and-shoulders close-up, you can use soft-edge oval mattes on two additional shots (placed on higher tracks than your head-and-shoulders shot) to position a pair of "good conscience" and "bad conscience" characters over your main subject's shoulders. You'll have shades of the "devil-and-angel" gag that's been a staple on the Conan O'Brien late-night TV program.

This is also a great place to use the "edge feather" feature that most modern computer editors provide. Instead of oval-shaped insets with hard edges looking like a pair of antique photos, a softly feathered edge will help to integrate the two mattes into the overall composite image.

All Keyed Up

To take the same multiple-picture composite idea a step closer to professional, spend

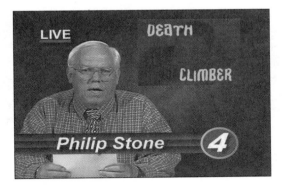

Figure 50.3 *Classic PIP—the picture-in-picture is one of the most commonly-used and easily-achieved composite effects.*

some time investigating your software's *chromakey* and *lumakey* capabilities.

A chromakey occurs when you tell your software package to take all the pixels of a particular color and replace them with the live video from another shot. Traditionally, the colors used for chromakeys are either bright green or bright blue—two of the basic colors that form a typical RGB video signal.

In blue-screen or green-screen compositing, video scenes are recorded with the characters appearing in front of an evenly-lit green or blue surface, then the software replaces the key-colored pixels with live video or a computer-generated background (see Figure 50.4).

Keying is one area where you need to experiment in order to get good results (see *Shooting for Chromakey* sidebar), but once you achieve a decent key shot, a world of creative options emerges.

For amateur weathercasters or kids who want to suspend their model spaceships over a field of stars, chromakeying or lumakeying can be just the ticket. An effective chromakey setup can take those competing angels in the above example and matte out the backgrounds to let them float over the master shot, without the background oval shapes spoiling the effect.

A close relative to chromakeying is lumakeying, which pulls mattes using brightness rather than color values. A somewhat dark scene with one character appearing in a bright white T-shirt could be a likely candidate for a lumakey composite. Using this technique you can do anything from simply turning the T-shirt the precise color you choose to something as wild as allowing a shot of ocean waves

Figure 50.4 *Angel-key—use a chromakey to achieve a seamless and realistic composite.*

breaking on the shore to replace the area of the T-shirts. Creatively, the sky's literally the limit.

And that's the real magic of compositing. It frees you from the need to show your audience only what your camera can record at one moment in time. Composites can be simple and realistic, or invoke multiple layers of live video, motion graphics, titles and effects.

Have Some Fun

Now that you know some of the secrets of compositing, watch for examples in the shows you see on television. You can expect to find scores of good examples in the openings of network entertainment programs and even in nightly local newscasts. But what you might not expect is that many of the seemingly sophisticated effects you'll see are not far from the capabilities of your own NLE program.

All that's required is that you master the tools you already have! So whether your goal is to get your audience to believe that two or more composited elements are actually part of a single scene, or just to have some fun with this cutting-edge technology, compositing is a creative joy. So dive right in and let the fun begin!

Sidebar 1

Basic Compositing Terminology

Layer: A plane of video or graphics. Imagine them as pages stacked on top of each other on your computer desktop.

Tracks: In most NLEs layers correspond to the program's video tracks. Lower-numbered tracks appear further back on the screen.

Matte: The electronic equivalent of cutting a shape out of a piece of cardboard and holding the results over a picture.

Wipe: A way to replace one picture with another when editing between scenes. In compositing, a slowly or partially executed wipe can create the same effect as a matte.

Alpha channels: A way to encode an image or an area of an image so that it is partially transparent.

Feathering: An automated alpha channel process in which the edges of an image are gently transitioned from opaque to transparent.

Sidebar 2

Shooting for Chromakey

The key to effective chromakeying is always the lighting setup you use. In order for a chromakey to be effective, the key background must be illuminated evenly without hot spots or harsh shadows. The pros typically use color balanced fluorescent arrays or large "scoop"-type fixtures with plenty of diffusion in order to make the light hitting the key background as even as possible.

51
The Art of the Edit

Janis Lonnquist

See video clips at www.videomaker.com/handbook.

When Oliver Stone turned over the massive amount of raw footage that became *JFK*, editor Joe Hutshing knew it would be a challenge. "I wondered if it could even be watchable," Hutshing says. "It was so incredibly complicated. It was like looking at a schematic for a TV set and then imagining actually watching the TV."

From the mountain of raw footage, to the first five-hour cut, to the final three-hour-and-eight-minute editing masterpiece, Hutshing had to make decisions, consider choices and re-examine goals. This is editing.

Editing systems may range from sophisticated digital suites with all the bells and whistles to basic single-source systems consisting of a camera, TV and VCR. Still, the functions of editing remain the same:

1. to connect shots into a sequence that tells a story or records an event,

2. to correct and delete mistakes,

3. to condense or expand time and

4. to communicate an aesthetic.

Whether you're creating a Hollywood feature film or tightening a vacation video, the challenge is to take raw footage, and within the limitations of equipment and budget, transform it into something compelling and watchable.

Shooting With the Edit in Mind

Editing may be the final step of the production, but to make a truly successful video, you need to begin making editing choices in the concept stage. What will the overall look of the piece be? The mood? The pacing? Will you cut it to music? What kind of music?

There are several techniques that will help you plan. Prepare a shooting script, a storyboard or—if it is not a scripted production—an overview for your program. This will be the blueprint for your production.

A *shooting script* lists the action shot by shot, along with proposed camera angles and framing.

253

In a *storyboard*, actual sketches illustrate each scene. It's a good opportunity to see what will work before you shoot it.

An *overview* should include: the chronology of shots as they will appear in the video; approximate timing for each shot; and information about accompanying audio, graphics and titles for each scene.

Next, prepare a *shot sheet*. Make sure it includes every shot listed in your script or overview. Get several shots of each item on the list.

"You need a variety of shots," says Kevin Corcoran, vice president of Pacific Media Center in Santa Clara, California. "In a basketball game, for example, you get shots of the crowd, shots of the scoreboard, shots of the referee, shots of the environment. In action that's typically long and drawn out, you need to consolidate information. You need to have images to cut to in order to make it look smooth."

Even in scripted productions, Corcoran recommends getting a variety of shots.

"I always try to get a wide shot and a head and shoulders shot for each block of text," says Corcoran. "Who knows what you'll find when you go into an edit? There may be something that bothers you with continuity in the background of a wide shot. Now you have a place to go."

While Joe Hutshing had massive amounts of material to edit for *JFK*, Corcoran says the more common problem is too little material.

"Often there are large sections to be removed and no smooth way to cut," says Corcoran. "This is especially true when you're editing on a two-machine, cuts-only system. Ideally, you will have some other framing, another angle, a reaction or some other activity happening in the environment. If it's a person at a podium talking, you need an audience reaction shot or two or three. You must have cutaways to consolidate a half-hour speech without jump cuts."

You also invariably end up with footage you can't use, often due to the unexpected appearance of objects on tape that you never noticed during the shoot. Once, when editing the "dream house" segment of a TV program, I discovered a power supply right in the middle of the kitchen floor. Nobody saw it in the field and every sweeping pan—all wide shots—included the ugly box. Other than featuring a dream house with no kitchen, we had no option but to use the embarrassing piece of footage.

"There will always be things in shots you don't see when you're shooting," Corcoran says. "Things reflected in mirrors or windows, things in dark areas of the picture. It's important to change your framing to avoid having problems like this in the edit."

If you will edit your video to music, select the music in advance and time zooms and pans accordingly. If this isn't possible, shoot a slow, medium and fast version of each camera move. In general, shots should be five to 15 seconds in length. Know the pacing and shoot accordingly.

You'll enjoy a lot more options in your edit sessions if you aren't desperately "fixing it in post." Taking the appropriate technical precautions saves you from having to scrap otherwise good footage due to lighting, audio or other technical problems.

"In an event, things will only go wrong," Corcoran warns. "In weddings, for example, the light is nearly always bad. A camera light is essential, especially if you don't have gain control. And you'll need a lot of batteries for that light."

Good lighting greatly enhances the quality of your videos; invest in a lighting seminar if you need more information. As a rule, the brightest spot in your picture should be no more than 20 to 30 times brighter than the darkest spot or you'll be editing silhouettes.

You'll have trouble in your edit if you don't white balance several times during an event. This is particularly true during weddings, which may move from bright sunlight, to a dimly lit church, to fluorescent lights in a reception hall. If you don't white balance, the shots won't match—you may end up dissolving from a well-lit scene of groomsmen decorating the getaway car to a blue, blue reception.

Production Pains

Production can be exhausting, with long days of hard physical labor, but it's vital to stay alert.

On a particularly grueling corporate production a few years ago, a camera operator, who was also monitoring audio, removed his headset during a break and forgot to put it back on. Our talent, the president of the corporation, removed his lavaliere microphone to stretch, and sat down on it for the remainder of the production. Try to fix that in post.

Mikes can fall down, batteries can die, a cable can go bad. Without headphones, you may not know until it's too late.

"If you know from your headphones there's no hope for that microphone," Corcoran says, "You can unplug it and let the camera mike try. It's going to be better than what you'll get otherwise. Nothing can kill a production faster than bad audio. Wear your headphones all the time."

For most productions, steady images make the most sense. Always use a tripod. Hand-held looks, *well*, hand-held. There's a trend right now to overuse this technique, but avoid the *cinema verité*, or "shaky cam" look unless you're after a strobed look or the effect is actually motivated by something in the script.

Be sure to allow for preroll. When you switch a camera from the *stop* mode to *record*, it rolls back several seconds before it achieves "speed" and begins taping. Allow five seconds, 10 to be safe, before cuing the talent to begin speaking or executing your shot.

Unless your edit system is very precise (plus or minus two frames) you will have trouble editing to the word, so make sure that you have two seconds or more of silence before your talent begins.

This is better than saying "action" to cue the talent: if the narration begins too quickly, you may end up losing two seconds of narration in edit to cut out your cue. Instead, count "five, four, three"… and cue talent after a silent count of two and one.

With high-end systems, you can encounter a similar problem. If the tape is checked and action begins too soon, you won't be able to back up over the break in control track to execute the edit.

To allow time for a good transition, instruct your talent to fix a gaze on the camera for two seconds before and several seconds after a narration. A quick, sideways glance for approval, a swallow or a lick of the lips before or after speaking may be difficult to edit out.

If you don't have control over the talent's timing and delivery—or example, when shooting a training session or wedding—your cutaways and reaction shots will be critical to mask cuts. Remember to shoot plenty.

In the Frame

Good framing and composition are vital in achieving aesthetically pleasing video that is cohesive and makes sense. A well-composed shot provides viewers with the information needed to follow the story. It reveals, through spatial relationships, the comparative importance of individuals and objects, and the effect they have upon each other. It focuses attention on details, sometimes subtly, even subliminally. Good composition can also disturb, excite and/or heighten tension if the script calls for it.

You can't fix poor framing and composition in post. A lack of head room will make your subject seem suspended from the top of the TV monitor. Framing a shot to cut at the subject's ankles, chin, hands or hem line is an uncomfortable look that doesn't allow "closure," a process in which the mind fills in the missing elements.

Remember the rule of thirds: place important elements in the top or bottom third of the screen. In a closeup, place the eyes at the one-third baseline. In an extreme closeup, the eyes are at baseline of the top third, the mouth is at the baseline of the bottom third, and, through closure, the chin and forehead are filled in.

Distracting or inappropriate backgrounds are nearly impossible to work around so pay attention to every detail when you shoot. In one production, a children's singing group performed a number in front of a blackboard. In the edit, I noticed one little girl standing directly in front of a large letter "M"—creating the look of two perfect, pointed ears. Again, saved by the B-roll.

Sometimes even balanced and thoughtfully composed shots don't cut together well. For example: if you're editing an interview or dialogue, cutting between head shots of the interviewer and guest, you need the heads angled slightly toward each other (to imply the interaction of the two) and off center, leaving "look space" or "nose room." Without look space, your interviewer will appear to address the edge of the TV screen. Centered, we have no sense of the spatial relationship of the two. They could be sitting back to back.

Similarly, maintain "lead room" for your subject to walk, run, bike or drive into.

Walk the Line

One production basic that can cause major consternation in the edit suite is "crossing the line."

Let's say you're shooting a parade passing in front of you, from left to right. A politician waves from a passing float, her back to you. You dash across the street and resume shooting, getting a great shot of her smiling face. When you go to edit, however, you'll find that you crossed the line: half of your parade marches left to right and the other half marches right to left. Cutting together footage from both sides of the line will create a bizarre montage where bands and floats and motorcades seem to run into one another.

Respecting the line is especially important in shots that track movement or where geography, such as movement toward a goal post, is critical to the viewer's understanding of the action.

Camera angles also play a role in the viewer's ability to interpret and believe the action. Let's say you want to show a child trying to coax a kitten from a tree. First we see the child looking up. We cut to the kitten cowering on a branch. We cut back to the child. The scene gains impact with the right camera angles. We see the child, framed left, looking up. Cut to a reverse angle shot looking down at the child, over the cat's shoulder, with the cat framed right. The camera angle duplicates the cat's line of vision. Cut to a low angle shot of the cat from the child's point of view. The edited sequence is fluid and believable.

There are two kinds of continuity you should monitor for successful editing. First: continuity of the environment. A made-for-TV movie has a scene in which a man speaks to his doctor. He wears a shirt with the collar turned up. Cut to the doctor. Cut back to the man, and his collar is flat. Cut to a two-shot and the collar turns up again. Productions on all levels are full of goofs like this one. To avoid adding blooper footage of your own, pay close attention to detail both in production and in the edit.

For the best possible editing situation, you also need to watch continuity of action. If your talent can give you numerous takes with identical blocking, you'll have lots of editing options. Cuts-only editing is at its best when you can achieve a multicam look by cutting to different framing on action. Look for the apex of the action—the full extension of the arm, the widest part of the yawn, the clink of glasses in a toast—and use that apex as the marker to cut to a new angle of the same action.

Motivate It

Transitions should occur only when motivated by something in the story.

A *cut* is the instantaneous switch from one shot to another. The most common transition device, it duplicates the way we see. (Just try panning or zooming with your eyes.)

A *dissolve* is the gradual replacement of one image by another. Use it to show a passage of time or create a mood.

A *wipe* is a special effect of one image pushing the other image off screen. With digital technology, the options are nearly endless. A wipe can erase, burn, fold, kick or flush the first image from the screen. Wipes signify the end of a segment and the complete transition to a new time, place or concept.

A *fade* is the gradual replacement of an image with black or vice versa, used primarily to begin or end a program or video segment.

Creative editing, using a variety of transitions, is still possible on a cuts-only system. If you can't fade in or dissolve, begin your shot out of focus and gradually make the image clear. A very fast pan—15 frames or so of light, color and motion flying across the screen—is almost as effective as a dissolve. Allowing your subject to exit the shot ends a scene with the finality of a wipe. Cutting to a static shot, such as a close-up of a flower, a sign or a building, defines and separates scenes.

For greater insight, learn from the pros. Rent a well-done video and create an overview and shot sheet.

There are also seminars and many excellent books available on framing, composition and technique. For an in-depth study of media aesthetics, look for Herbert Zettl's *Sight, Sound and Motion*. Of course, editing is a practical as well as an aesthetic skill. On to the practicalities.

Editing Systems

Practically speaking, editing is simply copying selected video from the source tape to the edit master or record tape. A wide variety of systems and methods are available.

Single-Source Editing. You can perform single-source editing from your camcorder to your VCR. Your owner's manual will include complete directions; basically, you control the edit by pressing PLAY on your source deck (camera) and RECORD on the record deck (your VCR), pausing and releasing as you go. The transitions are cuts only.

This type of editing becomes frustrating quickly. As the editor you must locate edit points, manually set preroll, start the machines at the same time and react at precisely the right moment to control the edit. Frame accuracy is usually a problem. If you hit RECORD too soon, you suffer video noise between edits. Too late, and you lose frames on the edit master.

Expanded Single-Source Systems. The first investment single-source editors usually make is an edit controller. Most edit controllers allow you to shuttle to locate scenes, to mark in and out points, to read and display frame numbers either from a pulse-count or time code system such as SMPTE or RCTC.

These editors perform the preroll function automatically and start the machines together. Many systems give you: 1) the option of insert or assemble edit, 2) the ability to "trim" add or subtract a few frames without resetting in and out points and 3) the ability to preview your edit. Some perform audio or video only edits and interface with a computer to store an Edit Decision List (EDL).

You can also expand single-source edit systems with an audio mixer, a switcher and character generator.

Multiple-Source Systems. These give editors the capability of A/B Roll Editing. The typical system consists of two or more source VCRs (A and B), which supply material to the video switcher or computerized editing control unit. There, the material is edited, combined with effects and sent to the record VCR. Audio from the source decks is also mixed and sent to the record VCR.

Multiple-source systems allow an editor to connect two moving video sources with dissolves, wipes and other transitions.

In nonlinear systems, every frame is stored in digital form and is instantly available to the editor. Once you've designated an edit and transition on the computerized EDL or storyboard, the computer executes the edit instantly. You can grab a scene from anywhere in your source footage without waiting for a tape to cue. Experimentation becomes effortless.

As you move up to the more complex systems, do your homework. Read product reviews before you make the investment. Find out what peripherals you need for basic operations and efficient editing.

Investigate the availability of classes and users groups in your area. Is there a local production facility that rents a suite featuring the same system? You may need a back-up plan if your system goes down and you're facing a deadline.

Advanced Editing Systems. These systems feature Digital Video Effects (DVE), better compression, exciting animation, special effects, pro titles and more. They are revolutionizing editing, providing greater options, accuracy and speed.

The ramping of capabilities means a ramping of complexity; you'll need education and practice to get up to speed. The systems are relatively expensive and the technology is constantly changing. It isn't easy to know when to make the investment. Some videographers complain that editing functions have not been designed with editors in mind; they're waiting for upgrades to correct this. Others have found systems that meet their needs well, and are using them to produce amazing programs.

Again, do your homework. If you can, rent a suite and actually do an edit on a given system before you buy.

The Final Cut

It's pay off time. You planned ahead, you paid attention during production, and now you can relax.

Why? Because editing is going to be great fun. Enjoy.

52
Title Talk

Bill Harrington

You've created the perfect video, great lighting, clean audio and beautiful editing. But be careful. All your hard work can be overshadowed if you are not careful with your titles. Titles, also called CGs (short for character generator), are the words you see on the screen. But adding titles is more than typing words onto your video. Good titles look balanced on screen and add to the message. Bad titles are like an out of tune instrument—they make the whole orchestra sound bad.

When it comes to making great titles, there are a few rules to follow. Just like making good video, it takes a certain amount of planning, knowledge and a lot of experimentation. An eye for composition doesn't hurt either. Here are some basic concepts you can use to enhance your titles.

Location! Location! Location!

Watch network television tonight and see if there is logo in the bottom corner of the screen. It's not there by accident. The big guys understand that when it comes to the video screen, every pixel is a precious piece of real estate. In real estate, location is everything. We read from left to right, top to bottom. The bottom right corner of the screen is the last thing you will read. That logo stays imprinted on the mind, and when the friendly folks at Nielson ask you what station you watched, you can remember quite easily.

You can use that same knowledge to your advantage when you build your titles. The corners of the screen are the most powerful place for small informational graphics like logos or names. They also work well because titles placed there are less likely to interfere with the action in your video.

If you want to make a major statement, then place a title in the center of the screen, demanding your audience to take notice. This is where you would typically find the title of a program. Placed in the center of the screen, the title becomes the most important thing on the screen. More

Figure 52.1 *Safety first—remember to observe the safe area whenever you're creating titles.*

important than even the video that plays beneath it.

Play it Safe

There are some places that you really cannot put titles, though. Most CG software now has a safe title reference built in (see Figure 52.1). These lines represent recommended limits to where you place your titles within the viewing area. Any titles outside of the safe title zone risk being unreadable due to the cropping and curvature of the TV screen. Keeping your titles within a safe title area is not an absolute, but you reduce the effectiveness of your titles if they are outside of the safe title zone.

Lastly, the text on the screen has to work with everything else the audience is seeing. Your subject's name won't look good superimposed over his face. It has to balance with the video you're using. If you interview a vet about his WWII memories and he's on camera left, try putting the title on the right to balance the overall picture.

The Font is the Message

Sometimes it's not what you say, but how you say it. This applies to the fonts you use for your titles. Graphic designers can spend years learning about font theory, but you don't need a master's degree to understand that the font—the actual shape of the letters—sends a message to the viewer. Does the text look like ancient Greek writing or is it more futuristic? There are thousands of fonts available, and the font you choose will have a direct impact on the final product.

Let's say you videotaped a local Christmas pageant and want to add a graphic as an introduction. A font that has a cowboy feel wouldn't make any sense. Unless the name of the pageant was *Christmas on the Prairie*, such a font would just confuse the viewer. A Christmas pageant screams for something with a holiday feel. Scripted letters would look nice and would convey the holiday spirit more effectively.

Look to the video itself for clues as to what font to use. The font you use should tie into the theme of the video (see Figure 52.2). Don't overwhelm your

Figure 52.2

audience with a lot of different fonts either. Stick to just one or two. If you need two separate lines of text to stand out from each other, try making one line bold or italicized rather than changing the font.

Now We're Styling

The style of a title is the sum of all the specific attributes that give it a particular look. The font plays a crucial role, but so does the color, edge, shadow and framing of the text. These characteristics, or the lack of them, also contribute to the message you are sending. For example, lighter colors tend to be easier to read and seem happier, while darker colors can add a more urgent or even ominous tone to the title.

Color is a great tool to reinforce the theme of the project. Let's go back to the Christmas pageant title. Should you use black and orange for your text? Of course

not. That would be more appropriate for a Halloween project. Christmas colors—like reds, greens and whites—would work better.

Adding color can be a tricky task. Video tends to have problems with certain colors, particularly shades of red. The concentration of chroma/color tends to bleed across the screen. If you must use red, try adding a thick black outline to contain the bleeding. Remember, colors will look brighten on TV then they do on your computer. Make your reds and greens slightly darker than you'd like them to appear on tape. Many titling software applications have a "safe color" mode that will warn you against using a color that will over-saturate the video. Yellow tends to be the easiest color to read (next to white) and is often used for video titles.

What Did That Say?

After learning all of the different ways to present your title, you still need to ask the most important question, what will your title say? First, determine if you need graphics at all. Your titles should be limited to only those that advance the story in some way. Video artists often use titles extensively to add a poetic layer to their work, however graphics with no real purpose tend to irritate the viewer more than anything else.

How long should a title stay on the screen? Rule of thumb says that a title should stay up long enough for the viewer to read it aloud three times. Any shorter is too short. Any longer and your viewers may become distracted by the presence of the title. Obviously, the longer the title the longer it must remain on the screen. A person's name may remain on the screen for as little as two or three seconds, a graphic spelling out a five-sentence quote may need to stay on the screen for thirty seconds or more. Of course, there are exceptions to every rule. If you have the quote read by a narrator, you can take it out after he has read it through just once.

Putting it all Together

Great titles don't just happen, they take knowledge, planning and a lot of experimentation. Like good video, the better you plan your project the better off you are in editing. Titles are no exception. Remember, your titles are written in video, not in stone. When you're building your titles, look at them critically. Do they make sense visually? Is your spelling correct? Do they add to the message? Don't hesitate to experiment with your titles. Try something different. If you go too far and the visuals just don't work, you can always change them before going to tape.

When it all comes together well, the titles compliment the video and *vice versa*. This seamless integration of titles and video can make a word worth a thousand pictures.

Sidebar 1

Glossary of common titling terms

Font: The shape and style of the letters. There are thousands of fonts available; each unique font can send a different message.

Border: The border of your font is the edge surrounding the letters. Changing the size or color of the border can have a dramatic impact.

Shadow: Separate from border, the shadow can either attach to the letters or not. Shadows can be solid or have a degree of transparency.

Justification: Where the words are in relation to the screen: left, center or right.

Kerning: The spacing between the letters of a word. Some fonts are not consistent with their spacing and may need some manual kerning.

Leading: The spacing between lines of text.

Safe Title Area: The area of a video screen where titles are easily read and without distortion: roughly the inner 60% of the screen.

Sidebar 2

Shadows & Outlines

Whether or not your text has a soft drop shadow or a hard outlined edge can add a subtle difference. Soft shadows and outlines communicate a softer message, while hard edges often imply boldness or urgency.

Sidebar 3

TV is the Key

Want to make better titles? Watch more TV! Study the titles that you see on television, note the colors, fonts and styles that are used and try to copy them when you build your own titles.

53
Adventures in Sound Editing:
Or How Audio Post-Production Can Make Your Videos Sound Larger Than Life

Armand Ensanian

See video clips at www.videomaker.com/handbook.

Imagine the tape you made of your kids' last campout. It's got some crickets on the sound track. At night, didn't those crickets seem to chirp louder as campers grew quieter and the sky grew darker?

When Bobby started telling Billie Jo the story of the cricket that ate sisters, didn't those chirpings seem even louder to her? With some equalization, reverb and creative mixing of your original sound track, you could let your viewers hear those monster crickets the way Billie Jo heard them.

Sound editing can turn commonplace video events into adventures that seem larger than life. With some simple electronic equipment—some of which you may already have on your stereo system—you can polish up any raw sound track. Here's how.

Know your Sound

To make good video, you need to understand light; likewise, to make good audio, you will need to understand sound.

Webster defines sound as "mechanical vibrations traveling through the air or other elastic medium." How many times these vibrations occur in a second is the *frequency* of the sound. A tuning fork vibrating back and forth 1,000 times per second generates sound with a frequency of 1,000 cycles per second or Hertz (Hz). If it vibrated 200 times per second, we'd hear a frequency of 200 Hz.

Variations and combinations of frequencies account for all the sounds we hear. At best, the human ear can recognize frequencies between 32 and 22,000 Hz.

We can perceive frequencies below 32 Hz, but as vibration, not sound. This range deteriorates with age or abuse. It is not uncommon for senior adults to top out at 9,000 Hz, while losing all low-frequency sounds below about 150 Hz.

People with ear damage will adjust sound to match their deficiency. For example, a sound engineer at a rock club may set up the PA to produce ear piercing highs to compensate for such a loss of his high frequency sensitivity. So if you plan to use the services of a studio, make sure your sound engineer can hear.

The interaction of two or more frequencies creates a third sound called *harmonic*. Harmonics, also known as overtones, give sound its life, allowing the human ear to distinguish one voice from another. Poor recordings reduce or eliminate harmonics, turning sound into an unintelligible mess.

Good recordings recognize the harmonics of a sound track, and enhance them—with the help of some snazzy audio post-production devices.

The Mixer

The single most important tool for audio production is the *mixer*.

A mixer's number of input channels determines how many different signals—read sounds—you can work with simultaneously. You need at least two for mono recordings and four for stereo. More inputs allow you to control more sound sources.

Remember that the tape speed and audio recording format will determine the frequency response of the recording medium. A VHS tape recorded on the linear track at EP speed may yield a frequency response no higher than 7,000 Hz. So stick with hi-fi audio if possible.

The first step is to hook up the right cables to the proper inputs and outputs. Do not scrimp on cables, because bad connections can create a lot of buzz and noise. A good mixing console will allow an input signal to be either mike or line level. This compensates for low-level

microphone signals and high-level line inputs, such as those arriving from VCRs, cassettes or CD players. Output will be mono or stereo, depending on your VCR.

Mixers have sliders, or *faders*, that control volume for each channel. A master fader controls overall volume. Mixers will also feature all or some of the following: attenuation, equalization, cue sends, pan pots, solo switch, monitor control, Volume Unit (VU) meters or Liquid Element Displays (LEDs) and echo/reverb.

Attenuation cuts down high input signals to prevent overloading.

Equalizers allow precise tone adjustment of selected frequency ranges.

Cue sends can send the signal to the video tape, headphone or monitor speaker.

Pan pots control the spatial position between right and left stereo channels.

The *solo switch* "listens" in on any individual channel without interfering with the recording process.

Monitor controls adjust headphone or speaker volume. We'll look at echo and reverb later.

The Equalizer

An *equalizer* (EQ) is the most common piece of signal processing equipment. It allows you to divide the entire (human) 32–22,000 Hz audio spectrum into separate bands you can adjust independently. With an EQ, you can raise or lower the levels of these bands to change the tonal characteristics of a sound, reduce noise and even create certain audio effects.

Many mixers have a simple EQ built-in, allowing you to adjust high and low frequencies independently. This is fine for broad tonal changes, but for more control, you'll need a graphic equalizer. Though a handful of mixers offer this level of tonal control, most graphic EQs are external units.

Whereas simple EQs use knobs—one for treble, one for bass—graphic equalizers have vertical sliders that show the amount of correction you applied to each band of frequencies. Thus you can tell, at a glance, what the graphic EQ is doing to the audible spectrum. Hence the term graphic.

Think of the graphic EQ as a vastly expanded bass/treble dial. The more sliders, the greater the selective control.

Say you have some music on your soundtrack that sounds flat and unexciting. Try boosting the 100 Hz and 10,000 Hz sliders, while lowering the 1,000 Hz to 500 Hz sliders. The graphic pattern on the equalizer will look like a suspension bridge—what you'll hear is rock concert sound.

If you're working with classical music, you may need to elevate the middle frequencies to bring out specific instruments. And Aunt Trudy's squeaky voice may require you to slide down the high and upper midrange frequencies.

Hooking up a stand-alone EQ is easy— simply connect it between the source output and mixer input. Or, if you want to alter your whole sound mix, place the EQ between your mixer and record deck.

On the Level

In the world of audio post-production, the strength or "level" of an audio signal is as important as the way it sounds. We have our ears to tell us that a sound is tonally correct; for clean recordings we need something to tell us about the signal's level.

VU meters and LEDs monitor the levels so you can prevent overloading and distorting the signal. VU meters use a unique scale calibrated in decibels (dB), which measure actual signal strength.

VU meters boast an ascending scale of values that start with negative numbers. Instead of being at the bottom, zero is near the top of the range. Why? Because zero dB indicates a full-strength signal. This way it's easy to remember that if a signal strays much above zero, distortion may result.

Sometimes, simply setting a record level based on the VU meter isn't enough.

Some sounds jump wildly from loud to soft, making them distorted one second

and virtually inaudible the next. The difference between these very loud and soft sounds is the *dynamic range*.

Changes in dynamics, at least within reason are good. It's the dynamic range of a recording or vocalist that coveys realism and power. Streisand's vocal style is dynamic, my grandmother's isn't.

But when recording sounds, too much dynamic range can be a problem. Thankfully, there's help available from a nifty device called a *limiter*. A limiter reduces instant signal peaks, such as a loud scream or feedback from an electric guitar. A limiter allows you to set a maximum signal level; the unit holds all sound under that limit.

A *compressor* works somewhat like a limiter, though its effects are less dramatic. Radio stations use compressors to maintain high signal levels without fearing distortion. The small sacrifice in realism may be worth it if you plan on taping loud live concerts or monster truck rallies. Good production mixers have limiters built in, for controlling sounds at the time of recording.

Reverb

Sound loses energy as it moves through the air. Sound strength drops 6 dB every time you double the distance between a mike (or ear) and the sound source. This is why good microphone technique includes moving the mike close to the sound source during live shooting or narration dubbing.

Sound waves bound off walls and hard objects. Echoes are bouncing waves that follow more than 1/20 second after the original sound; reverb is repeated reflecting waves that sound almost continuous.

Post-production electronics can simulate both these effects. Echo and reverb units can run the gamut from simple tape loops, playing back what you record immediately, to sophisticated digital reverbs simulating rooms of all shapes and sizes.

Reverb units bring fullness to sound. With a reverb you can make a three-piece band playing in the basement sound like a major concert hall event. Reverb emulates the sound of a big hall. But watch out—too much reverb will make things muddy.

Reverb also adds authority to a narrator's voice. Rock and roll's ultimate DJ, Cousin Brucie, uses a lot of reverb.

Reverb, particularly when applied to drums, can make a band sound bigger than life on tape. Now you know how rock bands maintain the ambiance of the concert hall on recorded media.

Once it's on tape, you can't eliminate reverb easily from a recording. That's why recording engineers add it later for maximum control. Use sound-absorbing dampeners—rugs, blankets, egg cartons—in small studios whenever recording to capture a clean dry sound. Then employ electronics in post-production to simulate real room resonance.

Digital delays are similar to reverbs. They electronically delay the input signal for a selected amount of time. You can produce echoes of extremely short duration. Use digital delays to double a vocal, and you can make it sound as though two people are singing together. And, if you take one output channel from the delay and run it through an EQ, you may even make it sound like two different people. The possibilities are infinite.

Phase shifters delay the incoming signal slightly, causing the delayed signal to partially cancel the original. This causes whooshing sound effects—good for planes, trains and other speedy objects.

Going for the Take

Okay, you've got your mixer and your equalizer. Now you must decide which sounds you need for the mixing session.

Much pre-recorded material is available, but you may want to experience the thrill of creating you own sound effects (SFX) like they did in the old radio shows. Crumpled cellophane, for example, makes good rain or eggs frying. But keep in mind you only have two hands to

work with and will need them for the mixing board. If you can, have an assistant with you during a mix.

Say you're audio mixing a wedding tape. You can "sweeten" up all your location audio through use of both technique and equipment. You may need to clean up and equalize the live audio vocals a bit.

You'll also want to work on the sound from your outdoor segments—selectively equalizing background noises or reduce them manually during spoken passages. That waterfall, for example, near the wedding party blocked out some of the vocal interaction. An EQ can help, as well as a touch of reverb on the vocalists' voices.

When possible, record musical interludes preceding the ceremony—such as a soloist's number—on cassette rather than relying on a room mike during the shoot itself. If the bride doesn't object, the artist may have a professionally recorded tape of the same material you can use to replace the live track. After all, we are not focusing our attention on the soloist unless there are a lot of close-ups requiring lip sync.

In almost any kind of production, consider using background or "wallpaper" music track for continuity. It will fill in those silent gaps often associated with live footage. One cheap trick; try an inexpensive keyboard with built-in rhythm sounds as background. Use the individual slider on the mixer to boost the volume of the background gently during these silent periods.

If you're relying on pre-recorded music, find selections that don't clash with the theme of your video. For a wedding, don't use anything overly aggressive or dynamic; instrumentals are a safe bet. You may wish to sprinkle in some sound effects like ambience or laughter. Stock music of applause and laughter may follow special introductions at the reception.

By now you will have run out of hands. Starting the CD player just in time while cross fading from the live track to an overdub makes this a job for an octopus. Pro studios use computer sequencers and remote controls to help. It is best to try a few dry runs before actually recording onto the final tape. While practicing, send the mixer output to a cassette recorder so that you can listen later. It is very difficult to be objective while working the mixer.

With most projects, you'll find it challenging at best to audio edit the entire length in one pass. Use cuts and scene breaks in the video for audio transitions and segues. Have an assistant keep records of tape count and time passed as editing cues. Have them act as audio directors, coaching you through the moves.

Complicated editing may require sound recording the output to a tape recording before laying it on the videotape. A minimum of two output channels will be sent to corresponding tracks on a tape recorder. You may use the individual left and right channels of a stereo cassette recorder for two-track mono recording. This is ideal for adding narratives that may require numerous takes. You can then mix the two-track master directly onto the video. You'll have control over each individual channel.

Successive generations do add noise, but what a small price to pay for such flexibility. You can also add noise suppression or filters for the final mix-down. Four, eight, twelve, sixteen and twenty-four track audio recorders are available at recording studios for complicated mixes of numerous audio elements.

It takes a lot of practice to learn proper audio mixing technique. Even a small video switcher/audio mixer demands a lot of attention. The results, however, are light-years ahead of what you produce in-camera.

54

In The Audible Mood:
Sound Effects and Music, Evocative, Legal and Inexpensive

Armand Ensanian

Imagine *Popeye* without *toot toot*, *Casablanca* without *As Time Goes By*, *Jaws* without *bum BUM bum BUM bum BUM*. The soundtrack is the very lifeblood of a video, setting the mood and enlivening each scene of your work.

The trick is to find the right set of sounds to accompany your video. The options are many, from creating sound effects yourself—a la old-time radio—to buying mood music from a music library. In this chapter, we'll explore these options, and discuss the legal and financial ramifications of your choices.

The Copyright Challenge

The availability and affordability of a simple special effects generator (SEG) with built-in audio mixing has prompted many videographers to try adding music to video during editing.

It's harmless fun, attaching a favorite song to a tender moment between mother and child, a hot rock tune to fast-paced footage at the track or some Benny Goodman to Grandma and Grandpa's 50th anniversary party tape. After all, you're not planning to make thousands of copies for distribution. What are the chances that the composer, publisher or lyricist of the songs will ever see this tape, anyway? Slim at best; no one's going to bust you for borrowing a tune or two for personal use.

The trouble begins when you turn pro or even semi-pro.

Every serious videographer will eventually land a real-world assignment: a wedding video, local commercial or contest entry video. Whatever the application, you cannot use someone else's work without permission in any video offered for sale, profit and/or distribution. Music is like photography, sculpture or any art you can hold in your hands. Yet the fact that you can't hold it in your hands makes music ripe for theft by otherwise law-abiding citizens.

You needn't stoop to theft. You can buy great sound effects and music for your videos from a number of sources. The first is the most expensive. It involves buying the rights, for one-time use, of a pop song performed by a noted artist.

Your clients will request this sort of thing often. After all, most clients can only relate to what they know and hear on the radio. You'll have to explain that you simply can't use the pop song without getting permission from the artist's representatives first.

This means the artist's publisher or licensing agency, such as the American Society of Composers, Authors and Publishers (ASCAP). You've seen the name on almost every record, cassette tape or CD you own. ASCAP operates like a big collection agency, collecting fees for the use of their artists' material. It's a fair system that keeps artists from getting ripped off—but it's an expensive one for videographers.

The price you pay for one-time use rights of a pop song depends on how you distribute the tape. Radio stations, TV stations and local bars with a jukebox pay agencies like ASCAP a blanket fee.

This fee may range from thousands of dollars for a radio station to a few hundred dollars a year for that jukebox. (For more info, call ASCAP in New York 212-595-3050.)

Unless you expect your video to make a big profit, paying for rights to use a hit tune may be unwise. There are cheaper ways to go.

One way is to create your own music. If you've the talent and the time, this is a worthwhile option. You can use your desktop video equipment to make music; MIDI interfaces to Macs and PCs provide the musically inclined with unlimited creative potential.

Software and sound cards can produce digital sound that rivals the best CDs. Some even come with hundreds of digital sound samples, ranging from pianos to xylophones.

Despite all this automation, you'll still need to have a musical ear, something that's not included. If you don't have an ear for music, find local musicians to participate in your production. They'll have both the equipment and the ear you need. You'll find, however, that the more people involved, the longer the process. Just make sure all parties sign an agreement transferring the rights to use the material over to you. Handshake deals don't carry the weight they once did.

The simplest solution, and perhaps the best bang for the buck, is to buy the music from a music library. The quality of the material will be as good as or better than you'd expect. You have heard music library soundtracks all your life. Commercials, opening scenes to sport events, TV news shows and presentation videos all use music made to augment video productions. In fact, most of the music is so much like what you hear on the radio that it's often easy to persuade clients to use music library tracks. Moreover, much of what's available was written and composed by award-winning musicians; the quality is first rate.

Libraries

You'd be surprised at how well music libraries categorize music ... broadcast promotional, broadcast show theme, corporate imaging, corporate icon build, credit roll, documentary, events such as weddings birthdays and anniversaries, industrial presentations, news and information, movie soundtrack, retail presentation, retail promotional, sound-alike, sports/action and underscore—to name a few.

All of us have a good sense of what these many categories sound like. Just watch some TV or look at a promo tape at the local travel agency. Still unsure?

Music libraries will gladly send you a tape or disk of material for approval for a specific tune; some even offer sample CDs.

There are many ways to buy music from music libraries. The traditional method charges per needle drop. This means you pay only for a specific selection of music used from their records, tapes or CDs. The term comes from the days of the phonograph, but applies to tapes and CDs as well. Most large music libraries will help you find exactly what you need. Computer databases allow quick searches from tens of thousands of titles.

The dollars add up quickly here, but you may obtain a very distinct tune, for a one-time production, that's not available from any other source. This is ideal for videographers who don't produce a lot of videos, but who need a unique style of music when they do.

Music library charges for needle drops depend mostly on the extent of use. For example, the charge for broadcasting the same music on the same video will vary, depending on whether it's broadcast in Smalltown, USA or Metropolis. Determined by the number of viewers, needle-drop fees may range from $150 for a network TV broadcast opening title to only $50 for a local TV program. The only other cost: $20 for leasing the CD that contains the material. You make your choice from the CD, report the piece of music you will use and pay for it.

There are other methods of dealing with music libraries. You may buy a production-blanket where you pay only for the music for a given production. Typically you select a CD with a variety of musical themes from a library, and use as much of it as you wish, provided you restrict that use to that production. Costs depend on the size of the project and distribution, but average in the hundreds of dollars.

Annual-blanket fees allow you to buy licensing rights to a group of CDs for unlimited use during a given year. Popular with high-volume videographers, radio and TV stations, fees from reputable large firms are around $1,000 for a group of over

a dozen or two different theme CDs for the year. You can also sign multi-year contracts with CD upgrades.

The best value: a buy-out library. Here you pay a one-time price for a CD, or set of CDs, that contains the music you need. You may use the CD as often as you wish, for as long as you live. You can better appreciate this deal when you know that you can purchase buy-out libraries for as little as $5 per sample tape from small independent producers advertising in the back of magazines.

But cheap can also mean poor quality. Listen to sample disks and tapes before you buy.

Sound Subscription

You may want to subscribe to a library service. Here you receive a CD every month or two, and have the option to keep it for a one-time fee. Beware, though: you may soon find yourself way overstocked, and stuck with soundtracks you'll never use.

It's like that videotape collection you started a few years back; despite the variety you always seem to stick with a few favorites. A variation on the subscription theme: lease the entire contents of a music library for a term, such as a year, and receive new CDs every month or two to add to that library.

One last note of caution: music libraries are licensed to individuals or production companies. Borrowing a library CD from a friend, and then putting your name on the finished product is a direct violation of copyright.

Stay honest. It'll pay off in the long run.

55
Dig 'm Out, Dust 'Em Off

Jim Stinson

Sooner or later, you'll come upon that drawer awash in color print packets, that carton bulging with slide boxes, that crate stuffed with round rolls of movie film and you will feel regret and a sort of mild guilt. All those precious records. All that effort and money. And you never look at them.

Why? Because there has never been a quick, convenient way to do so. Sure, you can arrange prints in albums, but for slides or movies you have to haul out the projector, wrestle with the screen, load the trays or thread the film and round up a patient if unenthusiastic audience.

So you don't, and there your family pictures sit, year in and year out, in mute but eloquent reproach.

But now that you have a camcorder, you have a way to turn your photographic archives into video programs that are as exciting as they are easy to show. You can transfer your movies, slides and prints to tape. And in doing this you can enjoy the fun and satisfaction that truly creative work delivers, because you aren't just copying materials, you're transforming them into video programs.

So this chapter offers a bundle of tips to help you copy photo materials to video. We'll start with suggestions that apply to all video copying, whether the source material is movies, slides or prints. Then we'll cover transferring movies and slides.

The chapter that follows this one concludes with a look at the challenge of videotaping photographic prints and other artwork.

General Tips

Here, then, are tips that apply to all types of video copying.

Copying with a Monitor. First, always use an external monitor to set up and check your work. It will give you a far more accurate image than you can obtain from any camcorder viewfinder, and in copying it's essential that you frame your originals precisely. You can run a cable from most camcorders to a monitor through composite or S-video jacks.

Adjust the monitor to show color, brightness and contrast as accurately as possible.

If you can't generate color bars and set up your monitor on a vectorscope, use a good quality store-bought video as a reference standard. Once you figure out how the tape should look, you'll be able to use it to dial in almost any monitor.

I set up my monitors with a commercial exercise tape. It has high video quality, carefully lit flesh tones for many skin colors and bright but realistic colors.

Rely on your monitor as you check and adjust focus, composition and color balance.

Controlling Color. Color balance is critical in copying. Usually you want to match the colors of the original, but sometimes you need to change the original colors to correct them or create special effects. To help control color, make sure you set the camera's white balance correctly. Most modern movie and slide projectors—as well as the lights on pro copy stands—use lamps with a color temperature of 3,200 K (degrees Kelvin). That is exactly the color temperature of your camera's "indoor" white balance setting, so set your camera to indoor—or "incandescent". If the color balance seems off when viewed on your well-adjusted external monitor, warm the light or cool it with photographic color compensation (CC) filters obtainable at photo stores.

For more color control, run the image through a color processor before recording it. To do this, don't use the "corder" part of your camcorder. Instead, just run the video signal out of the camera section to a color processor. From there, run the signal to a VCR.

Then, using your camcorder as if it were simply a camera, record the processed image directly on the VCR.

Steady as She Goes. Since a still image shows no movement of its own, it reveals the least little bit of camera shake; so be sure to set up your camcorder on a sturdy tripod. Here's a cheap trick if you need to set your camcorder securely on a table or other flat surface. Obtain a bolt threaded to match the unit's tripod socket and use it to secure your camera to a simple plywood base plate. Recess the bolt into a single piece of plywood, or put small feet on either side of the bolt.

If your camera has a remote control, by all means use it. You'll find many camera *on/off* buttons on the handgrip, so pressing them will no doubt jiggle the camera. Using the *record/pause* button on the remote guarantees jitter-free images. On some camcorders, you can even control the zoom, add titles and engage autofocus from the remote. Perform photo transfers, and the infrared remote becomes your best friend.

Keeping Things Quiet. Your final program will probably have sound—narration, music or both—but when you're recording you don't want to pick up projector noise or other ambient sound. To prevent this, disable your camcorder's microphone by inserting a plug into the external mike jack. The trick: use a plug that's not connected to anything. I find that a mini-to-RCA converter plug works fine with my camcorder.

On the other hand, you may wish to use the video soundtrack as a notepad to record data about your pictures as you transfer them. ("That's Aunt Florrie and the film can says Lake Runamuck, Summer, 1956.") When you assemble this raw footage into your final program, you can use these vocal notes to help create your final narration.

These tips cover all types of copying. Now let's look at copying movies and slides, beginning with some suggestions that apply to both media.

Copying Projected Images

First of all, decide whether you want to use conversion hardware or simply record the projected image off a wall or screen. You've seen film/slide transfer systems—arrangements of screens and mirrors that let you set up projector and camcorder at right angles and videotape the projected image.

While these can be quite useful, they sometimes limit your flexibility in selecting which portion of the image you want to record. It may be better and cheaper for you to project the original images onto a white surface and aim your camcorder directly at that surface. To make high-quality copies with this front-projection system:

- Make sure that projector and camcorder are perfectly level and that their lenses are at the same height.

- Place projector and camcorder as close together as possible, at equal angles to the screen. This will keep the image borders rectangular and the pictures undistorted.

- Use a smooth, white screen—never a beaded movie screen. I find that the white back of a poster printed on glossy stock works fine. Almost any high-quality white paper will work. Don't be afraid to try many types of papers—after all, they're cheap.

- Place the screen as far away as you can, while still getting an acceptably bright image (use your external monitor to check). The farther the screen from the projector and the camera, the shallower the angle between them—and the smaller the chance of picture distortion. Put it too far away, and the camcorder may try to compensate for the dimmer image by cranking up its gain. The result: a grainy image.

By setting up your copy operation like this you can make high-quality transfers and retain better control over the images. If those images are 8 mm or 16 mm films, you'll need to make a few extra adjustments.

Copying Movies

Movies are simple to copy to video because the screen proportions of the two media are the same: 4 to 3. Simply adjust your camcorder lens so that the projected image fills the frame and you're in business.

But movies are also hard to copy because of differing projection speeds. Your camcorder, of course, records thirty frames (images) per second. Film, on the other hand, runs at 24, 18 or 16 frames per second. The trouble is, these are only nominal speeds, and none of them matches the 30 fps of video. As a result, an unpleasant flickering effect often marks video transfers.

Fortunately, most film projectors have speed controls that you can use to vary the actual number of frames per second. The best way to use the speed control is to change the film projection speed gradually while eyeballing the effect on your monitor. When you've found the best setting for your video outfit, leave the projector at that speed and transfer your footage.

You can also stop many projectors so that they project a single frame as a still image; you can transfer these frozen moments to video. The problem is, once the movie film stops in the projector gate, it's protected from the hot projector lamp by a thick glass heat filter that degrades the quality of the image. If you have a good four-head video system you may get better results by transferring the movies in real time, displaying a selected frame as a video still and then re-copying that.

A final tip: because of the magnification required of tiny 8 mm film images, they often show dirt, fuzz and fingerprints. Clean movie film by pulling it gently through a fine, lint-free cloth saturated with film cleaner bought at a photo store (or with carbon tetrachloride).

Never use a water-based solution; film emulsion is industrial Jell-O and you can guess what happens when it's soaked in water. Also, be sure to clean the gunk out of the projector's film gate—that's the pair of metal plates holding the film as it's projected.

Copying Slides

Whether you use rear-screen or front-screen projection, copying slides is much like copying movies. But copying photographic transparencies can be trickier because their shape does not match that of a video screen in two crucial ways. First, slides orient ver-tically—portrait—as well as horizontally—landscape. Secondly, even horizontal slides will not fit a TV screen because the ratio of their sides is three to two instead of four to three (see Figure 55.1). So, in transferring slides, you must compensate.

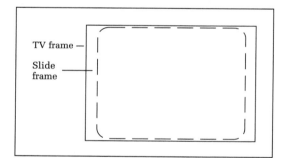

Figure 55.1 *Copying slides can be tricky due to their shape.*

Timing Your Slide Transfers

A slide will sit there on the screen until you advance the projector tray, so how long should you roll tape on each photo? I find that between 5 and 20 seconds per image is ample, depending on how much there is to see. Clearly, you don't need as long to look over a simple road sign as you do the ceiling of the Sistine Chapel. If you doubt that 20 seconds is longer than anyone wants to stare at even the most visually interesting slide; try it, you'll see.

Pre-Programmed Slide Shows

Many dedicated slide photographers show their programs on two or more pro-jectors, dissolving between them with a programmer unit controlled by pulses on an audiocassette. The cassette also carries a synchronized sound track.

By far the easiest way to transfer slides to video is by creating a complete pro-gram in this manner, plugging the cassette player audio into the camera's line-in jack and recording the program in real time. Another advantage: your complete pro-gram is first generation video! The big dis-advantage: you can't compose your video frame for each slide.

But whichever way you choose, you'll end up with video footage that you can edit into a program you'll be proud to show.

56
Easy Copy

Jim Stinson

Video is probably the most convenient and effective way to display precious movies, slides and photographic records. The preceding chapter showed you how to transfer movies and slides to video. Now we'll look at the fascinating process of copying photographic prints and other forms of flat art.

To transfer flat art to video, you'll need a copy stand, copy lights and suitable backgrounds on which to place your subjects. You can put these elements together cheaply and easily.

Your Basic Copy Stand

A *copy stand* simply holds the camcorder, lights, and artwork (see Figure 56.1) Still-camera copy stands, available at better photography stores, aren't always suitable for video, however. Many video lenses won't focus close enough at the camera-to-subject distance imposed by copy stands intended for 35 mm cameras. You'll often get better results by assembling your own video copying stand.

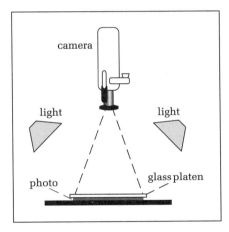

Figure 56.1 *A copy stand.*

In building a stand, consider how to orient it. You can use your tripod as camera mount for a horizontal stand, but holding the artwork in place vertically can be a nuisance (see Figure 56.2).

On the other hand, a vertical stand requires you to build a special mount for your camcorder, since it's usually impractical

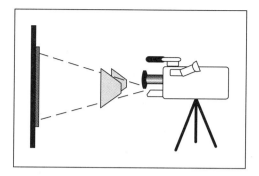

Figure 56.2 *A horizontal stand using a tripod.*

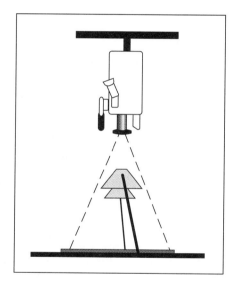

Figure 56.3 *A vertical stand requires you to build a special mount for your camcorder.*

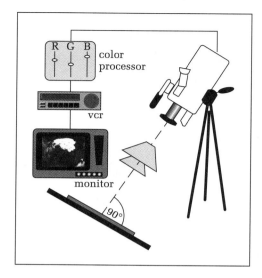

Figure 56.4 *A rig set at about 30 degrees works well.*

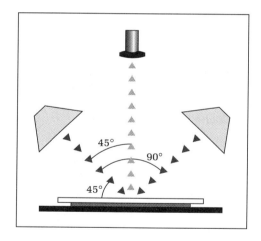

Figure 56.5 *Lights placed at 45 degrees off lens axis won't reflect into the lens.*

to shoot straight down from a tripod (see Figure 56.3).

I find it's best to compromise. A rig set up at about 30 degrees from horizontal lets you use your tripod, but still prevents photos from sliding off their backgrounds (see Figure 56.4).

Elemental Light

Now that you have a place to shoot your photos, you need to light them. Rig your lights on either side of your artwork support, at 90 degrees from each other and 45 degrees from the artwork and camcorder. Since the angle of incidence equals the angle of refraction (as you recall from high school physics), lights placed 45 degrees off the lens axis will not reflect into the lens (see Figure 56.5).

What kinds of lights? If you copy nothing but black and white originals, a pair of fluorescent shop lights work great and cost very little. You can't use them for color, though. They may seem to match daylight white balance, but they really don't and the mismatch will be visible when you copy color prints.

For color, use halogen (quartz) lights, whose 3,200-degree Kelvin color temperature exactly matches your camcorder's "indoor" or "incandescent" white-balance setting. (Never use standard household bulbs. Their lower color temperatures create a slight orange cast.)

For inexpensive halogen lighting, buy a couple of clamp-on work lights and fit them with halogen PAR floodlights.

Or modify a halogen work light -the kind with two heads on an adjustable floor stand- for a better and more versatile lighting setup.

If you're at all handy, you can modify one of these work lights for use as an all-purpose video light. Or dismount its heads and rig them as individual copy lights. Simply replace their electrical cords with plugged power cords, add a junction box to the lamp yoke, and remove the lamps from their yoke to use them with your copy stand (see Figure 56.6).

If you don't care to mess with electrical modifications, you can buy these same halogen heads as individual work lights that squat on low feet.

With camcorder and lighting in place, you need a way to support-and display-your photos or artwork

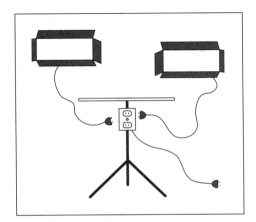

Figure 56.6 *A work light modified for use as an all-purpose video light.*

A Little Background

For simply copying drugstore color prints, you may not need a background for your artwork. Instead, simply set your rig so each print fills the frame. But to transfer images that don't fit the 4-to-3 video proportions, you need a background to fill the rest of the frame around them.

For an "invisible" background, you can place your photos on black cloth or cardboard. But this is rarely successful since bright copy lights invariably bring out some backing texture, resulting in tattletale gray on your screen. It's better to back your artwork with a dark, pleasing color like burgundy or rich blue.

Textured backgrounds (like burlap, monk's cloth, or velvet) contribute even more. The 45-degree lighting accents the background texture, adding dimensionality to the shot. For variety, try inexpensive dining table place mats. They come in a wide range of colors, patterns, and text- and they're just the right size.

Perfectly flat prints and artwork are rare, so you may need to press them against their backing with a *platen*—a simple pane of glass. Professionals use "optically flat" glass free of imperfections, but you'll do well enough by checking the glass sheet for ripples and distortions before you select it.

Be careful—glass is notoriously reflective and hard to light.

Overcoming Problems

To light materials for copying, you must cope with reflections and excess heat from the lights.

To defeat reflections from a glass cover or from glossy color prints, make sure to set your lights at the recommended 45-degree angle. If that doesn't work, try a polarizing filter on the camera lens.

To completely kill reflections, some professional copiers use polarizing gels on the lamps as well.

Heat from your lamps can cause problems. Halogen bulbs put out enough of it to damage delicate artwork if positioned too close. Fortunately, two 500-watt halogen lamps throw plenty of light on the subject from four or five feet. (Be careful how you handle hot lamp housings. Professional gaffers wear gloves.)

But you need to keep the lights as close as you prudently can, to increase "depth of field"—the zone behind and (especially, in copying) in front of what you focus on that's still acceptably sharp.

In copying, you're usually working with your zoom lens set at its longest focal length and focused at its shortest distance. Both reduce depth of field to the minimum. Since the size of the lens opening also affects depth of field, you need lots of light to achieve the smallest possible aperture.

As an experiment, I aimed a camcorder at a copy surface and held a ruler at right angles to that surface. I studied the resulting image on a monitor to see how much of the ruler remained sharp as its markings got farther from the plane of focus. In ambient room light the depth of field extended less than 1/4-inch from the plane of focus. But when I turned on two 500-watt halogen lights the zone of sharpness jumped to over an inch.

You need as much depth of field as possible for two reasons. First, despite your best efforts, your camcorder may not be absolutely at right angles to your artwork. Part of the art will be soft if the depth of field is too shallow.

Second, you need a bit of focus leeway. In copying, you often have to focus by moving the camcorder instead of by adjusting the lens. You generally have your lens set at its closest focus, and can't adjust it any further. To fine-tune the focus you have to move the camcorder slightly instead.

Why not get around the problem with your lens's macro setting? Many camcorder lenses offer macro capability for close work, and yours may be fine for copying.

I tested the same camcorder with it's 8–80 mm zoom and 4-foot minimum camera-to-subject distance and found that at 80 mm, the minimum field was 2.25 by 3 inches—small enough to copy wallet-size pictures.

When I switched to macro (which operates only at the winde-angle end of the zoon range), the minimum size was almost the same, but the lens hood was now only half an inch from the artwork! Needless to say, this makes lighting the art impossible.

In shooting photographic prints a color processor patched between camcorder and recording VCR can be indispensable.

You can color-correct age-faded photos. Typically, elderly color prints that have been exposed to light show a sickly magenta cast. Adjusting color balance can reduce this somewhat. And color adjustments can improve the originals: pump up the orange glow of a sunset or enhance the blue-white of snow. Add a slight sepia tone to black and white prints for an old-time effect (but don't overdo it—it can look hokey). Or set the colors to zero to guarantee black and white originals don't take on a color cast when viewed on a color monitor.

The Copy Session

Changing camcorder distance, focus, lighting, backgrounds, and such can be tedious, so the best procedure is to gang all similar artwork together. Sort photos by size, and then by portrait (vertical) or landscape (horizontal) orientation.

Sort by proportion, too: prints from 35 mm originals are usually 3 to 2; instamatic or Polaroid prints have different proportions. The more originals you can copy before you have to change the setup, the faster the process will go.

One nice thing about copying is that your finished programs can be first generation video. To do this, I create a complete music track, dub it to an assembly tape, and then load the tape into a VCR.

Next, I set up my camcorder to copy photos and cable it to the VCR. Using the video insert mode, I record the camera signal, timing it to the music as I would any editing element.

For stereo hi-fi sound and/or narration, copy the finished tape, relaying the music and adding voice-over narration. The final program tape will still be only second generation.

What's in Store?

The exciting future of video copying is already here! You need only a desktop computer, a card that accepts and outputs NTSC video, and a software package for retouching images.

You import a photo from your copy camcorder to your computer, which digitizes the video signal from NTSC. You take all the time you need to revise and improve the picture to your taste, reconvert it to NTSC and export it to your VCR.

You can remove Junior's acne; improve color, brightness and contrast; erase cracks and spots from that priceless family daguerreotype. Software packages will combine photos, mix photos and artwork, and "morph" a person into somebody (or some thing) else!

All the hardware and software you need for a "Digital Darkroom" is currently available and—with the rapid decline in prices—widely affordable. But even without computerized retouching, you can use your skills to pull those wonderful photos out of dark drawers and dusty albums and put them up on the screen where everyone can enjoy them.

PART V
Television Distribution

Broadcasting your programs through cable and over-the-air TV.

57
Commercial Distribution: Mapping Your Way to Financial Success

William Ronat

See video clips at www.videomaker.com/handbook.

Making video means working with motion, sound, color, words, composition, light—all combined in a maximum creative effort. That's fun.

Many have produced enough video to get good at it. This means putting in long hours planning, shooting and editing programs. That's work.

When you work for a company, you expect a paycheck when you finish your work. That's reasonable.

When you work for yourself, however, you can expect to work just as hard to sell your product as you did to make it. That's life.

Fun and Profit

To sell your product, several things have to happen. People have to know your product exists. They have to decide that the product is something they want. Then they have to pull their money out of their pockets and hand it to you.

This exchange can take the form of tickets at a theater, credit card information over the phone, money from the advertisers running commercials on your show or checks from all those networks buying your product. It all boils down to this: you get paid.

That's what you want. You may travel many paths to this destination. You can sell directly to the consumer through magazine ads or direct mail; you can work through a distributor; you can sell your program to broadcast TV: or you can buy airtime from a cable company, and then sell commercials during your show.

The path you choose (Figure 57.1) depends on your product and, to some extent, how deep your pockets are. Being in business involves taking risks, which means you sometimes have to shell out some cash before it starts to flow back to you.

Is It Good?

The first step in the process is to take a long, very critical look at your product.

Is this a show that other people will want to watch? Would they pay money to watch

283

Figure 57.1

it? Would you? Ask your friends to watch it and tell you what they think. Now do the same with your enemies. That should give you a nice range of viewpoints.

Is the target audience large enough to justify the production costs? You can produce the greatest video ever on *Growing Beans in Sandy Soil*, but if this subject doesn't appeal to enough people, then you may not get your investment back—even if every potential member of your target audience buys your product. You have to believe strongly in your product—just make sure you can justify that belief.

Your next consideration: production value. Producing on consumer-level equipment will work for some uses, but if you plan to sell your show to a broadcast or major cable network, you may want to work with professional gear. Also, use the best crew and talent that you can afford. If your show is perfect, *except* for the lighting, *or* the audio, *or* the on-camera spokesperson's delivery, you could be in trouble; one of these flaws alone could flag your project for rejection.

Let's say that (based on your long and successful track record) your product is

intellectually compelling and technically flawless (congratulations). Now you're ready to distribute that perfect video. Let's start with the cheapest way to do it—by yourself.

Birth of a Salesman

This method seems fair and natural to most people. You worked hard on your video; it's only right that you should enjoy all the profit from this effort. Remember, however, that this also means assuming all the risk and fronting all the money for the advertising, postage, dubbing costs, shipping and so on. Also figure in time and effort for answering inquiries about your product, as well as packaging and addressing these packages when you do make a sale.

Let's say your glorious video details the proper maintenance of inboard marine engines. Is this program any good? You think so. Your friends think so. Even your enemies admit to liking it. But these opinions won't do you much good when it comes time to sell. What you need is a review.

Check all the magazines covering your subject (*Inboard Boating Illustrated, Marine Engine World* and so on) and read them. Do they review books or videos of interest to their readers? If they do, write a professional cover letter to the editor of each, describing your show in a straightforward manner. (If they don't, send out letters (Figure 57.2) anyway; your product may be good enough to set a few precedents.) Don't hype your product at this point; journalists don't like that approach. Also send along VHS dubs of your program for the editors to pass on to their reviewers.

Don't expect replies, unless you also enclose a SASE (Self-Addressed Stamped Envelope) in each letter. If you want your dub back, then send a SASE with enough postage to cover its weight.

Getting a review is not a quick process. The reviewer has to view your show, write up the review and get the review to the magazine. Depending on the publication,

Figure 57.2

it may be two to three months from the point the review reaches the editor's desk until it actually gets into print.

If the review is favorable, your show has just taken a big step toward legitimacy. A major publication (*Inboard Boating Illustrated*, no less) has complimented your show in print. This tells your potential buyers that your program is for real, that you did not just fall off of a turnip truck and that the video is worth spending their money to see.

Another way to lend legitimacy to your tape is to have an expert introduce the material. You can also put the expert's picture on the cover of the tape's package. Potential buyers see their favorite inboard engine expert on the tape and say to themselves, "Hey, I trust Joe Inboard. This tape must be good." Of course, Joe Inboard will probably ask you to pay for his image, or he may even ask for a piece of the action (such as a percentage of the profits).

If *Inboard Boating Illustrated* uses a rating system (four little boats equal excellent, and three little boats equal good), then you have a perfect element for your next step in selling your product—advertising in the magazine. In your display ads, you'll feature "FOUR BOATS—*Inboard Boating Illustrated*" as prominently as possible.

The cost of your ad will vary according to the number of people who read the maga-

zine, how much space your ad takes up and how many colors appear in the ad. As you might expect, the price goes up as readers, colors and space requirements go up. If you run an ad run more than once (which you almost always have to do to have any impact), the amount per issue goes down. Magazines often offer breaks for running an ad three times (3×) or six times (6×).

Fulfillment

Once the ad runs, the orders start to pour in.

But how do you get them? Do customers order by credit card over the phone (any time of the day or night)? Or do they send you a check? Do you wait for checks to clear before you send customers their tapes? What if the check bounces? Which—if any—credit cards will you accept? What about a money-back guarantee?

You can avoid some of these headaches by working out a deal with a fulfillment house. I once used a service from a company that made dubs of my show and kept them on hand. The company provided me with its 800 number, which I used in my ads. My customers placed their orders with this company. The company performed a number of services for me:

- recording the pertinent customer information,
- accepting credit cards,
- waiting for checks to clear and
- sending out the videos, using a preprinted slip sleeve that I provided.

At the end of each month, the company sent me a statement telling me how many units sold during that time, along with a check—minus the fees they charged for their fulfillment services.

This is a good, convenient service; but it does mean additional expense. Also, fulfillment services typically require the assurance that they make a minimum amount of money per month, which means selling a minimum number of your videos each month. If the total falls below this, you may pay a penalty.

Direct Mail

Another method of reaching potential customers is direct mail. You get direct mail from advertisers at home all the time; you probably think of it as junk mail. But it's only junk if the ad is trying to sell you something you don't want. That's why you must make sure that the people you mail your ad to are the people who want your product.

There are companies that sell lists of business names, preformatted on sticky labels for easy use. These lists break down according to type of business, number of employees, region of operation and so on. Be selective, and you can buy the right list for your target market.

Also, *Inboard Boating Illustrated* probably sells its subscriber list to advertisers. Consider buying subscriber lists from appropriate publications.

Once you buy the right list, find a local company that handles large mailings. This way, you won't have to stuff any envelopes. If you've ever licked more than twenty stamps at a sitting, you'll know this service is worth the expense.

When you determine the price of your program, remember to figure in the advertising costs. For example, if you buy a list of 10,000 names from a magazine, print up 10,000 ads and stuff 10,000 stamped envelopes for your direct mailing, you've shelled out some serious money. The direct mail industry considers a one percent response rate "good;" that's 100 orders from a mailing of 10,000. So you could lose money if you don't charge enough for your product.

Libraries & Video Rental Stores

After you've fully exploited the inboard boating market, exploit libraries.

There are public libraries, college libraries, high school libraries and more. Most have videotape departments stocked with a variety of videos; especially popular are how-to programs.

Check out the magazines covering this market: *Booklist* (you won't find it at the newsstand, it goes out directly to librarians); *School Library Journal; Library Journal*; and *Wilson Library Bulletin*. Each of these publications reviews videotapes, so getting a review is a good place to start.

The local video rental store (Figure 57.3) is another option. One method would be to walk in, ask to see the owner and try to sell the show then and there. But this would be much like trying to teach a pig to sing. It wastes your time and annoys the pig.

Rental stores buy their programs almost exclusively from major distributors that publish catalogs every week. One is the Major Video Concept catalog (800-365-0150), which boasts lots of four-color ads for Hollywood features. One page advertises foreign films and other videos.

Figure 57.3

Distributors

When you distribute a product, such as a videotape, there is a certain amount of infrastructure that has to be in place. You must let the customer know that the product is available, you must be able to take orders and fulfill them. This is true whether you have one product in your line or a thousand. Obviously, this infrastructure is less expensive per product if you have a thousand products. This is why there are companies called distributors.

In the early years of the motion picture industry, there were no major film studios. The people who owned the theaters needed product. Viewers didn't ask for much, they would watch a man petting a dog or a horse running down a road and be happy. But they always wanted more.

Finally, the people who owned lots of theaters and thus needed the most product decided to make their own movies. That's how the major studios were born. Distribution was the key.

For video, there are hundreds of small specialty distributors. One distributor might serve a market of gardeners. Every few months the distributor sends a catalog to these gardeners featuring all the books and videos on pruning and planting. The gardener can pick out several and order all of them at the same time. Convenient.

You can usually find a list of distributors at your local library. Books listing all the video products available for the current year often include a list of distributors for ordering purposes.

The names may not tell you much about the distributors. So before you send out copies of your program to distributors, call the companies and chat with the owners about your product. Even if these people show no interest in your video, they may recommend distributors who might.

When a distributor decides to handle your show, you'll negotiate a contract. You won't sell the show, but rather license it. This means that while you still own the material, the distributor will receive a percentage of the retail price of product sold. This could be a healthy percentage, like 75 percent. Or it could be less, depending on how good a negotiator you are and how much the distributor wants the product.

When negotiating remember that the distributor is paying for advertising, fulfillment, storage and so on; you assume none of the risk. These services are worth something.

The Big Screen

You've always dreamed of seeing your work on the big screen. This means selling your work to film distributors—not an easy sell.

Major film festivals are a good place to show off your work to distributors. Events such as the Berlin Film Festival and the Sundance Film Festival are places to see and be seen by "the players". Before you can enter your show, however, check the entrance requirements. Pay particular attention to format. If you shot on video, you will have to transfer the master to 16 mm or 35 mm. Expect to pay a couple of thousand dollars for this process.

There are many video festivals as well. Entering and winning prizes for quality and great content can't hurt your chances of interesting a distributor in your show. And the price of a dub for your entry will be less expensive than a 35 mm film print.

Seeing your work "on the air," either on a broadcast or a cable station, is always a thrill. Again, there are many avenues you can take to reach this goal.

Vid News is Good News

Many local news shows encourage videographers to be on the lookout for newsworthy events. (Figure 57.4.) Even in large markets, a news director has only a limited number of crews to cover the station's area. Given the improved quality of consumer gear, stations are more likely to get footage of dramatic events as they

Figure 57.4

Figure 57.5

happen if a quick-thinking videographer happens to be on the scene.

The value of the footage depends on its newsworthiness; most stations pay $50 to $100 for short news pieces. You can expect a lot more if you get the Loch Ness monster, Bigfoot or some natural or man-made disaster on tape.

If you live in an area which has a low-power television (LPTV) station or a small cable company, you might be able to get on the air by forging a partnership. If the station or company doesn't have a production arm, make yourself useful to them by offering to: (1) cover city council meetings, (2) produce promotional spots, and (3) shoot public service work.

Could you do this out of the goodness of your heart? You could, or you could offer to do all this work in exchange for airtime on the channel, say an hour a week.

On the Air

Now you own an hour of airtime; how do you profit by it? There are a number of ways to boost your bottom line. If you live in an area that attracts lots of tourists, create a show that reviews restaurants, profiles interesting people and recommends local hot spots. Sell 30-second spots on the show to some of these same businesses.

Then produce the 30-second spots for them, charging for production services.

Or take your hour of airtime and sell it to a syndicator. The syndicator will then fill the time with an infomercial or an entertainment program, commercials included.

Or you could run a telethon and ask for donations from viewers in order to keep your telethon on the air. (If you succeed at this one, be sure to tell me about it.)

Leased Access & Satellite Time

If you have a great programming idea and live in an area where the cable company carries more than 36 channels, you may be able to lease your own time. The Cable Act of 1992 requires cable operators to set aside a certain percentage of their channels for lease by independent programmers.

This sounds good; but some cable companies hesitate to sell time to independents, and others charge too much when they do. Contact your local cable operator (Figure 57.5) and ask about its leased access policy; be ready to fight for the time that is legally yours.

If national exposure appeals to you, try a satellite TV network such as Channel America. Channel America is a 24-hour satellite channel affiliated with 110 full and low-power TV stations and cable affiliates in the U.S., reaching some 25 million households.

On-air hours are open to programming in the following categories: Talk, Events, Emerging Sports, College Network, Nostalgia, Travel, Lifestyle, Talent Showcase, Outdoors, Hunting, Fishing, Financial Opportunities, Your Money, Music Across America, New Age, Hobbies, Crafts and Collecting, International and Health and Fitness.

Airtime on Channel America isn't free, however. And the satellite channel won't pay you for your programming. There are ways around these financial obstacles, however. Say you've reformatted your inboard marine engines video; it's now a half-hour show with breaks for commercials. Approach national inboard engine manufacturers; ask them to buy the time on Channel America for your program, in exchange for exclusive commercial time. Of course, they would also pay you for the production.

Destination Distribution

Distribution paths are many. Some involve risking your money; some involve spending your time; and others involve sharing your profits with others.

The key is to find the ones that work for you and your video. Persevere and you can sell your show.

All it takes is a little effort and a little luck … and a great product.

58
Public Access:
Produce Your Own TV Show

Sofia Davis

You can have your own TV show. It's easier than you might think and best of all, it's absolutely free! How, you ask? The answer is public access.

Public access television is noncommercial airtime made available to the public, free of charge. The only requirement to utilize public access, it that you live in the community where the show will be produced. Most public access facilities offer training in shooting, audio and editing, and provide all the equipment you'll need.

While the law no longer requires that cable companies air public access programs, a certain percentage of cable revenue in any market must go to the host city or municipality. A portion of this money goes towards public access television, so most markets (even small ones) have a public access channel and a modest studio.

Does producing and broadcasting your own public access TV show sound enticing to you? This article will tell you how to get started.

Getting Started

The first step is to contact your local public access station and sign up for an orientation class. Most facilities have ongoing seminars and continuing education to help you increase your production knowledge. If you have questions during a shoot, a staff person is usually available to help you (see Figure 58.1).

Once you finish the orientation and get tested on the equipment, you're ready to produce your show. Usually, you must submit a finished program to the public access facility before it airs so someone can view your tape and make sure it fits the station's guidelines. Once approved, you will receive a time slot for your show to air.

Remember, your program has to be noncommercial; that means you cannot say or show phone numbers, dates of events, prices or store names within the show itself. You can put phone numbers at the end of the show, typically for no longer than 10 seconds. Anything longer than that is considered advertising.

Figure 58.1 *Teach me—you often need to be trained to use the equipment this is a great opportunity to learn.*

Figure 58.2 *Equip me—the gear at the station might be ancient or it might be the latest and the greatest.*

Everything You Need

If you have no experience with video or TV production, public access can be a great place for you to start. At most public access stations everything is provided for you—a studio for shooting, editing facilities, digital video cameras for location shooting, computer editing systems, microphones and audio cables, dressing rooms and more. This is a big help for a beginner or a person that does not have equipment (see Figure 58.2).

Although most studios now have well-maintained digital equipment, this is public access, so don't necessarily expect cutting-edge equipment. They will, however, provide everything you need to shoot and edit a program.

Other producers are usually available to crew for you, and in turn, it is expected that you will crew for them. Most facilities have a book that lists people who are certified and available to work on a production crew.

Different Time, Same Channel

Depending on your city, you may have to wait for a time slot before your program can air. And, you don't always have the option of choosing the time slot you like.

Typically, you will not have a time slot for more than 13 weeks, so it can be hard to build an audience to follow your program. You may be on Saturday at 8 p.m. and then moved to Wednesday at 7 a.m. Your 8 p.m. audience will wonder where you went. You cannot advertise the move in advance, because you won't know where you're going until the move has been made. There is typically nothing you can do about this. The facility has to make space for new producers.

If you are in a facility that has a lot of producers, you may be asked to go off the air (if your show has been airing for a period of time), to give new producers a chance.

The Golden Rule

Each station will have it's own rules and regulations about the use of equipment, crew and timeslots. Check with your local access station for specifics. However, there is one guideline to which all public access programs must adhere: You cannot make any money from the show.

The station staff will watch your show carefully. If they find that you've produced a commercial show, you can be banned from having a show, or using the facilities and editing equipment.

You've Got Access

The opportunity is there for you to take your own program to the airwaves. Despite some restrictions and scheduling irregularities, managing your own public access time slot is a wonderful opportunity.

Sidebar 1

Insurance?

Since your show is non-commercial, insurance is not required. You do not have to have Errors & Omission Insurance to produce a show.

Sidebar 2

Public Access Hints

- Take as many educational classes as possible.

- Crew for everyone you can. If there are people that are particularly experienced, crew for them; you will learn a lot.

- Volunteer to help edit someone else's show. Sit in with them to learn how they edit and why.

- Follow the rules of the facility. Most provide these services free; if you had to pay for it, it could really cost you. Therefore, be respectful of the rules.

59
Leased Access:
A Unique Cable Opportunity

Sheldon I. Altfeld

Broadcasting your program on leased access cable, an opportunity offered by most U.S. cable systems, can be an extremely cost-effective way to launch new programming concepts or sell products. And best of all, leased access can actually provide you with a revenue stream.

The practice has been used successfully by videographers and producers in a wide variety of programming concepts, including how-to's, infomercials, travelogues, talk shows, children's programs, comedy shows, restaurant reviews and local music videos, to name just a few.

The Federal Communications Commission got the leased access ball rolling when it established the Cable Communications Policy Act of 1984. The legislation compelled cable operators of systems with more than 36 channels to set aside 10 to 15 percent of their stations for commercial use.

"Leased access," the act stated, "is aimed at bringing about the widest possible diversity of information sources for cable subscribers."

Locally produced infomercials tend to be the most popular form of leased access programming because of their money-making potential. The process for getting your program on leased access is rather simple.

Leased Access and Public Access—Two Separate Animals

It is important not to confuse leased access with public access. Public access is one arm of a three-part federal program that mandates each cable system to provide public access, educational access and government access programming. Cable systems allocate these non-commercial channels to serve their communities. Leased access, on the other hand, offers a commercial programming channel, or channels, to enable producers time to display their programs. The only restrictions are programs deemed "inappropriate for the community standards, due to gratuitous sex, violence or profanity."

The Cost of Leased Access

Leased access on-air time is extremely reasonable. Generally, the cost is approximately $100 per half-hour for leased access time on larger cable systems, and as little as $10 on smaller systems (see Figure 59.1). The cable system is permitted, however, to charge different rates for different time-slots (as is common in broadcast television), so the time for a program carried in peak-time would be more expensive than one in off-peak.

You may also be required to provide proof of a $1 million general liability insurance policy (and possibly a $2 million errors & omissions policy) naming the cable system as co-insured. Once that policy is in place, your insurance agent can add each additional cable system you work with as a rider for a very nominal fee.

Since you are paying for the time on the cable system, you are at liberty to sell advertising for your program. Aside from the leased access time and perhaps a few operational fees, the cable system generally does not take a percentage of your advertising revenue.

Let your Advertisers Pay for It

Let's assume that you're producing a show about gardening, and you're going to lease broadcast time on your local cable system. Potential advertisers, who would include nurseries, gardeners, flower shops, tree-trimmers and landscapers should offset your broadcast costs. Not only could you charge them an advertising fee, but a production fee as well, since most small businesses haven't already produced a commercial. You'll provide the service of creating one for them (see Figure 59.2).

You might take out an ad in a local newspaper to promote the fact that your program will be on XYZ Cable at such-and-such a time. Mention the advertisers in the ad. It will act as another incentive for them to buy their advertising time from you.

Also, contact the cable operator about placing cross-channel promotional ads for your program, where they'll promote your show on other channels.

The general rule-of-thumb to determine how much to charge for your advertising is to take the total expense of producing

Figure 59.1 *Such a deal—leased access on-air time costs only about $100 per half-hour on larger cable systems and as little as $10 in smaller markets.*

Figure 59.2 *Ad Dollars—when you lease cable time for a show, you can sell ads to offset the cost. If your client doesn't have a commercial, you can create one charge a production fee too.*

your show and divide that figure by the number of 30-second spots you have available to sell. That will tell you how much to sell each ad for in order to break even. Add 15 or 20 percent to determine your basic ad rate.

Many leased access producers maximize their profits by purchasing time (and selling ads) for the same program on several cable systems in their area. And by running the show on additional cable systems, the advertising rate can be reduced and the profit-per-spot can increase.

Don't Forget the Quality

One of the most important aspects of producing leased access programming is the overall production quality. Unlike public access, which generally features "talking heads" in a very bland setting, with a wilted plastic plant in the background, leased access programs reflect the reputation of the videographers and producers putting the programming together. Like everything else a professional does, the

leased access programs need to be professional. Decent production values are crucial—not only for the advertisers, but for the audience as well. Remember that what people see on television with your name on it is your only real promotional brochure.

Get the Format Right

The cable system may accept your program in 3/4-inch U-Matic, BetacamSP or a digital format, so check with the system to determine which format they prefer. It is highly unlikely that a cable system will accept a VHS tape, as the quality would not generally be up to acceptable engineering standards. While digital formats that record high quality images are becoming the format of choice for producers, many cable stations still do not accept submissions on Mini DV or Digital8. Many stations do, however, provide a large format record deck so producers can transfer their footage to the proper format for broadcast. Producers should discuss format requirements and tape transfer options with the cable company up front. Also, when you bring the tape to the cable system, it needs to include everything in it—program, commercials, credits etc.

Leased access can open a whole new medium for videographers. As cable television becomes more diversified and digital set-top boxes begins to offer consumers literally hundreds of new channels, leased access enables entrepreneurs the opportunity to be an integral part of an exciting and ever-growing industry.

Sidebar 1

The Down Side of Leased Access

Some cable operators present leased access producers with obstacles in order to buy time on their systems. Some common roadblocks include:

- Expensive (and required) $1 million general liability insurance policy premiums.

- Arbitrary program schedule changes.

- Refusal of some systems to make any leased access time available.

- Exorbitant fee charges for tape playback, tape changes, viewing of tapes for indecent content, etc.

Since the FCC mandated leased access in 1984, every cable system is obligated to accommodate producers. Friendly negotiations with the system will generally overcome most hurdles and establish long-term working relationships between the entrepreneur and the cable operator.

Sidebar 2

A 20-minute Half-hour

The total running time of the average half-hour program is actually 28:30; with 90-seconds used by the cable system for its own internal promotion. The standard format for a 30-minute show that includes commercials would look something like this:

Time	Item	Cumm.
00:30	Opening Tease	00:30
02:00	SPOT BREAK #1	02:30
10:00	Segment I	12:30
02:00	SPOT BREAK #2	14:30
10:00	Segment II	24:30
02:00	SPOT BREAK #3	26:30
02:00	Bye Bye/Credits	28:30

Sidebar 3

Trying to Create a Network out of Leased Access

The good news is that nearly all of the 12,000-plus cable systems in the United States have a leased access channel. The bad news is that the cost of getting a program on all of them would be astronomical.

Imagine buying leased access time on 100 cable systems for a 30-minute program. At an average of $50 each, it would cost $5,000. Believe it or not, most cable systems are still using 3/4-inch U-Matic tape. At $12 each and you're looking at another $1,200 expense. And finally, add $1,500 for shipping and your cost thus far is $7,700.

The premium for the requisite general liability insurance policy runs abound $5,000 a year, and add approximately $150 per system for each system named as co-insured.

So, to establish a "network" of 100 cable systems, you can figure on spending nearly $28,000. And by the way, you still have to employ a staff to sell advertising for your 100-system network.

60
PBS and ITVS:
Fertile Soil for Independent Videographers

Alessia Cowee

See video clips at www.videomaker.com/handbook.

If you've ever dreamed of seeing your video production on television or bringing your vision to a broader audience than friends and family, now is the time and PBS is the place. PBS—both independently and through its liaison with ITVS—offers unparalleled opportunities for videographers with unique vision and a compelling story. You'll find a surprising number of opportunities with ongoing series (such as *Frontline, American Masters, POV*, and *American Experience*), limited jointly-curated series (like *Digital Divide* and *Independent Lens*) and one-offs (stand-alone, independent films). This article will help you evaluate whether your project is PBS/ITVS material and show you how to break into this ever-expanding market.

PBS, ITVS and You: The Time is Now

PBS has a strong tradition of working with independent producers. It's a common misconception, but PBS is not a television network. Instead, it is a membership organization made up of independent public television stations around the country, funded, in part, by the Corporation for Public Broadcasting, a private corporation created by the US Congress in 1967. PBS is available to 99% of US households and strives to reach all portions of the population with quality, accessible, relevant programming. Pat Mitchell, PBS President and CEO, says key components of the PBS mission are "to inform, to inspire and to educate."

Independent producers frequently challenge convention and provide in-depth analyses of complex topics. PBS makes available programming designed to spur discussion and active community involvement in social issues. Their goal is to provide thorough examination of a story, theme or issue, including all conflicting points of view.

The Independent Television Service (ITVS) was created in 1991 in response to demand from independent media

Figure 60.1 *Acting as guide and gateway into the public television arena, ITVS links independent producers with public television programming opportunities.*

producers and community activists for programming by and for diverse, under-represented audiences (such as minorities and children) not adequately served by the networks or by PBS.

Acting as guide and gateway into the public television arena, ITVS links independent producers with public television programming opportunities (see Figure 60.1). ITVS offers producers feedback during the creative process (including programs which apply, but are rejected for financial aid), content development assistance, funding options and an extensive marketing and publicity package in conjunction with Community Connections Project (CCP—a network of community organizers).

Content Confab: Programming Possibilities

What are PBS and ITVS looking for and how do you know if your program is right for them? The most obvious question is often the most overlooked: Do you want to produce a program or a series? If your long-range goal is theatrical release, PBS is probably not the proper venue for your project. Some films, however, do get additional play after a public TV release, for example, in educational distribution, at festivals and in home video and foreign broadcast markets.

Though the guidelines and needs vary for each program and funding initiative, it can be said that PBS and ITVS seek

innovative, adventurous, compelling stories told in distinctive, contemporary and
engaging formats. Of special interest are
projects that provide interactive opportunities for community participation. No subject is taboo, though projects too narrow in
scope may not have many market options.
Wide-market appeal creates more programming possibilities, but success is not
strictly about raw ratings in public broadcasting. You should also avoid controversy
for controversy's sake. Journalistic integrity
in research, documentation and development is expected.

Is it easier for emerging or established
videographers to break in with a one-off or
with a series segment? ITVS Executive
Director, Sally Jo Fifer explains, "It's always
difficult to get funding because the competition is so fierce. The one essential is to
have a great idea and tell it in a creative,
thorough, smart proposal. Tell a great
story in a unique, 'the viewer can't stop
watching' way."

Funding

ITVS offers several initiatives for producers
seeking financial support for completion of a film, although it actually funds
less than five percent of proposed projects. Open Call accepts proposals in any
genre and funding rounds occur twice
yearly (in February and August). LinCS
(Local Independents Collaborating with
Stations) provides matching ITVS funds
for producers who pair up with a specific
public television station and is perfect for
programs with a more local appeal.

PBS is currently implementing a program, called In The Works, to support
production on a limited number of projects
for use with its series, POV as funding
becomes available. An excellent way to
keep abreast of developments is to subscribe to the Beyond the Box newsletter
(see Figure 60.2). Available funding and
application procedures vary for each
program and initiative.

Public television is commercial-free, but
other outside opportunities exist for acquiring financial assistance. Corporate and
minority consortia funds are available for
resourceful producers, as are grants from
state and national arts councils.

Getting the Green Light

ITVS uses a peer-reviewed process to
screen applicants for funding. ITVS
selects juries based on diversity of ethnic-
ity, vocation, religion, geographic region
and other demographic criteria. The jury
considers each application on its own
merits, individually evaluated and scored.
The screening process has three levels,
with weaker proposals eliminated at each
stage. The panels often request additional
application materials from producers who
advance to the next level during the
review process. At the full panel meetings,
members advocate for their favorite projects
until they can arrive at a consensus on
which proposals to fund for that round.

Criteria the panel may consider when
reviewing your project:

• Is the project accessible, relevant, formatted in the most effective manner?

• Is the treatment thorough, concise, written with passion? Does it clearly show
  the project trajectory and structure?

• Is the audience easily identifiable? Is it
  broad enough? Does it represent ITVS
  and PBS mission statements?

• Is the producer or the team experienced
  enough to complete the project on budget
  and on deadline?

Ms. Fifer warns that producers frequently do not read the application guidelines carefully enough. She also suggests
that producers weigh the appeal of their
projects, "Programmers tell us repeatedly
that they don't need six shows on one
subject. They especially don't need six

Figure 60.2 *An excellent way to keep abreast of developments is to subscribe to the* Beyond the Box *newsletter.*

okay shows on one subject. What they need is one great show on that subject."

Sample materials and written treatments must outshine their competitors. There are not nearly enough programming hours available for the number of submissions received by PBS and ITVS, of course, and top-notch productions often do not make the cut the first time around. You may find the keys to the public programming kingdom in the feedback you get even if your proposal is rejected. But remember, not all venues are suited to all programs. Keep reevaluating your project to determine where it fits best.

Technical Specifications

Almost any shooting format is viable for PBS/ITVS programming. Choose the format that most effectively showcases your subject matter or the one that is most readily available. In the end, however, the final video must be digitally mastered and must meet all of the very rigorous PBS technical requirements, as set forth in the Technical Operating Specifications (TOS) (see Figure 60.3). This handbook and the ITVS Production manual are available for purchase online. Standard program lengths for PBS/ITVS are 26:40 and 56:40. Feature films of non-standard length are considered on a case-by-case basis.

Ready, Set, Video

You've set your sights on PBS and chosen the appropriate funding initiative. You've studied existing series strands and talked with producers who have worked with

Figure 60.3 *Your video must meet all of the very rigorous PBS technical requirements, as set forth in the Technical Operating Specifications (TOS).*

PBS. Your sample and treatment are flawlessly prepared and you can meet all of the technical specifications. The story you've chosen to tell is unique, passion-filled and appeals to a broad audience while remaining interesting and diverse. Now what?

Once you mail your application, the review process may take up to six months. If your proposal is selected, you must typically complete the project within one year of acceptance. Should ITVS license your film, they may offer it to stations directly, without benefit of a time-slot or an airdate. The film could be distributed over PBS Plus or on a soft-feed, which allows member stations to fit the program into available airtime. It might even earn a spot on the National Program Service (hard-feed) or another subscription services such as *Independent Lens* or *POV*.

It takes perseverance, persistence, resourcefulness and a dedication to vision, voice and mission, but dozens of independent video producers share compelling stories and unique perspectives via PBS every year. This could be the year the spotlight shines on your work.

Sidebar 1

Electric Shadows

ITVS is breaking ground with digital technology. If interactive media and Web release is what you crave, check out *Electric Shadows*, an extraordinary blend of digital audio, video, interviews and still photography, enhanced with feedback forums and lesson plan suggestions.

Sidebar 2

PBS.org

Stay current with the needs of PBS. PBS updates their Web site frequently with content priorities. Preview the strands you are interested in producing for before submitting your film or applying for funding. Does your format, vision, style and subject matter fit within the program's parameters? If not, consider another strand or funding source.

Sidebar 3

ITVS Information

Independent Television Service
501 York Street
San Francisco, CA 94110
Phone: (415) 356-8383
email: itvs@itvs.org

Sidebar 4

Online Resources for Producers

Producing for PBS
http://www.pbs.org/producers/

Online Version of PBS Redbook
http://www.pbs.org/insidepbs/redbook/index.html

PBS Production Guidelines
http://www.pbs.org/insidepbs/guidelines/index.html

Beyond the Box Online Content:
http://www.beyondthebox.org/

ITVS Funding Applications and Guidelines
http://www.itvs.org/producers/funding.html

61
Paths to Broadcast Television

Mark Steven Bosko

See video clips at www.videomaker.com/handbook.

Let me relate to you the story of a fellow videographer who "made good." John started like most of us, goofing around with his parents' film equipment. Though just a child, the creative art of cinematography really clicked for him. He created one film after another to the delight of his family and friends.

Though the passion for this "art" festered inside John, he became frustrated with the what seemed like a wasting of his time. The whole purpose of producing a movie was for an audience's enjoyment. After five years of basement screenings, family and friends hardly qualified as a legitimate audience anymore. John knew there just had to be a better way, but didn't latch onto it quite yet. Much later, in college, John enrolled in the school's teleproduction class. He knew a little bit about TV production, but was still mainly a "film" guy. It was here that he discovered what would later "rule" his world—videotape.

Even with excellent marks, John still yearned for that elusive "audience". Luckily, he was outspoken about this

need, and a professor took notice. The professor, as it happens, was on the board of the local public television station. He was primarily responsible for development of new local programming.

Thinking of John's desires, and some of the super productions the students were showing, the teacher came up with a "Young Filmmaker's" showcase program. The show would give aspiring film and videographers (now John's medium of choice due to cost and time considerations) a place to present their programming to a potentially large viewership.

Happy ending: John got his audience, the station got quality programming, and viewers got some alternative shows to watch.

Not all stories involving broadcast TV are so inspiring, and sometimes PBS networks are the hardest nuts to crack. But the example above does point out the many opportunities that exist for videographers looking for distribution of their productions within these "hallowed halls." For some reason or another, broadcast television stations have the image of an "insider's club." You've got to know someone or already work there in a lower capacity to get an in. If you weren't a part of the community's filmmaking "elite," your chances for broadcast were nil. Maybe ten or so years ago that was true, but today, this is simply not the case. Especially for dedicated, experienced videographers.

One of the reasons for this "opening" may be attributable to the increase in number and types of broadcast outlets on the map. Before everyone in America had cable, there existed a strong distinction between broadcast and cable fare. Broadcast programming was free, contained a some locally produced programming (created at the station, not by independents), and carried the network shows as they "came down the line." Cable, on the other hand, carried new movies and other, non-traditional television material. It was also perceived (rightly so) as being very costly.

As the years passed and more media moguls developed, the number of cable stations quadrupled, the cost for the service plummeted and the demand by consumers who "wanted their MTV" skyrocketed. This led to the confusing mix of cable and broadcast stations that currently exists on your channel selector. This influx of new entertainment choices spurred a huge void in the supply of programming able to fulfill the scheduling needs of the stations.

Another reason broadcast stations unlocked their doors to outsiders was the fact that now they wanted to compete with the trendy and popular cable networks. The old, stodgy rules of operation were changing, and any new face that had something to add to the party was welcome.

And, in recent years, a new broadcast outlet, Low Power Television (LPTV) became popular. The limited signal put out by these stations reaches a relatively small, geographically close audience. The LPTV stations tend to be carriers of downloadable national satellite programming, mixed with an unusually high amount (for broadcast) of local fare.

While all of this is certainly encouraging (if not educational) for the future of aspiring videographers, what real opportunities exist now, in the present, for those of you who can't wait a lifetime for their dreams to be fulfilled? What does broadcast television offer you in the form of distribution?

VHF

You've got a job (that you like) and possess some fine-tuned production abilities. You own a little equipment, no Industrial Light and Magic, but a respectable "studio" on your own right. You've made some industrials, a whole slew of weddings, even an instructional tape on gardening for your spouse. You got some good ideas for programming that you think will go over big with the locals, but how do you get it on the tube?

Time saving tip number one: skip the VHF channels in your broadcasting area. VHF slots, usually reserved for network affiliates, offer the independent videographer little in the form of finding an audience. The stations are network controlled, meaning they have mega-bucks at their resources. They're not rude, but why would they want to mess with your $1.98 Talent Show when they can program a re-rerun of *Who's the Boss*? It just doesn't make sense for the big boys to play with you.

About the only exposure you may achieve through a VHF outlet is sale of news-type footage. And this comes from personal experience. My town was literally burning down. A huge fire started in the historical district, and I happened to be at the right place at the right time with my camcorder. I got some great shots before any of the large news crews showed up. They were aware of my presence and asked to buy the footage for inclusion in the coverage of the story. I was only too glad to succumb to their wishes. But don't plan on getting rich from selling news footage. These deep-pocketed network guys could only scrape together $50 for the whole 30-minute tape. And then I didn't even get an on-air credit!

UHF

If you've seen the Weird Al movie of the same name, then you are aware of the possibilities available for independent programming to air on these channels. While it's not quite as zany as the Weird Al film, opportunities do exist (especially in smaller markets) for videographers to find an audience.

Many UHF stations are becoming network affiliates (FOX has conquered quite a few), so the chances with these stations are slimming. If you live in a large TV city (one with more than four or five UHF channels), then you should be able to locate a willing outlet. In the Cleveland-area, a late-night television host on a UHF channel hosts a viewer's film's series. It's a great show comprised of shorts (one shot-on-video feature has played) broken up with interviews of the videographers. There is no pay involved, but the audience is pretty big, and loyal. The program is also popular with local advertisers who recognize the local customer base tuning in.

If there is a late-night gig in your city, why not hit up the host with this idea? It makes his or her job infinitely easier, and becomes attractive to sales personnel at the station.

Sunday morning talk and "city" shows also seem popular with UHF channels. Easily produced, these programs focus on community events and personalities. Often, the production may center on one specific area, and the show is a submission from a freelance videographer.

Fairly new to the broadcast arena, Low Power Television Stations are basically UFH stations, only with less signal amplification. These stations function much like their big cousins, only with a greater concentration of the local goods.

Cashing In

Knowing that there's some distribution avenues available in UHF and LPTV is good news, but, you'd like some compensation

for your efforts, right? Well, just like the VHF networks, these stations pull in the reins when it comes time to pay. In fact, you may be the one paying them to show your program.

WAI-TV, part of a three-channel LPTV network in Cleveland and Akron, offers airtime for sale. Going for $250 and up per half-hour (depending what day and time you buy) the channel is a natural for independents. "We have space for sale just like every other television network. It just happens that ours is available to the independent," says Bill Klaus, owner of the station. Klaus makes it clear that the reason an independent can buy time from his network is because it is affordable. "Sure, someone with a home-grown production could go to their local VHF station and buy a half-hour of time to broadcast the show, but they'd probably have to mortgage their house to do it. My network makes it affordable, and we often barter time as well so the videographer can actually make a buck."

Bartering, as Klaus mentioned, is another favored option of UHF and LPTV programmers. What this means is that you retain some of the commercial time allotted within your programming block. As an example, let's say you buy a half-hour of air time for $200. That's the flat rate. With that price, you are the owner of all 8 minutes of commercial space. You can deal with the station, letting them keep 4 minutes of ad time, dropping your payment to $100. And, it also works in reverse. If they want to buy your show (yes—that actually happens sometimes), they may offer you the commercial time in exchange for any payment. This way they don't have a cash outlay, but fill their schedule. You, on the other hand, have found a profitable distribution outlet.

The large, network-affiliated stations will not likely be interested in your bargain broadcasting, but many independent stations will take a look. Local interest, interview shows, documentaries, community affairs and sporting events are all good ideas to present to any small broadcaster in your neighborhood.

When you go door knocking, bring an attractive demo and a professional presentation package outlining your programming ideas. This packet should present your work in its best possible light. While you may think you are the only indie out there (or at least the only one in the neighborhood), the fact is that programming managers deal with many proposals from many people. "It's probably hard to believe, but I get at least a proposal a week from independent video producers," states Klaus. "Most of the production ideas have no substance. If I got one backed by a demo, or put together in a professional manner, I might pay more attention to them. But too many of them look like a half-hearted effort to get a show on the air."

"I don't mind working with independents," Klaus continues. "In fact I like it, but they just have to be more professional in their approach. If a videographer wants to make some money by getting his programming on the air, instead of spending it to buy time, he should prepare the idea as completely as possible. That would be the type of producer I would look to work with."

There are no set rules here. Just remember that it's the fact that people are able to view your production through their television sets for free that's important, not the amount of bills you have wadded in your pocket.

The multitude of small and low-power broadcasting outlets has created a void of original, low-cost scheduling alternatives. There are only so many stations that can broadcast The Andy Griffith Show at any one time, and it's that fact that opens up the audiences to you.

62
Promotion Strategies:
Fame and Fortune on a Budget

Mark Steven Bosko

See video clips at www.videomaker.com/handbook.

If you don't tell people about your video, they won't even know it exists. The more aware the public is of your work, the greater fame and fortune you'll eventually achieve.

You can promote your work in many ways—from buying expensive full-color magazine advertising to sending out a simple press release. Full-blown promotional plans practically guarantee increased video sales, but they're often too expensive for the first-time videographer.

But there are less expensive ways to promote your work. In this chapter, we'll survey a selection of promotion strategies that will cost you little more than the price of pen and paper—and some hard work.

The Press Release

The press release is the most widely used and abused promotional technique. This one-page synopsis tells the media what you want them to know about your video. Media outlets such as newspapers,

magazines and broadcasters receive hundreds of these daily; to make sure yours receives proper attention you need to (a) submit it in regulation form and (b) make it stand out from all the others.

Press releases follow a standard format. Deviate from this format and no one will read it. This sounds harsh but it's true. If you want the press to read it:

• *Keep it short.* You don't need 10 pages to communicate your message. One page is best, two is the maximum. If it is longer, re-write it; include just the basics.

• *Title it.* Without a headline, they won't know what the release is about. Trust me: they won't take the time to read it to find out. The best headlines are short and to the point.

• *Say who sent it.* The upper left-hand corner of the page should set out the following information: your company's name, address, telephone number and—most important—a contact to call for further information. You're the best contact; if you can't do it make sure you choose a contact well versed in all aspects of your video.

• *Provide a release date.* Write "For Immediate Release" on the press release; this tells the press that they can use the information revealed in your release right now. If you don't want the information released until a specific date, then provide this "embargo date" in place of the usual "For Immediate Release" (i.e., "For Release October 10, 2003").

• *Use the standard form.* Type the release, double-spaced with ample margin areas. Check for any errors in spelling, punctuation, grammar or content; this kind of mistake screams amateurism.

Now you think your press release is going to look like all the others—and if the format is correct, it probably will. But Joe Reporter down at the *Daily Globe* doesn't care about fancy formats; he's looking for interesting content. Write your release so it not only answers the stock journalism questions—who, what, where, when, how and why—but also leaves the reader wanting to know more. Appeal to the natural curiosity of the reporter—without getting cute—and no doubt your video will see some press.

Mail, fax, transmit electronically or hand deliver your release to every possible media outlet. The wider the distribution, the better your chances of getting press.

Radio and TV Interviews

Turn on the radio. Flip through the stations. Listen. You hear a lot of talk, don't you? Radio stations live on music and talk; they have plenty of music, but they need the talk. That's where you come in.

More than 80 percent of the 11,000 radio stations in the United States air some sort of interview program; getting on one of these interview shows is easier than you might think. Best of all, it's free.

Call the stations you know that air interview programs and ask how they book their guests. Send the person in charge of booking a press release, some data sheets naming the subject, cast, crew, locations and length of your video and a cover letter. The cover letter is important; think of it as a sales letter selling you and your video. This letter should persuade the booking manager that your video is an ideal choice for the program—due to its exploitative elements, controversial theme, local interest or whatever "hook" will prove irresistible to the station.

With any luck, someone will give you a call to find out more about your project and determine if you would make a suitable guest for the show. When you get the call, be sure to answer all queries with confidence and grace; you want to prove you're a coherent, interesting individual who won't freeze up during the program.

Interviews are great promotional vehicle, but they do offer one distinct disadvantage: lack of control. You don't have the benefit of complete pre-planning. You can't predict what the interviewer will ask you or what part or parts of the interview will air. With live, call-in formats, you face the additional challenge of fielding questions from the listening public, who may or may not approve of you and your video. Two suggestions for handling radio interviews:

1. Restrict contact with the media to yourself or one or two other people associated with your production. You should coach these people—talent, director, producer—on appropriate responses to possible questions. You certainly don't want to hear your cameraman giving out details that contradict your press release.

2. Listen to the radio program before appearing on the show. Observe how the DJ deals with guests. By listening, you'll discover if the host and callers are friendly or abusive, the show is live or taped and whether the focus is

straight news or fluff. Prepare your answers based on your observations.

Now that you've successfully conquered radio, turn your attention to the other half of the broadcast spectrum: television.

Compared with radio, the market for TV guests is small; the chances of landing an interview are smaller still. To boost those chances, approach the TV station about an interview in the same way you approach the radio stations, but do more follow up. Don't wait for someone to call you; make those return calls yourself. TV people are always busy, and they believe that if you want to book yourself on a show you should do all the work.

You do have one advantage: you're promoting a video. Videos are visual and naturally lend themselves to the medium of television. Include a trailer of your best scenes—those most visually compelling—with your press release. This way the person in charge will know you have something unique to offer.

Most local television interview programs are not overwhelmed by low-budget video producers trying to land spots as guests on a regular basis. You're one of a kind; play up the glitz and glamour you bring to your hometown.

Tell the show's producers about any publicity stunts you plan and ask that they cover it to air with your interview. Keep the subject exciting and visual, and you shouldn't have any problems.

Screeners/Trailers

"We want to see the video."

That's what you can expect to hear hundreds of times while promoting your project. The press wants to see a *screener*. A screener is a full-length, promotional copy of your tape, provided free of charge to media personnel upon request.

They need to see first-hand what your video is all about. Screeners allow reporters to check out such considerations as budget, acting, effects and production values. Now your video must live up to the expectations you've created for it. Did you exaggerate too much in your press releases?

The press uses screeners most often for reviewing purposes; media outlets occasionally request them as well, primarily to check out authenticity. Nobody wants to devote space to a "phantom" video, especially national magazines.

Providing these screeners for everyone who asks becomes an expensive proposition. There is, however, a low-cost alternative: the *trailer*.

Short compilations of your best scenes, trailers can accomplish all a full-length screener can—at less than a third of the cost.

A general rule of thumb: use screeners for press outlets that want to review your program and trailers for those who just want to "take a look." Some suggestions:

- Use a disclaimer on screeners. When duplicating screeners to send to media outlets, superimpose or key the words "For Promotional Use Only" over the video during its entire duration. Not that the press is dishonest, but if your video lands in the wrong hands, nothing will stop those hands from selling the video as their own. The practice of using a disclaimer offends no one; it's always better to be safe than sorry. This tip comes from a video newsletter in California investigating a small cable station making illegal dupes to sell in Mexico. So protect your property!

- Duplicate screeners and trailers on B-grade tape. Most of these videos will be viewed only once or twice, making a high-grade tape unnecessary. The press outlets can handle a little dropout.

- Use a copyright. Place a copyright notice prominently on all screeners and trailers. Put a notice physically on the tape and within the program itself.

- Limit trailers to 5 minutes or less. This is adequate time to show your tape's highlights. Keep it "lean and mean."

- Make your trailer available in broadcast formats. Some broadcast press outlets may want to include your trailer as part of the story on your project. Don't miss out on this free advertising by not having the proper tape available. Most stations can work with three-quarter-inch format. It's cheap and widely available.

- Include any televised press on distributors' screeners. Tag a mini-trailer of any televised news stories about your project onto the beginning of the screener. How impressed will that distributor be when he sees your story as it appeared on *Entertainment Tonight*? A lot more impressed than he'll be when you just tell him about it. Be sure to check with news agencies concerning legalities of duplicating such stories.

Press Kit

It's now time to compile all of the press you've received thanks to your promotion strategies and organize it into a *press kit*.

The most useful weapon in your promotional arsenal, a press kit represents the culmination of all your efforts. Its purpose: to show the attention your project has received, proving that your video is worthy of further coverage such as newspaper space and TV airtime.

Some people say to include only the big "headline" stories. I say include everything—from that one-paragraph blurb in your local new paper to the full-page story in *Variety*.

Press is press. The more you can show a media outlet, the easier it is to get more coverage.

Some tips on putting together a decent press kit:

1. Use a high-quality bond for reproduction of the originals. The heavier weight paper lends a classy look.

2. Check the clarity of copies, especially when articles include photographs.

3. Place articles in descending order of importance, starting with the most prestigious—usually national media.

4. Articles buried in the editorial section should be shown with the cover or masthead of the publication; copy it and place it on the reproduction with the article.

5. Allow for only one article per page, unless the articles are extremely short and from the same publication.

6. Use the proper tape formats when including televised or radio coverage.

7. Put all the print elements along with a cover letter into a slick folder.

The press release P.R. strategy alone should garner enough press for a substantial press kit. And if you've employed the other promotional strategies as well, you may find you cannot include everything—your kit would be so thick, you'd go broke on postage. So choose only the best of your material for your press kit.

Publicity Stunts

Publicity stunts can be a great low-cost promotional technique, attracting both media and public attention to your video project.

Used with great success by the film industry, publicity stunts have traditionally accompanied the release of new movies. The "golden age" of publicity stunts was the 1950s, when the following tactics drew big crowds:

- Nurses in theater lobbies, placed there by smart promotional men asking viewers to sign medical releases, in the case of heart attacks brought on by the shocking subject matter they were about to see. A particular favorite of science fiction and horror film promoters.

- Bogus pickets, carried by "protesters" hired by a film company's publicity department to demonstrate against a film's sex and violence quotients.

- Film "banning," which implied that a movie's subject matter was so offensive it should not be shown in certain areas.

Your own publicity stunts don't have to be so melodramatic, however. Try setting up a live magic act in the video stores stocking your *Magic Made Simple* video. Or, celebrate the release of your *Keep Our Town Clean* video with a litter collection contest for local school kids; offer the winners some free production time. Any stunt you can think of that involves the public and creates interest in your video makes for good publicity.

To ensure success: keep the press informed and keep it legal. Check out all local laws that may apply to your particular stunt.

9 Ways to Cut Promotion Costs

Mailing and distributing press kits and screeners can prove expensive. Still, there are ways to economize:

1. Don't use envelopes when mailing press releases. Tri-fold the paper and staple the bottom.

2. For big mailings use pre-printed post-cards—they're cheaper to mail and cheaper to produce.

3. Order return address stickers bearing your company name from one of the many mail-order catalogs that offer such merchandise. They look good and cost substantially less than printed versions.

4. Shop for supplies and copy services at a large office supply store. Many of these places duplicate the same document for as little as two cents a page.

5. Mail screeners fourth class. Fourth class costs less than half the first-class rate and takes only two to four more days to deliver.

6. Save on postage by using air bubble envelopes instead of cardboard VHS tape mailers for screeners.

7. Put together a trailer instead of mailing out full-length screeners; this reduces postage and duplication costs.

8. Save big on phone bills by using toll-free phone numbers when calling distributors, TV/radio stations and publications. You'll find them listed in the toll-free directory at your local library.

9. When making long-distance toll calls, place them when it's most cost effective; keep time zone changes in mind. Contact your long-distance carrier for specifics.

The Bitter Fruits of Publicity

Execute a proper and thorough low-budget video promotional campaign, and your life will drastically change.

The good news is people will see your work. The bad news is more complicated.

First, you're apt to lose much of your leisure time to your publicity efforts. Sure, it is great to come home, pop open a beer and settle in to watch *Divorce Court*. But you're not going to get on any magazine covers that way. Not that you must devote every waking minute to the promotion of your video—we all need some time to relax—it's just that sooner or later the marketing machine you create will take on a life of its own. Instead of playing cards with the guys or hitting the mall, you will probably find yourself fielding phone calls and writing letters. If the process threatens to consume you, write "free time" right into your work schedule.

Promoting your video does not have to alienate you from friends and family, though this often proves the case. So go shoot hoops with friends or spend some quiet time with your spouse when you can.

The second source of grief that accompanies promotion efforts: reviews. Reviews are a necessary part of the marketing process; you'll need to develop a "thick skin" to survive the nastier negative criticism. Remember, you are sending out your video to literally hundreds of outlets, hoping to generate publicity and resources for a press kit. Among all these people watching your tape there will undoubtedly be some who don't like your work, for whatever reasons.

Who cares? What do critics do, anyway? They sit in front of a monitor all day, pointing out faults in something they never had the guts to try to do themselves. These people make their living by proclaiming what—in their own minds—is good and what is bad.

At least this is what you must tell yourself when bad reviews come in. You will, on the other hand, admire the intelligence and good taste of the reviewer who raves about your show.

There's one sort of criticism to which you should pay special attention—that of your fellow videographers. Send your video around to other producers who have "made it" in your field. Suggestions and insight from such individuals are very valuable, often saving you time and money on your next production.

A final thought: prepare yourself for the fame that will haunt you after your name begins to appear in the media. No longer will you be able to venture out into the world a nobody. You'll become a local celebrity and if your video is a big hit, national fame will follow. Standing in the limelight is fun, but it can be dangerous.

If you're flitting around like some self-important media butterfly and your project takes an unexpected turn for the worse, your fall from grace will hurt all the more.

Promoting your video should be a fun and exciting experience. Be sure it stays that way!

Tell 'Em and Sell 'Em Again

With the right promotion strategies, fame and fortune can be yours. The key is persistence. It takes time to create and execute a promotion plan, but it's worth it.

If you believe in your video's success, as you surely do, nothing can stop you.

63
The Demo Tape

Mark Steven Bosko

See video clips at www.videomaker.com/handbook.

With so many of today's ideographers relying on their video skills and equipment for income, marketplace competition is keener than ever. To succeed, these courageous entrepreneurs (or hopefuls) need all the help they can get.

A good demo tape should be your number one marketing tool. There's nothing like it to showcase (and sell) your videography talent. A well-done demo attracts new clients, creates good public relations, and can even lure competent employees.

Unfortunately, a good demo is not that easy to make. In this chapter we explore elements of the demo tape—its reason for being, its creation, its uses. Once you see what a demo can do, you'll wonder why you never got around to making one before.

Why You Need One

Say Uncle Bob, the dentist, needs a marketing video. He wants to feature basic information on his facility—friendly staff, low prices, after-work appointment hours.

He'll show the tape around to factories and large corporations. The vast numbers of employees within these companies permit him to offer attractive discount plans.

In production terms, the video sounds easy. Some interior shooting. A couple of staff interviews. You'll finish it off with narration and graphics. You're a member of the family, so getting the job's no problem, right?

But during your meeting with Bob, he asks to see something you've done. A representation of past work. Some evidence you're competent to make a video to his liking.

Uncle Bob wants a *demo*. You have one, don't you?

If you're like many small video companies and independent producers, the answer is probably no. But it takes more than smooth talk to convince clients—even Uncle Bob—that they can trust you with their money. Videos aren't tangible things. Until a camera comes out of the bag, they're just talk and writing. Investing in someone's videography skills without having viewed his work is like buying a car based on nothing but a sales pitch.

Videos often record those once-in-a-lifetime events. A potential client must be certain you'll get it right the first time. He can't stage his daughter's wedding again because you forgot a microphone. He needs a good look at your "credentials."

The demo also is a simple way to attract new business. It shows off the power of the medium. It gets your foot in the door.

As a fund-raising tool, a demo can't be beat. Whether you hope to make a low-budget feature, a social issues documentary or an instructional tape, it takes more than expendable income to pay for a vision.

To paraphrase, "Demos talk. Bragging walks." Investors must see proof of your abilities. No amount of pipe-dream description will get you the cash you need.

Low-budget producers often shoot a couple of scenes of the planned work, and present this "demo" to potential investors.

J.R. Bookwalter of Akron, Ohio, is the definitive real-life example. He admired the work of Hollywood producer Sam Raimi (*Darkman, The Evil Dead*), and pegged him as a possible backer. Raimi screened the novice filmmaker's previous efforts. He was so impressed by the badly exposed Super 8 "demos" he agreed to finance a low-budget film.

To the tune of $125,000.

"Raimi told me that of all the proposals he'd received at that point, only mine was accompanied by a representation of my experience," Bookwalter says. "I'm sure if I hadn't screened my films, the deal would never have gone through."

This isn't a common scenario, but it proves the demo's potential.

Just remember: No demo has more impact than a bad demo, while a great demo pays the bills.

Creating a truly effective demo tape takes more than some assemble edits and a blank tape. Careful planning is the first step.

Consider the Content

You want to show off only your very best work in your demo tape. Scan all your videos, noting outstanding shots, imaginative camera-work and good production values. You want to show a broad spectrum of abilities.

If a particular vacation video looks good, include it. Earmark for use any wedding footage that came out better than normal. Sporting events, community functions and film-to-video transfers all provide raw material for a demo.

Don't be impatient. Getting the best possible footage may mean scanning three entire weddings to find that gorgeous sunset kiss sequence. Any extra effort invested at this point will only make the demo that much more powerful.

Let's say your video services have just become available. Let's also say that you really haven't had any legitimate (paying) jobs yet. Sure, you've goofed around with camcorders for a couple of years. But until now, videography wasn't something you'd considered a career choice. How can you put a demo together without footage?

By creating what you need.

For example, to target the wedding and event video market, you'll need footage of a wedding or two. Check nuptial schedules of area churches and get permission from some couples-to-be to shoot some footage. You don't have to cover the entire wedding. Just get a few shots good enough to convince a prospective client you can handle the job.

Nobody wants to be your first client. If you include wedding footage in your demo you'll appear to have experience in this area.

One caveat. Be certain you really can adequately produce a wedding video. Acquiring a few stray shots and actually shooting and editing a cohesive and attractive ceremony are two very different things. You don't want to misrepresent yourself.

Which leads us to another option for acquiring demo footage: Shoot it for free.

Don't cringe. I realize making money is the whole point. But we all should pay a few dues. Free production work is one way to do this.

Hundreds of organizations gladly accept the donation of video work. Any nonprofit entity (your local food bank? SPCA?) is a good place to start. Call. Explain your situation. Make your offer of free service. Beyond getting demo material, this philanthropic practice increases your working experience. And it's not bad for your reputation, either.

Inform local press of your charitable video "donations." This is great free advertising. Doesn't it feel good to help out others?

A Manual of Style

How you edit your demo can have as much impact as its contents.

First, set an appropriate length for your tape. Your projected audience pretty much determines this. A 3-minute demo isn't really long enough to warrant an award of cash.

Nor would you want to solicit a commercial account with a half-hour production. The client wants a 30-second spot, not a TV series.

Rule of thumb: Keep it short. For the general production market, 5 to 10 minutes is about right. It's not so long the viewer gets bored but not so short a potential client will question your experience. There's ample time to display your best work, professionally and courteously.

Applying the term "courteous" to a demo tape may seem odd, but your customers lead busy lives. They have better things to do than sit through your 30-minute extravaganza. Like anyone else, they want to get their information as quickly as possible. (You can always include supplemental materials with tapes you send to major funders.)

You've decided on a 5-minute demo. Now you're ready to edit footage, right?

Wrong. We're not done planning: Determine the order and style for presenting your experience before you start cutting. And it's a good idea to create a detailed script. Map out the order of each segment of footage.

Now consider style. Who's your target market? How can you reach them most effectively?

If they're serious business people, try a straightforward presentation—interspersing your footage with defining graphics and augment it with a clean voiceover. The key here is quick-paced editing with a clear demonstration of your abilities.

Perhaps you plan to approach several markets using a single demo tape. Intersperse interviews shot expressly for the demo—remarks from enthusiastic past clients—with cuts of your footage.

Taping these interviews means a little extra work, but it's well worth it. The boast of a satisfied customer impresses potential clients more than any claim you can make.

The testimonial is popular for all facets of advertising—just check out the commercials during network prime time. Using this technique in a small-town framework pays off especially well.

Business people and ordinary citizens see neighbors and friends—familiar faces—on the tape. If a prospect's competition or friend up the street is using you, chances are good you've found a new client.

The truly motivated may want to host their demos. The hosted demo is an innovative approach most smaller production companies seldom take advantage of.

If you're not a smooth talker, find someone who is. Create a script and have the emcee introduce each clip or segment. You can structure this many ways, for a serious, comedic or down-home feel.

Take care, though, if you're going for laughs. Your sense of humor might not be that of the general public. It's less risky to be serious.

Consider your host's setting, wardrobe and narrative. All these play a big part in the presentation's effectiveness.

Experiment. You may want to combine styles. Try a hosted demo that includes interviews with satisfied clients. Voiceover client comments while rolling footage from a particular job. Incorporate shots of your equipment in the demo.

Interview yourself—talk about customer satisfaction, your state-of-the-art gear, your sincere goal of creating the best possible product.

Shameless self-promotion adds a personal touch, and it's as popular as the testimonial. Again, just take a look at any network TV program for abundant proof.

Technical Concerns

Planning and assembling a slick demo does you no good if the tape itself is defective.

This sounds obvious, but it's a legitimate consideration. When putting your production together, work with the lowest-generation tape available. If you use a wedding shot, pull it from the original footage.

This applies to any material included in the tape.

If raw footage isn't available, be sure your editing set-up allows for the cleanest possible dub. Remember—you'll dub the demo again for client copies. If you use a second-generation shot, it will be fourth-generation when a client views it.

Seen much good-looking fourth-generation footage lately?

Keep a quality-control check on footage, graphics and narration recorded specifically for the demo. Your amazing shots won't impress if they're book-ended by amateurish on-screen intros from an inexperienced host. Be sure graphics and voiceovers complement the rest of the tape. It may seem funny to have your voice talent talk like Elmer Fudd, but does this really show you in a professional light?

Distribute your demo on VHS. Other video formats are gaining popularity, but VHS is still most widely used. Businesses, organizations and individuals welcome this tape size. If someone requests a different format, make it available. Conversion services are plentiful and cheap. It's worth the expense if you get the job.

Packaging affords you another chance to get a jump on the competition. True, you can't judge a book by its cover. But it doesn't hurt to impress when theres a chance to. Most demos I see come in plain cardboard or plastic sleeves. *Boring*. Why not take advantage of those nifty full-sleeve insert shells? Create a cover or design with photos from your business, high-tech images or even your logo. The 8-1/2 by 11-inch layout facilitates low-cost color copies. Slip your custom cover in the sleeve and you've got a package that really stands out.

Or you can print professional face or spine labels on colored stock. Consider dubbing onto tapes with colored shells. It costs a bit more, but it separates you from the masses.

Mail your demos in bubble-lined envelopes—they cost less to mail than cardboard shippers, and they allow you to insert additional materials. Always include a cover letter, a short note informing the recipient of your intentions.

If you're sending the tape in response to a request be sure and point this out. Enclose any press you've received. Letters of recommendation are good, too. Praise from past clients impresses potential ones.

Show It Around

There are a surprising number of additional ways to get your tape to roll where it counts most:

- Event videographers should keep a tape available for loan at photography studios. Drop a couple at local bridal and tux businesses.

- Film-to-tape transfer specialists might leave a copy at film shops.

- Attend county fairs, business expos or video industry trade shows with demo in hand. These functions are tailor-made to sell your business. You'll meet business owners and potential clients face-to-face.

- Present your demo to church, school and community groups. These organizations always have some sort of function in the works. Allow them to witness the advantages of having videotape recording of their event.

Following Up

People can be lazy. Your demo may pique their interest, but you're dreaming if you think it's enough to inspire every viewer to make the call. It often takes some additional sales effort to get the job.

Back to tooth-man Bob. As he considers a marketing plan, he gets your demo tape in the mail. Until now, direct mail, print ads and weekly shoppers had seemed the way to go. They require little effort on his part, pricing is reasonable, and audience delivery is good.

But now he's struck by the impact of live, talking images. Potential patients can "tour" his high-tech facility. Nurses and staff can show their friendly faces. Bob himself can make an earnest plea for healthy teeth. Done well, the demo may intrigue Bob enough to give you a call.

Or you could call him. Dispel the high-cost myth associated with video production. Explain how the video will attract clients just as it attracted him to your work. Let Bob know he can be as involved as he wants in making the tape.

Putting together an effective, professional-quality demo is not something you do one afternoon out of boredom. It takes patience, planning, creativity and hard work. You want to show yourself at your best.

To do just that, keep a few key ideas in mind.

- Include only your best work. Don't be impatient when scanning your videos for footage. You want to show a broad spectrum of ability. If necessary, create the footage you need.

- Set an appropriate length. Rule of Thumb: Keep it short. Five to 10 minutes is about right.

- Plan order and style before editing your footage. Keep in mind your target market. When possible, create a detailed script. Try incorporating testimonials and self-promotion. You may even want to host your demo.

- If you need funding, shoot a couple of scenes of your planned work. Present this "demo" to potential investors.

- Work with the earliest generation tape available. Remember, it will be about fourth-generation by the time your client views it.

- Distribute your demo on VHS. If someone requests a different format, make it available.

- Package your demo creatively. Use full-sleeve insert covers and colored spine labels and tape shells.

- Mail demos in bubble-lined envelopes. Be sure to include a cover letter and supplementary materials.

- Follow up your demo presentations with a personal sales effort. Dispel the high-cost myth. Explain how your videos will benefit your client.

Rely on these key ideas and you'll create a demo impressive enough to convince even Uncle Bob.

PART VI
Internet Distribution

Getting your videos seen on screens all over the World Wide Web.

64
The Web:
Little Screen, Big Opportunities

Carolyn Miller

Natalie MacGowan Spencer produced her first video for the Web just a few months ago, but by Internet standards that makes her an "old timer." It's been plenty long enough to convince her that the Web is a viable and exciting new medium for up and coming video producers. "It's allowed me to spread my wings and fly," she declared recently. "All the video editors I know want to try it out, to play with it. We don't know what it can do yet, and we want to check out its creative possibilities. We're all stimulated by it and tickled by it."

Before discovering the Web, London-born Natalie had made short films and done hair and makeup for music celebrities and commercials. Her debut piece for the Web was a music video of the British band Olive. Created specifically for the Web, it was made for Eveo (www.eveo. com). Its bold, assertive style swiftly attracted a great deal of attention and it became one of the hits of the site.

"When you're making something for the Internet," she said, "the screen space is so much smaller that you want your visuals to be extremely strong, so they really pop out at you, almost like a 3-D effect. And when you're shooting on video, you should build on what video does best and not try to imitate film. Film is soft and subtler, but video is very literal and the images are very striking. In my opinion, you shouldn't fight it, you should go for it."

Developing a Distinct Format

Eveo, the site that Natalie made her music video for, is one of many Web sites that feature shorts. However, the site is of special interest to videographers because of its emphasis on pieces created on video. Most of the other sites feature shorts first made on film, often for the film festival circuit, and then transferred to video.

Alan Sternfeld, Chief Content Officer of Eveo, explained recently that the goal of Eveo is to give videographers a forum for making and showing short, self-expressive pieces, "little movies." Sternfeld says these original pieces, each termed an "eveo" (short for "e-video"), "can be made by anyone about anything." He sees Web shorts as a distinctly new format and said they are being introduced at his site much in the same way music videos were first developed and promoted by MTV. Eveo has an open-door policy and solicits work "from people who just got a camcorder for Christmas right up to the pros," according to Sternfeld.

Eveo's library contains a large portion of non-fiction pieces, an area that often appeals to video hobbyists operating on lower budgets or with less experience. The subject matter is wildly diverse— everything from true stories about homeless people to a love triangle involving three kindergartners (see Figure 64.1). To create a successful non-fiction video for the Web, Sternfeld advises that videographers do something based on personal experience. "Use this as an opportunity to reveal something about the world you live in," he recommended.

Sternfeld believes working in this new arena can be a tremendously liberating experience and unlike television, with its rigid formulas and set program lengths, the Web offers uncharted creative freedom. He also applauds the fact there are fewer human roadblocks. "The Internet is a great disintermediary phenomenon," he asserted. "It cuts out all the middlemen and gatekeepers."

Charting New Territory

One team of creators who has benefited by the Web's freedom is the small group of friends who made a startling short called *Sunday's Game* (see Figure 64.2). According to David Garrett, one of the short's two producers, the group deliberately set out to make something that would both shake people up and showcase their sensibilities. The short tells the story of a seemingly bland quintet of elderly ladies who spend Sunday afternoon playing a lethal game of Russian Roulette. Although the four creators of *Sunday's Game* had shot it on film and envisioned it as a calling card piece to be shown at film festivals, every festival they

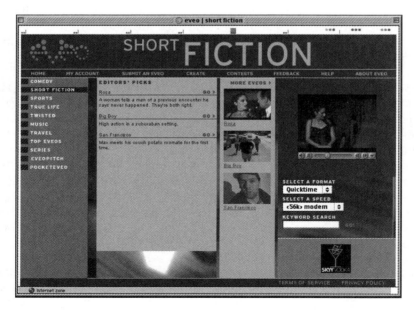

Figure 64.1 *Take your pick—eveo offers a wide selection of categories for submitted videos.*

Figure 64.2 *Sunday's game—a video that breaks new ground and takes risks—a recipe for success on the web.*

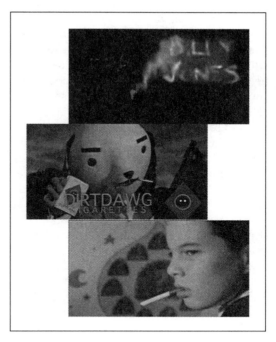

Figure 64.3 *Billy Jones—A Web short that won top honors in Yahoo's online film festival.*

approached rejected it. It wasn't until executives at the Web site Ifilm (www.ifilm.com) recognized its merits—and saw its strong subject matter as an asset, not a liability—that the short got its chance. When the piece debuted on Ifilm, it received so much positive attention (as well as stirring up heated controversy) that members of the team now have various TV and motion-picture deals at top Hollywood studios.

Their story is real-life rags to riches: at the time they made *Sunday's Game*, they were unemployed. One of them even had his car repossessed before success hit. None of the team had gone to film school; Garrett, for example, was an attorney. "Our school was the school of hard knocks," he commented recently. "We broke a lot of rules. The pace of *Sunday's Game* was really slow, especially for MTV fans, and it had a lot of old lady talk. In fact, it broke three taboos: against using old people, against guns and against suicide." Garrett believes that one of the main reasons *Sunday's Game* was so successful on the Web was because it was

unique in both viewpoint and subject matter. His advice for making shorts for the Internet? "Make something you can't see anywhere else," he said.

A New Place to Shine

Like David Garrett, Christopher Bell is convinced that content is critically important. He, too, originally set out to make a film to be shown at film festivals, but his quirky labor of love, *Billy Jones*, took him three years to complete, and by the time it was finished, the Web had matured enough to be a desirable venue (see Figure 64.3). Like *Sunday's Game*, it made its debut on the Internet site, Ifilm. And it seems to have brought Bell the kind of attention that would be hard to attract in the film festival world: he won top honors at the first annual Yahoo Internet Life Online Film Festival, and he's had a flurry of meetings at top studios and talent agencies.

Billy Jones is a dark comedy about a 12-year-old smoker, and not only contains a strong anti-smoking message, but is done in a highly original visual style. Bell said that he was inspired to make the film because a good friend of his was hooked on smoking. "It's a story I really wanted to tell," he commented recently. "And I got other people to believe in what I was doing, too, and to do top quality work on it... sometimes for free." Though produced on a small budget by Hollywood standards, Bell paid close attention to every detail. "Everything in a frame should have a reason for being," he stressed. "Especially on the Internet, you need to avoid visual clutter."

Another director whose work unexpectedly found a home on the Internet is Rafael Fernandez. His short, *Oregon*, is a minimalist, chilly sci-fi story that has received glowing comments from viewers who have watched it on the Web. Made on film, *Oregon* debuted simultaneously on Ifilm and at the prestigious South by Southwest Film Festival.

Like a number of other Internet success stories, it was Fernandez' first production. Before making *Oregon*, he had spent five years working as a computer programmer. Though he had studied writing in college, he had no other skills relating to making a film. So, to make up for his lack of production experience, he assembled a "kitchen cabinet" of friends and acquaintances that were experts in various specialties. He was still working at his day job while shooting the short. "It almost killed me," he confessed recently.

Like Garrett and Bell, Fernandez believes that to be successful on the Internet, you must first start with the subject matter. As for shooting, he advises keeping the real

Figure 64.4 *Post it—think you've got the next big Web title? Post your work at a site like ifilm.*

estate—the small screen space—in mind, and avoiding such obvious pitfalls as giant establishing shots or shots of tiny, intimate details. Overall, though, he believes it isn't necessary to worry about the technology or the limitations of the Internet (see Figure 64.4). "You can get around the limitations," he asserted recently. "And the technology is going to catch up, anyway. I think of the story I want to tell first, and the venue second."

Although he was initially hesitant about putting *Oregon* on the Web, it proved to be a good move for him. It led to numerous professional contacts and opportunities. Overall, he feels that the gamble he took in making his short has more than paid off. Currently he has a contract to make music videos and a possible deal with the Sci-Fi Channel. "It's been a life-altering experience," he affirmed.

Sidebar 1

Creating Your Own Web Calling Card

Do you want to make a video that will shine on the Web? The experts offer the following tips, which apply equally well to non-fiction and story based pieces:

1. *Choose a strong concept.* A concept that's original or has a surprising slant—especially something that is meaningful to you. Don't be afraid of a controversial theme, as long as it doesn't involve gratuitous violence or explicit sex. Craft your topic so it can be explored in a short span of time.

2. *Don't sacrifice production quality.* The higher the production quality, the better it will look on the Web.

Remember that strong visuals, close-ups and extreme close-ups work better than wide and long shots on the Web. If you'll be streaming your production, keep your backgrounds simple and avoid rapid camera movements, moving backgrounds transition effects and quick cutting.

3. *Pay attention to lighting.* Keep things on the bright side; dark scenes tend to be hard to see on the Internet, and any grain, caused by low light, will be interpreted as motion when you encode your video for streaming, making your files more complicated and harder to stream.

4. *Don't neglect your sound.* Use good mikes and avoid shooting where there's background noise. Sound is especially important on the Web, since visual quality and small screen size make images more difficult to "read."

5. *Select a catchy title or "log line" (short description).* These can help put your short in the limelight.

Sidebar 2

Sites to Check Out

The following list of sites, while by no means exhaustive, is a good starting place to investigate some of the many venues for shorts on the Web. Be forewarned, however: the fortunes of Web sites rise and fall like the tides.

- Ifilm (www.ifilm.com): largest venue for shorts on the Web; extremely democratic, inclusive polices.

- AtomFilms (www.atomfilms.com): smaller library than Ifilm; highly selective; prides itself on top quality offerings.

- Eveo (www.eveo.com): specifically designed for videographers; open-door policy; good venue for non-fiction shorts.

- MediaTrip (www.mediatrip.com): highly popular destination; showcases some of the biggest hits on the Web.

- RealNetworks (www.realnetworks.com): home of major streaming media tools; also shows shorts and offers useful information.

- Cinemanow (www.cinemanow.com): specializes in independent films; offers free home-pages for directors and others to promote their own work.

Sidebar 3

Three Elements of Success

David Garrett, one of the producers of the Web hit *Sunday's Game*, believes there are three keys to maximizing the potential benefits of having your short on the Internet.

1. BUZZ. For your short to stand out, it needs to create buzz. The pieces that generate buzz, he feels, are the ones that are highly original and that are top quality products.

2. ACCESS. Buzz gains you access to places you couldn't go before—to top talent agencies, studios and money people.

3. IDEAS. Even though buzz will open doors for you, this access is of little use unless you come in with good ideas, Garrett believes. You need to be prepared to discuss new projects in order to take advantage of your moment in the sun.

65
Eleven Easy Steps to Streaming

Charles Mohnike

Whether your pet video project is *Exposing The Chattanooga City Council* or *Baby Timmy Makes a Mud Pie* it's likely you've been tempted by the possibility of streaming it over the Internet. Putting video on the Web is a great way to show your work to others, whether you plan to offer sample clips that might lead to a lucrative sale of your tape, or to just display your work to friends, relatives and admirers. If you're new to the Web, you might think that getting your video into streaming formats requires lots of tricky mouse-jockeying and a hefty wallet, but that's no longer the case.

The latest crop of streaming-media packages makes it easier than ever to incorporate streaming video into your existing Web site—whether or not your Web provider runs a video-streaming server. In the following 12 steps, we'll show you how to start with a standard Windows movie file (.avi) and turn it into a streaming video presentation.

Our example uses RealNetworks' *Real-Producer Plus*, one of the most popular streaming video tools, but by no means

the only one. The concepts in this example also apply to stream-building packages such as Sonic Foundry's all-in-one *Stream Anywhere*, Terran Interactive's *Media Cleaner Pro*, the native Macintosh application *QuickTime Pro* as well as Microsoft's *Windows Media Tools*.

The Process

On launching *RealProducer Plus*, you'll be asked a series of questions to find out what type of video you want to create and what to do with the thing once it's created.

Step 1: Select Recording Options. Turning this feature on will allow others to "record" your streaming video by saving it to their hard drives as it plays. If you're working with copyrighted material or have worries about others stealing your thunder, it's best to turn this feature off.

Step 2: Choose a Recording Wizard. Fortunately, RealNetworks has followed the lead of many software providers and ditched the animated wizard characters.

Instead they use the term to describe a series of dialog boxes that guide you through an otherwise tooth-gnashing process. There are three to choose from.

- *Record from File*. Allows you to convert an existing .avi, .mov or MPEG-1 movie file into streaming RealVideo.

- *Record from Media Device*. Allows you to record video directly from an input device such as a VCR, camcorder or WebCam, but you'll need the necessary capture hardware installed in your computer if you intend to record from an external source/device.

- *Live Broadcast*. Sets up your computer to serve streaming video to a compatible RealServer elsewhere on the Net for a live Webcast. This method might be used to broadcast a meeting, a television newscast or even your appendectomy if you're so inclined.

Step 3: Choose a File. When you choose the "Record from File" option, RealProducer prompts you find the movie file on your hard drive using a standard dialog box. Again, this example assumes that you're working with a single existing movie file. In most cases, an edited project rendered to a single .avi or .mov file (see Figure 65.1).

Step 4: Supply RealMedia Clip Information. RealProducer next prompts for details to include in your video file. It's a good idea to include things like copyright information (to thwart the thunder-stealers), a description and some pertinent keywords.

Step 5: Select a File Type. The selection you make in this Window determines

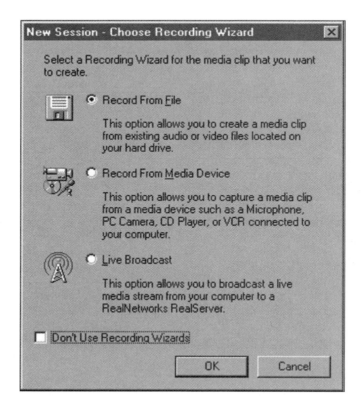

Figure 65.1 *Take your pick—you can encode footage from a file on your hard drive, from tape or from a live camera.*

the type of file RealProducer will create from your video.

- *Multi-Rate.* If your Web site host uses RealServer G2, count yourself among the truly privileged. G2 servers automatically detect the user's connection speed and then serve up an optimized video, meaning that your users always see the best quality video for their connection whether they're on a cable connection next door or a budget modem somewhere in the Himalayas.

- *Single Rate.* If your Web host doesn't run RealServer G2, you can still serve streaming video on any standard Web server with this method. With Single Rate, you have to create one or more video files optimized to different connection speeds, and then allow your users to choose one that suits them (see Figure 65.2).

Step 6: Select your Target Audience. We'll assume that you don't have access

to a RealServer G2 and that you'll serve your video from a standard Web host. When you select "Single Rate" you'll be prompted to choose one or more "target audiences" that will view your file. If you choose more than one, RealProducer will create a separate video file for each. For example, if you choose 28.8k modem and ISDN RealProducer will make two files, one with smaller file size and lower video quality to serve over 28.8 modems, and one with larger file size and better video quality to take advantage of broader bandwidths.

Step 7: Select an Audio Format. RealProducer next asks you to select the audio quality for your video. Lower selections like "Voice Only" mean smaller files and more room in the stream for better-looking video. The trade-off is that lower rates can also make certain audio sound like someone with a mouthful of enchilada shouting into a tin can. In general, it's best to try the lower-quality options first and use the

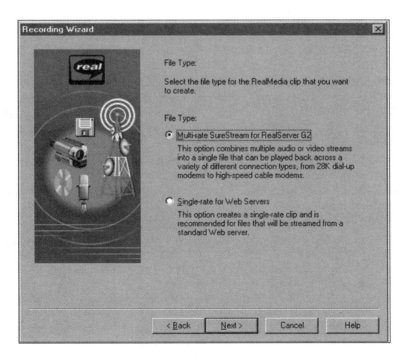

Figure 65.2 *The right rate—select multiple file types for viewers with various connection speeds.*

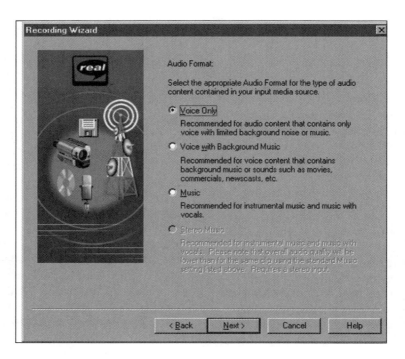

Figure 65.3 *Sound off—select lower audio quality in favor of high quality video.*

higher rates only if your resulting audio is unintelligible, or if your project has a more complex audio track with music and sound effects (see Figure 65.3).

Step 8: Select a Video Format. Like the Audio Format dialog, this screen allows you to choose the quality of your resulting video. In practice, we have found that "Smoothest Motion" delivers pretty fair video quality, but "Normal Motion" occasionally makes actors appear as if they'd been painted during Picasso's Cubist period. Sorrenson video compression used in products like Media Cleaner Pro has a *Developers Edition* that uses Variable Bit Rate (VBR) to dramatically smooth out some of these artifacts. Experiment to find the best rate and product for your content (see Figure 65.4).

Step 9: Choose an Output File. RealProducer next prompts you to specify a filename and location to save your RealVideo file. It supplies a filename based on that of your input file, but if that title doesn't grab you, choose the "Save As" option to customize it.

Step 10: Encode your Video. Finally, RealProducer provides a summary of the options you've chosen and returns you to its main screen. If you need to make any last-minute changes to the encoding options, this would be the time. Press the Start button to begin the encoding. You'll see your video whiz by in the display, letting you know that RealProducer's magic fairies have begun their handiwork (see Figure 65.5).

Step 11: Publish Your Video to the Web. You now have a properly encoded RealVideo file on your hard drive, but it's not doing you much good *there*. You'll need to create a Web page to announce your clip to the world. To begin, choose "Create Web Page" from RealProducer's pull-down Tools menu. The wizard will prompt you for the name of the video file and ask whether you want users to view it in their browsers (Embedded Player) or in their stand-alone RealPlayer (Pop-Up Player). Finally, the wizard asks you to provide a caption for the Web page and a location to store the page on your hard drive.

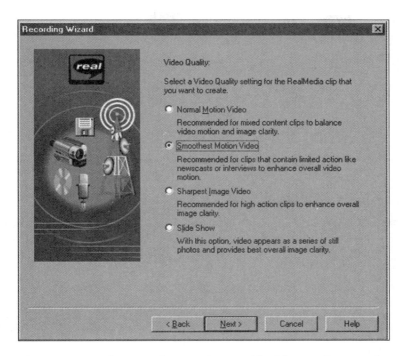

Figure 65.4 *Looking good—experiment with video quality to make the most of your bandwidth.*

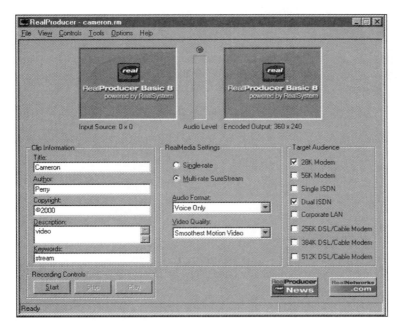

Figure 65.5 *Ready to roll—review your settings, then press start to begin.*

Once the Web page is saved, you can upload it and your video file to your Web host using standard methods such as an FTP program, or you can choose Publish Web Page from the Tools menu to have RealProducer automate the process with another nifty Wizard.

That's it. Your streaming video is now publicly available and it's likely you'll soon be contacted by eager fans around the globe, assuming you put your *actual* e-mail address into your video's information boxes instead of using me@you.com as you do with all those Web forms. Good luck.

Sidebar 1

Five Tips for Better-Looking Streams

1. Balance encoding rate with image quality. The higher the encoding rate or "target audience," the larger the video file that will be stored on your server. If your Web host is stingy with the storage space, you can get more bang for your buck by using lower encoding rates at the expense of video quality.

2. Avoid Stereo. Even if your source video contains stereo audio, it's best to avoid the tempting "Stereo Music" option unless it's absolutely required by your content. At lower encoding rates, mono audio will usually sound better than stereo because the single track won't require as much compression.

3. Let your content drive quality. When choosing a video quality, consider your program's content. For example, if your presentation contains mostly still images, definitely choose "Slide Show"—your users will see extremely clear picture quality even if their modems date back to the Reagan-Bush administration.

4. Filter to reduce artifacts. If your resulting RealVideo contains artifacts like interlacing or noise, choose Preferences from the Options menu and select the Video Filter tab. There you'll find some optional filters that may help you pull your picture and audio out of the muck.

5. Capture the best quality you can. It's usually best to first capture your video using the software that comes with your capture card and convert it to RealVideo later. Capturing directly from RealProducer saves you a step, but if your computer's processor can't cut the mustard you'll get ugly glitches in your final RealVideo.

66
Squish! Shooting for Streaming

Bill Davis

In order to get your video creations to fit within the bandwidth limitations of Net-delivered streaming video (and storage/-playback media such as VCDs), your video is going to be subject to compression.

While the "data pipes" available to the general public are getting bigger, in order to use them for something as data intensive as streaming video, you'll want to condense your video data stream as much as you possibly can.

The Holy Grail

The overall goal of video compression is to reduce the bandwidth requirements of your data stream so that it can travel quickly and efficiently through the copper and silicon that make up today's computerized video systems.

It's the electronic equivalent of making sausage. You take a big bunch of stuff (data) and figure out a way to squeeze it into its smallest possible form.

But don't get me wrong. Compression can be a good thing. In fact, every digital video format that enjoys widespread popularity already incorporates some form of video compression. But how much, and what kind of compression can have a big effect on how your video will look.

Of course, the ingredients of digital video are numbers—and without a doubt, data compression is a lot less messy than making sausage. But as I learned watching my mother-in-law in her kitchen, trying to stuff a lot of something into a little space, no matter what type of compression you're contemplating, isn't likely to be pretty.

The Basic Concept

The root concepts behind most data compression schemes are easy to understand. Imagine that you and a friend are sitting at a table in front of 100 coins. Set up in 10 rows of 10 coins each; they create a simple grid. Your job is to tell your friend how to make patterns in the coins. You could develop a pattern from the coins by describing them one at a time. You could say, "Make the first coin heads, the second one heads, the third one tails," and so on. And continue along for each of the 100 coins.

And that's similar to what an uncompressed digital signal represents. The information describing each separate pixel is stored, transmitted and translated into the picture raster separately.

Since each pixel has to have enough code to represent the required levels of its specific color and brightness, you end up with a whole lot of descriptive numbers, i.e. a whole lot of data.

But what if you could simply tell your friend, "Make the first 50 heads and the rest tails." Bingo. In one simple instruction, you can describe a whole range of coins.

Most compression schemes take a similar approach. They look for repetitive patterns in the data and instead of describing them in discrete steps, they attempt to express them in condensed mathematical shorthand (see Figure 66.1).

If your goal is to shoot footage that will compress well, the first step is to pay close attention to how much detail your shots contain.

If you put your subject in front of a flatly lit, solid color wall, your software will have lots of excellent compression opportunities (see Figure 66.2).

But there's a danger here. Putting every subject in front of such a flat background can make for pretty boring video. So, the challenge is to learn about how to create shots that are both compression-friendly *and* visually interesting.

On the opposite extreme, putting a subject in front of a large, leafy tree on a windy day is a classic example of footage that will compress poorly. Your poor pixels try to portray millions of leaves alternating between light and dark, and as the breeze blows, nearly every pixel in every frame changes. The result is that there's hardly any chance for your compression software to find repetitive patterns from frame to frame.

Combine that kind of compression-hostile scene with a video system that applies a large amount of compression to

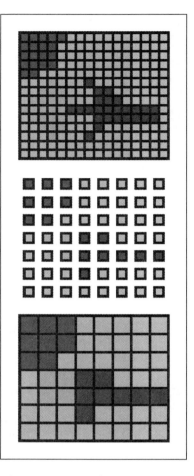

Figure 66.1 *Intraframe compression is accomplished by averaging pixels. In this example, four pixels of information are averaged and stored as a single piece of information.*

Figure 66.2 *Solid-colored backgrounds compress better than complex or busy backgrounds.*

the signal and you can be left with some pretty ugly footage.

The results are often described as "compression anomalies" or "compression artifacts," convenient shorthand terms for a range of picture problems, including blockiness, which can result from poor compression results.

Spare Change

Since the object of making compression-friendly video is keeping the intraframe (between pixels within a given frame) and interframe (between adjacent frames) differences to a minimum, anything that makes one pixel different from the preceding one works against you. This includes such simple camera moves as pans and zooms. Think about it; when you zoom into a scene, the view constantly changes. And the same holds true for pans and tilts. Under certain circumstances, these moves can decrease the ability of your software to compress your scene. Even the slightest camera move can cause compression problems. Thinking of shooting handheld? Forget it! A tripod is essential when shooting video for streaming.

But Not Always

Consider a shot of a white wall with a solid black square on it. Simply panning across the scene won't change the ability of your software to compress it. After all, the differences between the elements aren't increasing, only changing location on the raster. And if you zoom-in on a similar scene, the compression penalty will also be small. The black square gets larger, but with only two simple colors (or two regions to describe), your software will still be able to do a good job of decreasing the size of the data stream.

So, if you've established a compression-friendly scene, it's not always necessary to be super-conservative with your camera work. Make your own judgment. And

Figure 66.3 *Complex moving backgrounds, such as the plants shown here, do not compress well. The first order of business when you're thinking about compression-friendly shots is to look at your landscape with an eye to detail.*

understanding how compression works will help you make better judgments.

The Devil's in the Details

If a major obstacle to compression is scene detail, it stands to reason that simply removing some of the fine detail from your scene will help increase your ability to compress it (see Figure 66.3).

If there are busy patterns in paintings, wall hangings or light and dark details, such as narrow window blinds, try to reframe with an eye on minimizing and eliminating compression-unfriendly material.

A good example might be a shot that uses a large bookcase as a background. Row upon row of colorful book jacket spines, with contrasting type, is another type of scene that would typically compress poorly.

Moving the subject in front of a plain background would make a big improvement.

Plumbing the Depths

If, however, you're faced with a scene where background detail is unavoidable,

Figure 66.4 *Clever us of depth of field to create a soft focus on the background can also improve compression.*

one of the easiest ways to improve your compression results is to use the tricks of depth of field to throw the background out of focus (see Figure 66.4).

If you've been reading **Videomaker** for long, you already know about controlling depth of field, leaving your subject in sharp focus while allowing your background to go soft. Because soft backgrounds have less detail, they will compress much better than sharp backgrounds.

If you have ample camera-to-subject-to-background room available and can keep your scene's light levels low enough, open up your iris or increase your shutter speed to make your depth of field shallow, throwing your background out of focus.

Another great compression trick (if you have the technical capabilities) is to shoot your subject against a blue screen or green screen and matte in a still photo instead of a "live" background. Then no matter how complicated the background image, the complete lack of motion between frames will make it easy for your computer to compress the interframe differences.

The key here is to keep a sharp eye out for anything that will lead to large interframe changes.

Compress the Future

As video migrates from television sets to the Web, VCDs and other cutting-edge storage media such as Flash memory cards, memory sticks and more, compression is going to be an increasingly important part of video content delivery.

A part of effective video production in the future could be the ability to judge how well a scene will compress for streaming. As with most other video skills, trial and error is a good teacher. So, as you start to prepare your video for these new delivery technologies, pay special attention to the effects of compression on your work. Keeping your eye tuned to shooting compression-friendly video is a skill you'll likely be using for a long time to come.

Sidebar 1

A Compressionist by Trade

As compression gets more and more important in the delivery of video content, there is a growing trend of individuals who are specializing in this field.

The video compressionist is an individual who either understands how to deliver the largest amount of content in the smallest stream of data, or who understands the best type of compression to employ in order to get the best looking video playback on a particular system.

The fact that there are specialists doing this work is a good indicator of how complicated the underlying technology can be. But don't worry, for the vast majority of us, the hardware and software tools we use do an excellent job of compression without the need for any human input at all.

Sidebar 2

Be Afraid of the Dark

Well lit shots cut back on grain, making the image easier to compress, easier to send and easier on the eye of the Web viewer. As strange as it may seem, you will want to use bright lighting for roughly the same reason as limiting movement in the frame. Grain (also known as noise) in an image is seen as motion by compression programs, eating up file space and resulting in degraded images. A simple, stable, grainy image can be as difficult for a compression program to work with as a complicated image with lots of motion. Good looking streaming video requires that you shoot well-lit raw footage.

67
A Step-by-Step Guide to Encoding for the Web

John Davis

When you started your production, you had a vision; you may have had a simple message to communicate, a joke to tell or a story to share. After shooting, you spent time editing your footage and making your masterpiece come to life. Finally, your work is at an end and your finished production sits in an .avi file on your hard drive. Now what do you do? The only thing left is to output your production so you can share it with others.

How can you share your project with all the people that you want to see it? You could output your project to tape and make duplicates to send to your friends. Or, you could put your finished program on the Web, either as a downloadable file or as streaming media for the entire world to see. In this article you will learn how to take your video file from your hard drive, create a streaming media file and then post it to a Web site.

Although the specific mouse clicks may vary depending on the software you use, the basic steps are the same. Using this article as a guide, you'll be able to get your project ready for your audience to view.

Video on the Web

You can post video files on a Web site and make them available for downloading just like you can any other type of file. Because video files can be quite large, with correspondingly large download times, many people choose to offer their video as streaming media. Streaming refers to media files that can be viewed as they are downloaded. Since viewers watch streaming video on the fly, they don't have to wait for long downloads. Only a small part of the file stays on your computer while you are watching the video.

The first thing that you must do if you're going to stream your video is to convert your video file into a streaming format (see Figure 67.1). There are several different software programs that will perform the necessary file conversions; some

Figure 67.1 *A Complete video—once you've finished your production, it's ready to be converted, to a streaming format.*

will also help you clean up your project and tweak it for the smaller format and ower quality that's required for the Web. Before you go out and buy encoding software, you might want to check the editing software you now have. Some of the newer versions, such as Sonic Foundry's Vegas Video, have encoding options built into their output choices. Similarly, encoders from both RealMedia and Microsoft Windows Media are available as free plugins to popular editing packages like Adobe Premiere and even Microsoft's PowerPoint. For more products you can see a detailed list in the Streaming, MPEG and QuickTime Encoders Buyer's Guide, on page 9 in this issue.

We have selected one of the products featured in that buyer's guide, Media Cleaner Pro 4 from Terran Interactive, to illustrate the necessary steps to get a video from your computer to the World Wide Web. Although other programs will

operate differently, the concepts will be universal and consistent.

Getting Started

First, make sure you have your finished video project and the encoding software. For our example, we will encode a 60-second video for a project that we shot and mastered on the Mini DV format. The final edit of the video resides on our hard drive as a 720 × 480, 30-frame-per-second, 32-bit color .avi file with 16-bit stereo audio, sampled at 44.1 kHz. Sound complicated? Don't worry. These are standard settings for video captured to a computer from a digital camcorder using an IEEE 1394 (FireWire) cable. Your settings may differ, but that doesn't matter. You simply need to have the video you'd like to stream on your computer's hard drive to begin.

When you start the encoding program, you will likely have two choices: you can

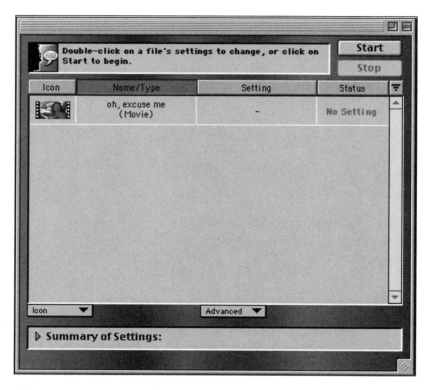

Figure 67.2 *Capture it—load your video into the Batch window to begin the encoding process.*

use the program's wizard to help you customize your project or you can specify all the advanced settings yourself. Choosing the wizard is a good way to start, as it walks you step-by-step through the encoding process. For this article we'll discuss the advanced settings option.

When you're ready to begin encoding, you first need to load the video that you want to encode into the encoding program. You can do this by dragging the actual .avi file you'll use into the Batch window or you can choose Add to Batch from the File Menu (see Figure 67.2). If the Batch window is not available, simply select New Batch from the file menu. Once you have your production in the Process window, you can then go to the Advanced Settings dialog by selecting Advanced Settings from the Windows menu. It is here where you will tell the software how you would like to encode your streaming media file.

Output Options

The first settings in the Advanced Settings window are on the Output tab. The most basic decision is the output file format: do you want a Real Video, QuickTime or Windows Media file? Or do you want all three? Although there are significant differences in the way that each format is encoded, the image quality of each is on par with the others. You may end up choosing one format over another out of personal preference or due to where you will ultimately post your file. Some formats have features that the others don't, so be sure to read up on each of the formats. Depending on the encoder you use, you may not have many choices. Not all encoders output all of the file types. We are using Media Cleaner Pro for this example because it handles all of the common file formats.

The output options that follow depend on the format you've chosen (see Figure 67.3).

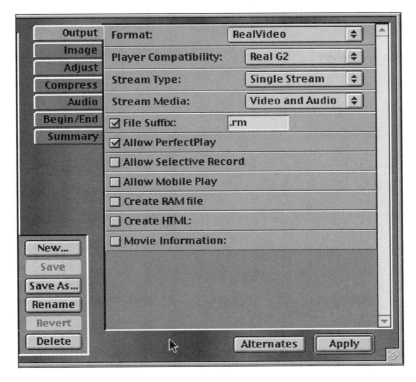

Figure 67.3 *Focus on format—the output window is where you decide what type of format you'd like to use to stream your video.*

If you choose RealVideo, for example, you will see choices for RealPlayer compatibility. You can also choose to encode using SureStream, which automatically adjusts to the viewer's connection speed, or you can choose to encode to a single stream.

Next, you need to choose the frame size (see Figure 67.4). You do not want to use 720 × 480, as the file size would be enormous and take forever to view. Often, to ensure speedy delivery, Internet video is quite small, sometimes less than 100 pixels wide and/or tall. Generally, the smaller the frame size, the smoother the stream. For our project, we chose to create a streaming file at 160 ×120 pixels.

Now it's time to consider frame rate. Each frame adds to the total size of your file and slows down the whole streaming process. The human threshold for discerning motion happens to be 12 images per second. Anything less than that (roughly) will appear as a fast slide show.

With this in mind, many streaming media files are lowered to 12 FPS. This reduces file size so that viewers are able to watch your video with less pauses, glitches and stutters.

Keeping in mind that both audio and video travel down that same narrow modem line, let's turn our attention to the audio portion of our project. Some file formats support different codecs than others. The RealVideo format, for example, allows you to adjust audio gain, low pass, high pass, noise removal, dynamic range (difference between highest high and lowest low frequency), noise gate, notch and oddly enough, reverb. Play with these settings to find what works best for your project (see Figure 67.5). Because Internet audio tends to be low quality, you may choose to cut some corners with the sound quality so you can preserve precious bandwidth for your visuals (see Figure 67.6).

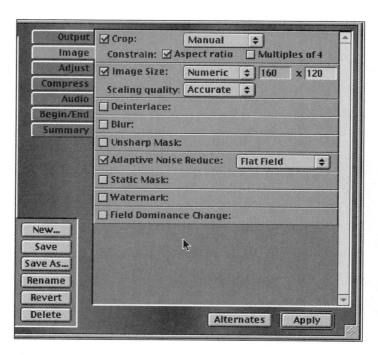

Figure 67.4 *Size matters—choose a frame size that will ensure speedy delivery of your video over the Internet. The smaller the better.*

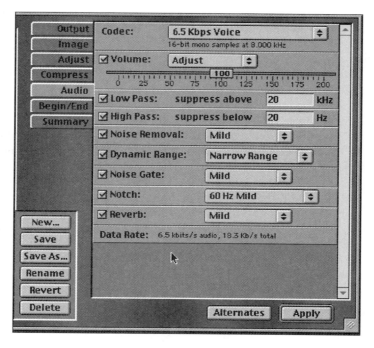

Figure 67.5 *Sound it out—work with the audio settings to get good sound without compromising the video image.*

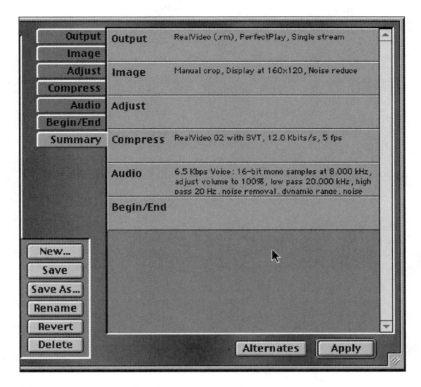

Figure 67.6 *Review it—the summary tab allows you to verify all your settings options before you encode the video file.*

Encoding the Output File

Once you have set all the options, go back through and verify them. Many of these programs have a setting's summary which you can view before you encode. In Media Cleaner Pro, the summary is always available as another tab in the Advanced settings.

After you verify your settings, click Apply. It is here that you might consider adding alternate outputs, like QuickTime and Windows, so that you can walk away and come back to find several output files finished. For our project, however, we selected RealVideo as our only output file and pressed Start.

It took 10.5 seconds to create the output file for this 60-second project. Encoding speed depends on several factors, including processor speed. Media Cleaner Pro has a cool feature that lets you watch a split-screen view of the before (source)

and after (destination) (see Figure 67.7). This can be especially helpful to see what you have selected, if you are making adjustments such as cropping or color correction.

After you have encoded your file, you should view it before you put it on the Web. Make sure it looks okay on your computer before you send it to someone else. This step can save you time and trouble later. If everything looks good, you can now upload your file to the Web.

Publishing to the Web

The last step in this process is getting your encoded file to your Web host. You can send it electronically from your computer via the Internet to your Web host, you can send a floppy disk with the encoded file via snail mail or you can send the edited project on tape and have the Web host

Figure 67.7 *Before and after—media Cleaner Pro has a split-screen feature that allows you to view the original as the new file is created.*

encode it (see sidebar). For more information on hosting services, check out "Web Hosting," in this special guide.

When you publish to the Web, you're really just storing your file in a folder or directory on a host computer. That computer runs specialized server-software that allows it to share files to users all over the world. Getting your streaming media file to the server is the same as moving it to another folder on your computer. The main difference is that the folder where you are moving your files might be 3,000 miles away!

Some programs that encode media files also help publish your finished products to the Web. Depending on who your Web host is, you may have some online uploading aids or step-by-step instructions available to you. In either case, consult the host site's technical support for directions. Typically, you will upload the file via FTP (file transfer protocol) to your Web host (see Figure 67.8). You can almost always accomplish this by using a shareware FTP

client such as Cute FTP (Windows) or Anarchie (Mac).

Once you have uploaded your file to your host, you will need to make it available to your viewers. Follow your encoding software's directions for serving and embedding your streaming media files in Web pages, as the directions will vary between formats.

Surf's Up

Once you've invested your time and effort into a production, you want it to be seen by as many people and as easily as possible. Getting it onto the Web can accomplish that. By learning to encode your original project into a streamed file, you can make it happen in a way that will get more viewers to your show.

Using encoding software can be extremely simple. These encoders can take your finished product and squish it down to the size of a postage stamp, if need be. Their

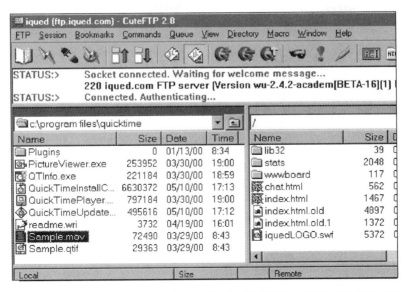

Figure 67.8 *Post it—an FTP shareware program can upload your encoded project to your Web host.*

specialty is keeping your carefully-wrought images intact when they squish the file.

If you haven't already experienced the thrill of publishing on the World Wide Web and having people from all over watch your productions almost as fast as you can make them, you do not know what you've been missing!

68

Why and How Would
I Get a Streaming Server?

Larry Lemm

To provide video over the Internet, you need to have a server. Hosting your own streaming server is a good idea only if you already have a Web server with at least a T1 line running to it. If you have a Web server with no more than phone or ISDN lines you will not be able to stream video effectively.

Many people who create video content would rather spend their days shooting and editing video than maintaining an ordinary Web server, much less one that streams video. For them, a remote server hosted by someone else is a good idea.

If you do have your own Web server, you can provide a hyperlink to the video hosting company's Web site. Alternately, you could keep all your Web content—including your video content—on a remote video streaming server and avoid the need for maintaining a Web server of your own. Another advantage of enlisting a remote host: a large video serving company could also draw more people to your video than you could draw to your own web page alone.

There are many considerations to keep in mind when choosing a streaming server. The first and foremost is how many "streams" you are allotted. A single stream would allow only one viewer to watch one video clip at a time. The more streams that are available, the more viewers can be watching at one time. For many Web sites, 10 streams would be plenty. If you had 20 minutes of streamed video on demand, 10 streams would allow up to720 people to watch that video in a 24-hour period.

Some servers charge you by the number of streams you want available to potential viewers, while others charge you by the number of streams they actually served to viewers of your video.

If you are going through the trouble of having someone else host your video, you should choose one of the multiple protocol streaming software packages. Along with choosing a server, you will need to decide what software you want to use to serve your video. Each package has its own features and drawbacks. Some programs require clients to download browser plug-ins to watch the video; others do not; still others cram a plug-in into your browser with the power of Java.

The streamers that don't require a plug-in transmit video through the Web's HTTP protocol. These are convenient for the user because they are easiest to setup and use. However, they do not take advantage of alternative protocols that are designed to deliver video more quickly and accurately. Non-HTTP software packages use "non-reliable" protocols to send everything but the control information and are thus inherently faster.

When shopping for a streaming server company, consider the amount of bandwidth that it makes available for your content. The more bandwidth you have, the faster and better your video will stream to viewers. Some servers may use a process known as multicasting. Multicasting sends only one stream of video to a collection of servers. Those servers then re-transmit the video to viewers in their area. This process saves bandwidth on the backbone of the Internet, and allows for more video to be streamed without clogging the 'Net with video. The downside is that multicasting eliminates the on-demand aspect, you can watch a multicast only while it is being transmitted; you can't initiate one on your own.

Choosing the right server is the most important decision you make after deciding that streaming video is for you. If the idea of setting up a high-bandwidth video server makes your head spin with unknown acronyms and arcane nerdspeak, then choose a remote video hosting company to stream your video for you.

69
Slide into "Thin Streaming"

Larry Lemm

See video clips at www.videomaker.com/handbook.

Someday soon Internet video-on-demand will democratize video distribution, allowing everyone the opportunity to distribute video to a worldwide audience without having a multi-billion dollar television-broadcasting studio.

But what is there to do in the meantime? How can I put my productions on the Internet today?

The answer lies in the slideshow. I remember the first time I watched video-on-demand via the Internet. "Amazing," I thought to myself as I clicked on the button that started the video. Having already downloaded and installed the utility that allowed this technological miracle, I was ready to experience "click-and-watch" video. What a letdown.

The video was tiny, roughly the size of a saltine cracker on my 17-inch monitor. The picture was barely discernible, with large digital-artifacts appearing where the software's compression utility hadn't quite done its math correctly. The most obvious problem was the lack of motion. The video sputtered along at two or three frames per second. I had almost given up hope for Internet video, when I remembered how I was connected to the Internet: through an old, slow, copper phone wire.

Then I imagined the super-fast connection the phone companies are promising over the next couple of years. If they can transmit almost-video over my ancient phone line now, full-motion, full-screen video-on-demand will be a reality when the super-fast Internet connection comes. Until then, I can distribute my work on the Web in the form of a slideshow.

Internet slideshows are a fast and inexpensive way to get your ideas out to a mass audience, without having to resort to slow, chunky and tiny video. By using the basic story-telling concepts of a storyboard, you can easily turn any video into a multimedia web-based slideshow. Slideshows also play great on a television, opening your Web slideshow to a wider potential audience of Web TV surfers.

Making Slides to Show

There are two basic ways to create digital slides. First, you can use a still camera. Your still camera can be either a standard film-based camera, in which case you would have to use a scanner to digitize the photos, or a digital camera that saves stills on a disk in an Internet-ready format. Or, you can use a video camera, and take stills from video (Figure 69.1).

The first method requires little or no special equipment, save a scanner if you are using a film-based still camera. If you have a FireWire based digital camcorder it is easy to create stills that are transferable to your computer through a simple connector. If you want to use existing analog videotape taken from a standard camcorder, making digital stills requires a special piece of equipment called a digitizer. This can be either a special video-capture board that you install into your computer, or an external device like Play Inc's Snappy (Figure 69.2), that plugs into the ports in the back.

Either way, you can use these tools to capture "still frames" from your video. These devices will usually save the still frames in any of the standard digital photo formats including .gif, .jpg, .bmp, and .tga. After you have selected the stills you want to use, you'll need to put them in an order that tells a story. For example, if you are making a how-to slideshow about organic gardening your first slide could be of your untilled garden. The next could be a slide of tilling the garden, followed by slides of rebuilding the soil with compost, planting the garden, chemical-free pest control techniques, harvesting and so forth. After you have selected your slides, you can create an audio track that explains each step, and match the changing slides to your audio track.

Tools to Slide the Show

Now that you have slides to show, you are ready to put them on the Internet. For

Figure 69.1 *Your camcorder is all you need to gather images for your Internet slideshow.*

Figure 69.2 *Video stills can be captured using an inexpensive device like Play, Inc.'s Snappy.*

those of you who aren't experienced in HTML Web programming, I'd recommend using an existing video streaming program like the Real Video Producer (Figure 69.3) or a special slideshow program such as InMedia's Slides and Sounds.

To make a slideshow in Slides and Sounds (Figure 69.4), simply place your

Figure 69.3 *RealVideo allows you to make streaming slideshows by showing a video frame every four seconds.*

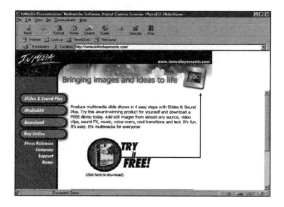

Figure 69.4 *InMedia's Slides and Sounds is designed to make creating Internet slideshows easy.*

selected slides in order in the slideshow creation menu. Captions and sound effects can be added to each slide by simply clicking the "add sound" and "add caption" buttons. Transitions between slides can then be selected from the F/X menu. Blank slides can also be created to add simple titles at the start or finish of your slideshow. It's that easy. To finish the slideshow, save it as a file that can be e-mailed to family and friends, or select the "save as HTML" option from the file menu.

This will create a Web ready HTML file that will play on most browsers (in Internet Explorer, you might have to go to the "view" menu, "options" section, "security level" button, and select the medium security setting to permit a small file to be temporarily used to play the slideshow).

Getting Your Slideshow on the Web

Now that your slideshow is ready for the web, you'll need to publish it to your Web page. There are numerous Web hosting companies, and each offers its own package of options for your site. Users of InMedia's Slides and Sound who don't want to host their own Web site can have a slideshow served by InMedia.

If you plan to use a video-streaming package to create your slideshow, make sure that the hosting company you choose supports the streaming package you plan on using. There are some sites on the Web that will even give you a free web site to display your slideshow. Geocities (www.geocities.com) and Tripod (www.tripod.com) will host a small site for free as long as it is a not-for-profit endeavor. (See Figure 69.5.)

Until the majority of the wired world has a high-bandwidth Internet connection that streams video full-size and full motion, slideshows are the low-bandwidth alternative of choice for camcorder enthusiasts.

Making a Slideshow in HTML

It is easy to make a series of Web pages act like a slideshow is you already know the basics of HTML. To perform this feat of coding magic, simply use this tag above of your HTML header (make it the first thing listed in an HTML source).

<META HTTP-EQUIV="Refresh" content="5;
URL=http://www.yoururl.com/nextslide.htm">

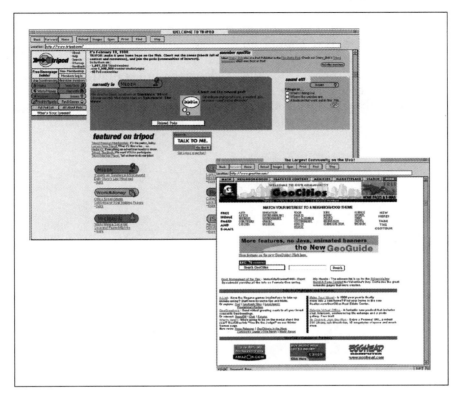

Figure 69.5 *An easy way to get your show on the Web (if you're a non-profit outfit) is to utilize a free host like Geocities or Tripod.*

In this example, the refresh call is the "slideshow" command, the content number (5 in the example) is the number of seconds the page will wait before cycling to the next page in the slideshow, which is the URL listed in the tag. To use this bit of HTML magic, replace the sample URL with the URL of your next slide, and replace the 5 in the content call with the number of seconds you want your slideshow to be displayed.

Create your web pages for the slideshow with the images and text you want displayed, as you would create any web page. If you use an HTML generator such as Pagemill, you can create the pages normally, then add the Meta-Refresh tag above any other coding. An example of this style of slideshow is available at www.adventureliving.com/home/slideshow/ index.html.

Using RealVideo to Make a Slideshow

Video streaming software such as VivoActive or RealVideo can also be used to make an Internet slideshow. The downside of this method is that viewers will have to download a special player plug-in to watch your slideshow. On the upside, the streaming packages allow for a continuous soundtrack of narration or music to be added to your slideshow.

The RealVideo encoder, for example, has a pre-defined slideshow setting that will take a video clip, and stream it with high-quality sound, and a single frame from the video is shown every four seconds. This is the easiest way to make a slideshow from a video. Another way to use RealVideo to make a slideshow is to make an audio-only RealMedia file.

Then you create a series of web pages holding the images you want shown in your slideshow. The next step is to make a text file that will list the web pages you want synchronized to the audio with a time marker next to each, and it will begin loading that page at that point in the audio file. As the audio file plays, the web pages are automatically displayed.

A stellar example of a RealVideo slideshow is at www.starwars.com/dewback/index.html. Here you will see George Lucas explain some moviemaking magic while his Web site employs some Web-Jedi tricks.

70
Put MPEGs on Your Home Page

Joe McCleskey

See video clips at www.videomaker.com/handbook.

MPEG (emm-peg): *Moving Picture Experts Group* 1) A working group of digital video experts who meet regularly under the auspices of the International Standards Organization (ISO) and the International Electro-technical Commission (IEC) to develop standards for compressed digital video. 2) A compressed digital video clip, often found on the World Wide Web or in multimedia CD-ROM products.

If you've spent any time at all on the World Wide Web, you're probably familiar with the MPEG acronym by now. That's because MPEGs are one of the main types of digital video files available on Web pages, some of the others being Microsoft's Windows Media (formerly known as Video for Windows), RealNetworks' RealMedia and Apple's QuickTime. MPEG compression is the older brother to MPEG-2 compression which is used to encode video for DVDs as well as DSS. MPEG compression has been designed to compress digital video to manageable size while retaining picture quality.

"Okay," you say, "that's all very well and good, but how do I get these MPEGs onto my home page?"

Glad you asked. What follows is a concise guide to putting your own short video clips onto the World Wide Web. We'll cover the shooting and digitizing of these clips in somewhat less detail; what we're really after here is the simplest way to 1) compress your digital video files using the MPEG-1 CODEC, and 2) post these files to a Web page using the store-and-forward method.

When you've finished with the article, you'll be able to put the entire Web audience just a few mouse clicks away from viewing your short video clips.

Store and Forward

Currently, the most popular method for distributing digital video on the Internet is known as the "store and forward" method. The concept is pretty simple: a videographer makes a digitized video clip available on his or her Web page, where the Internet public at large may download it onto their own computer and play at their leisure. It's nearly identical to the shareware concept of computer software distribution, with one condition: the shared software is a video clip instead of a software package or application.

There are some drawbacks to this method. The biggest problem is time; video files tend to be rather large, so it takes some time to download them on a typical (56.6 kilobaud) modem. A thirty-second MPEG clip, for example, can easily occupy 1 MB of hard drive space—which, in turn, will take approximately five minutes to download on a 56.6 Kb modem.

Fortunately, there are ways to make the process a little bit more palatable. Common practice is to place a single frame of the video clip onto your Web page near the location of the MPEG itself; this gives potential viewers a look at what they're getting before they commit some of their valuable online time.

Limitations

Before you get ready to start digitizing your favorite video clips, you'll need to consider the method that your audience will most likely use to view your MPEGs. Most multimedia systems offer only a small, low-res window for viewing digital video.

Brand-new computer systems can handle bigger window sizes and better resolutions, but you can't count on everyone in your potential audience having a brand-new computer. For this reason, we suggest offering your MPEGs in a 320 × 240 format or smaller, and 15 frames per second or less. This tiny window will place limits on the kind of video clips you can use. The most obvious limit is size; if you want to show a stunning wide-angle shot of a mountain range, for example, it won't look like much once you've reduced it to fit, stutteringly, into a tiny little box on a computer screen.

These and other factors will unfortunately make most of your existing video footage difficult to watch in a small window. The solution: either sort through the footage you have for the appropriate shots, or start from scratch and shoot a video project with the above-mentioned concepts in mind.

Another problem with MPEGs is audio. Many software MPEG encoders won't handle MPEG audio, and just as many software MPEG playback applications won't play MPEG audio even if you take the time and effort to include it in your video clip. For this reason, MPEG video artists might find themselves operating in a visual-only medium. (The easiest way to get around this? Go with the standard .avi or .mov formats instead of MPEG.)

Shooting Video for Multimedia

Once you decide on what footage to use, you'll have to get the video into the computer with a video digitizer. Digitizers are available in a wide range of performance levels and prices. Note that a 60-field-per-second, full-screen video digitizer is not necessary to produce a suitable digital video clip. Many of the older low-cost digitizers were designed with the small multimedia video presentation in mind, so if you've got one of these, you're set to go. If you're in the market for a new video digitizer, however, and you're willing to spend a little extra, it's a good idea to get the best model you can afford. A better digitizer will not only give you a better overall image (even at these small sizes); it'll be there for you when you're ready to upgrade your DTV workstation.

One more thing to look for if you're in the market for a video digitizer: check to see if the model you're interested in comes with MPEG encoding software bundled. Many of the newer video digitizers come complete with software for nonlinear editing, 3D animation, photo enhancement and other applications. For our purposes, a software-only MPEG encoder is a direct hit.

Software MPEG Encoding

Now that you've digitized your shot-for-multimedia footage, it's time to use MPEG to bring your video files down to a more manageable size.

You can accomplish this by two means: through a hardware MPEG encoder, such as might be integrated with your capture card, or by using a software MPEG solution. An hardware encoding solution is usually faster (real-time or better), but generally costs more, while a software solution might leave you waiting, but with more money in your wallet.

Once you've successfully encoded them to MPEG, your video clips should occupy a much smaller space, requiring less online time for your audience to download. Now it's time to post it to a Web page. In order to do so, you'll either have to pay someone who knows how (i.e. an Internet service provider or consultant), or roll up your sleeves and get friendly with HTML, the language of the Web.

Post It

Don't panic: the basics of HTML (hypertext markup language) are quite easy to learn. For a primer on Web production fundamentals, take a look at "A Beginner's Guide to HTML". (www.ncsa.uiuc.edu/General/Internet/WWW/HTMLPrimer.html.) An alternative would be to use one of the WYSIWYG ("What You See Is What You Get") Web page editors, such as Microsoft's FrontPage or Adobe's PageMill, which handle all the "coding" for you. There are also shareware and even free-ware editors available for download, so don't feel compelled to learn HTML.

Besides knowledge of the basics of HTML (or at least a method of creating it), you're going to need access to the right kind of Internet service. Specifically, you'll need the type that allows users to create and post their own Web pages. The major online service providers (AOL, CompuServe, etc.) offer limited Web pages to their clients, but the large number of individual pages this creates makes it necessary to severely limit them in size. For this reason, your best option for Web publishing is likely to be one of the many free web-hosting service providers, such as iDrive (http://www.idrive.com), Driveway (http://www.driveway.com) or K-Turn (http://www.kturn.com).

Here's how it usually works: you create your HTML files, then "post" them to your assigned site, either through FTP or through the HTML editing program you're using (e.g., Microsoft FrontPage allows you to manage your site through an Explorer-like interface, with folders and file icons).

Students who are lucky enough to attend schools that offer them Web space can take advantage of this opportunity, but bear in mind that you'll probably be on your own for the actual posting. Consult your campus information center to find out how your school handles student Web pages.

For those who already have some experience producing Web pages, here's a tip: posting MPEGs (or any other kind of video file, for that matter) is easier than it may seem. Just link the MPEG file (video.mpg, for example) the same way you would create an internal link to another Web page. The HTML might look like this: Click <a href="video.mpg">here</a> to download my latest MPEG.

When you do this, a person viewing your page has only to click on the word "here" to download your video clip. (Note: in the above example, you'd have to make sure that the file "video.mpg" was in the same directory as the page listing the link. Otherwise, you'd have to put the directory information ahead of the file name, e.g. "mpegs\video.mpg".)

Confused? Don't worry; a visit to the above-mentioned HTML tutorial should help to sort things out a bit. And if all else fails, you can always bribe one of your computer-nerd friends with a six pack of Jolt Cola; this always works for me.

What For?

Now that you know how to post MPEGs on the Web, what will you do with this knowledge? Here's a short list of applications you might consider: Illustrate a process. Provide talking-head narration. Make a preview of a longer work. Create a weekly 30-second Internet TV show. Advertise a product. Smile and wave to your Web audience. Give the Web a "virtual" tour of your backyard. Introduce your pets. Expose a scandal. Sell your car. Create a video personal ad. Or anything else you might think of.

PART VII
Authoring DVDs and CDs

Burning video onto discs that will play in DVD players and computer drives.

71
Getting Your Video
Onto a DVD

Matthew York

DVD players were the only category in consumer electronics hardware that showed major growth last year. At least three factors have fueled this rapid adoption. First, the quality of DVD-video is far superior to VHS, especially the sound quality. Second, most video rental stores carry a wide selection of DVD titles for rent. Third, the retail price for a DVD player has plummeted below $100, so they are quite affordable. This is important to people who make video because we now have another distribution medium to use.

VHS videotape has been the standard video format for distribution for years because nearly every home has a VHS VCR connected. Now, there are enough DVD players in use for everyone making video to consider making duplicates of their videos on both VHS and DVD. The price to duplicate DVDs has dropped dramatically within the past year. Individual copies made at home might cost as little as 70 cents per disc and the cost to professionally duplicate 1,000 copies of a DVD is about the same as 2-hour VHS tape.

DVD is clearly becoming the new standard video format for distribution. But what does that mean for video producers?

DVDs can be played back on personal computers or living room DVD players. When played on a personal computer, other information can be included like still images, games, software applications, documents and even Internet links. These bonus features are something that all videographers should consider when they have the chance to use DVD to distribute their work.

The most important aspect of using DVD for video is navigation. With a VCR, the remote control is the only navigation tool available. The menu choices are crude and inaccurate: pause, stop, rewind, play and fast-forward. The content creator has no control over the navigation and, therefore, it is assumed that the viewer will simply play the video from the beginning to the end. Since videotape is a linear medium, this is a good assumption. It is impractical to instruct the viewer to press the fast forward button on their VCR's remote to simulate random access of the video. Besides, the fast-forward button is imprecise and the TV screen may be blank while the tape is fast-forwarding to another spot on the video.

DVD, on the other hand, is nonlinear. This means that the viewers can jump to any point of the video at any time. DVD menus, when properly designed, are a boon to multimedia presentations. This one seemingly simple capacity actually transforms the entire video production (and viewing) experience.

From the outset, video production has really just been an extension of radio. Early TV shows where comprised of cameras pointed at radio personalities as they did their radio shows. These shows were, in turn, an extension of motion pictures, theatrical plays and Vaudeville acts. Collectively, it is all really story telling, which is in turn largely what being human

is about. Stories are linear. They start with a beginning, have a middle and conclude at the end. Since most videos are stories on a TV screen, the linear nature of videotape is perfectly suited for this purpose.

Of course a series of loosely related short stories can be collected together in a single volume. The Bible is a good example of this. The Bible is not one long story, but is instead a series of short stories arranged in books and chapters. Vaudeville acts were also comprised of short individual live performances. Variety shows (on the radio or TV) are also collections of short stories.

This fundamental idea of making a video that is, in essence, a series of short stories is enhanced by DVD. DVD authoring will challenge all video producers to consider the idea of a nonlinear presentation. Creating this type of video is an entirely different endeavor right from the first stages of planning.

72

Burn Your Own:
A Guide to Creating Your Own CDs and DVDs

Loren Alldrin

See video clips at www.videomaker.com/handbook.

Been to a video store lately? If so, you've probably noticed that you can rent movies on something other than good-old VHS tape. More and more releases are now available on DVD, a shiny disc that holds moving images and sounds in a digital format. DVD delivers excellent audio and video quality plus the potential for inter-activity: viewer-selectable camera angles, alternate edits, multiple languages and much more. Intrigued? As a videographer, you should be!

Unfortunately, due to the high cost of hardware putting your own videos onto DVD has been an unaffordable dream for most. But this is rapidly changing—hard-ware prices are dropping to the point where burning your own DVD (or CD-ROM or Video CD) isn't outrageously expensive. What it *still* is, though, is confusing. Many videographers have tried to burn their own video discs but found themselves lost in a maze of acronyms, technical jargon and fast-moving standards.

Sound familiar? If so, you've come to the right place. We'll do our best to explain the basic concepts of recording to DVD-Video, CD-R video and Video CD discs.

The Big Picture

When you boil it all down, there are two main issues at work when it comes to recording video onto a disc. First, you have the physical disc format itself. There are just two to consider—CD and DVD. Both use tiny pits in a reflective medium to represent digital data, but the newer DVD technology packs much more data on the disc. You can think of both as sim-ple storage devices that store any type of data without bias.

The bigger issue is what type of data a given disc holds and how that data is structured. DVD-Video, for example, is simply a DVD disc with MPEG-2 video, audio and a file structure that makes sense to a DVD player. A Video CD's medium is just like that of an audio CD, but the video and audio files are saved in the specific format a Video CD player expects.

Keep in mind that CD and DVD can store any type of information, not just the latest DVD Video movie or Microsoft Office 2004. This means you can use a CD or DVD to hold digital video and audio that's *not* formatted for a specific hardware device (such as a DVD player). Since this is sort of like a cross between the strictly data and strictly video applications, you'd use a computer to read and play back these files. It's just good to remember that DVD Video, for example, represents just one way to store digital video and audio on a DVD.

If you're reading between the lines, you've probably already figured out the good news—computers that have a CD-R drive are physically capable of writing a Video CD, and those with a DVD-R drive can write a DVD Video disc. When it comes to burning 1s and 0s into that shiny silver disc, you're already equipped.

But as we mentioned above, the physical format of the disc is only half of the equation. The other half is getting your video and audio files in the correct format—and in the right place—for playback in a stand-alone player. This is where specific software comes into play to encode and author.

Blend, Pour, Bake

Whether you're making just one copy for yourself or creating a master to send off for duplication, the DVD and CD-ROM creation process is essentially the same: digitize, encode, author and burn. (See Figure 72.1.)

The encoding step converts digital video and audio files from one format to another, usually reducing their size dramatically along the way. Encoding for a DVD Video, for example, involves compressing video files with the MPEG-2 standard. The software then encodes audio files into any of several formats (surround, 5.1 surround, stereo, etc.) recognized by DVD players. The encoding process is similar for a Video CD, but software uses lower-quality MPEG-1 compression for the video and audio.

At the encoding stage, DVD makers have numerous parameters at their disposal for controlling image and sound quality, as well as the amount of video that will fit on the disc. Good DVD encoding fits the required amount of video on the disc at the highest-possible quality, with no wasted space. For a major motion picture, this might equate to roughly two hours of

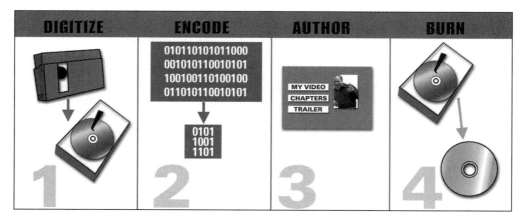

Figure 72.1 *1) Transfer your video from tape to hard drive. 2) Apply the appropriate compression/decompression (codec) scheme to your video. 3) Design the operating interface for your video. 4) Copy your finished video to a disc.*

video. Drop the quality down to the VHS level, and you could fit 10 or more hours of video on the smallest-capacity DVD. Be forewarned: depending on quality settings, the software you use and the speed of your computer, encoding MPEG-2 can be a lengthy process.

Authoring software then takes the encoded video and audio files and formats them according to their intended purpose. For DVD, the encoding software records various special codes required for correct playback, as well as such optional goodies as chapter points, navigational aids, menus and overlayed graphics. Because capabilities of the Video CD aren't as advanced, Video CD authoring software is simpler and less costly than DVD authoring software. Some software packages combine encoding and authoring into one step.

The final step is to actually burn the audio, video and other special files to a blank DVD-R or CD-R disc (about $30 and $1 respectively). Everything is just a series of numbers at this point, and the recorder will lay these bits onto the disc as fast as the burner hardware (or the operator) will allow. Since DVD and CD-R burners range in speed from 2x to 12x and beyond (CD-R), the process doesn't happen in real time. If your hardware is very fast, for example, you may be able to burn a full 74-minute Video CD in about 5 minutes.

Burning For You

Is everything rosy in the world of home-cooked DVDs? Not entirely. DVD-R drives record permanently on a disc, offer the best compatibility with home DVD players, but still cost several thousands of dollars. Most professional DVD authors use DVD-R drives.

Rewritable DVD drives have dipped below the $1,000 mark, and may be available for less than $500 by the time you read this. Unfortunately, the rewriteable DVD market is in the middle of a bitter format war. Three competing standards (DVD-RW,

DVD+RW and DVD-RAM) are available and each has its advantages and disadvantages. Compatibility with existing home DVD Video drives and computer DVD-ROM drives is one of the hottest topics, so be sure to check for late-breaking news before you purchase a drive.

Folks wanting to burn their own Video CDs have it easy. They may already have everything they need, provided their CD-R bundle included the correct software.

ABCs of Acronyms

One of the first obstacles to get over when moving from a video cassette to a silver disc is the mountain of acronyms that seems to pile up with every new technology. Here are some of the key acronyms and terms that you need to know:

CD (Compact Disc): a digital "bit bucket" that can store any type of data, be it audio, video or computer software. One CD holds roughly 650 megabytes (MB) of data.

- CD-R (CD Recordable): a CD you can record your own data on. You can't erase or re-record a CD-R.

- CD-ROM (CD Read Only Memory): a CD pre-recorded with computer data that can't be changed or erased.

- CD-RW (CD Rewritable): a CD you can write and re-write to thousands of times.

DVD (Digital Versatile Disc): like a CD, holds digital data of any kind. Today's DVDs hold roughly 5, 9 or 13 gigabytes (GB) of data on one, two or three data layers. A 13 GB DVD holds the equivalent to about 20 normal CDs.

- DVD-R (DVD Recordable): a DVD that you can record your own data onto only one time. DVD-ROM (DVD Read Only Memory): a DVD pre-recorded with computer data that can't be changed or erased.

- DVD-RW, DVD-RAM, DVD +RW: competing rewriteable DVD standards embroiled in a heated format scuffle.

- DVD-Video: a DVD disc that holds MPEG-2 video and any of several different types of audio. When you rent a DVD, this is what you get.

MPEG-1 (Motion Picture Experts Group, first standard): a highly efficient way of compressing digital video for lower resolutions (i.e. 320 horizontal lines).

- MPEG-2 (MPEG, second standard): offers better quality and higher resolution than MPEG-1. DVD players use MPEG-2 with a horizontal resolution of 720 lines.

- VCD (Video CD): just like a regular CD, but holds MPEG-1 video and audio for playback in reasonably fast CD-ROM and DVD-ROM drives and current-generation DVD video players; as well as Video CD players not readily available in the U.S.

For a look at the physical differences between a rewritable CD and at recordable CD, take a look at Figure 72.2.

Keeping up with digital video is all about learning new technology and new techniques and the latest trend away from tape and toward DVD is no exception. Someday soon, a silver disc may be the final destination for all your video projects.

When that day comes, you'll be ready to burn.

Web Links

The Internet is one of the best places to stay abreast of rapid-fire changes in the DVD and CD-ROM markets. Visit these informative Web sites for the latest news and product information.

General Info
DVD FAQ (Frequently Asked Questions)
www.videodiscovery.com/vdyweb/dvd/dvdfaq.html

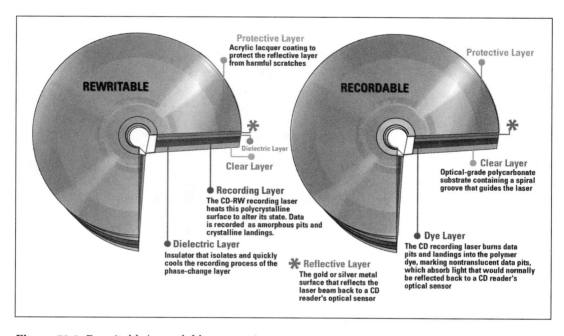

Figure 72.2 *Rewritable/recordable comparison.*

DVD for Not-so-Dummies
www.nimbuscd.com/dvd.html

MPEG Home Page
www.cselt.stet.it/mpeg

MPEG Pointers and Resources
www.mpeg.org

Canopus
www.canopuscorp.com

Creative Labs
www.soundblaster.com

Digigami
www.digigami.com

Fast Multimedia
www.fastmultimedia.com

Vitec Multimedia
www.vitecmm.com

73

DVD Authoring Software:
Special Buyer's Guide

D. Eric Franks

A year ago, we were excited, but conservatively optimistic about home DVD authoring. High prices and compatibility loomed large in our thinking. With second and third-generation recorders dropping below $300 and blank media dipping well under $1 a disc, price is no longer prohibitive. Software is also entering a new generation, with fewer bugs and greater stability. Fierce competition has also meant better quality, more features and lower prices. This is good news for the would-be home DVD maker, as it means that you can concentrate on the art of making DVDs, and not the technology.

Easier than Editing

DVD authoring software typically performs three functions: encoding video, menu authoring and burning the disc. Perhaps surprisingly, almost all basic applications support all three functions, but some of the more advanced, professional and specialized authoring applications only author and do not encode or burn.

• *Encoding.* Most people do not want to deal with the complexities of encoding, so you'll want to make sure that your authoring app has an encoder (which is in most products from Main Concept). For those of you who are interested in the art of the compressionist, there are advanced applications such as Canopus ProCoder or Discreet Cleaner, as well as MPEG specialists like the Tsunami encoder (TMPGenc).

• *Burning.* Burning is even less interesting than encoding and should probably not be any more complex than clicking the Burn button. You should make sure your authoring application can burn if you need it, however. Most do have burning capabilities.

• *Menu authoring.* DVD authoring applications are primarily about creating attractive and functional menus. A typical menu will have a background image, a title and smaller thumbnail images that represent the various chapters or movies on the disc. The focus of authoring is layout and design, which is really pretty fun. For those of us who do not have degrees in layout, many programs offer professionally designed templates. Not only are attractive templates a boon to the artistically challenged, but they can also be huge timesavers. The only *potential* downside to templates is that they might limit your freedom. For DVD novices, we really like applications like Apple iDVD and Sonic MyDVD that start you out with templates, but also give you the freedom to change anything you want later. Another approach we like, used in applications like Dazzle DVD Complete, is a software Wizard which can walk you through the DVD menu creation process step-by-step.

Bells and Whistles

We're not going to tell you how to create your DVD (in this article), but we will suggest that once you have a single attractive menu with thumbnails to navigate to the various chapters, that is probably all you need. When you design your disc, always keep your view in mind, especially when you consider the extra bells and whistles offered by some programs, such as Ulead DVD Workshop or Sonic DVDit!

- *Submenus.* Complex DVDs might need submenus, but you should always count the number of clicks it takes users before they can actually play the movie. Also consider that your viewer isn't you and a complex disc structure might result in people getting lost or confused when all they really want to do is watch your video.

- *Animations.* Many authoring applications allow you to animate the background and the individual menu thumbnails (referred to as motion menus and backgrounds). These features typically add rendering time to the disc creation process and often add nothing to the actual information, content or ease of navigation of

the disc. But we must admit that it sure is cool and it is an optional feature we like.

- *Background music.* Background music can also be annoying, but not if it is done well. It can be tricky to get the music to loop properly (making the end transition seamlessly back to the start of the music), but most Hollywood DVDs have a music bed.

- *Start up splashes.* When you first pop that disc in the player, wouldn't it be neat to have a logo swoosh in? This is called a "first play" movie and, again, is completely optional. You should make sure that you don't have a horrible intro before or between every menu. You may personally think it is cool, but trust us: like Web sites with annoying Flash Intros ("Skip Intro"), your viewers will be vexed if they repeatedly have to see your extreme cleverness. Seeing it once as a "first play" is enough.

Advanced Features

We consider the previously mentioned Bells and Whistles to be fun but optional extras (unless your client or boss demands them). The following list highlights a number of important advanced features that that might not be a part of more basic authoring applications. Some reasonably priced applications that support some or all of these more advanced features are Apple DVD Studio Pro, Pinnacle Impression and Sonic Reel DVD.

- *Subtitles.* If you need subtitles (and widely distributed productions should have them to accommodate the broadest audience), make sure your chosen authoring application allows you to insert them. Subtitling is an extremely labor-intensive task, so you should carefully consider your subtitling needs beyond simply finding an application that supports this feature.

- *Audio compression.* DVD audio compression is more complex than it should be. Uncompressed PCM audio is officially a part of the DVD specification and is widely supported, but this type of audio takes up inordinate amounts of precious disc space. A more efficient solution is MPEG-1 Layer 3 audio and you should look for this feature if you decide you want it. Although it is not officially in the DVD specification, it is widely supported in Asia, which is where almost all DVD players are manufactured, which means that most DVD players here in the US also support this type of audio. But it isn't universal.

• *Dolby surround.* Many applications support AC-3 Dolby audio, but (as of this writing) only a few actually encode Dolby. Even stereo Dolby encoding is rare and still slightly expensive, but this is changing very quickly (see sidebar). 5.1 Dolby surround encoding is even more rare and also needs an application that can mix six channels (5 + 1) to take advantage of this very cool DVD feature. Dolby AC-3 is a very important technology, since basic AC-3 stereo audio takes up much less room on your disc than uncompressed PCM audio and is more widely (and officially) supported than MPEG-1 layer 3 audio.

• *Alternate video tracks.* Part of the original hype of DVD was that you could include multiple video streams in a single track, which would allow the viewer to press the Angle button on the remote to see the same scene from a different angle. While this is only rarely used in Hollywood DVDs, it is an advanced feature you might be interested in for multi-camera shoots at concerts, weddings or plays.

• *Multiple languages.* Like multiple video streams, you can also place multiple audio streams on your DVD. This is most often used for multiple languages, but is also frequently utilized for director's comments.

• *DLT output.* If you need to mass-produce your DVD, duplication houses often require you to submit your project on digital linear tape (DLT). This may change as time goes on, but the reason for this is at least partially pragmatic: home-burned DVDs are limited to 4.7 GB while dual-layer professionally stamped DVDs can hold 9 GB.

Almost Perfect

Home DVD authoring is here and now. From a small handful of first generation products a year ago, DVD authoring applications are now maturing and diversifying. Independent professionals may be disappointed to learn that while we have seen almost every sub-$1,000 application available, we haven't found one that does everything described in this article. Novices and home hobbyists will be pleased to hear that there are many excellent programs for putting your video on disc to share with your family, friends or small organization (see the figures below). Our recommendation: get the hardware, try out the included software and troll the Web for free trial versions before you decide. Perhaps the best news about home DVD for jaded video veterans: DVD authoring is (relative to shooting and editing) fun and easy. Nothing since the invention of the Star Wipe has generated so many "wow, cool" responses from our viewers.

Figure 73.1 *Ahead Software: Nero 5, $69.*

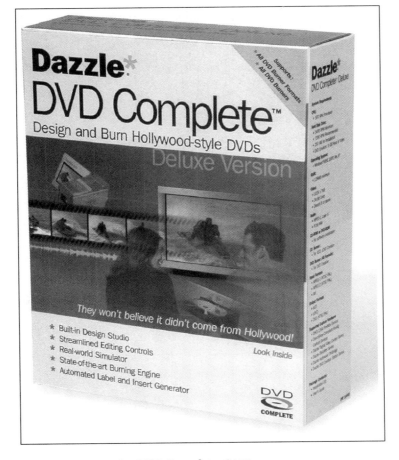

Figure 73.2 *Dazzle: DVD Complete, $100.*

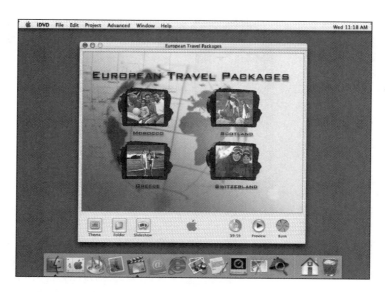

Figure 73.3 *Apple: iDVD 2.1, $20.*

Figure 73.4 *Mediostream: neoDVD plus, $50.*

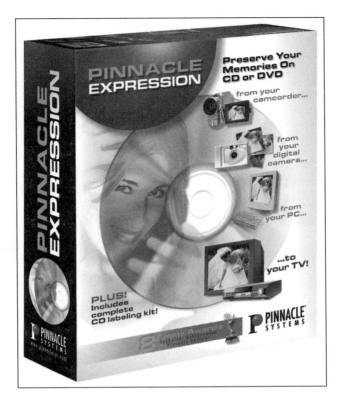

Figure 73.5 *Pinnacle: Expression, $50.*

Figure 73.6 *Sonic: ReelDVD, $999.*

Sidebar 1

Compatibility

During the past year, we've learned that compatibility, while important for authors, is largely out of their control. Some DVD players play home-burned DVDs and some don't, and there is very little you can do to change this. In our tests, we've found that the particular piece of software used to create the disc is mostly irrelevant to the final compatibility of the disc.

Sidebar 2

DVD-R vs. DVD + R

The short answer for the relationship of authoring software and the DVD format war is that it is irrelevant. Most authoring software just doesn't care what kind of media you are using. Just make sure your burning software supports the particular drive you want to use (e.g. Pioneer DVR-A05) and you are good to go.

Sidebar 3

Dolby Encoding

Until recently, Dolby Laboratories was charging premium fees for encoding licenses. By "premium" we mean that you could not find end-user Dolby 5.1 surround encoding software for much under $1,000 and even simple stereo encoding was at least $100. Fortunately, that appears to be changing, with Dolby charging roughly $50 per unit to the software manufacturer (this is still a huge licensing fee per box). As of this writing, proper surround mixing starts at around $350 for Sonic Foundry ACID, plus another $200–300 for the Sonic Foundry 5.1 encoding plug-in.

74

Burner Basics: An Introduction to DVD Burners

Charles Fulton

When the first CD burners hit the market, the equipment was very expensive, but prices fell rapidly and, today, most entry-level computers come with a CD burner. One could safely expect that this will soon be the situation with DVD burners.

Times were simpler back when the first CD burners came out, though. There was really only one standard with two types of discs: the write once discs (CD-R) and the rewritable discs (CD-RW). DVD is a little more complex. The first recordable DVD formats developed by the DVD Forum were DVD-R, DVD-RW and DVD-RAM. The DVD+RW Alliance, led by Philips and Sony, created a different format: DVD+RW and DVD+R. Both the DVD Forum (-R) and DVD+RW Alliance (+R) claim better compatibility. For the consumer, this can seem confusing. Rest assured, this format war shouldn't cause the end user to lose too much sleep.

Will It Play in Peoria?

Naturally, both the proponents of the DVD+R/+RW and those of the DVD-R/-RW formats claim that *their* discs are the most compatible with the installed base of living room DVD players. Who's right?

Many factors contribute to whether a given disc will play in a given player. For the home DVD author, the hardware burner, the authoring software and type of blank media are all part of the equation. In the end, however, we've found that the bulk of compatibility problems are with the player. In our tests, living room DVD players that play DVD-R discs also tend to play DVD+R discs, and vice versa. This is a broad generalization and is not 100% true across the board.

That said, it is our responsibility as content creators to do everything we can to make the most compatible discs possible and the material on the disc itself is sometimes the problem. Many complex projects must be tweaked and re-built before the project can be widely distributed. We've experienced this firsthand when building our own *Basics of Videography* DVD. It can take a lot of patience (as well as a tall rack of DVD players and an intern to do some quality assurance tests) to find all of the problems that might crop up in a disc.

Who Makes 'Em?

The big players to watch are the manufacturers of the drive mechanisms, primarily Pioneer for DVD-R/RW mechanisms and Ricoh for DVD+R/RW mechanisms (and Panasonic for DVD-RAM mechanisms). There are a wide cross-section of computer peripheral manufacturers that are offering branded-DVD burners, including Verbatim, TDK, Memorex, Pioneer, Panasonic, Toshiba, HP, Sony and LG. (See the *DVD Burner Manufacturer Listing* sidebar for the entire gamut.) There are also companies who repackage drives in their own enclosures, and bundle them with software and cables to create a convenient and consumer-friendly single-box DVD authoring solution (such as Pacific Digital, QPS, EZQuest, Fantom Drives and LaCie). Shop around and you're sure to find something that meets all of your needs, whether it's a complete kit or a bare drive.

Speed Demons

Need that disc yesterday? Drives get faster every day, with the fastest Pioneer drive currently burning at 4x. (This drive initially had a firmware problem that has since been corrected. If you have an older drive with a Pioneer mechanism, be sure to visit Pioneer's Web site at www.pioneerelectronics.com/hs/.) Confusingly, 1x for DVD (1,321 KB/s) is not the same as 1x for CD (150 KB/s). In other words, 1x DVD = 9x CD. DVD burners, whether +R/RW or -R/RW will burn CDs also, although they can't burn CDs

as fast as some of the newer CD burners on the market.

A Bigger Buffer is Better

A feature to watch for when buying a DVD burner is the size of the internal buffer. The buffer is a bit of RAM on the drive that temporarily stores data before it is burned onto the disc. The disc-mastering program that you use will try to keep the buffer as full as possible. There is an important reason for this: DVD burners (and CD burners, for that matter) need a steady flow of data. The buffer on the burner compensates for a certain amount of variability in the data stream, with larger buffers able to handle more difficulties. Most DVD+R/RW drives have a 2 MB buffer, while newer DVD-R/RW drives generally have a more generous 8 MB buffer (we'd expect this to change very rapidly). Buffer underruns were a common cause of CD-coasters a few short years ago, but modern technologies can easily deal with interruptions in the data flow, using such tactics as throttling down the drive to a lower speed when the buffer level falls below a specific point.

Interfaces

Among internally mounted drives, IDE (ATAPI) drives are by far the most common. Only a handful of SCSI drives exist anymore, although they once were common. Externally, FireWire is the interface of choice, but a number of drives using the fast USB 2.0 standard also look very promising. Several companies that market off-the-shelf drives in custom enclosures offer external drives with both FireWire and USB 2.0 connections.

Laptop DVD burners are not common at this point. If the trailblazing CD-R drives have taught us anything, it's that DVD drives will become faster, smaller, less expensive and more available. Currently,

Toshiba and Apple offer recordable DVD drives on laptops, but we fully expect that other manufacturers will have this feature in the near future.

The War is Over

At the beginning of this article, we told you not to worry about the DVD Forum vs. DVD+RW Alliance format war too much. In a very real sense, the war is over for consumers, although a winner has not been declared. TDK and Sony now offer writers that burn both DVD-R/RW and DVD+R/RW discs. We'd expect more manufacturers to offer more format agnostic burners over the coming year. These drives are a little more expensive, but if you are concerned about compatibility, this is the way to go. You'll still have to decide on the media you use, but at a dollar or so a disc, the cost of burning incompatible discs is not high.

The Future

Recordable DVD is still a young technology, although second and third generation devices are making it to market as we write. We expect the combination of future drives and future software to yield discs that are even more compatible than discs authored with today's drives and software. Prices will also continuing to fall somewhat, although not as rapidly as they did over the last year. Of course, better living room players are also coming out, and that should help home authors as well.

Witnessing the rapid rollout (and rapid price drop) of recordable DVD technology makes us wonder what will happen when the recordable version of the next high-capacity optical format comes around. We're brimming with excitement to see what the future will bring, but we are also very happy with the state of today's technology (see the figures below).

Figure 74.1 *Memorex: DVD+RW/+R Internal Rewritable Drive, $380.*

Figure 74.2 *Sony: DRU-500A, $349.*

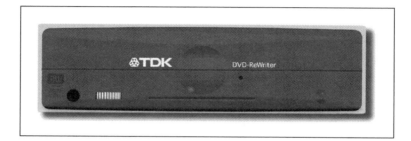

Figure 74.3 *TDK: Indi DVD AID+420N, $349.*

Figure 74.4 *Pioneer DVR-A05, $299.*

Sidebar 1

No Computer? No Problem!

One of the latest consumer electronic products to hit the shelves is the standalone living room DVD burner. Externally, these devices look exactly like the DVD player already connected to your TV. Functionally, they work more like your VCR: just press Record. All have inputs for analog video, but we are especially excited about the recorders that have FireWire input. While prices may be a bit high this year, with so many products from so many manufacturers, we expect standalone DVD recorders to be the next must-have product for the living room, and a neat extra for videographers who want simple DVD-recording functionality. Would-be DVD authors should note that while these standalones will record video to disc, they do not offer a means of creating custom menus or fancy navigational structures.

Sidebar 2

General vs. Authoring Media

If you've ever shopped for blank DVD-R discs, you've undoubtedly seen references to authoring discs (as opposed to general purpose discs). These discs are written with a different laser wavelength (635 nm, as compared to 650 nm for general discs). Authoring discs can't be burned in drives meant for general media, and vice versa.

So why in the world are there authoring DVDs, anyway? Authoring DVDs were originally designed for professional use, and can hold information that general discs can't. For example, an authoring DVD with standardized Cutting Master Format (CMF) data can be submitted to a duplication house instead of a DLT (digital linear tape). Authoring burners are, of course, significantly more expensive than the general burners discussed in this article.

Sidebar 3

Don't Call it "Minus!"

When the burnable DVD world consisted solely of DVD-R drives, everyone just called them "Dee Vee Dee Arr." When the first DVD+RW drives came out, a distinction had to be made. Many people instinctively said "Dee Vee Dee Plus Arr Double-You." And, logically, the opposite of "plus" is "minus" and many people began talking about DVD-R as "Dee Vee Dee Minus Arr." The DVD Forum folks in charge of marketing DVD-R are not terribly fond of the negative connotation of "minus" and would respectfully request that you call it "Dee Vee Dee Dash Arr" instead. We suppose you could refer to it as "Dee Vee Dee Hyphen Arr," but, officially, it's a dash.

75

DVD Flavors:
What's the Deal with
DVD Compatibility?

Roger B. Wyatt

Good-bye, stretched tapes and dropouts—hello, pristine digital images, generation after generation. With the right hardware and software you can simply burn an edited project to DVD with the click of a mouse. Sound like a dream? It's not. The first affordable DVD recording devices are already in stores, in mail-order catalogs and on the Net. While first generation units were in the $5,000 range, today's recorders list for under $1,000, with street prices below $800.

Unfortunately, there is more to DVD than meets the eye. When DVD manufacturers told us that the initials "DVD" stood for "digital versatile disc," they weren't kidding. The recordable standards vying for your dollars are DVD-RAM, DVD-R, DVD-RW, DVD+R and DVD+RW. The good news is these are all very exciting technologies, some excelling at high capacity data storage and some offering convenient distribution. The bad news is they aren't all compatible with each other, and most won't play in the DVD player you have in your living room. Before you commit to a DVD format, you'd better know the difference. To help you understand these emerging formats, we've developed this handy guide to bring you up to speed on all of the issues.

DVD-Video

The standard that started it all was DVD-Video (and DVD-Audio, too), those discs you pop in your DVD Player to watch feature films and interactive productions. The standard supports a capacity extension up to 8.5 GB per side, but this is not available at this time. DVD-Video is a playback-only format.

DVD standards (including DVD-Video) have been developed over the years by the DVD Forum (dvdforum.org), which is composed of over 220 companies including Hitachi, JVC, Matsushita, Mitsubishi, Philips, Pioneer, Sony, Thomson, Time Warner, IBM, Intel, NEC, Samsung, Sharp and Toshiba, among others. It's a veritable who's who of consumer electronics. When it came to DVD-Video, this broad consortium spoke with one voice, and an industry standard was born.

Somehow, that group unity on the playback-only standard fractured when recordable DVD standards were developed.

DVD-RAM

DVD-RAM is a recordable and rewritable standard that the DVD Forum supports (see Figure 75.1). The current second-generation discs store 4.7 GB per side (for a total of 9.4 GB), and cost as low as $20, although other sizes and capacities are available. DVD-RAM discs come in a plastic cartridge or housing that makes them physically incompatible with non-DVD-RAM drives and therefore can only be played back in DVD-RAM drives.

An interesting variation on DVD-RAM is the small 80 mm (8-centimeter) disc. Those little discs hold 1.46 GB per side and are used in the new MPEG-2 digital camcorders, such as the ones from Hitachi, and in some digital still cameras from Sony.

With this feature, you can shoot and edit without the tedious step of capturing; assuming you had a DVD-RAM drive or hybrid DVD drive on your computer. (However, see the *MPEG-2 Cams—Not the Ultimate* Sidebar for an important caveat.)

DVD-R and DVD-RW

DVD-R is a write-once format, fully supported by the DVD Forum (see Figure 75.2). It is single-sided, has a top capacity of 4.7 GB and is rapidly extending into the emerging DVD-RW format. Like DVD-R, DVD-RW (the format formerly known as DVD-R/W) is optimized for video, but can be written to numerous times. Clearly, this format is very significant to videographers. These formats strive to be analogous to the now standard CD-R and CD-RW formats. DVD-R discs are rapidly falling in price, approaching the $6 per disc range, while DVD-RW disc prices are also falling, but remain more expensive at about $16 per disc. The first DVD-R/ DVD-RW drive,

Figure 75.1 DVD-RAM; (a) best for multiple rewrites, (b) good for data and files, (c) often needs a cartridge, (d) DVD-RAM: $12. DVD-RAM discs act similar to a hard disk, allowing you to write and rewrite with random access.

Figure 75.2 DVD-R and DVD-RW; (a) best for sequential writes, (b) good for large files, such as movies, (c) claimed compatible with DVD video players, (d) DVD-R: $4, (e) DVD-RW: $13. The DVD-R/RW format is touted as the logical extension of CD-R/RW technology we are all used to.

the Pioneer DVR-A03, is very reasonably priced. Expect to see a number of competitors and a corresponding drop in price soon. DVD-R and DVD-RW discs are designed to work with DVD-ROM drives as well as standalone DVD players, provided the disc is correctly formatted. There are, however, occasional compatibility problems mostly associated with older devices. These issues will disappear as the format matures. The DVD-R and DVD-RW format is good for creating standard DVD-Video formatted discs as well as long format data such as video files.

DVD+RW and DVD+R

DVD+RW is the rewritable standard that Sony, Philips and Hewlett-Packard originally developed to compete with DVD-RAM (confusingly, not with DVD-RW, although it is now a competitor of that format as well) (see Figure 75.3). Note the use of the plus sign (+) instead of the

hyphen (-). Philips and Sony (both members of the DVD Forum) argue that their non-DVD Forum-sanctioned DVD+RW format is more compatible than DVD-RAM, largely because DVD+RW discs do not use a physically incompatible cartridge. They are right, but the compatibility argument was largely rendered mute by the DVD-RW format, which also use no cartridge. At press time, we couldn't find any DVD+RW discs for sale, but we expect the price to be competitive with DVD-RW. DVD+RW is designed for greater compatibility with existing standalone DVD-Video players, but this claim is impossible to test at this time.

The DVD+RW camp has also announced, a bit backwards chronologically perhaps, that it will support a DVD+R format that will allow write-once capabilities. The DVD+R and DVD+RW formats are theoretically good for creating standard DVD-Video formatted discs (although, at press time, there were no DVD+RW units on the market to be tested) as well as long format data such as video files.

Figure 75.3 *DVD+RW and DVD+R. (a) best for sequential writes, (b) good for large files, such as movies, (c) claimed compatible with DVD video players, (d) DVD+RW: $14, (e) DVD+R: unavailable, The DVD+RW format is the newest format and claims to be more compatible than others. DVD+R has not yet been rolled out.*

RAM vs. RW

The RAM in DVD-RAM stands for random access memory. DVD-RAM discs read and write much the same way as your hard disks. This is an important aspect of this format and differs from the other read/write DVD formats (-RW and +RW), which are optimized for sequential recording. In other words, DVD-RAM is a data storage format that is perfectly happy scattering thousands of tiny files (and parts of files) here and there across the entire disc. This allows for faster access times and yields a more robust rewriting and erasing format. DVD-RW and DVD+RW, in contrast, do not offer random access in the same way, are not as robust as rewriters and are not designed to act like a hard disk. They are, however, optimized for long, sequential reads/writes and occasional rewrites of large chunks of data, which is exactly what videographers need.

Standards Shmandards

Do multiple standards guarantee trouble? Not really. The DVD Forum came up with a plan to prevent conflicts among DVD formats and assure compatibility between DVD products. They call it DVD Multi, a set of hardware specifications that enables disc and manufacturer compatibility for virtually all DVD Forum consumer electronics and personal computers formats. Look for a logo identifying DVD Multi products. The specification covers many formats including DVD-Video, DVD-ROM, DVD-Audio, DVD-RAM, DVD-R and DVD-RW.

You can measure these discs' capacities in two ways. First, for finished productions, MPEG-2 DVD-Video can have a duration as long as two hours. MPEG-2 video is compressed, often resulting in compression artifacts, which can range from unnoticeable to debilitating, depending on the quality of the encoding. Compressed video is not suitable for editing, mastering or storage purposes. Second, capacity can be measured in terms of data storage and expressed in gigabytes. At S-VHS quality, each minute of video data might occupy 120 MB of storage (although it could be much more). So, 4.7 GB works out to almost 40 minutes of recording capacity, per side. DV data occupies roughly 216 MB of space for a minute of video, or approximately 22 minutes per side, per DVD disc.

New hardware devices are hitting the market almost every day. The first DVD-R, DVD-RW drives, such as the Pioneer DVR-A03 or the Panasonic LF-D311, are widely available at less than $500. Also, watch for hybrid DVD-R, DVD-RW, DVD-RAM combo drives (called DVD Multi) that can read and write the three DVD Forum formats. One model from Panasonic (LF-D311) sells for just under $500. This drive allows you to avoid much of the format war controversy, writing and rewriting to DVD-RAM for your personal use and writing DVD-R discs to play on your television. We are extremely excited about this technology and hope that is does not suffer from the compatibility problems that plagued the first CD-R drives.

The DVD+RW camp, on the other hand, is aggressively marketing recordable and rewritable DVD+RW drives. Other computer manufacturers, like Apple and Compaq, are shipping boxes with DVD-R drives built-in.

Early Adopters Only?

Is it time to move to DVD optical recording? For data purposes, permanently saving your video projects, media and all, has become a distinct possibility for the first time. And burning your productions to DVD for playback on standalone DVD players gives you a very high quality way to conveniently distribute your work. At $500 for a recorder and $6 per disc, DVD recording is at a very tempting price point for the home video enthusiast, although we certainly expect prices to fall over the next year. With the right purchase, you can enjoy recordable DVD products that will play on all your gear.

Sidebar 1

MPEG-2 Cams—Not the Ultimate

Are they the best things since sliced bread? Probably not. While the quality of DVD-Video is very high, it is nonetheless MPEG-2 compressed video. As such, it is very problematic to edit and you should not consider it for mastering, archiving or editing purposes. A good digital strategy is to shoot and capture at the highest quality (e.g. DV or MJPEG), edit at highest quality, master at highest quality and finally, distribute MPEG-2 on DVD.

Sidebar 2

Yes, Master

One undeniably exciting aspect of the latest multi-format hybrid DVD recorders is the possibility of burning DVD-Video discs to send high-quality versions of your movies to your friends and then burning a DVD-RAM disc (two-sided 9.4 GB) of the project as a master. How many times have you watched a movie you created two years ago and cringed, wishing you could fix it up? Although burn speeds and transfer rates mean taking some time to backup and restore a project, it is undoubtedly faster than recapturing and recreating a project from scratch.

Sidebar 3

The Media

Format:	DV	DVD	VCD	SVCD	MiniDVD
Resolution	720 × 480	720 × 480	352 × 240	480 × 480	720 × 480
Recording Time	60 mins tape	2 hrs	74 mins	35 mins	15 mins
Video Compression	DV	MPEG2	MPEG1	MPEG2	MPEG2
Audio Compression	PCM	MPEG2, AC3	MPEG1	MPEG1	MPEG2, AC3
Size/min	216 MB/min	30–70 MB/min	10 MB/min	10–20 MB/min	30–70 MB/min
DVD Player Compatibility	None	Excellent	Great (2/3)	Good (1/3)	Poor
Quality	Excellent	Great	Fair	Good	Great

Table by Scott Anderson.

76

Step by Step Guide to Making DVDs

D. Eric Franks

More and more of this magazine is being devoted to DVD each month. DVD gear, DVD media, DVD software, but we're afraid we are missing the forest for the trees. If you've been reading the magazine and have a good grip on what you need, here is a path through the trees: our Step by Step Guide to Making DVDs.

Overview

First, a little encouragement: DVD creation on a computer is considerably easier than editing video. The entire process can be summed up in four steps (but see the sidebar for a One-Step Solution).

XX Capture. You need to get video onto your computer. How you edit it is entire up to you and is not what this article is about, so we are going to assume that you have a tape with video on it that you want on DVD.

XX Encode. Once your video is on your computer, it needs to be transformed and encoded into DVD-friendly MPEG-2

video. This process can be one-click easy or hardcore technical and tedious.

XX Author. Authoring is what we call the process of actually designing and creating the DVD menus. This is the fun part.

XX Burn. Yawn. This process should definitely be one-click easy.

Capture

So you have a video tape that you'd love to distribute on DVD. What is the easiest way? We have two answers for you, one for digital video and one for analog tapes.

First, for those of you with digital video (DV) source material, you should use your FireWire port on your computer to dump your digital data to your computer. You don't need a fancy computer or expensive editing software, but you will need a ton of hard disk space, about 20 GB for an hour of video for a complete DVD project. On a Windows XP or Mac, the capture tools you need are included with your computer.

DV is so easy because the video is already in a format your computer can handle. If you have analog video tapes (such as VHS), you need to convert that video into digital data for your computer. To do this, you'll need some kind of capture card, otherwise known as a digitizer. Some computers come with analog capture cards (e.g. an Ati All-In-Wonder card), but most do not. If you are not interested in hacking about inside of your computer to install a new card (and who is), there are a few devices that digitize your video and then send the data to your Windows computer via a USB 2.0 connection. ADS Tech's Instant DVD 2.0, Adaptec's VideOh! DVD and Pinnacle's Dazzle Digital Video Creator 150 are three competitive products (all less than $200) worth researching. The most convenient aspect of these boxes is that they digitize straight to MPEG-2 video.

Encode

If the video on your computer is not DVD ready, you will need to encode it to the MPEG-2 format. This is what you will need to do with FireWire-transferred DV video and DV video projects from your editing software. The encoding process (also called compression or transcoding) can happen immediately when you finish editing, although most DVD authoring programs now automatically encode any video of any format that you use on your DVD. In your editing software, you'll usually be able to find an Export or Render As option that will open an encoding dialog. In this dialog, select a DVD MPEG-2 encoding template and render away. Encoding is very computationally intensive, so get ready to wait a long time for the process to finish, typically twice as long as your video's duration. We usually start encoding before we go to bed at night.

Of course encoding can be much more complicated. There are entire applications dedicated to the task (e.g. cleaner, ProCoder, Squeeze), books explaining the

technology (like the ones from Ben Waggoner) and experts in Hollywood who are Career Compressionists. For this article, it is only important that you know that all of your media (video, audio and stills) needs to be in DVD-compatible MPEG-2 format before it can be put on a disc. Hopefully, your authoring software will take care of it for you.

Author

Authoring is the fun part of creating a DVD. The process requires some organizational skills, a little design talent and a dollop of artistry, but you can usually get by even if you aren't particularly gifted in these areas.

The first step is to start a new project and collect your media together. This will of course include your video, but also might involve stills for a slide show and music for menu backgrounds. Again, everything, even stills and audio, will end up in a DVD-compatible format, but for now you only have to organize the pieces and parts.

The next step involves designing the navigation of your disc. Like the Web, DVD discs have buttons that you can highlight and click, although you use your DVD player's remote control to make the click. DVDs are much simpler than Web pages, however, and you basically need only a Play button to allow folks to watch your movie and maybe a Scenes button to allow them to jump to the various parts of your movie that they want to skip to. You can have more complex navigation schemes and special features, but work conservatively and cautiously so that you don't overwhelm and confuse your viewers. The dozens of Hollywood discs you've rented can serve as examples, both good and bad, for you to emulate or at least learn from.

The final part of authoring is the best part: designing attractive menus. From backgrounds to buttons, the DVD menu is going to be the first impression your viewers will get of your project. Most DVD authoring programs come with a bunch of templates that can be used as-is or that can be used as jumping off points for your own unique discs. In our reviews of DVD authoring programs, pay careful attention to what the writer says about the templates and how much they can be customized. If you only need a quick disc and aren't very interested in authoring, templates may be all you need. If you are a production house with a talented design professional onboard, make sure your software lets her do her thing.

Burn

We call the actual process of writing a DVD "burning" and it is just about as boring as can be. Usually, it involves inserting a blank disc into your DVD drive and clicking a button or, at most, selecting a menu item. It either works or it is broken. Fortunately, it almost always works nowadays.

Compatibility with stand alone, living room DVD players is a serious issue. In almost every case, compatibility problems are not caused by the burning process. In fact, almost all compatibility problems are caused by the DVD player and not by the DVD authoring process outlined here. It doesn't much matter whether you are using an HP 300i or a Pioneer DVR-105, or whether you are using DVD-R or DVD+R (don't use rewritable discs for distribution). The discs are designed to play back in the same players. Once you find a DVD player that plays one kind of disc, you'll find that it plays back most kinds. Of course we are skimming over many issues

here that are covered in much more depth in other articles in this magazine (such as the Winter 2003 issue).

As far as media goes, there are two approaches. You can play it safe and go with a branded media, like Verbatim or TDK (or even Ritek) or you can get a spindle of generic discs. The advantage of going with a branded disc is that you get a guarantee from the company and can be assured that there was some quality control during the manufacturing process. Generic discs are cheaper, of course, and can be of very high quality, but the problem is that you just don't know until you have some experience. Some blank media companies offer sampler packs of various kinds that you can test. As of this writing, we look for 4x certified media, which is required for newer burners. Ultimately, you shouldn't sweat the media too much: if it is going to fail, it'll fail during the burn process.

Best Thing Since Sliced Bread

Capture, encode, author and burn. That's all there is to it. Sure, each step warrants its own article and that's part of *Videomaker*'s goal each month, but we hope this article has encouraged you to give DVD a shot. It's not nearly as hard as other computer video tasks. Durable blank discs cost less than a dollar, postage costs less than a dollar and nearly everyone you know has a DVD player in their living room. Home DVD authoring is the best thing to happen to us since the advent of digital video.

Sidebar 1

One-Step DVD Solutions

OK, we hear you: four steps are too many, especially the part about capturing video. If you can operate a VCR, we have a one-step solution for you. If you haven't already seen them, go down to your local electronics store and check out the standalone living room DVD burners on sale. Prices have dropped significantly below $600 on many models and they work just like a VCR. Pop in a blank disc, hook up your camcorder and press Record. The menus usually aren't very attractive, but they get your video onto a disc and you don't even have to think about capture/encode/author/burn.

77

Video Out:
MPEG-2s for Me and You

Larry Lemm

In the last year, DVDs have really taken off in popularity. Consumers are embracing them at a pace faster than they ever embraced VHS or any other video format. As a videographer, you'll soon want to burn your videos into DVDs, lest you get left behind as the one guy who still uses videotape. Not only that, but there is so much more you can do with a DVD than you can with videotape. It opens new levels of creativity for the video artist.

DVD Basics

Most of you are probably familiar with DVDs by now, but just for the record, let's run down some of the advantages and disadvantages of the format.

First, DVDs are digital. This is both an advantage and a disadvantage. For the most part, the picture on a DVD will blow the doors off of VHS (see Figure 77.1). It is much sharper (400–500 lines of resolution for DVD versus 200ish for VHS) and it has brighter colors. If there is a disadvantage to

DVD, it is that an improperly compressed DVD can have visible artifacts. Many of the early Hollywood-released DVDs were not compressed properly, and you can see their artifacts in scene after scene. However, when done right, the format's picture is sharp and clean.

Second, DVD offers more sound. Instead of the hi-fi stereo of VHS, you get Dolby™ Digital AC-3 audio. This allows you to output five separate channels of audio, just like a professional filmmaker. Unlike the mono "surround" channels of "Dolby surround" the rear "surround" speakers of AC-3 are themselves stereo.

Third, and here's where you get into features of DVD that you may not have known about: you can make your own interactive menu systems and provide several different versions of the same basic movie on the same disc. You can make a director's cut of your video without having to record the whole second version on the disc. You can just have the different scenes and have the DVD piece it together seamlessly as it plays by, skipping

Figure 77.1 *Crystal Clear—DVD nearly doubles the resolution of VHS, and it reproduces richer color and sound.*

certain chapters and including others. This makes the DVD disc an option for non-linear video entertainment because you don't have to store your video on the disc in the order in which it will play. With these options, DVDs are a whole new world for video creativity.

Harnessing the Power

If you want to make your own DVDs, you're in luck these days. Easy to use, consumer-oriented, DVD-creation tools are already on the market. They all aim toward the same basic goal of creating the necessary introductory menu system and allowing you to include whichever additional multimedia files that you want such as graphics, text, sound or video files. Most of these software packages even come bundled with newer MPEG-2-based capture boards. This way, if you buy the capture board that captures video into the MPEG-2 format, you'll already have the software necessary to make those MPEG-2s into DVD files.

The bundled programs include titles such as Minerva Impressions, Sonic Solutions' DVDit! and Spruce Technologies' DVD Virtuoso. These aren't the only fish in the sea of DVD, but they are some of the

big ones. You'll be in good company if you choose one of these programs because they have established themselves in this first wave of consumer DVD authoring packages (see Figure 77.2).

Minerva Impressions comes bundled with hardware from Pinnacle Systems. Impressions competes directly with the Spruce DVD Virtuoso, which comes bundled with Canopus' Amber DVD hardware. You don't have to buy hardware to get these DVD authoring software, however. Sonic Solutions' DVDit!, for example, isn't bundled with hardware, but it offers discounts to owners of other hardware/software packages. This way, you can afford to use this other software, even if you've invested most of your available DVD-authoring cash into MPEG-2 capture hardware.

If you get MPEG-2 hardware, you won't have to perform a lengthy re-encoding of the video from whatever format you're using into MPEG-2. Having the hardware will usually result in a better picture than using software alone, and it will be a lot faster to output onto disc. Even if the software isn't bundled with the hardware, you won't pay much more for DVD-creation software than you would for editing software.

You don't use these DVD software packages to edit video. For editing, you still

Figure 77.2 *Author, Author!—DVD authoring software is becoming more common and less expensive. In the near future price will no longer be an issue.*

use the same video editing software that you've grown to know and love. Once you have a final rendered edit of your video, complete with titles, trailers and whatever else you want to include, you're ready to create a DVD. These packages can make your DVDs play like Hollywood's or you can add even more interactivity than most of what Hollywood offers up today on DVD (see Figure 77.3).

First, you take all of your clips and make them into "chapters" on your disc. This way, the viewers can freely fast forward and rewind through your video, like using the track markers on a CD. If you plan on making several different versions of the same movie on the same disc, pay special attention to where you mark your chapters. The order of these chapters will let you include and discard certain clips in the video when you play it back, depending on the version of the video the viewer has chosen to play.

After you've specified the chapters of the video, you'll want to create the menu system that your DVD will use to let viewers navigate through the disc to see exactly what they want. You create your

menus in a program like PhotoShop and import them into the DVD-creator program. Then use the DVD-creator program to link together the hot spots you want. These links act much like hyperlinks do on a Web page. This way you can build a computer-like multimedia page that you can use from a standard DVD player. This is exactly what you are looking for in DVD-creation software.

Basically, you keep adding clips to the disc and create a menu system that allows you to access the clips in whatever order you specify. Normally, this would include putting the clips of a movie in a linear order, but seeing as this is a new medium, and most videographers are not making two-hour feature films, this approach to DVD may not be appropriate for you. Make full use of the options that DVD offers because the first people to use these options in a creative fashion will be the vanguard of the DVD generation.

There is also a language option available on DVD that lets you include several different versions of the soundtrack. Many Hollywood discs include a soundtrack that includes the director, producer and

Figure 77.3 *DVD Video—VHS may soon be abandoned by video editors in favor of DVD.*

actors talking "behind the scenes" about the production of the movie. You could also use this type of approach to allow your video to be "kid-friendly" and omit any adult language, if that's what you want to do.

Getting it on Disc

Once you've completed your DVD file, you'll have to take it to a DVD-duplicating house (making your own discs is still expensive). Many duping houses will accept masters on DVD-RAM. Find one that does, then copy your project to a DVD-RAM cartridge. A DVD-RAM cartridge is a bit expensive (about $40 a pop) to use for making simple copies, but its great storage capacity makes it great for making masters to send to the duplicating house. You can get DVD-RAM drives from companies like Panasonic for around $500.

Once you've finished creating your master disc and the graphics for your cases, you'll be ready to have your production-run of discs. Then it's up to you to get enough people to buy them. Or you can just get your DVD-making skills down pat, and in a year or so, the tools to duplicate your own discs for mass production probably will have dropped enough to make it cost-effective to do from your home or office.

When that price shift happens, you can be sure that burning a DVD will be as common and as easy as burning a CD is today. Think of how exciting it will be to watch your own multimedia creations right on your television set. DVDs are the wave of the future for video. Get ready to ride it.

78

Burning Down the House:
Creating Video on CDs

Don Collins

My brother, who lives in Europe, shoots almost as much home video as I do. For years, we've wanted to send each other family videos, but we haven't been able to get past the PAL/NTSC barrier. The two broadcast formats, PAL in Europe and NTSC in the U.S. are incompatible. I looked into transfer services that convert NTSC signal to PAL, but the cost was exorbitant. We even tried sending each other video e-mails but the files were huge. Then it hit me. What if I recorded video onto a CD-ROM and sent that to my brother? After all, CD-ROMs are universal. They'll play in any computer: PC or Mac. We wouldn't have to fiddle with tapes or try to open humongous e-mails.

I had created a few audio CDs before, but I never tried to put video onto a disc. I decided to go for it and send a home video on CD-ROM to my brother for his birthday. Guess what? I found that it's easy, fast and best of all, I already had everything that I needed on my new computer. In this article, you will learn the basic steps it takes to put your own video onto CD-ROM.

Virtual Studio in your Computer

If you already edit video on your computer, chances are you've already got everything you need. Here's a quick checklist of hardware and software that you'll need to create a video CD.

- Video input: You're going to need to be able to get your video onto your computer either through a digital FireWire or USB port or through a digitizing card or external device.

- Editing software: You need to edit your video for length and size. The software can be as basic as Windows MovieMaker or as complex as Adobe Premiere.

- CD-R/CD-RW drive: Of course, you'll need a CD-R or CD-RW drive and CD-recording software.

- CD-R discs: Discs are cheaper than VHS tapes. As far as I can tell, the biggest difference in the cost of CD-ROMs is the jewel cases that come with them.

Getting Started

First, you need to edit your video. If you already have a video project that you've created you can open the project and make a new movie to export. If you haven't already done so, render your project and watch it to make sure you're happy with the way it plays.

We'll Adobe Premiere to illustrate the basic steps required for editing video for CD. Though every editing program is unique, the basic steps will be the same.

Creating a Movie for CD

Once you've loaded your project and rendered your video, you're set to export your movie. In Premiere 6.0, go to the File menu, select Export Timeline and choose Movie. A settings dialog window will open to show you the current settings (see Figure 78.1). Click the Export Settings button and then click on Load. This will open another dialog window with a list of settings. Choose Multimedia Video for

Windows, which has a 320 × 240 frame size and a frame rate of 15 frames per second (fps). You can customize your settings as well. I chose to work with 15 fps so it would run smoothly on an older (and slower) machine and a newer Pentium III or 4. If you know your audience has a fast computer, you may want to choose 30 fps for a smoother picture. Experiment with a few different settings and see how they look to you.

One thing to remember, the larger the frame size and the more frames per second, the larger the final .avi file size will be. At 15 fps, one minute of video will take up about 24 MB of CD space. Since most CD-ROMs hold about 650 to 700 MB, you can fit 25 to 30 minutes of video on a CD-ROM. Audio takes up significantly less space than video, so don't be too concerned about space (see Figure 78.2).

Burning Your Video to Disk

If you've got a CD-burner on your computer or if you recently bought one, chances are

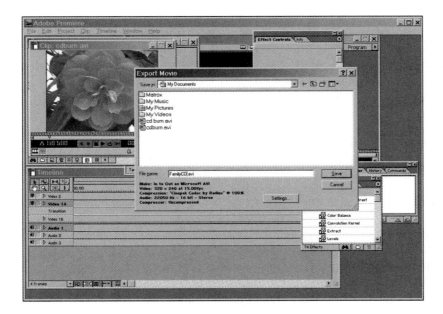

Figure 78.1 Finishing touch—in Premiere 6.0, finish your project by going to the File window, then choosing Export Timeline and saving it to a folder.

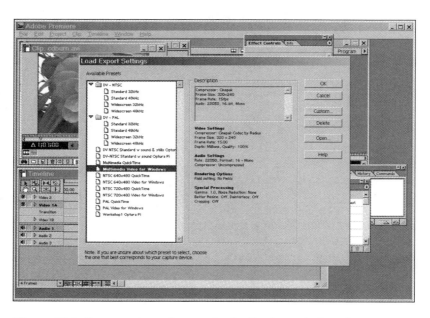

Figure 78.2 *Compression scheme—in the Settings window choose Multimedia Video for Windows to compress your project so it fits nicely on a CD and can be played back in most computers.*

it came with some kind of CD-creation software. This software makes the process very simple. It's basically a drag-and-drop operation. You choose the files you want, record them and seal the disk. My computer came bundled with Adaptec Easy CD Creator 4. This application copies data, image, audio and video files to disc. But since this was my first go at this, I wanted to keep it simple and record only one .avi file to the disc.

Open your CD-creation software (see Figure 78.3). With Easy CD Creator, you simply launch the program and choose Data from the opening dialogue window. Open the folder where your .avi file resides. Select the file and drag it to the CD Layout window. Easy CD Creator will then automatically indicate how much space is left on your targeted CD.

Once you've loaded all the files that you want to record to disc, hit Create CD. The CD-creation Setup window will open. It is here you can indicate drive, record speed, and whether you want a test file or not. I first selected the CD-R drive. Then I selected a moderate recording rate of 8X 1200 Kb/sec to ensure a quality recording.

With CD-RW (rewritable) drives and the proper CD, you can record over the same CD as many times as you like. With CD-R drives, however, you can only record to a disc once.

Sealing the Deal

The final step for recording to a one-time only CD-R disk is closing the session or sealing the disc, indicating that you like what you've got and don't want to add or delete anything else. If you've got a CD-RW drive, this step won't apply.

In the CD Creation Setup, you can choose to close the session after the software records to the disk or you can choose Test, which puts the file on the CD but does not close the session (see Figure 78.4). Since I was happy with what I had, I chose create Disc-at-Once method so that it would automatically close my session, thus sealing my CD and my video fate. I hit OK and in less than five

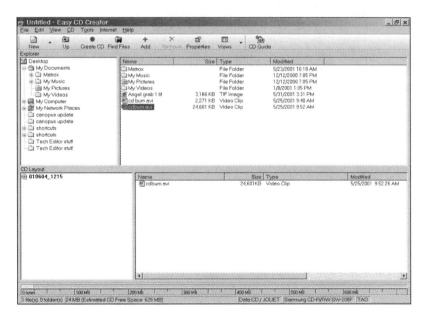

Figure 78.3 *Ready to burn—from inside the CD-creation software, open the file of your finished movie and drag it to the CD layout window.*

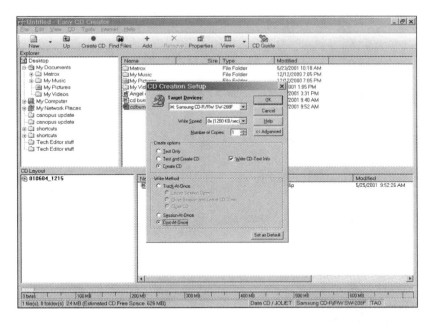

Figure 78.4 *Creation theory—when you're ready to finish your CD, the Creation Setup windows allows you to select the destination of your finished movie.*

minutes, I had my very first video on CD-ROM.

When I first told my brother I was going to create a video on CD, he sounded a little skeptical. But after he received the CD and played it in his Mac, he was amazed. It was the first time his family got to see and hear my family. When I outlined the basic steps to him, he practically dropped the phone to start creating his own video on CD.

If you've got a CD-R drive on your computer or if you've been thinking about buying one to make video CDs, go for it. It's one of the easiest, least expensive, most efficient and universal modes of distribution. CD-R drives have come down so much in price, it doesn't make sense not to own one.

Sidebar 1

CD-R Versus CD-RW

- CD-R (recordable) drives can record once to a CD-R disc. Once you've finished recording files to the disc, you have to close the CD so that you can later play it in a CD-ROM drive.

- CD-RW (rewritable) drives and discs allow you to record to a CD as many times as you like. In many ways, CD-RW has become even better than Zip disks, with much larger storage capacities.

Originally, CD-RW drives were far more expensive than CD-R drives. But that's changed. Although they still cost more, the difference is nominal. CD-R drives can be found for about $100 while CD-RWs typically cost around $250.

Sidebar 2

Five Tips for Creating Video for CD-ROM

1. *Select 320 × 240 Frame Size.* This half-screen-size option seems to be ideal for computer-based playback of video. It balances screen size with file size. If you want to fit more video on the CD you can save space by choosing a quarter-screen (160 × 120) setting.

2. *Plan your recording session.* If your CD-creation software offers it, look at the available space total. You will encounter an error if your clip's file size is larger than the space available.

3. *Edit for the computer.* If you're taking an existing video and editing it for CD, take the time to delete any unwanted or unnecessarily complicated scenes. Complex your scenes (including transition effects, etc.), can slow your computer down and impair playback. This is particularly noticeable on older computers.

4. *Shoot Tight.* If you're shooting with CD in mind, it's best to frame your subject large in the frame. Since your video will occupy a small part of the viewer's screen. In order for viewers to see details, you'll need to shoot in closeup. Also, limit your camera movement. Avoid excessive zooms and pans.

5. *Keep it Short.* When the file size is smaller, it's easier to handle and less likely to undergo problems while playing back on a computer. Hone your editing skills and make less more. An added bonus of keeping it short: your audience will be left begging for more, not turning your video off because they get bored.

79
Video Out:
Make Your Own
CD-ROM Videos

Joe McCleskey

Now that CD-R (recordable compact disc) drives have become affordable and a blank CD-R disk costs about the same as a blank VHS videotape, isn't it time to think about putting some of your videos onto CD-ROM? It doesn't take a super-powerful computer to get the job done; all you really need is a video capture card that's capable of recording video at 320 × 240 resolution or greater, some sort of video editing software, a sound card and a CD-R drive.

The benefits of recording video onto CD-ROM are many. Though the size and resolution of CD-ROM-based videos are not as good as videotape, CDs are a better archiving medium than tape. Also, making multiple-generation copies for family or friends is a snap, and results in perfect duplicates with no generation loss. It's also easy to incorporate your home videos into your own CD-ROM multimedia presentations, using the right software.

So if you're interested in making your own CDs full of home video, fire up your camcorder, buy some blank CDs and get ready to burn some home movies.

Planning and Shooting

Before you begin shooting your CD-ROM video masterpiece, take some time out before hand to plan the production.

The most important thing to remember when you're planning a CD-ROM-based video production is that whatever else your video is going to be, it's certainly going to be small. The typical resolution used for CD-ROM video is somewhere in the range of 320 × 240 (or, if you're working with DV video, 360 × 240). This resolution is handy because it's one-fourth the resolution of a typical full-screen digital video file (640 × 480, or 720 × 480 for DV). At such small resolutions, it's difficult to make out any kind of detail, so the most important things to remember are: get close and keep it simple (see Figure 79.1).

Imagine, for example, that you've shot a lineup of 50 or more people at a family reunion. If you simply set up a wide shot of the whole group, you might be able to pick out Aunt Louise when you later watch the videotape on a TV monitor.

Figure 79.1 *A. Shoot close-ups and keep movement to a minimum. B. Avoid busy clothing and background patterns.*

Digitize the footage at 320 × 240 resolution, however, and you'll be lucky if you can tell the men from the women. A good solution for this kind of problem would be to get closer and shoot a slow pan or handheld dolly shot of each face.

Also, when shooting for CD-ROM video, be sure to keep the camera moves to a minimum. The small size of the video makes it more difficult to follow busy, confusing shots. As always, you should move the camera only when you have a good reason to do so. The above example of the pan or dolly shot illustrates a good reason to move the camera; even better, however, might be to get a succession of static shots with only a few people in the frame for each shot. This will make it much easier for the viewer to keep track of who's who and what's going on.

What you're aiming for here is simplicity, and that includes the location you shoot in as well as the patterns of the clothes that people wear. When advising your talent what to wear, stick to solid colors, and avoid busy patterns like paisley or plaid.

Time to Edit

Once you've finished shooting your CD-ROM video footage, it's time to capture those clips onto your hard drive and begin editing. Probably the most important thing to remember when capturing your clips is to set the resolution to what it will be when you output the finished video. This will help you to avoid the horrible artifacts that sometimes result when you re-size a clip. If you find that you must capture at a higher resolution than you plan to output (this may be the case with some FireWire capture cards), then plan to output your video at a resolution that's an exact multiple of the capture resolution. So if you capture DV at 720 × 480, set your editing software for output at 360 × 240 (exactly one-fourth the resolution of 720 × 480).

The rules for editing pretty much follow the rules outlined above for capturing: keep it simple. A few effects might be nice, but highly complicated, high-resolution filter effects may not be visible in the tiny screen that CD-ROM video relies on for playback.

When choosing titles, be sure to use a font that's relatively large in comparison to the overall size of the video, or else you may have a readability problem. Also, resist the urge to use complex patterns with your titles, and choose a color that contrasts well with the background video (see Figure 79.2).

Rendering Issues

When you've made all of your editing decisions and it's time to render your final movie, it's important to consider the most limiting factor in CD-ROM video: space. There just isn't that much room on a CD-ROM (around 650 megabytes) and what space there is gets taken up fast by digital video.

Of primary importance is the type of codec (compression/decompression scheme) you use to compress the video.

Figure 79.2 *A. Keep titles and graphics large and simple. B. Use basic colors and avoid complicated high resolution effects.*

For maximizing space at the expense of resolution and overall quality, MPEG-1 is hard to beat. Remember, too, that your production won't have to be output to videotape, so you don't have to worry about using hardware-assisted codecs (like MJPEG and DV) when you render the video. This may make rendering times a little slower, but it'll result in a video that can be viewed on anyone's computer.

Don't hesitate to try several test renderings of your video, just to see what it looks like and how much space it takes up at several different compression ratios. If you have a lot of video you'd like to fit onto one CD, and you can squeeze the video a bit more without a major drop in quality, then go ahead and crank up the compression ratio a notch or two. Conversely, if you don't have that much video to fit onto the disc, then ease back on the compression a little and get the best quality you can.

One final note about compression and rendering: it's important to bear in mind that the CD-ROM drive you use to play back a video may be faster or slower than someone else's CD-ROM drive. This means that although your lightning-fast 44x speed CD-ROM drive plays your video just fine, your friend's old-school 12x drive might not be able to keep up. So before you render, decide what speed you'd like to be able to play the CD-ROM at, and then adjust your compression accordingly.

In general, video that's more highly compressed will play better on slower CD-ROM drives. If your MPEG compression software or video editing software allows you to dictate the playback data rate you desire, use the following formula to determine the rate you want:

Desired data rate $<$ target CD-ROM playback speed $\times$ 150 Kilobits/second

If, for example, you want your CD-ROM video to be viewable on a 12x CD-ROM drive, then your finished video should play back at something under 1800 Kilobits per second. Note that the desired data rate should be less than, and not equivalent to, the target CD-ROM's playback rate, because the listed speeds for most drives are maximum speeds, not sustained speeds. If you shoot for half or maybe three-quarters of the listed speed of the drive, you shouldn't encounter any playback problems.

Burn Baby Burn

Before you begin to burn your videos onto a CD, consider your options. Would you like to present your videos in an organized graphical format, like a CD-ROM-based Web page or a Microsoft PowerPoint presentation? Or do you prefer to conserve space and simply burn a list of video files onto the CD, with maybe a text file to describe the contents of each clip? The choice is yours.

If you know a little HTML, or if you have access to an HTML editing program, then building a simple CD-based Web page with links to your videos is a good way to organize your project (see Figure 79.3). Almost all computers nowadays have

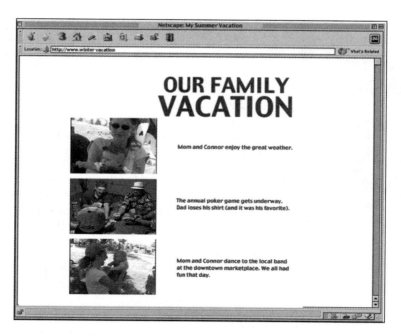

Figure 79.3 *If you know a little HTML, or if you have some Web-page creation software, you can create a simple index of your CD-ROM videos.*

Web browsers, so all a potential viewer of your CD-ROM-based videos would have to do is double-click your index.html file to launch a Web browser and begin viewing your clips.

Now that you know how to create your own CD-ROM videos, go ahead and give it a try for yourself. It's much easier than it looks, and it's a great way to share your videos with friends and family.

Jargon:
A Glossary of Videography Terms

.asf Active Streaming Format

.avi Short for Audio Video Interleave, the file format for Microsoft's Video for Windows standard.

.gif Graphics Interchange Format—a bit-mapped graphics file format used by the World Wide Web, CompuServe and many BBSs. GIF supports color and various resolutions. It also includes data compression, making it especially effective for scanned photos.

.jpeg Joint Photographic Experts Group image format. A popular Internet compression format for color images.

.mov File extension used with Quick-Time movies.

.mov File extension used with Quicktime, a popular file format for video on a computer developed by Apple.

.rm Most common file extension used with RealMedia files.

.wav A sound format for storing sound in files developed jointly by Microsoft and IBM. Support for WAV files was built into Windows 95 making it the de facto standard for sound on PCs. WAV sound files end with a .wav extension.

8mm Compact videocassette format, popularized by camcorders, employing 8-millimeter-wide videotape. [See Hi8]

A/B roll editing Two video sources played simultaneously, to be mixed or cut between.

A/V (Audio/Video) A common shorthand for multimedia audio and video.

action axis An imaginary line drawn between two subjects or along a line of motion to maintain continuity of screen direction. Crossing it from one shot to the next creates an error in continuity. It is also referred to as the "180-degree rule."gree rule."

ad-lib Unrehearsed, spontaneous act of speaking, performing, or otherwise improvising on-camera activity without preparation.

aDSL Asymmetric (or Asynchronous) Digital Subscriber Line. A 'fat pipe.' New technology to carry high-speed data over typical twisted-pair copper telephone lines. ADSL promises be up to 70 times as fast as a 28.8 modem.

AFM (audio frequency modulation) The analog soundtrack of the 8mm and Hi8 video format. [See PCM.]

AGC (automatic gain control) A circuit on most camcorders that automatically adjusts a microphone's gain (volume) to match environmental sound levels.

ambient sound (ambience) Natural background audio representative of a given recording environment. On-camera dialog might be primary sound; traffic noise and refrigerator hum would be ambient.

amplify To magnify an audio signal for mixing, distribution and transducing purposes.

analog An electrical signal is referred to as either analog or digital. Analog signals are those signals directly generated from a stimulus such as a light striking a camera picture tube. You can convert an analog signal to a digital signal by using an analog to digital converter.

animation Visual special effect whereby progressive still images displayed in rapid succession creates the illusion of movement.

aperture/exposure A setting that manipulates the amount of light falling onto the camera's CCD(s). This control adjusts the size of the camcorder's iris.

apps (application) Software that performs a specific function.

artifacting The occurrence of unwanted visual distortions that appear in a video image, such as cross-color artifacts, cross-luminance artifacts, jitter, blocking, ghosts, etc. Artifacting is a common side effect of compression, especially at lower bit rates.

artifacts Unwanted visual distortions that appear in a video image, such as cross-color artifacts, cross-luminance artifacts, jitter, blocking, ghosts, etc.

artificial light Human-made illumination not limited to "indoor" variety: fluorescent bulbs, jack-o'-lanterns and

a car's headlights all qualify. Typically, it has lower color temperature than natural light, and thus more reddish qualities. (See color temperature, natural light.)

aspect ratio Proportional width and height of on-screen picture. Current standard for a conventional monitor is 4:3 (four-by-three); 16:9 for HDTV.

assemble edit Recording video and/or audio clips in sequence immediately following previous material; does not break control track. Consecutive edits form complete program. [See edit, insert edit.]

ATV (amateur television) Specialized domain of ham radio, transmits standard TV signals on UHF radio bands.

audio dub Result of recording over prerecorded videotape soundtrack, or a portion thereof, without affecting prerecorded images.

audio frequency modulation (AFM) Method of recording hi-fi audio on videotape along with video signals. Used in VHS Hi-Fi Audio, and also the analog soundtrack of the 8mm and Hi8 video formats.

audio mixer The piece of equipment used to gather, mix and amplify sounds from multiple microphones and send the signal on to its destination.

automatic exposure Circuitry that monitors light levels and adjusts camcorder iris accordingly, compensating for changing light conditions.

automatic gain control (AGC) Circuitry found on most camcorders that adjusts incoming audio levels automatically to match environmental sound levels.

available light Amount of illumination present in a particular environment: natural light, artificial light or a combination of the two.

AVI (Audio Video Interleave) One of the oldest file formats for digital video on PCs.

back light Lamp providing illumination from behind. Creates sense of depth by separating foreground subject from background area. Applied erroneously, causes severe silhouetting. (See fill light, key light, three-point lighting.)

balanced line Audio cables that have three wires: one for positive, one for negative and one for ground.

bandwidth A measure of the capacity of a user's data line. Video looks its best on a high-bandwidth connection, like DSL, cable modems or satellite modems. Conversely, trying to download or stream video on a low-bandwidth connection like a dial-up modem can be a frustrating experience.

bandwidth compression Reducing the bandwidth that is required for transmission of a given digital data rate.

barndoors Accessories for video lights; adjustable folding flaps that control light distribution.

batch capture The ability of certain computer-based editing systems to automatically capture whole lists or "batches" of clips from source videotapes.

Betamax More commonly known as "Beta," half-inch videotape format developed by Sony, eclipsed by VHS in home video market popularity. [See ED Beta.]

bidirectional Microphone pickup pattern whereby sound is absorbed equally from two sides only. [See omnidirectional, unidirectional.]

black box Generic term for wide variety of video image manipulation devices with perceived mysterious or "magical" capabilities, including proc amps, enhancers, SEGs, and TBCs.

bleeding Video image imperfection characterized by blurring of color borders; colors spill over defined boundaries, "run" into neighboring areas.

BNC (Bayonet Fitting Connector aka British Naval Connector) A durable "professional" cable connector, attaches to VCRs for transfer of high-frequency composite video in/out signals. Connects with a push and a twist.

boom Any device for suspending a microphone above and in front of a performer.

booming Camera move above or below subject with aid of a balanced "boom arm," creating sense of floating into or out of a scene. Can combine effects of panning, tilting, and pedding in one fluid movement.

C See chrominance.

cable/community access Channel(s) of a local cable television system dedicated to community-based programming. Access centers provide free or low-cost training and use of video production equipment and facilities.

cameo lighting Foreground subjects illuminated by highly directional light, appearing before a completely black background.

Cannon See XLR.

capacitor The part of the condenser mike that stores electrical energy and permits the flow of alternating current.

capture card A piece of computer hardware that captures digital video and audio to a hard drive, typically through a FireWire (IEEE 1394) port.

cardioid A microphone that picks up sound in a heart-shaped pattern.

CCD (charge coupled device) Light-sensitive integrated circuit in video cameras that converts images into electrical signals. Sometimes referred to as a "chip."

character generator A device that electronically builds text which can be combined with a video signal. The text is created with a keyboard and program that has a selection of font and backgrounds.

chroma Characteristics of color a videotape absorbs with recorded signal, divided into two categories: AM (amplitude modulation) indicates color intensity; PM (phase modulation) indicates color purity.

chromakey Method of electronically inserting an image from one video source into the image of another through areas designated as its "key color." It is frequently used on news programs to display weather graphics behind talent.

chrominance Portion of video signal that carries color information (hue and saturation, but not brightness); frequently abbreviated as "C," as in "Y/C" for luminance/chrominance. [See luminance.]

clapstick Identification slate with hinged, striped top that smacks together for on-camera scene initiation. Originally used to synchronize movie sound with picture. [See lip-sync.]

closeup (CU) A tightly framed camera shot in which the principal subject is viewed at close range, appearing large and dominant on screen. Pulled back slightly is a "medium closeup" while zoomed in very close is an "extreme closeup (ECU or XCU)."

CODEC (compressor/decompressor) A piece of software that converts a raw stream of uncompressed video to a compressed form. The same piece of software can also play the compressed video on-screen.

color bars Standard test signal containing samples of primary and secondary colors, used as reference in aligning color video equipment. Generated electronically by a "color bar generator," often viewed on broadcast television in off-air hours. [See test pattern.]

color corrector Electronic device that dissects the colors of a video signal, allowing them to be adjusted individually.

color temperature Relative amount of "white" light's reddish or bluish qualities, measured in degrees Kelvin. Desirable readings for video are 3,200 K indoors, 5,600 K outdoors. (See artificial, natural light.)

comet tailing Smear of light resulting from inability of camera's pickup to process bright objects—especially in darker settings. Object or camera in motion creates appearance of flying fireball. [See lag.]

component video Signal transmission system, resembling S-video concept, employed with professional videotape formats. Separates one luminance and two chrominance channels to avoid quality loss from NTSC or PAL encoding.

composite video Single video signal combining luminance and chrominance signals through an encoding process, including RGB (red, green, blue) elements and sync information.

compositing Superimposing multiple layers of video or images. Each layer may move independently. Titles are a simple and common example of compositing.

composition Visual make-up of a video picture, including such variables as balance, framing, field of view and texture—all aesthetic considerations. Combined qualities form an image that's pleasing to view.

compression An encoding process that reduces the digital data in a video frame, typically from nearly one megabyte to 300 kilobytes or less. This is accomplished by throwing away information the eye can't see and/or redundant information in areas of the video frame that do not change. JPEG, Motion-JPEG, MPEG, DV, Indeo, Fractal and Wavelet are all compression schemes.

condenser mike A high-quality mike whose transducer consists of a diaphragm, backplate and capacitor.

continuity [1:visual] Logical succession of recorded or edited events, necessitating consistent placement of props, positioning of characters, and progression of time.

contrast Difference between a picture's brightest and darkest areas. When high, image contains sharp blacks and whites; when low, image limited to variations in gray tones.

control track A portion of the videotape containing information to synchronize playback and linear videotape editing operations.

Control-L A two-way communication system used to coordinate tape transport commands for linear editing. Primarily found in Mini DV, Digital8, Hi8 and 8mm camcorders and VCRs. (See Control-S, synchro edit.)

Control-S A one-way communication system that treats a VCR or camcorder as a slave unit, with edit commands emanating from an external edit controller or compatible deck. Primarily found on 8mm VCRs and camcorders. (See Control-L, synchro edit.)

cookie (cucalorus) Lighting accessory consisting of random cutout shapes that cast patterned shadows when light passes through. Used to imitate shadows of natural lighting.

crawl Text or graphics, usually special announcements that move across the screen horizontally, typically from right to left across the bottom of the screen.

cross-fade Simultaneous fade-in of one audio or video source as another fades out so that they overlap temporarily. Also called a dissolve.

cucalorus (cookie) Lighting accessory consisting of random pattern of cutouts that forms shadows when light passes through it. Used to imitate shadows of natural lighting.

cue [1] Signal to begin, end, or otherwise influence on-camera activity while recording. [2] Presetting specific starting points of audio or video material so it's available for immediate and precise playback when required.

cut Instantaneous change from one shot to another.

cutaway Shot of something other than principal action (but peripherally related), frequently used as transitional footage or to avoid a jump cut.

cuts-only editing Editing limited to immediate shifts from one scene to another, without smoother image transition capabilities such as dissolving or wiping. [See cut, edit.]

D1, D2, D3, D5, Digital-S, DVCPRO, DVCAM, Digital Betacam Entirely digital "professional" videotape recording formats.

decibel (dB) A unit of measurement of sound that compares the relative intensity of different sound sources.

decompression The decoding of a compressed video data stream to allow playback.

deinterlace To convert interlaced video into progressively-scanned video, for use with computers.

depth of field Range in front of a camera's lens in which objects appear in focus. Varies with subject-to-camera distance, focal length of a camera lens and a camera's aperture setting.

desktop video (DTV) Fusion of personal computers and home video components for elaborate videomaking capabilities rivaling those of broadcast facilities.

diaphragm The vibrating element in a microphone that responds to the compressed air molecules of sound waves.

diffused light Indistinctly illuminates relatively large area. Produces soft light quality with soft shadows.

diffuser Gauzy or translucent material that alters the quality of light passing through it to produce less intense, flatter lighting with softer, less noticeable shadows.

diffusion filter Mounted at front of camcorder lens, gives videotaped images a foggy, fuzzy, dreamy look. [See filter.]

digital audio Sounds that have been converted to digital information.

digital video effects (DVE) Electronic analog-to-digital picture modification yielding specialty image patterns and maneuvers: tumbling, strobing, page turning, mosaic, posterization, solarization, etc.

digitization The process of converting a continuous analog video or audio signal to digital data for computer storage and manipulation.

digitizer Device that imports and converts analog video images into digital information for hard drive-based editing.

directional light Light that illuminates in a relatively small area with distinct light beam; usually created with spotlight, yields harsh, defined shadows.

dissolve Image transition effect of one picture gradually disappearing as another appears. Analogous to audio and lighting cross-fade. [See cross-fade.]

distribution amp (distribution amplifier) Divides single video or audio signals, while boosting their strength, for delivery to multiple audio/ video acceptors. Allows simultaneous recording on multiple VCR's from the same source, especially useful for tape duplication.

DivX ;-) A recent codec for MPEG-4 video, developed on the Internet.

dolly dolly Camera movement toward or away from a subject. The effect may seem to be the same as zooming, but dollying in or out results in a more dramatic change in perspective than using the zoom.

dollying Camera movement toward or away from a subject. Effect may appear same as zooming, which reduces and magnifies the image, but dollying in or out maintains perspective while changing picture size.

dongle A device that prevents the unauthorized use of hardware or software. A dongle usually consists of a small cord attached to a device or key that secures the hardware. The term is also used to signify a generic adapter for peripherals.

download and play A way of viewing Web video that requires a user to download a video before playing it. Download and play files are usually higher quality than streamed video.

dropout Videotape signal voids, viewed as fleeting white specks or streaks. Usually result of minute "bare spots" on a tape's magnetic particle coating, or tape debris covering particles and blocking signals.

DTV Desktop video.

dub [1] Process or result of duplicating a videotape in its entirety. [2] Editing technique whereby new audio or video replaces portion(s) of existing recording.

DV (Digital Video) With a capital "D" and a capital "V," DV is a specific video format; both a tape format (like Hi8) and a data format specification.

DVE (Digital Video Effect) Electronic special effects and picture modification yielding specialty image patterns

and maneuvers, such as tumbling, strobing, page turning, mosaic, posterization, solarization, etc. [See F/X.]

dynamic mike A rugged microphone whose transducer consists of a diaphragm connected to a moveable coil.

ED Beta (extended definition Beta) Improved version of the original half-inch Betamax video format, yielding sharper pictures with 500-line resolution. [See Betamax.]

edit Process or result of selectively recording video and/or audio on finished videotape. Typically involves reviewing raw footage and transferring desired segments from master tape(s) onto new tape in a predetermined sequence. [See assemble edit, in-camera editing.]

edit control protocols Types of signals designed to communicate between editing components, including computers, tape decks and camcorders. Allows components to transmit instructions for various operations such as play, stop, fast forward, rewind, record, pause, etc.

edit controller Electronic programmer used in conjunction with VCRs/camcorders to facilitate automated linear videotape editing with speed, precision and convenience.

edit decision list (EDL) Handwritten or computer-generated compilation of all edits (marked by their time code in points and out points) to be executed in a video production.

edited master Original recorded videotape footage; "edited master" implies original copy of tape in its edited form. Duplications constitute generational differences.

editing appliance An self-contained machine, essentially a small computer, which only edits video. Editing appliances usually contain most features found in standard computer-based editing systems.

EDL (edit decision list) Handwritten or computer-generated compilation of all edits (marked by their time code in points and out points) planned for execution in a video production.

EFP (Electronic field production) Film-style production approach using a single camera to record on location. Typically shot for post-production application, non-live feed.

EIS (electronic image stabilization) A process of limiting shaky camera shots with digital processing within a camcorder. [See OIS.]

electret condenser Microphone type incorporating a pre-charged element, eliminating need for bulky power sources. [See condenser.]

electronic image stabilization (EIS) A process that limits shaky camera shots with digital processing found within a camcorder. [See OIS.]

encoder Device that translates a video signal into a different format—RGB to composite, DV to MPEG,etc.

encoding The actual process of compressing video for streaming or for downloading.

ENG (Electronic news gathering) Use of portable video cameras, lighting and sound equipment to record news events in the field quickly, conveniently, and efficiently.

enhancer (Image enhancer) Video signal processor that compensates for picture detail losses and distortion occurring in recording and playback. Exaggerates transitions between light and dark areas by enhancing high frequency region of video spectrum.

EP (Extended play) Slowest tape speed of a VHS VCR, accommodating six-hour recordings. [See LP, SP.]

equalization Emphasizing specific audio or video frequencies and eliminating others as signal control measure, usually to produce particular sonic qualities. Achieved with equalizer.

equalize To emphasize, lessen or eliminate certain audio frequencies.

essential area Boundaries within which contents of a television picture are sure to be seen, regardless of masking differences in receiver displays. Also

called the "critical area" or "safe action area," it encompasses the inner 80 percent of the screen.

establishing shot Opening image of a program or scene. Usually, it's a wide and/or distant perspective that orients viewers to the overall setting and surroundings.

extra Accessory talent not essential to a production, assuming some peripheral on-camera role. In movie work, performers with fewer than five lines are called "under fives."

f-stop Numbers corresponding to variable size of a camera's iris opening, and thus the amount of light passing through the lens. The higher the number, the smaller the iris diameter, which means less light enters the camcorder.

F/X Special effects. Visual tricks and illusions—electronic or on camera—employed in film and video to define, distort or defy reality.

fade Gradual diminishing or heightening of visual and/or audio intensity. "Fade out" or "fade to black," "fade in" or "up from black" are common terms.

feed Act or result of transmitting a video signal from one point to another.

feedback [1:video] Infinite loop of visual patterns from signal output being fed back as input; achieved by aiming live camera at receiving monitor. [2:audio] Echo effect at low levels, howl or piercing squeal at extremes, from audio signal being fed back to itself.

field Half a scanning cycle. Two fields comprise a complete video frame. Composed of either all odd lines or all even lines.

field of view Extent of a shot that is visible through a particular lens; its vista.

fill light Supplementary illumination, usually from a soft light positioned to the side of the subject, which lightens shadows created by the key light. (See back light, key light, three-point lighting.)

film-style Out-of-sequence shooting approach, to be edited in appropriate order at post-production stage. Advantageous for concentrating on and completing recording at one location at a time, continuity and convenience assured.

filter Transparent or semi-transparent material, typically glass, mounted at the front of a camcorder's lens to change light passing through. Manipulates colors and image patterns, often for special effect purposes.

filter effect Digital effect added to colorize or otherwise alter a clip in post-production.

FireWire (IEEE 1394 or i.LINK) A high-speed bus that was developed by Apple Computer. It is used, among other things, to connect digital camcorders to computers.

fishpole A small, lightweight arm to which a microphone is attached, hand held by an audio assistant outside of the picture frame.

flare Bright flashes evident in video. Caused by excessive light beaming into a camera's lens and reflecting off its internal glass elements.

flat lighting Illumination characterized by even, diffused light without shadows, highlights or contrast. May impede viewer's sense of depth, dimension.

floodlight Radiates a diffused, scattered blanket of light with soft, indistinct shadows. Best used to spread illumination on broad areas, whereas spotlights focus on individual subjects.

fluid head Tripod mount type containing viscous fluid which lubricates moving parts, dampens friction. Design facilitates smooth camera moves, alleviates jerkiness. [See friction head.]

flying erase head Accessory video head mounted on spinning head drum, incorporated in many camcorders and VCRs to eliminate glitches and rainbow noise between scenes recorded or edited. By design, all 8mm-family and DV-family equipment has flying erase heads.

focal length Distance from a camcorder's lens to a focused image with the lens focused on infinity. Short focal lengths offer a broad field of view (wide angle); long focal lengths offer a narrow field of view (telephoto). Zoom lenses have a variable focal length.

follow focus Controlling lens focus so that an image maintains sharpness and clarity despite camcorder and/or subject movement.

foot-candle A unit of illumination equal to the light emitted by a candle at the distance of one foot. One foot-candle equals 10.764 lux. (See lux.)

format Videotape and video equipment design differences—physical and technical—dictating compatibility and quality. In most basic sense, refers to standardized tape widths, videocassette sizes. [See Betamax, D1/D2, 8 mm, three-quarter-inch, VHS.]

FPS (frames per second) Measures the rate or speed of video or film. Film is typically shot and played back at 24 fps. Video is recorded and played back at 30 fps.

frame 1) One complete image. In NTSC video a frame is composed of two fields. One 30th of a second. 2) The viewable area or composition of an image.

framing Act of composing a shot in a camcorder's viewfinder for desired content, angle and field of view.

freeze frame Single frame paused and displayed for an extended period during video playback; suspended motion perceived as still snapshot.

frequency Number of vibrations produced by a signal or sound, usually expressed as cycles per second, or hertz (Hz).

frequency response Measure of the range of frequencies a medium can respond to and reproduce. Good video response maintains picture detail; good audio response accommodates the broadest range, most exacting sound.

friction head Tripod mount type with strong spring that counterbalances camera weight, relying on friction to hold its position. More appropriate for still photography than movement-oriented videomaking. [See fluid head.]

full-motion video A standard for video playback on a computer; refers to smooth-flowing, full-color video at 30 frames per second, regardless of the screen resolution.

gaffer Production crew technician responsible for placement and rigging of all lighting instruments.

gain Video amplification, signal strength. "Riding gain" means varying controls to achieve desired contrast levels.

GB (Gigabyte) Giga- is a prefix that means one billion, so a Gigabyte is 1,000,000,000 bytes. Most commonly used to measure hard disk space.

gel Colored material placed in front of a light source to alter its hue. Useful for special effects and correcting mismatches in lighting, as in scenes lit by both daylight and artificial light.

generation Relationship between a master video recording and a given copy of that master. A copy of a copy of the original master constitutes a second-generation duplication.

generation loss Degradation in picture and sound quality resulting from an analog duplication of original master video recording. Copying a copy and all successive duplication compounds generation loss. Digital transfers are free of generation loss.

genlock (generator locking device) Synchronizes two video sources, allowing part or all of their signals to be displayed together. Necessary for overlaying computer graphics with video, for example.

ghosting Undesirable faint double screen image caused by signal reflection or improperly balanced video circuitry. "Ringing" appears as repeated image edges.

giraffe A small boom that consists of a counterweighted arm supported by a tripod, usually on casters.

glitch Momentary picture disturbance.

grain Blanketed signal noise viewed as fuzziness, unsmooth images—attributable to lumination inadequacies.

grip Production crew stagehand responsible for handling equipment, props, and scenery before, during, and after production.

group master fader A volume control on an audio board that handles a sub-group of input channels before they are sent to the master fader.

handheld mike A microphone that a person holds to speak or sing into.

hard disk Common digital storage component in a computer.

HDTV (high-definition television) "In the works" television system standard affording greater resolution for sharper pictures and wide-screen viewing via specially-designed TV equipment.

head Electromagnetic component within camcorders and VCRs that records, receives and erases video and audio signals on magnetic tape.

headroom Space between the top of a subject's head and a monitor's upper-screen edge. Too much headroom makes the subject appear to fall out of the frame.

hi-fi (high fidelity) Generalized term defining audio quality approaching the limits of human hearing, pertinent to high-quality sound reproduction systems.

Hi8 (high-band 8mm) Improved version of 8mm videotape format characterized by higher luminance resolution for a sharper picture. Compact "conceptual equivalent" of Super-VHS. [See 8mm]

high impedance A characteristic of microphones that have a great deal of opposition to the flow of alternating current through them and therefore must have short cables; they are less likely to be used in professional situations than low impedance microphones.

hiss Primary background signal interference in audio recording, result of circuit noise from a playback recorder's amplifiers or from a tape's residual magnetism.

horizontal resolution Specification denoting amount of discernable detail across a screen's width. Measured in pixels, the higher the number, the better the picture quality.

IEEE 1394 (Institute of Electrical and Electronics Engineers) Pronounced "eye-triple-E thirteen-ninety-four" the institute establishes standards and protocols for a wide range of computer and communications technologies, including IEEE 1394, which is a specification FireWire data transmission widely used in DV. Sony refers to the ports on its products with the proprietary term, "i.LINK."

image enhancer Video signal processor that compensates for picture detail losses and distortion occurring in recording and playback. Exaggerates transitions between light and dark areas by enhancing high frequency region of video spectrum.

image sensor A video camera's image sensing element, either CCD (charge coupled device) or MOS (metal oxide semiconductor); converts light to electrical energy. [See CCD.]

impedance Opposition to the flow of an audio signal in a microphone and its cable.

in-camera editing Assembling finished program "on the fly" as you videotape simply by activating and pausing camcorder's record function.

incident light That which emanates directly from a light source. Measured from the object it strikes to the source. (See reflected light.)

indexing Ability of some VCRs to electronically mark specific points on videotape for future access, either during the recording process (VISS: VHS index search system) or as scenes are played back (VASS: VHS address search system).

input channel On an audio board, the control into which a microphone, tape recorder or other source is plugged.

insert edit Recording video and/or audio on tape over a portion of existing footage without disturbing what precedes and follows. Must replace recording of same length.

interlace To split a TV picture into two fields of odd and even lines. Under the interlaced method, every other line is scanned during the first pass, then the remaining lines are scanned in the second pass. All analog TV formats (NTSC, PAL and SECAM) use interlaced video.

interlaced video Process of scanning frames in two passes, each painting every other line on the screen, with scan lines alternately displayed in even and odd fields. NTSC video is interlaced; most computers produce a noninterlaced video signal. [See noninterlaced video.]

iris Camcorder's lens opening or aperture, regulates amount of light entering camera. Diameter is measured in f-stops. [See f-stop.]

jack Any female socket or receptacle, usually on the backside of video and audio equipment; accepts plug for circuit connection.

jitter Video image aberration seen as slight, fast vertical or horizontal shifting of a picture or portion of one.

jog/shuttle Manual control on some VCRs, facilitates viewing and editing precision and convenience. Jog ring moves tape short distances to show a frame at a time; shuttle dial transports tape forward or reverse more rapidly for faster scanning.

jump cut Unnatural, abrupt switch between shots identical in subject but slightly different in screen location, so the subject appears to jump from one screen location to another. Can be remedied with a cutaway or shot from a different angle.

Kelvin Temperature scale used to define the color of a light source; abbreviated as "K." [See color temperature.]

key light Principal illumination source on a subject or scene. Normally positioned slightly off-center and angled to provide shadow detail. (See back light, fill light, three-point lighting.)

keyframe A complete image, used as a reference for subsequent images. To keep the data rate low, other frames only have data for the parts of the picture that change.

keystoning Perspective distortion from a flat object being shot by a camera at other than a perpendicular angle. Nearer portion of object appears larger than farther part.

Killer app An application of such technological importance and wide acceptance that it surpasses (i.e., kills) its competitors.

lag Camera pickup's retention of an image after the camera has been moved, most common under low light levels. Comet tailing is a form of lag.

lapel mike A small mike often clipped inside clothing or on a tie or lapel.

lavalier A small mike that can be worn around the neck on a cord.

LCD (Liquid Crystal Display) Commonly used in digital watches, camcorder viewscreens and laptop computer screens, LCD panels are light-weight and low-power display devices.

LiIon (Lithium Ion) The most common battery type among new camcorders. More expensive, but has a higher capacity and fewer memory rechanging problems.

linear editing Tape-based VCR-to-VCR editing. Called linear because scenes are recorded in chronological order on the tape.

lip sync Proper synchronization of video with audio—lip movement with audible speech.

long shot (LS) Camera view of a subject or scene from a distance, showing a broad perspective.

LP (long play) Middle tape speed of a VHS VCR, accommodating four-hour recordings. [See EP, SP.]

LTC (longitudinal time code) Frame identification numbers encoded as audio signals and recorded lengthwise on the edge of a tape, typically on a linear audio track of VHS or S-VHS tape. (See time code, VITC.)

luminance Black-and-white portion of video signal, carries brightness information representing picture contrast, light and dark qualities; frequently abbreviated as "Y."

lux A metric unit of illumination equal to the light of a candle falling on a surface of one square meter. One lux equals 0.0929 foot-candle.

macro Lens capable of extreme closeup focusing, useful for intimate views of small subjects.

master Original recorded videotape footage; "edited master" implies original tape in its edited form.

master fader The audio volume control that is located after all the input channel controls and after the submaster controls.

matched dissolve Dissolve from one image to another that's similar in appearance or shot size.

media player A program that plays back audio or video. Examples include Microsoft Windows Media Player, Apple's QuickTime Player, and RealPlayer.

medium shot (MS) Defines any camera perspective between long shot and closeup, viewing the subjects from a medium distance.

memory effect Power-loss phenomenon alleged of NiCad—camcorder batteries, attributed to precisely repetitive partial discharge followed by complete recharge, or long-term overcharge. Considered misnomer for "voltage depression" and "cell imbalance."

MIDI (musical instrument digital interface) System of communication between digital electronic instruments allowing synchronization and distribution of musical information.

mike   (also "mic") short for microphone.

mix   [1:audio] Combining sound sources to achieve a desired program balance. Finished output may be mono, stereo or surround. [2:video] Combining video signals from two or more sources.

model release   Agreement to be signed by anyone appearing in a video work, protecting videomaker from right of privacy lawsuit. Specifies event, date, compensation provisions, and rights being waived.

monitor   [1:video] Television set without receiving circuitry, wired to camcorder or VCR for display of live or recorded video signals. Most standard TVs have dual-function capability as monitor and receiver. [See receiver.] [2:audio] Synonymous with speaker.

monopod   One-legged camera support. [See tripod.]

montage   A sequence of shots assembled in juxtaposition to each other to communicate a particular idea or mood. Often bridged with cross-fades and set to music.

mosaic   Electronic special effect whereby individual pixels comprising an image are blown up into larger blocks—a kind of checkerboard effect.

MPEG (MPEG-1)   A video compression standard set by the Moving Picture Experts Group. It involves changing only those elements of a video image that actually change from frame to frame and leaving everything else in the image the same.

MPEG-2   The highest quality digital video compression currently available. MPEG-2 is less blocky than MPEG-1 and is used in DVDs and DBS satellite TV systems.

MPEG-4   A recent data compression format that can get better quality out of a given amount of bandwidth. MPEG-4 can compress a feature film onto a CD-ROM disc with VHS quality.

natural light   Planetary illumination—from the sun, the moon, stars—whether indoors or out. Has higher color temperature than artificial light, and thus more bluish qualities. (See artificial light, color temperature.)

neutral-density filter (ND)   Mounted at front of camcorder lens, reduces light intensity without affecting its color qualities. [See filter.]

NiCad (nickel cadmium)   Abbreviation coined and popularized by SAFT America for lightweight camcorder battery type designed to maintain power longer than traditional lead-acid batteries. Rare among new camcorders, supplanted by Li-Ion and NiMH.

NiMH (nickel metal hydride)   Battery technology similar to NiCad, but more environmentally friendly, with higher capacity and fewer memory recharging problems.

NLE   (nonlinear   editor/editing)   Hard drive-based editing system defined by its ability to randomly access and insert video in any order at any time. This is in contrast to linear, tape-to-tape editing which requires rewinding and fast forwarding to access material.

noise   Unwanted sound or static in an audio signal or unwanted electronic disturbance of snow in the video signal.

noninterlaced video   Process of scanning complete frames in one pass, painting every line on the screen, yielding higher picture quality than that of interlaced video. Most computers produce a noninterlaced video signal; NTSC is interlaced. AKA progressive scan.

nonlinear   editing   Digital random access editing that uses a hard drive instead of tape to store video. Random access allows easy arrangement of scenes in any order. It also eliminates the need for rewinding and allows for multiple dubs without generation loss.

nonsynchronous sound   Audio without precisely matching visuals. Usually recorded separately, includes wild sound, sound effects, or music incorporated in post-production. [See synchronous sound.]

nose room The distance between the subject and the edge of the frame in the direction the subject is looking. Also called "look room."

NTSC (National Television Standards Committee) U.S. television broadcasting specifications. NTSC refers to all video systems conforming to this 525-line 59.94-field-per-second signal standard. [See PAL, SECAM.]

Off-line Until recently, the low quality of computer video images limits the DTV computer to "off-line" work. That is, making the edit-point decisions (EDL) for use in a later "on-line" session, using the original tapes to assemble the edit master. Today's editing systems are capable of on-line quality output by themsleves, relegating this term to history.

OIS (optical image stabilization) A process of limiting shaky camera shots with mechanical movement of the optical system within a camcorder. [See EIS.]

omnidirectional A microphone that picks up sound from all directions.

outtake Footage not to be included in final production.

over-the-shoulder shot View of the primary subject with the back of another person's shoulder and head in the foreground. Often used in interview situations.

PAL (phase alternate line) 625-line 50-field-per-second television signal standard used in Europe and South America. Incompatible with NTSC. [See NTSC, SECAM.]

pan Horizontal camera pivot, right to left or left to right, from a stationary position.

PCM (pulse code modulation) A popular method of encoding digital audio. [See AFM.]

pedestal A camera move vertically lowering or raising the camcorder, approaching either the floor or ceiling, while keeping the camera level.

phone plug Sturdy male connector compatible with audio accessories, particularly for insertion of microphone and headphone cables. Frequently referred to by their sizes, usually 1/4-inch and 1/8-inch. Not to be confused with phono plug.

phono plug (RCA) Shrouded male connector used for audio and video connections. Frequently referred to as RCA plugs, they only come in one size. Not to be confused with phone plugs.

pickup [1] A video camera's image sensing element, either CCD (charge coupled device) or MOS (metal oxide semiconductor); converts light to electrical energy. [See CCD.] [2] A microphone's sound reception.

pickup pattern Defines a microphone's response to sounds arriving from various directions or angles. [See omnidirectional, unidirectional.]

PiP (picture in picture, p-in-p, pix in pix) Image from a second video source inset on a screen's main picture, the big and small pictures usually being interchangeable.

playback Videotaped material viewed and heard as recorded, facilitated by camcorder or VCR.

playback VCR Playback source of raw video footage (master or workprint) in basic player/recorder editing setup. [See recording VCR.]

point-of-view shot (POV) Shot perspective whereby the video camera assumes a subject's view and thus viewers see what the subject sees.

polarizing filter Mounted at the front of camcorder lens, thwarts undesirable glare and reflections. [See filter.]

post production (post) Any video production activity following initial recording. Typically involves editing, addition of background music, voiceover, sound effects, titles, and/or various electronic visual effects. Results in completed production.

posterization Electronic special effect transforming a normal video image into a collage of flattened single-colored areas, without graduations of color and brightness.

POV (point of view)   The apparent position of the observer in a shoot that defines the camera's position.

pre-roll   [1] Slight backing-up function of camcorders and VCRs when preparing for linear tape-to-tape editing; ensures smooth, uninterrupted transitions between scenes.

preamp   An electronic device that magnifies the low signal output of microphones and other transducers before the signal is sent to a mixing board or to other amplifiers.

proc amp   (processing amplifier) Video image processor that boosts video signal's luminance, chroma, and sync components to correct such problems as low light, weak color, or wrong tint.

Progressive scan   A method of displaying the horizontal video lines in computer displays and digital TV broadcasts. Each horizontal line is displayed in sequence (1, 2, 3, etc.), until the screen is filled; as opposed to interlaced (e.g. first fields of odd-numbered lines, then fields of even-numbered lines).

props   Short for "properties," objects used either in decorating a set (set props) or by talent (hand props).

PZM (pressure zone microphone)   Small, sensitive condenser mike, usually attached to a metal backing plate. Senses air pressure changes in tiny gap between mike element and plate. Trademark of Crown International. Generically, "boundary microphone" is preferred.

QuickTime   Computer system software that defines a format for video and audio data, so different applications can open and play synchronized sound and movie files.

rack focus   Shifting focus between subjects in the background and foreground so a viewer's attention moves from subject to subject as the focus shifts.

RAID   Acronym for Redundant Array of Independent Disks. Hard drives installed in multiples that are accessed as a single volume. RAID 0 systems (stripe sets) are common in higher-end video editing systems, as they allow for faster access to video. Other RAID configurations are used in some servers to keep important data accessible and protected, allowing access to data even after one of the hard drives crash.

RAM (Random Access Memory)   The short-term memory of a computer which temporarily holds information while your computer is on. Distinct from storage, which is more permanent and is held on hard disks or some other media, such as CD-ROM.

raw footage   Pre-edited footage, usually direct from the camcorder.

RCA plug (Recording Corporation of America)   A popular cable connector for home audio as well as video components. The standard connection for direct audio/video inputs and outputs.

RCTC (rewritable consumer time code)   The time-code format used with 8mm and Hi8 formats.

reaction shot   A cutaway to someone or something showing their facial response to the primary action or subject.

real time   Occurring immediately, without delay for rendering. If a transition occurs in real time, there is no waiting; the computer creates the effect or transition on the fly, showing it immediately. Real-time previewing is different from real-time rendering.

real-time counter   Tallying device that accounts for videotape playing/recording by measure of hours, minutes and seconds.

RealNetworks   Developed the leading streaming technology for transmitting live video over the Internet using a variety of data compression techniques and works with IP and IP Multicast connections.

RealPlayer   A program developed by RealNetworks to play live and on-demand RealAudio and RealVideo files.

RealVideo A streaming technology developed by RealNetworks for transmitting live video over the Internet. RealVideo uses a variety of data compression algorithms.

recording VCR Recipient of raw video feed (master or workprint) and recorder of edited videotape in basic player/recorder editing setup. [See playback VCR.]

reflected light That which bounces off the illuminated subject. Light redirected by a reflector. (See incident light.)

reflector Lighting accessory helpful for bouncing light onto a subject. Often made of lightweight reflective material.

remote Video shoot performed on location, outside a controlled studio environment.

render The processing a computer undertakes when creating an applied effect, transition or composite.

render time The time it takes an editing computer to composite source elements and commands into a single video file so the sequence, including titles and transition effects, can play in full motion.

resolution Amount of picture detail reproduced by a video system, influenced by a camera's pickup, lens, internal optics, recording medium and playback monitor. The more detail, the sharper and better defined the picture. [See horizontal resolution.]

Rewritable Consumer (RC) Time code sent trhoug Control-L interface permitting extremely accurate edits. Each frame is assigned a unique address expressed in hours:minutes:seconds:frames.

RF (radio frequency) Combination of audio and video signals coded as a channel number, necessary for television broadcasts as well as some closed-circuit distribution.

RF converter Device that converts audio and video signals into a combined

RF signal suitable for reception by a standard TV.

RGB (red, green, blue) Video signal transmission system that differentiates and processes all color information in separate red, green and blue components—the primary color of light—for optimum image quality. Also defines type of color monitor.

ringing Undesirable faint double screen image caused by signal reflection or improperly balanced video circuitry. "Ringing" appears as repeated image edges.

RM (Real Media) A popular file format used for streaming video over the Internet.

roll Text or graphics, usually credits, that move up or down the screen, typically from bottom to top.

rough cut Preliminary edit of footage in the approximate sequence, length and content of finished program.

rule of thirds Composition theory based on dividing the screen into thirds vertically and horizontally and the placement of the main subject along those lines.

S-video Also known as Y/C video, signal type employed with Hi8 and S-VHS video formats. Transmits luminance (Y) and chrominance (C) portions separately via multiple wires (pins), thereby avoiding the NTSC encoding process and its inevitable picture-quality degradation.

S/N Ratio Relationship between signal strength and a medium's inherent noise. Video S/N indicates how grainy or snowy a picture will be, plus color accuracy; audio S/N specifies amount of background tape hiss present with low- or no-volume recordings.

safe title area The recommended area that will produce legible titles on most TV screens; 80 percent of the visible area, measured from the center.

scan converter Device that changes scan rate of a video signal, possibly converting it from noninterlaced to interlaced mode. Allows computer graphics to be displayed on a standard video screen.

scan line Result of television's swift scanning process which sweeps out a series of horizontal lines from left to right, then down a bit and left to right again. Complete NTSC picture consists of 525 scan lines per frame.

scan rate Number of times a screen is "redrawn" per second. Computer displays operate at different scan rates than standard video.

scene In the language of moving images, a sequence of related shots usually constituting action in one particular location. [See shot.]

scrim Lighting accessory made of wire mesh. Lessens intensity of light source without softening it. Half scrims and graduated scrims reduce illumination in more specific areas.

script Text specifying content of a production or performance, used as a guide. May include character and setting profiles, production directives (audio, lighting, scenery, camera moves), as well as dialogue to be recited by talent. [See storyboard.]

SECAM (sequential color and memory) 625-line 25-frame-per-second television signal standard used in France and the Soviet Republic. Incompatible with NTSC; PAL and SECAM are partially compatible. [See NTSC, PAL.]

SEG (special effects generator) Permits video signal mixing from two or more sources—cameras, time-base correctors and character generators—for dissolves, wipes and other transition effects.

selective focus Adjusting focus to emphasize desired subject(s) in a shot. Selected area maintains clarity, image sharpness while remainder of image blurs. Useful for directing viewer's attention.

sepia Brassy antique color effect characteristic of old photographs.

shooting ratio Amount of raw footage recorded relative to the amount used in edited, finished program.

shot Intentional, isolated camera views, which collectively comprise a scene. [See scene.]

shotgun A highly-directional microphone used for picking up sounds from a distance.

signal-to-noise ratio (S/N) Relationship between signal strength and a medium's inherent noise. Video S/N indicates how grainy or snowy a picture will be, plus its color accuracy; audio S/N specifies amount of background tape hiss present with low- or no-volume recordings. Higher figures represent a cleaner signal. Usually cited in decibels (dB).

Skylight (1A) or haze (UV) filter Mounted at front of camcorder lens, virtually clear glass absorbs ultraviolet light. Also excellent as constant lens protector. [See filter.]

SMPTE Time-code standard which addresses every frame on a videotape with a unique number (in hours, minutes, seconds, frames) to aid logging and editing. Format used for film, video and audio. Named for the Society of Motion Picture and Television Engineers, which sanctions standards for recording systems in North America.

snake A connector box that contains a large number of microphone input receptacles.

snoot Open-ended cylindrical funnel mounted on a light source to project a narrow, concentrated circle of illumination.

snow Electronic picture interference; resembles scattered snow on the television screen. Synonymous with chroma and luma noise.

solarization Electronic special effect distorting a video image's original colors, emphasizing some and de-emphasizing others for a "paint brush" effect. [See DVE.]

sound bite Any short recorded audio segment for use in an edited program—usually a highlight taken from an interview.

sound effects Contrived audio, usually prerecorded, incorporated with a video soundtrack to resemble a real occurrence. Blowing on a microphone, for example, might simulate wind to accompany hurricane images.

soundtrack The audio portion of a video recording, often multifaceted with natural sound, voiceovers, background music, sound effects, etc.

SP (standard play) Fastest tape speed of a VHS VCR, accommodating two-hour recordings. [See EP, LP.]

special effects F/X. Tricks and illusions—electronic or on camera—employed in film and video to define, distort, or defy reality.

special effects generator (SEG) Video signal processor with vast, but varying, image manipulation capabilities involving patterns and placement as well as color and texture: mixing, multiplying, shrinking, strobing, wiping, dissolving, flipping, colorizing, etc.

spotlight Radiates a well-defined directional beam of light, casting hard, distinct shadows. Best used to focus illumination on individual subjects, whereas floodlights blanket broader areas.

stabilizer Video signal processor used primarily for tape dubbing to eliminate picture jump and jitter, maintain stability.

star Filter Mounted at front of camcorder lens, gives videotaped light sources a starburst effect. Generally available in four-, six-, and eight-point patterns. [See filter.]

stereo Sound emanating from two isolated sources, intended to simulate pattern of natural human hearing.

stock shot Common footage—city traffic, a rainbow—conveniently accessed as needed. Similar to a "photo file" in the photography profession.

storyboard Series of cartoon-like sketches illustrating key visual stages (shots, scenes) of planned production, accompanied by corresponding audio information. [See script.]

Streaming Playing sound or video in real time as it is downloaded over the internet as opposed to storing it in a local file first. Avoids download delay.

strobe Digital variation of fixed-speed slow motion, with image action broken down into a series of still frames updated and replaced with new ones at rapid speed.

Super VHS (S-VHS, S-VHS-C) Improved version of VHS and VHS-C videotape formats, characterized by separate carriers of chrominance and luminance information, yielding a sharper picture. [See VHS, VHS-C.]

superimposition (super) Titles, video or graphics appearing over an existing video picture, partially or completely hiding areas they cover.

sweetening Post-production process of adding music and sound effects or otherwise enhancing the existing audio with filters and effects.

swish pan Extremely rapid camera movement from left to right or right to left, appearing as image blur. Two such pans in the same direction—one moving from, the other moving to a stationary shot—edited together can effectively convey passage of time or change of location.

switcher Simplified SEG, permits video signal mixing from two or more sources—cameras, time base correctors, character generators—for dissolves, wipes, and other clean transition effects.

sync (synchronization) Horizontal and vertical timing signals or electronic pulses—component of composite signal, supplied separately in RGB systems. Aligns video origination (live camera, videotape) and reproduction (monitor or receiver) sources.

synchronous sound Audio recorded with images. When the mouth moves, the words come out.

talent Generic term for the people assuming on-screen roles in a videotaping.

tally light Automatic indicators (usually red) on a camera's front and within its viewfinder that signal recording in progress—seen by both camera subject(s) and operator.

telecine converter Imaging device used in conjunction with a movie projector and camcorder to transfer film images to videotape.

telephoto Camera lens with long focal length and narrow horizontal field of view. Opposite of wide-angle, captures magnified, close-up images from considerable distance.

teleprompter (prompter) Mechanical device that projects and advances text on mirror directly in front of camera's lens, allowing talent to read their lines while appearing to maintain eye contact with viewers.

test pattern Any of various combinations of converging lines, alignment marks, and gray scales appearing on screen to aid in video equipment adjustment for picture alignment, registration, and contrast. Often viewed on broadcast television in off-air hours. [See color bars.]

three-point lighting Basic lighting approach employing key, fill and back lights to illuminate subject with sense of depth and texture. Strategic placement imitates natural outdoor lighting environment, avoids flat lighting. (See back light, fill light, key light.)

three-quarter-inch (U-matic) An analog video format utilizing 3/4" tape. Very popular in professional, industrial and broadcast environments in the past, though beginning to be supplanted by digital formats.

three-shot Camera view including three subjects, generally applicable to interview situations.

three-to-one rule A microphone placement principle that states if two mikes must be side by side, there should be three times the distance between them that there is between the mikes and the people using them.

tilt Vertical camcorder rotation (up and down) from a single axis, as on a tripod.

time base corrector (TBC) Electronic device that corrects timing inconsistencies in a videotape recorder's playback, stabilizing the image for optimum quality. Also synchronizes video sources, allowing image mixing. [See sync.]

time code Synchronization system, like a clock recorded on your videotape, assigning a corresponding hours, minutes, seconds, and frame-number designation to each frame. Expedites indexing convenience and editing precision. [See SMPTE.]

time-lapse recording Periodically videotaping a minimal number of frames over long durations of actual time. Upon playback, slow processes such as a flower blooming may be viewed in rapid motion.

timeline editing A computer-based method of editing, in which bars proportional to the length of the clip represent video and audio clips are represented on a computer screen.

titling Process or result of incorporating on-screen text as credits, captions or any other alphanumeric communication to video viewers.

tracking Lateral camcorder movement that travels with a moving subject. The camcorder should maintain a regulated distance from the subject.

transcode To convert analog video to a digital format, or vice-versa.

tripod Three-legged camera mount offering stability and camera placement/movement consistency. Most are lightweight, used for remote recording. [See monopod.]

turnkey DVD authoring system Any computer system designed to author (and usually burn) DVDs right out of the box, needing only trivial changes in its configuration.

turnkey nonlinear editing system Any computer system designed to edit video right out of the box, needing only trivial changes in its configuration.

turnkey system Any computer system which is considered ready-to-use right out of the box, needing only trivial changes in its configuration.

two-shot A camera view including two subjects, generally applicable to interview situations.

U-matic An analog video format utilizing 3/4″ tape. Very popular in professional, industrial and broadcast environments in the past, though beginning to be supplanted by digital formats.

umbrella Lighting accessory available in various sizes usually made of textured gold or silver fabric. Facilitates soft, shadowless illumination by reflecting light onto a scene.

unbalanced line Audio cables that have two wires: one for positive and one for both negative and ground.

unidirectional Highly selective microphone pickup pattern, rejects sound coming from behind while absorbing that from in front. [See bidirectional, omnidirectional.]

variable bit rate (VBR) A way of coding video to maximize image quality over a connection's available bandwidth, usually provided by more recent codecs.

VCR (videocassette recorder) Multifunction machine intended primarily for recording and playback of videotape stored in cassettes.

vectorscope Electronic testing device that measures a video signal's chrominance performance, plotting qualities in a compass-like graphic display.

vertical interval time code (VITC) Synchronization signals recorded as an invisible component of the video signal, accessed for editing precision. [See time code.]

VHS (video home system) Predominant half-inch videotape format developed by Matsushita and licensed by JVC.

VHS-C (VHS compact) Scaled-down version of VHS using miniature cassettes compatible with full-size VHS equipment through use of adapter. [See Super VHS.]

video card The PC card that controls the computer's monitor display. Don't confuse the computer's video (VGA, SVGA, Mac monitor and so on) which is non-interlaced, with NTSC video. PC cards for DTV are also called capture, overlay or compression cards. Most do not generate NTSC video output.

video prompter A mechanical device that projects and advances text on a mirror directly in front of a camera lens, allowing talent to read lines while appearing to maintain eye contact with viewers.

videocassette recorder (VCR) Multifunction machine intended primarily for recording and playback of videotape stored in cassettes.

vignette Visual special effect whereby viewers see images through a perceived keyhole, heart shape, diamond, etc. In low-budget form, vignettes are achieved by aiming camera through a cutout of a desired vignette.

vignetting Undesirable darkening at the corners of a picture, as if viewer's peering through a telescope, due to improper matching of lens to camera—pickup's scope exceeds lens size.

VITC (vertical interval time code) Synchronization signal recorded as an invisible component of the video signal, accessed for editing precision. [See LTC.]

VOD Abbreviation for Video on Demand. Usually only heard in the context of delivering full-frame, full-motion video to a television; since most video on the Internet is provided on-demand.

voiceover (VO) Audio from an unseen narrator accompanying video, heard above background sound or music. Typically applied to edited visuals during post-production.

waveform monitor Specialized oscilloscope testing device providing a graphic display of a video signal's strength. Plus, like a sophisticated light meter, aids in precise setting of picture's maximum brightness level for optimum contrast.

WebCam   Abbreviation for Web Camera. A small camera connected to a computer, usually through a USB port. Webcams usually produce small, progressive-scanned images.

whip pan   (swish pan) Extremely rapid camera movement from left to right or right to left, appearing as an image blur. Two such pans in the same direction, edited together—one moving from, the other moving to a stationary shot—can effectively convey the passage of time or a change of location.

white balance   Electronic adjustment of camcorder to retain truest colors of recorded image. Activated in camcorder prior to recording, proper setting established by aiming at white object.

wide-angle   Camcorder lens with short focal length and broad horizontal field of view. Opposite of telephoto, supports viewer perspective and tends to reinforce perception of depth.

wild   sound   Nonsynchronous   audio recorded independent of picture ie. rain on roof, five o'clock whistle—often captured with separate audio recorder. [See nonsynchronous sound.]

windscreen   Sponge-like   microphone shield, thwarts undesirable noise from wind and rapid mike movement.

wipe   Transition   from   one   shot   to another, where a moving line or pattern reveals the new shot. In it's simplest   form   it   simulates   a   window shade being drawn.

wireless   mike   A   microphone   with   a self-contained, built-in miniature FM transmitter that can send the audio signal several hundred feet, eliminating the need for mike cables.

workprint   Copy of a master videotape used for edit planning and rough cut without excessively wearing or otherwise jeopardizing safekeeping of original material. Also called "working master."

wow and flutter   Sound distortions consisting of a slow rise and fall of pitch, caused   by   speed   variations   in audio/video playback system.

XLR (ground-left-right)   Three-pin plug for three-conductor "balanced" audio cable, employed with high-quality microphones, mixers and other audio equipment.

Y   Symbol for luminance, or brightness, portion of a video signal; the complete color video signal consists of R,G,B and Y.

Y/C   Video signal type (also known as S-video) employed with Hi8 and S-VHS video formats and analog output -on digital camcorders. Transmits luminance (Y) and chrominance (C) portions separately via multiple wires, thereby avoiding picture quality degradation.

YUV (y = luminance, u = B-Y or blue and v = R-Y or red)   Video signal used to compose a component NTSC or PAL signal. [See RGB.]

zoom   Variance of focal length, bringing subject into and out of close-up range. Lens capability permits change from wide-angle to telephoto, or vice versa, in one continuous move. "Zoom in" and "zoom out" are common terms.

zoom ratio   Range of a lens' focal length, from most "zoomed in" field of view to most "zoomed out." Expressed as ratio: 6:1, for example, implies that the same lens from the same distance can make the same image appear six-times closer. [See focal length, zoom.]

List of Contributors

Dr. Robert G. Nulph
Dr. Robert G. Nulph is an Associate Professor of Communication Studies and an independent video/film producer/director.

Larry Lemm
Larry Lemm is a freelance writer.

Scott Anderson
Scott Anderson is the author of animation software and a book about digital special effects.

Jim Stinson
Jim Stinson is the author of the book Video Communication and Production.

Robert J. Kerr
Robert J. Kerr is a consultant, teacher and writer in the video industry.

Loren Alldrin
Loren Alldrin is a freelance video and music producer.

Michael Rabiger
Michael Rabiger teaches filmmaking at Columbia College, Chicago. He is the author of Directing the Documentary.

Joe McCleskey
Joe McCleskey is an instructional media specialist

Charles Bloodworth
Charles Bloodworth is a video hobbyist and DV enthusiast.

Bill Rood
Bill Rood is an engineer at KTXL Channel 40 in Sacramento, CA.

William Ronat
William Ronat is the owner of a video production company.

Stray Wynn Ponder
Stray Wynn Ponder is a writer and producer of television commercials and industrial training videos.

Stephen Jacobs
Stephen Jacobs is an English and data processing instructor at National Technical Institute for the Deaf at RIT.

John K. Waters
John K. Waters is a freelance writer.

Mark Steven Bosko
Mark Steven Bosko is a freelance writer and an independent video and film producer.

Randal K. West
Randal K. West is an award winning director of Broadcast television and is a Creative Director with Hawthorne Direct, Inc.

Bill Fisher
Bill Fisher is a documentary video producer based in Portland, Oregon.

Mark Levy
Mark Levy specializes in patent, trademark & copyright law and has won numerous awards in film and video festivals.

Brian Pogue
Brian Pogue is a news videographer/editor at KTXL-TV in Sacramento, CA.

Michael Hammond
Michael Hammond is a twenty-year communications veteran, teaching electronic media and producing independent video.

Michael Loehr
Michael Loehr is a foreign documentarian.

Hal Robertson
Hal Robertson is a 20-year audio/video production veteran and owns Sound Foundation - a consulting firm specializing in media production.

Michael J. Kelley
Michael J. Kelley is a freelance media production consultant in Kenwood, CA.

Carolyn Miller
Carolyn Miller is a Hollywood-based scriptwriter and journalist who specializes in New Media projects.

Tim Cowan
Tim Cowan is a freelance writer specializing in video and computer subjects.

Norm Medoff
Norm Medoff is a university professor, author, and video workshop instructor.

Bernard Wilkie
Bernard Wilkie designed special effects for the BBC for over 25 years.

Don Collins
Don Collins is a freelance writer and video producer.

Bill Davis
Bill Davis writes, shoots, edits, and does voiceover work for a variety of corporate and industrial clients.

Janis Lonnquist
Janis Lonnquist is a writer and producer with clients including Intel and America's Funding Source.

Bill Harrington
Bill Harrington has been a professional video producer for over ten years.

Armand Ensanian
Armand Ensanian is a professional videographer, photographer, and former columnist for Video Review.

Sofia Davis
Sofia Davis has been a leased access and public access producer for 18 years.

Sheldon I. Altfeld
Sheldon I. Altfeld is a freelance writer specializing in leased access.

Alessia Cowee
Alessia Cowee is a freelance writer, editor and mother of three.

Charles Mohnike
Charles Mohnike is a technology writer and co-owner of a web development firm.

John Davis
John Davis is a writer and video producer.

Matthew York
Matthew York is the Publisher-Editor of Videomaker and Smart TV magazines.

D. Eric Franks
D. Eric Franks is Videomaker's Technical Editor.

Charles Fulton
Charles Fulton is Videomaker's Associate Editor.

Dr. Roger B. Wyatt
Dr. Roger B. Wyatt is a partner in McLellan Wyatt Digital, a new media company, and on the board of directors of the Saratoga Media Arts Institute.

Index